TRACKER

TRACKER

Case Files & Adventures
of a Professional Mantracker

Joel Hardin
with Matt Condon

TRACKER

Case Files & Adventures of a Professional Mantracker

Sign Cut Graphics by: Robert Brady
Illustrations by: Janet Hardin
Cover and page design by: Anita Jones, Another Jones Graphics
Cover footprint from San Francisco Police Homicide Case File page 243

ISBN:0-9753460-0-8

First Edition, 2004
Printed in USA

Dedication

This book is dedicated to the United States Border Patrol and all of its unsung heroes who have worked faithfully and tirelessly without recognition to thanklessly stem the tide of illegal migration into the United States across the international boundaries. I would not have been able to accomplish the many successes that were achieved without the authorization and approval of Border Patrol Chief Patrol Agents and Regional Commissioners.

Border Patrol trackers or "Sign Cutters" were once the quiet, elite few, uncontested for place of honor and respect, deferred to even by the great "pistoleros" of the day, and recognized nationally by other law enforcement agencies. Time and place of honor has passed and both Sign Cutters and Pistoleros are historical tales. Tracking now is most often referred to as a lost art and the quiet few are the remaining ones that once knew a Sign Cutter.

Ab Taylor was a "Sign Cutter." I had the very good fortune to work closely with this man for several years and gained a lifetime education that has served as the foundation for my tracking career. Ab believed that tracking training could be delivered effectively to volunteer search and rescue responders and law enforcement officers. That belief and effort to save the lives of little children began the training program that I have redefined, developed and delivered for more than thirty years. The result of that beginning are the hundreds of SAR, law enforcement and military trackers that have learned to "see that which others look at and do not see" using Ab's "step-by-step" technique to acquire tracking understanding and skill to resolve issues and find missing persons.

Contents

Acknowledgements

I must acknowledge that throngs of tracking enthusiasts, students and others alike that have so often requested a written recording of the many tracking adventures during my career inspired this book. Many of these stories were told and retold by request around the Saturday night bon fire gathering of tracking students and often used as examples to reinforce teaching points.

The actual writing down of these stories may never have come to be but for the encouragement and insistence of Matt Condon, an accomplished tracking student and recognized freelance author of outdoors magazine articles. Matt offered to assist and focused my story telling into print with editing and rewriting talents. Then, when it seemed both of our energies were spent elsewhere, my good friend Ginny Turner picked us up with the project, and injected new energies and technical order bringing our efforts into a meaningful manuscript suitable to offer for publishing.

To my family from the beginning to this day, my lovely and thoughtful wife Janet and wonderful daughters Carrie, Cassa, Carma and Corina, without their love, encouragement, support and advice, my career, these adventures themselves and this book would never have been.

>-+-+>-0-<+-+-<

Preface

When I began to write this book, I decided that I didn't want to write a "how-to" book. I wanted a book to be a mix of stories about tracking and practical instruction. When I sit down with people and talk about some of the more interesting tracking tales I've been involved in over the years, I notice something interesting. Even people who couldn't care less about tracks on the ground listen intently. They lean in, their body language telling me that they want to hear more. They're sorry when the story ends. I wanted people who have not had the advantage of being in one of our tracking courses (or sitting around my dinner table) during the past thirty years to be able to "sit in" on some of those stories. The prospective tracking student will also begin to understand how each of these stories involves tracking and how people can learn to do the things that might well seem improbable, if not impossible.

CHAPTER ONE

The Most Dangerous Prey
Pursuit of a Murderer

It was Carma's birthday, a perfect May 24th in 1979, sunny and warm, one of God's good early summer days in northwest Washington. I was with our four daughters, aged 11 to 17, playing the Hardin family version of backyard soccer in the early evening when, amid the shouting, yelling and laughter, I caught the sound of numerous sirens not far away toward the north. I stopped to listen, holding up my hand to silence the girls. We lived in a farming community about five miles southeast of the town of Lynden, and approximately 12 miles south of the Canadian border. From time to time we would hear the siren of a fire truck or police cruiser, but this was unusual. The girls stopped to listen to the sirens, which were coming closer to our house. I had been a police officer when the girls were born, so they had grown up with police cars, cops, handcuffs, guns and sirens, and we all knew that this was more sirens than all of the cops in Lynden and Everson put together. The girls looked at me and asked if I were going to go see what was going on, which is what I would normally do. "No," I said to them, "they'll call me if they need me. Let's play." As we did, the sirens wailed their way past the road intersection a quarter mile north of us and drifted into the distance toward Everson, a small town four miles northeast of us. Then, they abruptly stopped.

That evening at about 10 p.m., as the girls prepared for bed, the phone rang. The Border Patrol radio dispatcher asked if I was available to respond to assist the sheriff's office. "We don't have any hard information yet, but some real bad guy, a left-wing military guerrilla of some sort, was coming back into the U.S. through the Point of Entry at Lynden and shot Jerry Ward. He died at the scene." I'd known the feeling before—that sudden empty, hollow, helpless feeling that I guess all law officers get when a fellow officer goes down. It is truly a brotherhood where we take care of each other and when one of us is hit, it affects us all.

The dispatcher went on to say that the guy had shot Ward, then fired a couple of shots with a handgun at the other on-duty inspector and at the Canadian inspectors before calmly getting into his car and driving south into the U.S. and toward the town of Lynden. "He got away from them near Everson, and that's where you come in, Joel. You'd better give them a call." I was about to hang up when she said, "And Joel? Watch yourself, the info we have from the FBI says this guy is bad news and he knows what he's doing. If he got Jerry Ward, you know he's good. Be careful."

I hung up and called the Whatcom County Sheriff's office. Their dispatcher was expecting my call and advised me that the command post was set up at the state highway maintenance yards at Strandell, a railroad siding located just south of Everson and about two miles from my house on my side of the Nooksack River. The Chief Criminal Deputy Doug Gill was in charge of the search/pursuit operation and wanted me over there as soon as I could get there. Doug and I knew each other well; we'd worked together often using tracking to resolve issues when other resources had failed.

By 10:15, I noted it because I'd have to put it in my report—I had gathered my tracking gear and my flashlight. Why was it that whenever something happened, it was always after dark before I got called? I was at the scene in five minutes and I could see why the sirens had sounded like a policeman's parade. Cop cars were everywhere, parked in every available place, including the shoulders of the highway and on the streets for hundreds of yards in every direction from the maintenance shops of the highway department compound. It wasn't just local cops—there were Highway Patrol, Border Patrol,

FBI, DEA (Drug Enforcement Agency), and Customs Agency cars, as well as sheriff's cars from the surrounding counties, even some from Seattle and Tacoma, more than 100 miles away. Many of them had their overhead light bars flashing red and blue, and their outside radio speakers crackled a jumble of radio traffic from the various agencies. It had been quite a time since I had seen this kind of law enforcement crowd.

I found a place along the highway to park safely and began to walk toward the huge overhead spotlights that focused attention in the center of the compound. I could see in the light and shadows a gathering of 50 or 60 officers around the command van, some carrying rifles and shotguns, some with flak vests and helmets. I didn't know all the details yet, but there was no doubt that this was a really big deal! As I approached the group of men, I noticed that many of them wore familiar dark windbreaker jackets—some had FBI, DEA or U.S. Customs stenciled on the backs. Others were plain-clothes agents.

I finally spotted Doug in the middle of the throng of officers and got his attention. He motioned for me to walk away from the group and he would join me. I did, and he joined me in a few minutes, bringing styrofoam cups of steaming black coffee to the shadows and far enough from the lighting generator that we could talk without having to shout at each other. We stood looking at each other trying to sip the too-hot coffee, and he shook his head.

"Damn!" he said, "This thing is totally out of hand! We've got people coming from all over. I don't even know who-all is here and I can't seem to get a handle on it. The FBI is trying to claim jurisdiction and they're trying to do their own thing, Customs is claiming that they're in charge because it was their man that got killed and they're trying to beat the 'febbies' to the glory. The sheriff is yelling at me that it's our jurisdiction because it happened in our county and to get a handle on it."

"Well, Doug, that's why you get the big bucks," I replied. "What do you want me to do? They said you needed me, but I can just as easily go home. You know I don't like crowds, and I surely don't want to add anything to your circus."

Doug glared at me and muttered, "Don't add to my problems, Joel. Just go get this damn thing figured out and find this guy for me! They've been down there with dogs and about 20 guys searching for over two hours and no one can figure how they got away. How much do you know?"

I shook my head to indicate nothing, and Doug began telling me a streamlined story. His office thought that they had the suspect identified as Artie Ray Baker, an Army Special Forces-trained man in his mid-thirties and rock hard. He was some kind of weapons, scout/sniper and defense expert. He did two tours in Vietnam but went bad and got crosswise with everyone over there, so was sent home hating the army, the government and the establishment as a whole. He got in some kind of trouble in California and was in prison, but he escaped. He got hooked up with and hired on as an advisor with some extremist left-wing guerrilla group in northern California. The group was supposed to be well organized, with lots of money, people and guns and the intent to overthrow the government. The FBI had been investigating the group for some time.

"They know this guy," Doug explained. "He was traveling in Canada with a girlfriend and came back to the Lynden Port of Entry this evening. Unfortunately, when Jerry Ward did the initial inspection, he smelled something fishy—nobody knows what yet. He sent them inside and went in to do the secondary inspection. No one is exactly sure what happened then, or at least they haven't gotten the story to me. The other inspector came out of the office to change places with Ward in the inspection booth. The next thing he knew, he hears a couple shots and looks out the window at the door to the office and sees this guy aiming a .45 at him. The guy fires a shot, hitting the window frame, and the inspector split, running for the Canadian port of entry. The Canadians heard the shots and see this guy Baker as he comes out of the office and touches off a couple rounds at their offices.

They dove for cover but could see the guy and the woman get in the car and drive off south toward Lynden."

Doug briefly outlined a weird series of coincidences. A DEA team had the Port of Entry under surveillance for a suspected drug deal at the time, and a DEA agent sitting in his car behind the POE building heard the shots that killed Ward. He saw the inspector running north and heard the shots aimed at the Canadian offices, then saw the car start driving south. The agent didn't know what had taken place, but he reported hearing the shots fired and began to follow Baker's car at a safe distance, radioing the car's description and location to the Border Patrol dispatcher. Then he heard the report from the Canadian officers that Ward had been shot.

At the same time, the FBI was conducting a training class at a grade school for local law enforcement officers at the northern city limit of Lynden. There were about 20 uniformed officers from all over the area present, and with their walkie-talkies they were all hearing everything that was being broadcast over the radio. Baker, with the DEA agent following, managed to drive right past the grade school and the startled gathering of officers. They scrambled into action, but it must have looked like a Keystone Kops movie as they all ran out of the school, jumped for their cars and took off on the chase. Speeds never got above 40 miles per hour on the narrow two-lane country roads and the chase actually went right through the middle of Lynden. Despite all the sirens and lights, Baker wouldn't stop and they just kept following like a damn parade!

"I think he was trying to get to the mountains he could see over there toward Sumas," Doug said. "The problem was he didn't know the area and how to get there. He turned south at Lynden and was trapped into crossing the river bridge, then he turned onto the Van Dyk Road and hit the highway back there. He sped up and went straight at that corner and was going too fast over the railroad tracks to make that 90-degree corner at Dwayne's house."

Baker hadn't seen the turn quickly enough and he had gone down the driveway and straight past the farmhouse and barn and onto a dirt field road alongside a newly planted potato field. As he sped down the field road, the dust billowed up, hiding the car from sight and causing the officers to stop. They gathered around the house and barn, waiting for the dust cloud to settle and watching for someone to appear. By the time the dust settled, officers could see the suspect's car about 200 yards away and apparently abandoned at the edge of the field. They couldn't see either of the fugitives. Officers called for canine units and picked a team of officers to approach the car. They found no one at the car, and the dogs were unable to find anything either. Officer teams searched the brush up and down the river. Some were across the river, searching in the brush over there in case they had swum across. Others went downstream in case fugitives were riding the river down.

"Reinforcements are coming in from everywhere, and I'm posted to form a perimeter around the area, including guys positioned along the north side of the river to intercept if they show up." Doug said. "Joel, this guy is good. He just slipped through us and we can't afford to lose him! I'm counting on you. What do you need?"

"Well, Doug, the one thing I don't need is all these people! Give me a couple of guys, someone who has been down to the car, and I'll go down and take a look."

"Done! Wait here, and I'll send Peterson and Baldwin over. Peterson can be your contact with me, and Baldwin has been down to the car." I had worked with both these officers on complex crime scenes and knew they'd do a good job—Ron Peterson was a Whatcom County deputy and Jim Baldwin was a resident State Police trooper. When they joined me it was nearly 11 p.m. We needed no introductions or briefing and headed out to where the car had been left.

Baker's car was nosed into the deep grass and weeds bordering the field; its tail end remained on the dirt of the field. I motioned for the two officers to remain in position outside of all of the footprints that we could see in the dirt by the light of our flashlights. The soil was dry and loose, light river-bottom silt, and it readily held the sign story for anyone wanting to read it. On top of everything were footprints of four officers approaching cautiously, several of them going to the side and along the car, looking into the windows and doors of the vehicle. It was obvious that someone had the forethought to caution all remaining officers to not invade the possible evidence scene area around the vehicle. I worked my way around the car, observing all of the footprint sign story. The dog teams had come next, their prints deep in the soft soil. The handlers had also been cautious in their approach, taking the dogs to the doors of the vehicle, probably to smell some of the clothing that had been left behind. I could see that dogs and handlers had been all around the car, then headed off toward the river following the footprints of others. The officer's footprints went through the grass and weeds up the bank of the river dike and down the other side toward the water's edge.

Equally clear, but not so obvious, were the footprints of the car's driver and passenger. The driver had gotten out of the car and joined the passenger at the center of the rear bumper. I could see their footprints as they reached repeatedly into the trunk. They turned and sat on the bumper and changed shoes. Each person had at least two different shoe patterns. There was also sign in the loose soil that two or three bags or parcels were placed on the ground. The pair, having changed shoes, turned and put things into or took things from the trunk then closed it, turned and walked side by side toward and into the brush and weeds of the dike bank. Their passage through the high weeds and small brush at this point made an obvious pathway for the officers to follow.

The fugitives' sign told me a couple things that I needed to show to Ron and Jim. I had told them both I would advise them of what I could see in the sign story and thereby alert all three of us to any possible danger from a man we knew to be armed and dangerous. This sign told me that the gunman was in total control of his emotions at the time the car stopped at the dike. Neither person had made hurried footsteps. They had calmly gotten out of the car, rearranged items in the trunk, and changed into comfortable walking shoes. They had probably taken with them at least one bag with other items, possibly additional guns, food, clothing and shoes. They weren't in the least concerned about the dozens of pursuing officers at this point. Possibly the dust cloud still obscured the area during this period. There was plenty of dust on the denim skirt and Levi's marks on the bumper. Apparently the FBI's information was right on, this guy was a "thinker" and wouldn't be easily caught.

I stood with Ron and Jim a short distance outside of all of the footprint sign, explaining that we didn't want to add our tracks to the mix and pointing out what I wanted them to see. They had heard me before warn that the mistake most often made during crime-scene investigations, from a tracker's point of view, was that officers often walk into a crime scene and begin to work before they stop to see what is there to begin with. I began helping my partners to see what I was seeing in the sign, explaining and separating the suspects' sign at the rear of the car from the other prints. Once I showed them what to look for, they could easily separate the officers' tracks from those of our suspects.

The woman had gotten out of the car and walked in flat-soled, sandal-type shoes to the back of the car. There the prints showed her standing close to the bumper facing the vehicle, her feet shuffling back and forth, showing that she was going through items in the trunk. She then turned and sat lightly on the bumper; two denim-textured curves of her skirt showed clearly on the chrome. She had changed into walking shoes with good heel and sole patterns. The driver, in Levi's, had sat on the other side of the bumper and changed into regular business street shoes. After they closed the trunk, they slowly, almost casually, walked toward the river side by side. I could sense the chill going up Ron and Jim's spines as they considered the implications of the footprints. This guy was cool and calculating. At least two dozen police cars had been just 200 yards away while they prepared to leave, yet their actions showed there was no panic, no worry, no fear. Baker wasn't running; he was thinking and planning. His actions were deliberate and well thought out. Such a man would be very dangerous. I thought about the officers who were even now positioning themselves in a perimeter to encounter this guy. They would be wary and fearful, but he would be bold and confident.

We were ready to get on with it. The trail over the dike and through the brush leading to the river was well defined in the tall grass and weeds that had been tromped down by the feet of the officers, dogs and dog handlers. We followed the corridor up and over the dike and down the other side toward the river, coming out onto an open gravel bar.

The Nooksack River was cold and swift. Its principal source is Mt. Baker's melting snow and ice rushing to the bay only 50 miles away. The river changes course often, with spring and fall high-water runoff creating a river bed that varies from 100 yards to nearly a half-mile wide. Cottonwood, alder, birch and maple trees mingle with willows, brush and wild roses in the sandy silt of the drift bars that cover the older, abandoned river bed and high-water areas. At this time, the watercourse was bordered by large rocks, old root balls, stumps and other tree debris unloaded by the receding flood waters. At this place, the river was making a half-mile-long sweeping curved bend toward the north and back toward the southwest. The path through the weeds and brush from the car opened onto the open gravel bar some 20 to 50 feet from the water. This was the back side of a large eddy that trapped sand and silt and, as the water level had dropped, left a dried scum of silt on the exposed rocky surfaces.

I stopped to study the sign of those who had gone before us. Once out in the open on the gravel bar, the various searchers' tracks fanned out as they first looked for some sign of Baker along the water's edge, then toward the bushes and willows through the evening hours. They had gone back and forth several times, generally traveling parallel with the river, although some distance from the water's edge. I told the guys to wait and keep an eye open while I walked along the river's edge looking into the water. The still water was shallow and held silt residue from turned and rolled rocks. I found an area in which the silt had been stirred up then settled back onto the rocks, marked by a contrasting color to the undisturbed silt around it. This disturbance went straight into the water 20 or 30 feet. As I scanned the area in front of me with my flashlight, my two anxious escorts stood silently behind me, not knowing what I was doing, but trusting that it was important. I had asked Jim to make notes of comments I made about the sign, should it come up later at some point. Ron carried our covering weapon, a shotgun, and extra ammunition, as well as the radio for contact with command. I showed them what I was seeing in the light beam gleaming on the water and the rocks beneath, and drew their attention to two nearly parallel lines of disturbance from the water's edge. I suggested to them that the two suspects had gone into the water and then retreated, walking backwards, as indicated by footprint pressure pressing rocks downward but rolled rearward instead of forward. We slowly followed the twin sign lines away from the water and toward the brush and willows.

The two lines of "tracks," consisted primarily of rolled rocks, some freshly wet with sand and silt, and these were crisscrossed by the dogs' and officers' sign. We were able to follow these slowly and with some difficulty into the willows, where the footfalls showed clearly on the sand and silt that the pair was walking backward. They abruptly turned and walked normally. Our suspects were definitely on this side of the river and possibly somewhere in the brush and trees of the old riverbed close to us. As my companions looked around cautiously, I assured them that the suspects had a four-hour head start and were probably not very close to us now. I told Ron to call command and tell Doug that they had not crossed the river at this point, that we had the sign and that we'd advise when we had an idea of where the fugitives were going.

We followed the footprints a short distance. They wove their way through the willows to where I could see that they had sat down and watched and waited as the officers came in search. The pair had sat side by side facing the river, probably watching as the first officers and dog teams went about trying to sort out the puzzle. They were close enough that no doubt they could hear the radios broadcasting instructions to the other units—positioning, speculating, discussing strategy, setting up road blocks and bringing additional resources in for the manhunt. They had remained here long enough to gather significant information, then picked up their bags and walked off through the willows upriver. Baker wasn't afraid and he wasn't going to run from anyone. Everything about his movements indicated that he was thinking, planning and coolly calculating his next move.

The sign showed the two suspects picked their way through the brush and willows, walking on dog-team tracks in some places. Their prints seemed almost deliberately placed on top of the officers' clear prints in the open soil. In other places the dog-team prints were on top of the fugitives' prints, indicating that the fugitives were there in the brush during the time the officers were searching. The teams had searched in front of and behind the pair without the dogs alerting. The pair had stopped momentarily in a small clump of brush grown that grew around a couple of upended stumps tumbled and dumped when they were being washed downstream. Moving on, we found additional dog-team prints and different officers' prints, indicating that canine teams had made a second sweep attempt to find the two. The fugitives had played a cat-and-mouse game with the searchers. Baker and his companion had hidden, let the teams move past, then moved and hidden again. They repeated this process several times. When I pointed this out to the others, Ron got big-eyed and again started looking around cautiously. He was our protection, and he took the responsibility seriously.

The fugitive pair then came to an area where several large cottonwood trees growing close together had survived years of high water, creating a substantial pile of drift debris. Here the fugitives sat for a short period of time. There were indications in the leaf- and debris-covered ground surface that a fair amount of activity had taken place.

Baker had left his Oxford-type shoes sitting neatly by the trunk of the tree. I worked the area carefully and located an unusual area and softly called the team over to where I was separating leaves on the ground carefully. I showed them that some of the leaves were weathered side down and mixed with others right side up. Sand and dirt was lying unnaturally on top of others. I probed carefully, exposing a portion of the ground surface, which had been freshly dug up, then covered again with dirt and leaves. We dug slowly into the disturbed ground, uncovering several items—socks, and other inconsequential things that obviously were no longer of value to the fugitives.

The pair left the clump of cottonwoods walking side by side. They headed upriver through the brush and willows lining the high-water river bank. Baker was now walking in coarse wool socks, and his girlfriend was wearing lug-soled boots with a good heel. I reasoned that his shoes had been left in plain sight against the tree trunk to so occupy the finder's attention as to prevent further search. This made me think I must have missed something of importance in the little cache that they'd left, and I determined to go back later to take a look. The tracks showed that they were still unhurried, picking their way through and around the brush, around a stump and into an open silt-bottomed wash. Here the dog-team prints showed plainly beneath the fugitives' prints, meaning the dog teams had searched and given up before the two had moved from the cottonwood tangle. The dogs had not alerted on the fugitives, even though they had been within a few yards on several occasions.

I glanced at my watch and saw that it was midnight. We worked the sign slowly. I assured the two deputies that there was no reason to rush. The area perimeter was being set up at the same time the canine teams were at the river searching. Now we knew that, at that time, the fugitives were still within a couple hundred yards of the car but in the deep brush along the river's high-water line. Only a few hours had passed and now the perimeter was a heavily guarded loose half-circle about four to five miles in diameter, with the river forming the eastern edge. More resources were arriving and being posted.

What Baker had in mind I didn't know, but it was evident that he was planning on evading rather than running. I thought he was somewhere within the circle.

The night wore on slowly as we carefully followed the sign. At one o'clock, the stars were shining brightly but the night's chill and dampness began to take a toll an us. We were lucky in that we had the moon that night, and it continued to get lighter as the moon slowly climbed the star stairway. I was getting tired—my eyes were burning from the intense search by flashlight—and our rest periods began to get a bit too often and a bit too long. I had restricted the flashlight use to just me and had advised the officers to follow at either side of me and behind any light spill, so they could see and not be seen.

The sign wasn't that difficult to follow, but it took a good deal of looking and I didn't want to miss anything. Our guy had put on lugged-sole hiking boots with a good heel now, matching the ones the woman was wearing. He had found that walking shoeless on the rocky ground was rough on his feet. The sign crossed several narrow open, sandy strips—giving me a definite print here or there—and went around brush clumps for cover, over gravel bars and finally came out onto a long open gravel bar that glistened silvery in the moonlight. Here it got tough—the river rock was bigger, the size of good cantaloupes, and there was less sand and gravel. It was step by step, looking for the occasional rolled rock or some other small indication of passing. The radio, turned very low so only Ron could hear, kept us constantly updated regarding the rest of the search, and so far nothing had been turned up. The perimeter of the area was secure, and Doug kept in close touch with us, hoping we would come up on the fugitives as they holed up near one of the perimeter lines.

We worked our way to and along an uprooted tree that had been carried along by the high water and deposited on the bar. This was just one of several that the pair had come to and crossed. At the root of this one, however, they had stopped. We looked closely and found, stuffed between the roots of the tree, a blue shoulder bag, books and miscellaneous items of clothing. We guessed that the woman was getting tired and had cached the items here. This was a good sign.

As we were looking at the bag and contents, the radio came alive with the news that two subjects matching the description had been sighted walking the railroad tracks about a mile upriver from our location by officers with night-vision equipment,. A coordinated ambush had resulted in the capture of the woman, but the man had managed to escape into the woods once again. Several fresh dog teams were being dispatched and a flood of officers directed to quickly close in to surround this smaller area. The three of us sat quietly on the tree stump in the moonlight and listened to the radio traffic.

The particular area of concentration formed a loose triangle, possibly a half mile across and bordered on two sides by roads. Residential drives and open fields would permit officers to close off the third side. The fugitives had gotten about four miles from the car and we had covered almost three of that distance, so we had been gaining on them. The area they were in now was filled with heavy underbrush, nettles, brambles and briars and was dotted with alder and birch trees. The woods would be dark and shadowy, even in the moonlight.

The deputies and I sat on a log and listened closely to the activity on the radio, and finally said, "Not much reason to sit here, I guess. Let's go get a cup of coffee." The command center was nearly abandoned by the time we trudged back in. Someone was still manning the coffee pot and we were grateful. The cook filled us in on what he had learned from

officers coming and going. A field command had been set up in Doug

Gill's patrol car. All available officers had been repositioned close enough to surround the area where the suspect was so that each one could see another officer on either side and ensure that the fugitive could not escape without being seen. It was 3:30 a.m. and Jim Baldwin was to go on duty at 6 a.m. He thought he'd better get home and grab a couple hours of sleep, if possible, to come back after daylight. We waved him a goodnight.

The cook related that the dog teams seemed not to be having much luck. The thick brush was taking its toll on the dogs and wearing them out quickly. The two suspects had been walking on the railroad tracks and apparently they were jumped by the officers and had bolted off of the railroad right of way headlong into six-foot-high nettles and blackberry briars. The woman had fallen and quickly been subdued by the officers. The male suspect had broken free of the tangle of nettles and briars, and officers could hear him running for several strides, crashing through the brush for a few yards, before it became silent. Suspecting that the subject had run until he fell, they figured he must be waiting for them with his gun cocked, so they stopped and waited for reinforcements. The dog teams arrived within several minutes and were ordered off into the darkness again following the fugitive trail through the brush, the handlers trying to light up every shadow with their hand lights. I knew the handlers would be following the dogs slowly, knowing full well that the fugitive had the advantage as he sat in the dark, waiting for them to come to him. The dogs were having a hard time with the nettles, which stung their noses, tongues and eyes. The brush quickly wore out the dogs and, as each one was brought out, another took its place. The minutes became half hours, and the half hours became an hour. It would soon be dawn. From radio traffic we understood that Doug was getting concerned that the subject wouldn't be caught before commuters and school children began to venture out for the day. He assigned additional officers to ride with each school bus and others to assist with the roadblocks. There was no question that Baker would do anything to escape, including taking a hostage.

When we'd finished a couple cups of coffee and light streaks were beginning to show over Mt. Baker in the east, I suggested, "Let's mosey over to where the action is." We got into Ron's car and drove to where the capture had taken place. As we got there, I saw a big, gruff Royal Canadian Mounted Police sergeant with tears rolling down his cheeks, carrying his scratched and exhausted dog from the brush to his car.

"Ron," I said, "Go ask Doug if that's the last dog team in the brush."

"Are we going in?" he asked.

"Well, don't tell Doug we are," I responded. "He has enough to worry about. Just find out what you can."

Ron came back with the news that all the dog teams were expended and out of the brush and that Doug was going to just sit tight with the area surrounded until after daylight. Ron brought with him one of the Bellingham Police detectives, David McNeil, who wanted to be a part of our little tracking team. We headed down the railroad tracks at 5:30 a.m. toward where we'd been told the woman had been captured. Tromped down as it was, the area was easy to find without a flashlight in the early morning light. Leading directly away from the tracks was a rough trail through six-foot-tall nettles and brush where the dog teams had gone in. We eased down the railroad track embankment and into the gouge through the brush. I cut for sign to the right and left, but there was no sign of anyone veering off the freshly beaten path. There was a 15-foot circle tromped flat, obviously where the woman had been pounced upon, wrestled around in the nettles and taken back to the tracks. The trail was clear and straight, continuing from that point for 40 or 50 feet and going into the mouth of a small wash, then jogging to the right and continuing along the bottom of the wash where the brush and high grass was a little easier to travel through.

Straight ahead, where the path took a jog, was a single set of tracks, easily overlooked in the darkness by handlers following their dogs through the path of least resistance. These undisturbed tracks were long running steps, hardly affecting the two-foot-tall grass and weeds between footfalls. Baker was obviously "high-stepping" in the darkness to keep from falling. He'd done pretty well until he hit a small clump of brush cut long ago and piled to be burned, which was now covered with weeds and nettles. This he hit full force and pitched into it, one leg getting tangled in the branches and holding fast, while his momentum carried him to the ground. This must have been the loud crashing the officers heard as Baker ran off into the brush. He had waited for a short time, kneeling at the brush pile, perhaps listening to what was happening to his girlfriend. The sign indicated that he had risen from the ground and continued, this time more deliberately, and once again in control. They had spooked him, but now that he was away Baker reverted to his previous cunning and caution. Now he walked quietly, picking his way in the dark, able to see enough in the scant light to make his way with confidence.

We worked the sign slowly and carefully as we paralleled the dog trail as it went up the wash. We crossed the bottom of the wash and followed Baker's sign climbing the bank. The dogs had continued up the wash, following the bottom. Dogs trained to "air scent" will parallel a trail downwind of the actual tracks. I couldn't tell if that's what they had been doing here or if they were just following the easiest route. The top of the bank was flat, probably three to five acres covered mostly with waist-high brush with scattered cedar, fir, maple and alder trees. The sign showed that Baker carefully picked his way. He was still wearing the lugged-sole hiking boots that we'd seen prints of earlier. I glanced at my watch—6:00 and nearly full light. I needed the flashlight only when I got down in the brush looking on the ground surface to see the sign. Here and there the sign of the dog teams crossed the fugitive sign line but, just as at the river, they hadn't alerted to his presence. We found a place where Baker had lain on the ground in the thick brush, avoiding the dog teams that must have been circling all around him. He had crawled a little way, waited for the teams to come through, then returned to where he had been originally. As his sign continued, his tracks were on top of the dog-team tracks, then beneath them again. The dogs had come within a few feet of his hiding place several times and must have known he was there. The only thing we could figure was that they didn't think he was the subject of their search. Whatever the reason, he continued his cool trickery until the dogs were exhausted and had left the area.

The tracking from that point was slow and painstaking work. It was light enough now that we could see the sign without the flashlights and we had worked it almost to the edge of the flat. At this point we were only about 300 yards from the railroad tracks. Here heavy traffic from officers and dog teams had all but eliminated the subject's sign and it was a real puzzle to work it out. I decided to make a cut and see if I could pick up where he entered the woods. I left Ron and Dave on the last known prints and began the cut. When I found the trail again, something different about it caught my eye. Besides the fact that he had his shoes off again, this guy was now traveling after the dew, knocking it from the grass blades and the stems and leaves of the bushes, which meant that he had been moving within the last hour. That told me he was probably just a short way ahead of us and still within the circle of officers. He must have been hiding close by as we worked out his trail through all the dog-team tracks. I found where he had been lying in the brush, close enough to hear us talking and moving on his sign. Because he knew we were so close on his trail, things could get dicey.

I marked the sign with a flagging tape then signaled for Ron and Dave to keep very quiet. I wanted to radio to Doug Gill and tell him that we were back on the sign and that the guy was still within the circle, but I felt that our guy would also hear everything that was said. I whispered this to Ron and Dave to ensure that they understood that I thought the guy was very close to us. I had told Ron when we left the railroad tracks to turn the radio off. We would have to stay radio silent, though the radios from the cruisers had been blaring all night and there was no doubt that Baker could hear everything that was going on. Even with our radio off, we could clearly hear the speakers blasting out the radio traffic on all sides of the triangle perimeter. As we stood listening, we heard Doug asking if anyone knew where Joel Hardin was!

He was saying he had a mission for me. I was sure he wanted me to do what I was doing right now and when Ron whispered, asking if we should tell him our location. I replied, "Absolutely not! This guy may be within a hundred feet of us right now!"

I also realized that Baker probably had been listening to us, even though we'd been talking very softly ever since we'd gotten up on the flat. He'd probably heard everything we'd said. He knew we were tracking him and were on to the tricks he'd played with the dogs, and he knew we weren't fooled.

I motioned Dave and Ron to put their heads close to me. "He'll be watching his back-trail more closely now," I warned quietly. "Ron, this is where you have to be on your toes. Any questions?" There weren't any and we moved on.

The sign showed our subject had picked his way very carefully, stepping over and beside obstacles, watching the placement of every step. We proceeded slowly, watching carefully ahead and all around us while trying not to make any noise. The terrain here was a series of humps and bumps and several gullies, all covered with brush and waist-high ferns, with clumps of brush and trees. This was like many elk hunts I'd been on, when we were moving slowly and trying not to spook the game. But none of the elk I'd hunted were armed. I tried to make out several footfalls ahead and once they were determined, I'd move to the last one while keeping my eye on the surrounding brush and trees. Ron and Dave, carrying shotguns, were to the right and left and slightly behind, where they could see and cover each other and me. I followed telltale signs of wool socks pressing down on the decayed leaves and mashing the soft lichen growing beneath the larger brush and weeds. This guy was being extremely careful now, even more so than before. He was doing his best to hide his sign, something he hadn't done up until this point. He put his boots on again and tried walking on logs, straightening grasses and weeds, and placing his feet carefully so as not to leave heel or toe marks. We stayed on the sign, not worried about hurrying, since he was now going very slowly and really had nowhere to go.

The edge of a ravine came into view a little way ahead and the sign turned and paralleled the ravine a short distance, then turned where an old fir tree had fallen across the void. The old fir, some two feet in diameter, was a blow-down and had been a very full tree in its day. Now the empty branches stuck from the trunk like spokes for the full length of the tree. Baker had made his way to the edge of the ravine, carefully combing and straightening the tall weeds as he made his way to the fir tree. Then the sign disappeared.

Ron and Dave stood waiting for me to proceed. They had lost contact with the sign completely, not even able to see the slight indications that I tried pointing out to them. The thought crossed my mind that neither cared whether there was sign or not—they just wanted to make sure they saw the guy before he cut loose on us. I examined the downed tree carefully. I couldn't see any evidence of a person having crossed the log. But on the other side of the ravine, I could see a disturbance, probably a footfall. As I looked more closely at the tree, I realized that Baker had worked his way across the ravine by stepping on the branches themselves, never touching the trunk of the tree. I motioned to my cover team and one by one we crossed to the other side on the fallen tree. I saw where Baker had carefully let his weight down on the other side, then tried to cover his sign by again straightening the weeds he'd disturbed. This was him, all right, and he was getting harder to follow.

We made our way up to an old maple stump in a cluster of new tree shoots on a hump that overlooked the tree over the ravine. Here the sign told me a chilling story. On the far side of the stump there was a clear knee and foot print where he had knelt to watch his back-trail. On top of the stump there was an indication where he had rested his arms across the stump. In my mind's eye I could see him taking careful aim with a gun over the top of the stump, trying to decide whether or not to shoot. As I whispered my interpretation to the two partners, the looks on their faces told me they were more than a little shaken. Here Baker had taken time to put his boots back on, having taken them off during the log crossing, so we had gained a little time on him. When I mentioned this, Dave whispered, "Yes, but it sure looks like he was thinking about leaving us back in that ravine!"

"Sure," I said quietly, "but we have some insurance."

"What's that?" said Ron.

"He doesn't want everybody else to know where he is," I explained. "That keeps him from touching off a round at us." I hoped I was right.

We stopped to listen and there was much to hear. Car traffic on the nearby road was increasing and radio traffic was crackling through the woods. We could hear the SWAT members talking to each other on the radio, arranging their perimeter, setting their men up in 50- to 75-foot spacings. We knew Baker was close and that he was hearing everything we were hearing. I looked around and realized that in following the sign we had made a large circle through the woods and were in fact headed back towards the railroad tracks near where the woman was captured. Where would he be least suspected to appear? Right where he was last seen! This guy was heading for the tracks and the road that ran along it and it was my guess he was going to try to slip through the perimeter line right between the guarding officers. Once he was through the line he would have quite a head start before anyone even began looking outside the circle. If he was discovered, it would be a foot race to the foothills, only about four miles away across the river and probably only six to seven more miles from the Canadian border and the uninhabited mountains. As we began moving again, I whispered to Ron to pay no attention to the ground or to what I was doing. I wanted his full attention on the surrounding woods. Evading us, Baker was cold and calculating. Surprised or cornered, he would be deadly.

We moved slowly with Ron totally vigilant, Dave torn between watching the woods and scribbling notes of the few things I was pointing out in the sign line. The sign was easier to follow here. He was no longer trying to hide his tracks, just moving quietly so as to make no noise and remain unseen. We were on a fairly short, steep hillside going down to the railroad tracks and the road. I could hear but couldn't see a car slowly going by on the gravel road. The radio announced the clos-est SWAT member's position. I began moving more quickly on the sign now, still trying to be quiet, but moving every time the radio broke silence. I wanted to get to the road's edge before Baker made his move. We were very close to wherever Baker was hiding and one noisy step would tell him exactly where we were. As the car's noise faded around a bend, everything got very quiet. I could hear Ron and Dave carefully placing each foot as they advanced. I remembered that the railroad tracks were between our position and the road. This guy would have to go down into the right-of-way barrow ditch and out into the open to get to the road. I was sure he would pause, waiting on the edge of the woods before making his move.

We were only about 30 feet from the edge of the brush line, still coming downhill, and I could see through the brush and leaves bits and pieces of the road. I could hear another vehicle coming along slowly, its tires crunching the gravel. I could see glimpses of the light bar and the numbers on the roof of the car, and recognized its colors as that of a Whatcom County Sheriff's patrol car. As I watched the car pass in front of us, I saw something else. A dark human form, perhaps 20 feet directly in front of me, standing in thick brush with his back to me. His arms and hands were nearly shoulder high as he leaned forward, parting the brush to get a better view of the road, his attention totally focused on the passing vehicle. I knew that it was now or never—the sound of the car tires on gravel would cover the sound of my move-ment. I took three or four large strides toward the man and said loud and clear, "FREEZE! DON'T DO ANYTHING STUPID! We're right behind you!"

Baker startled, and his hands started to move slowly downward as he straightened slightly. I com-manded again, "Don't do anything stupid! Lock your fingers on top of your head!" His hands froze, then began to move inward and downward. "You know we have you covered! Raise your hands and lock your fingers on top of your head!" I heard Ron and Dave moving up beside me. The hands slowly withdrew from the brush he was holding open and slowly began to rise, then hesitated again. This was being a little stupid and again I said, "You know what's behind you. You wouldn't have a chance. Don't be stupid!" Finally the hands raised slowly and the fingers interlocked on top of his head as he straightened up to full height and I could see and hear him exhale. I took two more giant steps, knowing that Ron and Dave were now up with me and covering every move. I grasped Baker's fingers on top of his head and, holstering my weapon, I reached around to remove the gun in his front waistband to my rear pocket. I frisked him for other weapons, but he had none. I said, "All right, let's put the cuffs on," and he complied without comment.

I turned him around to face us and asked, "Are you OK?" He looked tired—it had been a long night, his street clothes dirty from crawling around in the brush and dirt, his face had smudges of dirt and grime. He said simply, without emotion, "I didn't expect you to be that close yet."

Ron and Doug let out big sighs as well. The chase was over. We pushed through the remaining fringe of brush into the open upon the railroad tracks and across to a waiting car on the road. Within minutes we were in the middle of the circus with 20 or 30 officers all over us. Baker was turned over to the sheriff's officers and I selected one detective I knew well and gave him the .45-caliber automatic handgun that I had taken from Baker's waistband. Telling him I'd have a receipt for him to sign later for evidence purposes, I slipped out of the crowd and found David sitting on the railroad rail.

"How's about a ride back to my car?" I asked. He nodded and we walked away from the commotion. I glanced at my watch and saw that it was 8:30. Dave saw me looking and said, "We got him at 8:20—just for the record."

⊱─⊰⊱─◦─⊰⊱─⊰

Artie Ray Baker was later convicted of murder in the shooting of Customs Inspector Jerry Ward, as well as attempted homicide and assault on a Federal officer and was sentenced to life in prison. The female accomplice, Marie Ferreboeuf, Baker's wife, was sentenced to 15 years for her part in the crimes. A crucial portion of the prosecution's case was to establish the frame of mind of the suspects. The sign story showing their rational, calculated escape attempts greatly assisted in proving that they were in full charge of their faculties at the time of the shooting.

I learned the following about Baker's history during his trial period. In 1977, Baker was serving a life sentence when he escaped from the California prison. After his escape he joined the Wellsprings Group, a militant extremist organization that operated out of Honeydew, California. On October 14, 1979, while Baker was being held awaiting trial in Seattle, Washington, a jailbreak was attempted by members of the Wellsprings Group. The incident, resembling an Al Capone-era escapade, resulted in nearly 200 rounds being fired in the ensuing automatic weapons gun battle on the streets of Seattle. It resulted in the death of one Seattle police officer and one jail inmate. Humboldt County (California) police linked the Wellsprings Group to the Symbianese Liberation Army. The group maintained an armed compound in Honeydew, which has since been dismantled. Baker was recaptured and is, at the time of this writing, still in custody.

Chapter Two

On the Border
The Making of a Tracker

There are some who might say that I was born a tracker, but they don't really know me or my beginnings, as I don't think that's true of me or anyone else. I often tell tracking students, no one is a born tracker. Trackers are the product of interest and motivation and good instruction. There are individuals in every walk of life who have the natural attributes and attitudes to develop an extraordinary skill or depth of knowledge of tracking. I doubt that my three brothers or my sister could recall my ever doing any tracking out of the ordinary during our childhood years. But what would be out of the ordinary?

I was born in the spring of 1940, the second son of the family living in the small town of Ontario in eastern Oregon. Ontario in the early '40s was growing and prospering, characterized by small farms and industrious people. My father was a small contractor working on construction for himself and he subcontracted to other, larger contractors. His father, who at that time was working a small 40-acre farm near Ontario, had been a bridge engineer and builder in the Midwest. Grandpa Hardin worked on the huge construction projects that built the west, the dams, roads and buildings. During the 1930s, era of the Works Progress Administration, Grandpa was with the throng of workers who built the structures that are the envy of skilled carpenters and stonemasons today.

My father, born in Indiana in 1910, enjoyed the out-of-doors—all of his free time in his late teens and early manhood was spent hunting and fishing the mountains of Oregon and Idaho. He was independent, self-reliant and ambitiously adventurous. He read and studied historical accounts of early mining and miners, the explorers, trappers and hunters of the "Old West," which was not too far in the past at that time. With a buddy or two, he would drive an old model-T pickup and hike to abandoned gold-mining streams and fields to explore and relive the recent past. Marriage to my mother, who grew up in a ranching family, and the arrival of the first son slowed down his pleasure excursions into the mountains.

My mother, born in Mariposa, California, in 1911 to John and Rosella Roesbery, was the oldest daughter and fourth in a family of nine children. John Roesbery was a second-generation descendant of the Mormons who migrated to Utah. Rosella Alcanta was a second-generation descendant of an aristocratic Spanish family displaced when the United States voided all original Spanish land grants in declaring war with Mexico in 1846. Grandpa Roesbery was born in the "Old West" and lived the day-to-day life so often written about in novels. He rode a horse throughout the western states and worked as a cowboy, freighted borax out of Death Valley, mined for gold, joined the Mexican Revolution, hunted meat for hire, wrangled wild horses, ranched and most importantly, met and married Rosella, the beautiful Spanish lady, in 1904. Grandma remained a lady without fanfare or flair, while in saddle roping and working cattle, hunting game to feed the family, and moving the family from one place to another in an iron-wheeled wagon, following wherever Grandpa worked. I was fortunate to know them both well, lived close to them and had them around the ranch where I grew up.

My first job on the ranch was driving the derrick horse during haying season when I was five. Grandma helped me to harness the horse, an old white mare who knew far more about the job than I ever learned, then I rode her to the hay field. While waiting for the wagon loads of hay to come to the derrick to be put on the haystack, Grandma showed me how to weave baskets of grass, telling me the ways of the Indians whom she had known. The noon meal was a huge dinner cooked and served by my mother to all hands, and there was much talk among them of farming, ranching, hunting, fishing and "fooling." Grandpa was a noted storyteller, with yarns of the old days that captivated all within hearing distance. My imagination was stirred and inspired during the hearing of these "real-life" yarns.

The ranch raised hay, grain, corn and other crops to feed the beef cattle. In later years we added the dairy cow string. We rode horses and worked cattle, planted corn, hoed the garden, picked fruit, and had the best bird hunting and bass fishing in the valley. My brothers and I carried shotguns or rifles and learned to hunt, clean and fix game under the tutelage of my father. He demanded a kill for each shot fired, and a reason for every kill. Fishing was fun and fortune, fun to do and food for the table. We ate everything we killed and caught, sometimes only once, but were prone to try everything. Neighboring ranch kids of like age did the same and we joined forces whenever possible. My eighth-grade graduation present was a new .22 rifle.

During those years, we went hunting in the hills and mountains for deer and elk. Dad showed us the fundamentals of tracking such animals, the same as tracking a first-calf heifer when she was due and not on the feed ground. These were probably my first tracking lessons, not special, not acknowledged, just matter of fact and part and parcel of the job to be done. Basic tracking was just a part of what farming, ranching and hunting was.

I graduated from high school in June of 1958. At that time, every male reaching 18 years of age or graduating from high school was given three choices: volunteer for any branch of the armed forces; be accepted into an approved college program; or be drafted into the U.S. Army. We had nine months to make a decision and take that action, or the third choice took effect whether we liked it or not. I joined the Idaho Air National Guard (ANG). As this was a first choice of many young men, the only job category not flooded with applicants was air police. I signed up for it, and it was my introduction to a 35-year law enforcement career, neither by design nor preference, but merely by chance of times.

I was sent off to Lackland Air Force Base near San Antonio, Texas, with a buddy who later became my brother-in-law, Dan Steiner. We completed the basic air force training and returned to Idaho. The ANG Air Police were allowed to work with local police agencies to complete training requirements and this was my intro-duction to actual police work. I asked to work relief and vacation shifts for local agencies to gain experience and, when an opening came up in the local police department, my application was accepted. Between the return from air force basic training and going

to work for the police department, I managed to marry a beautiful girl named Janet who has over the years graciously forgiven more than another would have endured. Together we raised four beautiful, intelligent and talented daughters, of whom we're most proud.

I enjoyed police work, even the mundane aspects of cat-in-the-tree type of calls. There was always something happening and something different every hour of every shift. There were criminal matters to work on, police patrol

functions, bar fights and burglaries. Armed holdups, and street shootings, disrespectful youth and the "everyone for himself atti-tude" by the public was still in the future. These were still the days in which "good" criminals were respected as masters of their profession. (They often left a telltale indi-cator—their mark or sign—at the crime scene so investigators would know who had done it.) Leaders of crime conferences

distributed pictures of such respected criminals, and respected crimi-nal investigators talked with respect of these persons and their modus operandi.

I was fascinated with this professional respect for the opposing force and studied and listened to the older and more experienced officers. I attended every training class and course available and learned the latest developments and newest techniques in criminal investigation. I also learned that if you really wanted to "know" one of these professional criminals, the easiest way to get acquainted was to contrive to encounter the person and offer to buy him a cup of coffee or a lunch and talk. I became acquainted with several criminals, all older men, the age of my father and more. I bought the coffee and they gave me pointers for solving crimes.

In 1963 I made an application to the U.S. Border Patrol. I hadn't exhausted my source of law enforcement education, but I was looking ahead. Some police officers were retiring at age 50 or so, when they ended up on the bottom of the bar fight more often then not. There wasn't a retirement system for law enforcement in Idaho, and there were no "benefits" as we expect in employment today. No state civil service system. Cops who retired had to find another job to pay bills. I wasn't qualified to take the exam for the FBI or most other Federal law enforcement agencies because I had not gone to college. Border Patrol officers came through Emmett each summer and rounded up some illegal Mexican aliens, and they always dropped off a couple recruiting brochures. My wife Janet had a cousin who was an Immigration Criminal Investigator in Los Angeles who had been in the Border Patrol. I talked with him during a summer family reunion. The Border Patrol sounded like my kind of an outfit, a unique and highly respected small federal law enforcement force of about 750 men. Patrol stations mainly along the southern border constituted most of this force, but some were along the northern border.

In the summer of 1964 I applied and tested for the Border Patrol. I was told that only about 20 percent of applicants passed the test. The most difficult portion was the creation of an artificial language using specific rules. I had no idea what they were even talking about. English hadn't been my favorite subject in school. I had gotten by with Cs, but never understood what I was doing. Somehow, someway, I figured out the section on artificial language, and the rest of the test was actually quite easy for me. Turned out I had passed all three sections with flying colors! The examination board was intimidating, with two Border Patrol Chiefs firing all sorts of questions, for most of which there wasn't a right answer. They were asking questions that caused applicants to demonstrate common sense and reasoning. I got through it, but they didn't say with flying colors. I do believe that my time with the police, little though it was, was a deciding factor.

In the spring of 1965, I was invited to travel to Chula Vista, California, at my own expense, to join the Patrol. This was probably

 the most important decision I had ever made. On April 26, 1965, I was sworn into the U.S. Border Patrol at Chula Vista Sector Headquarters located at San Ysidro, a little town right along the border and directly north of Tijuana, Mexico. Eight other trainees and I stumbled through the paperwork and regimented orientation of the Patrol for six long days. One of these trainees, James D. Burns, was from Bonners Ferry, Idaho, and had contacted me prior to our coming to California. J.D. and I quickly became close friends and partners. He was tall and slim, a couple years older than I, and just as full of energy and enthusiasm.

During that first week of duty, we were privileged to wash and gas up the jeeps of journeymen Patrol Inspectors (commonly called PIs) prior to riding with them during their duty shifts. We learned the area and what the Border Patrol actually did. We quickly found that the border area they patrolled called for four-wheel-drive vehicles. From the Pacific Ocean beach on the west to the top of Otay Mountain on the east were about 35 miles of mostly farming and rough back country brush, rattlesnakes, tarantulas and several different kinds of cactus. Rough roads were bladed with the Patrol's D-8 Cat among deep and steep canyons, then dragged to produce a road-wide stripe of pristine dirt that showed the slightest mark of any human crossing, or "sign."

From observing and listening (the most effective of law enforcement skills), I quickly came to understand that sign was whatever visual evidence showed the means or manner in which someone passed through an area. Illegal entrants heading north had to cross these roads. Crossing a drag road successfully required maximum ingenuity of the individual, and those with effective means and methods were much respected by the PIs. They were usually caught, but much respected. On duty, Patrol Inspectors would drive these crude drag roads and do what was called "sign cutting," looking for the marks of those who crossed. Once  sign was found, a tracking operation would commence. Often the officer finding the sign would park his jeep and simply begin to follow the sign on foot through the brush and canyons to wherever it led to find the *alumbrista*, or "fence jumper." Sometimes two or more officers would work together in a coordinated operation that covered several miles, one following the sign until another found, or "cut" the sign ahead in another area. The same operations continued at night and we trainees of course were also assigned night shifts to ensure we fully understood that this was a 24-hour job.

There were 35 journeyman inspectors assigned to the Chula Vista station when my class of trainees arrived for duty. I came to understand that this was the first class of trainees in this sector since 1961. I was assigned to work the afternoon shift on the fourth day and well remember being with rather talkative Patrol Inspector Hal Kosic. First names I learned quickly in the Patrol as was usual within the military environment also, were most often discarded in lieu of a nickname or simple use of the last name. It was near dusk and lights began to show here and there in the houses. We were high on the rim of a mesa west of the Tijuana River bottom area. The night air was soft and the dust had settled. Mountain quail were calling, the doves were cooing and it sure seemed like the place to be. Kosic had been in the Patrol for years. He had been all over the country and knew both good times and bad with the Border Patrol. We could see along the border fence for a great distance toward Ports of Entry at I-5 and across the farmed fields of celery, cabbage, carrots and lettuce and tomatoes that lay north of the fence on "our" side between I-5 and the beach area. On the south side of the fence, kids and dogs played in the soft warm dusk. Men in straw hats walked with small bags home from long days working in fields and wherever they could find work. Women with brooms swept the doorways and dirt paths to houses that appeared to me unkempt, dilapidated and in need of immediate repair. Most were of adobe blocks, some were of wood, and some were a combination. Most had tin roofs. The calls and conversations were in a language that I had heard but couldn't understand. I sat thinking of all that I was seeing, now and then asking of the Patrol inspector a question of this or that.

Suddenly the two-way radio squawked and one unit spoke to another announcing that they had "an entry, a single, plain sole, single row of stitching, screen-wire heel within a heel, eight nail holes, about 150 yards west of the white gate." There was radio acknowledgment by two other units. I sat there trying to figure out what it was that I had heard. Finally, thinking I had gotten some parts of it, I asked for an interpretation. Kosic spit tobacco juice into the growing darkness and pointed, saying, "See where the lights of that jeep are along the fence? Someone crossed the drag road there and is headed north toward the freeway." He explained that the description of the shoe he was wearing was like a street shoe without marking in the sole, but was sewn onto the upper with one line of stitching. The shoe had a heel with markings that looked on the ground like the out-line of one heel inside of the other, and it has little lines crisscrossing that appear like window-screen marking. He went on to say that the location was where, in past years, long before his time at this station, there had been a large white gate in the border fence at that location. He noted that it was very important for new officers to learn such locations as the White Gate, the Red Barn, the Old Truck Trail, and he rattled off a dozen more, some names of old ranchers and homesteads that were long gone but still marked locations for memory. Equally important was to learn the different descriptions of footgear worn by persons that might come across the fence. *That* was our business, he said, looking directly at me, and me knowing that he was telling something for which I would be responsible, "and catching every one depends on your knowing one from the other."

He drove the jeep a little closer to the rim of the mesa. Soon the lights of four vehicles were on the table top below us. I was anxious to get down there and help. Sensing this, my partner said softly, "Let's just watch and see how it goes from here. We have a better view." I watched the sign cut vehicles work back and forth and Kosic helped me to understand the first tracking operation that I had witnessed. I could see the tracker with a flashlight slowly following the sign on foot. Other sign cutting jeeps with side-mounted lights slowly drove along the crop roads and the pavements. The sign was cut here and the operation moved up, then followed and cut again near the river bottom that ran through the farm ground. The entrant was in the river bottom and traveling through the brush and weeds, the tracker hot on his heels.

Ahead, another PI in a jeep was cutting sign along the roads. In two other places, jeeps now sat quietly in the dark, their drivers watching with binoculars into the darkness (this was called still-watching). The tracker reported his progress by radio, keeping all informed. Soon one of the still-watching units reported he had the fellow in view along the river bottom and 100 yards in front of him, and that he'd be out of the jeep. Five minutes, then ten went by, the operation continued silently below. Then the radio announced that the fellow was in custody by the still-watching unit. The officer I was with explained that by cutting the drag road along the fence where the first sign was found, then by following the person's footprints, other units were able to position themselves to intercept this illegal entrant. This was an example of a perfect Border Patrol tracking operation I learned. A similar operation had taken place in another location and resulted in an arrest. All the units then converged on the station so the new recruits could see and talk with the illegals.

I was intrigued with the whole sign cutting operation, which seemed very mysterious to me then. During that week a total of seven or eight illegal entrants were caught, and I was told that was about normal for that time of year.

On our fifth day at Chula Vista, we were all taken into a classroom and told that we would be leaving for the Academy the next morning. There we'd have eighteen weeks of basic training consisting primarily of the study of Immigration and Nationality Law and learning Spanish. Duties and Authorities, a third major study, was primarily the practical application process of getting the job done. I had learned from talking with journeymen officers that the instructors were much like

James "JD" Burns and Joel ready for post-acadamy training classes.

military drill instructors. All were regular Border Patrol inspectors except for a few Spanish teachers. Patrol Inspectors Andrew (Andy) Hattery and William (Bill) Fleming would be our post-Academy Spanish and Law instructors. They spent much of the afternoon preparing us for our stint there and said we'd be joined by trainee inspectors from other duty stations.

The Academy was at a World War II-era naval air station near Los Fresnos, Texas, a small town about an hour's drive from Brownsville. The Border Patrol would be the only people on this base except for an alien detention center that was active on another part of the base. The Academy facilities had been refurbished and were actually not bad, according to those who had been there. We would be required to stand inspection each morning, march to and from classes, etc. Most important was the Spanish tests, given each Friday, along with a crucial midterm and final exam. Fail the midterm or the final and you could kiss the job goodbye. Law tests were important but more forgivable; Spanish was not. Upon finishing the Academy, we'd continue on probation for a year.

When we were returned to our duty stations, we'd be expected to attend post-Academy classes on the sixth day of each week. We'd have a double-translation Spanish test at the end of six months and another at ten and one half months. A double translation consisted of being perfectly attired in dress uniform, entering a closed room to announce and address a board of three Chief Patrol Inspectors. One of these Inspectors would announce to you in Spanish that he was to be your "alien." We'd be handed a list of 20 questions in English that were to be asked of the alien in Spanish. The alien would answer in Spanish and we were to write the answer in English. The other two Inspectors would grade our accent, vocabulary, word usage, etc. both in Spanish and English. Failure to make a 70 percent on either was grounds for immediate dismissal. In addition, there would be weekly Conduct and Efficiency reports written by whatever journeymen officers we were assigned to work with during the week.

Early the next morning after the briefing, we were loaded up for our trip to the Academy. With bag and baggage, uniforms, leather gear and side arms, we loaded into "alien transportation" and taken over the mountains to El Centro, California. Alien transportation consisted of old buses used to transport apprehended aliens from BP stations to holding facilities and from holding facilities to the border or to aircraft for interior transportation. Five other trainees from the Temecula Station joined us.

We arrived at El Centro at about six in the evening. It was 106 degrees, we had been sweating in the bus for eight hours, tired, hot, dirty and as stinking as the frightened aliens who had used the bus days and weeks previously. The bus driver (a journeyman Border Patrol Inspector) stopped at an older and obviously second-rate motel. He characteristically said not more than absolutely necessary to any of us trainees, simply stating, "Get booked in. Each man has a room for the night, the clerk has your names. NO PARTYING TONIGHT! I'll be here in the parking lot at five in the morning and everyone had better be here and ready to go, understand! I'll take you to the airport for transport to the Academy." With that he turned, boarded the bus and drove off.

We got checked into our rooms and began to relax. We learned that there were a dozen or more trainees from other duty stations also booked into the motel for the night and we soon began to gather and get acquainted. Someone brought a case of cold beer and we congregated in one of the largest rooms and compared notes of our first week in the Border Patrol. Everyone drifted in and out taking showers and changing clothes. One thing quickly agreed upon was the universal character of the journeymen inspectors. A number of us had been in the military basic training and the unexpected and comparable environment gave cause for thought. Someone shouted, "Let's go get something to eat," and en masse we moved "uptown." The group split up into smaller units with different desires for dinner and drinking. The admonition of NO PARTYING was quickly forgotten. Many of the guys had a few more to drink than they could handle and the first rule of the Patrol was that you take care of each other. My new found ole buddy J.D. was a mess—he'd made a real spectacle of himself at dinner and it was quite a chore for me to get him back to the motel and into bed.

It seemed like only a few minutes till 4:30 a.m. I jumped up and hit the shower and by 5 a.m., I was pulling my baggage outside into the parking lot. The bus was there, and leaning against the front fender was the same ol' sourpuss looking PI. I got my things aboard and mumbled that I'd shake up the others. I hit J.D.'s door first and it was open—he was still in bed. It took nearly an hour to get everyone up and dressed and their gear gathered up. Already it was 106 degrees and the sun had been up less than an hour. We were finally loaded, the PI was mad, cussing and kicking and threatening. He drove us to the airport and at one end of the flight line I could see an old four-motor Super Connie.

We rolled up behind the wing and he braked to a stop. "OK, get the hell off of my bus! And get on the plane!" he shouted. We got off the bus and up the ladder onto the plane with our baggage.

Years before, when I was in high school and a member of the CAP cadet program, I had taken a trip to Casper, Wyoming, aboard a U.S. Air Force transport aircraft. I had seen canvas sling seats before, but not many of the others had. We got seated and somewhat strapped in before we noticed there weren't any crew members aboard. We relaxed; some with hangovers immediately went to sleep. Then we became aware that the heat was growing inside the aircraft. I also observed that here and there the side panels of the fuselage were taped to cover cracks between the panels. Before long we heard and saw through the open door a Border Patrol sedan and a maintenance van drive up alongside the aircraft. Two pilots boarded without a glance or word to any of us. A mechanic began to do a preflight check. As the time passed the temperature inside the plane went up steadily. We were sweating profusely. Finally the pilot shouted to the crew chief on the ground and I watched as the left outside prop began to rotate. Finally it caught in a plume of blue smoke and began to fire. Then the right outside began to turn and then to spin. The mechanic climbed up on the ladder and poured oil from a five-gallon can into the top of the inside right engine. I could see the oil leaking to the tarmac below. He gave the pilot a thumbs-up and the prop began to turn and then again in a cloud of blue smoke began to fire. The copilot came back and pulled in the ladder and shut the door, shot one look at all of us and shouted over the engine noise, "Hang ON!" We rolled across to the runway and with engines roaring at full throttle down the runway and into the air. The noise was deafening but at least the fuselage leaked enough air that now we could breathe and the breeze was refreshing. Several of the hangovers didn't take the takeoff well and turned a bit green. I enjoyed flying and didn't think it was too bad.

We had flown for about four hours when we landed and a couple people recognized that we were at the El Paso airport. A Border Patrol sedan rolled up to our plane now parked in the hot sun. The pilot and copilot climbed down the ladder and, looking back into the anxious faces, announced, "Wait here, we'll be back." We waited, the temperature climbed, the air died and the sick got sicker and prayed they'd die and never drink again! No one had anything to eat or drink of course, no one had told us to bring anything aboard with us. We waited well past an hour before they returned and we took off again. We flew for hours, it seemed, and it was nearing dark we descended into a gale-force wind. We could see in the dim light palm trees blowing wildly, and the old plane growled and groaned, roared and tossed, bucking in the wind. Those who could, got sick all over again. Finally we were low over a runway that seemed in the middle of nowhere. Wheels down and solid, we taxied and parked. Another alien bus was waiting to take us on another hour-long ride to the Academy. The new life had begun.

The Academy had a distinct military atmosphere. Trainees stood formation, uniform inspection, marched to and from, etc. We were the eighty-fourth Academy class and I guess proud of it. The Academy on the old naval base was at least 20 miles from the nearest town. Only a couple trainees were allowed to drive vehicles to the Academy; all others were transported by service vehicles of some sort. This was done to limit students' off-duty activities to whatever mischief they could get into on post. This was pretty much limited to study, supervised pistol practice, hand-to-hand defensive tactics, practicing Spanish, and looking for rattlesnakes. The rattlesnakes were something to behold—it wasn't unusual to find one six feet long and as large around as your upper arm. This was what the Border Patrol wanted—a cadre of captive students who concentrated on their studies. Only one little short-order cafe and beer garden to which the students had access was allowed on post. Otherwise we were afoot and it was too far to walk to anywhere.

For the most part, students were too concerned about studies and making sure to pass their tests to want to go to town. During the last half of the Academy, those with some measure of grade security ventured to Brownsville or across the river to Matamoros. Most stuck to their reason for being there. Somehow I managed to squeak by each of the "do or you're out" Spanish tests. I was more interested in the law and derivation of citizenship; on that side of the page I felt secure. I had no problems with the "confidence course"—pistol shooting, duties and authorities, etc.

The first week of August, an order came from the Border Patrol Chief in Washington, D.C., to the Chief at the Academy: "Graduate those trainees and get them back to their duty stations—we're being overrun!" The Bracero program had ended its treaty life on June 30, and the Mexican government had refused to reinstate the agreement. As a result, all contract workers were returned to Mexico. U.S. employers were immediately in desperate need of laborers, and previously contracted Mexican workers were equally in desperate need of work and wages. However, with the termination of the international labor-contracting treaty, there was no lawful means to bring these two needs together. Increasing daily were the numbers of these workers crossing the border illegally to work. The Border Patrol was called on to make an increasing number of apprehensions, perhaps ten times the arrests made previously. The system was flooded. The call came down from Border Patrol Headquarters in Washington D.C. to the Chief at the academy to get every available man out and on the border line.

Our Academy class was cut two or three weeks short and we all were graduated and sent again by the same service aircraft on the return flight back to El Centro, California, and then on the alien bus again to Chula Vista, arriving at about three in the afternoon. The Temecula guys boarded another bus and headed north to their

Chula Vista Trainees - L-R Back row: George Whitney, James Burns, Larry Haynes, Joel Hardin. Front row: D. Dunson, Robert Woytych Jr., Donald Myers, Clark Burrow

station and we reported in. The Shift Senior looked relieved and greeted the eight of us with a tired, but friendly, handshake. He said, "Well, guys, we're being overrun. I need four of you to start work now, and the other four to come back at midnight and relieve them." We looked at each other and I spoke first. "I'll work now, if someone will take my gear and stow it in a motel room." The others quickly sorted themselves out.

The Senior looked at me and said, "Here's keys to a jeep. Do you remember how to get out to the mesa off of Brown Field Road?" I nodded, trying to remember where he was talking about. "Okay, Patrol Inspector, go catch some! Go out to the mesa and, with whatever daylight you have left, get familiar with the area. When you get two or three, bring them back in here. You other three, go west along the fence." With that, I went out to find the jeep to fit the keys I had been handed. I found the jeep and checked the oil and gas as I had been instructed to do in the week prior to the Academy. Then, drawing a long breath, I started out.

I found Brown Field Road and drove to the eucalyptus tree line that I recognized as the road to the mesa. I drove out on the mesa and to the rim overlooking the canyon that separated the U.S. from Mexico. In the bottom, Mexicans played soccer on a field that they had leveled and set up goals. The fence that marked the border ended at the canyon's west bank and began again at the east side, leaving a mile or so in the bottom with only a steel fence post here or there to mark where the division was. It was now near five in the afternoon and the day's heat was beginning to ease, and people were beginning to move about on the dirt lanes and streets between the houses and shops across the canyon. I sat and watched and wondered just what I had gotten myself into. This was the first time I had been alone with my own thoughts and without the pressure of Academy classes, being and doing everything right in front of other journeymen officers. I just sat and watched the people across the line going about their late-afternoon routine. Here and there I could see a single individual with a small "triques bag," walking and looking north across to my side of the canyon. These would be the people coming across after it got dark.

I drove slowly around and down into the canyon, and followed the jeep roads around, getting familiar with the area. Just before dark as I was letting the jeep idle along the road, suddenly a head popped up in the brush ahead coming up out of a finger canyon. I quickly sped up, threw on the brakes, and jumped out and ran into the brush. I heard movement and trying to remember what to say, uttered something in Spanish and dug the guy out of the brush. He was shaking his head and apologizing to me. My first solo apprehension and he was apologizing, or I thought that was what he was saying. I patted him down and gestured for him to get into the jeep on the passenger side. He looked startled, but I opened the door and remembered to say *"Subase."* This was my opportunity to try to speak the Spanish I'd been learning. Later I caught several more individuals and by midnight I was feeling quite comfortable. My first real day on the job was a success with seven apprehensions.

During all of this, the "powers that be" insured that, as promised, one day each week was devoted to post-Academy studies. We trainees all worked at it when we could, tested and passed our six-month exam. The tenth month was the cutoff for eliminating those trainees that the senior men determined weren't Border Patrol material. Most made the cut and now that we were journeymen officers and the pressure was off, we all settled in to our steady activity.

Since I'd had more law enforcement experience than most of the newer officers, I was put in charge of a unit of six to eight officers working various assignments adjacent to the border. By the second year of duty we were beginning to be seasoned veterans. Most of us

1970 - El Cajon Station Outstanding Award
L-R Back row: Walter Pataya, James Burns, Richard Lensink, Walter Shulstrom,
Ab Taylor. Front row: Joel Hardin, Dennis Nichell, Jack Kearney, James Dorcy.

had already apprehended as many people as the officers with ten years of experience. We had worked all of the usual operations associated with what was called "line watch" operations. These consisted of actually watching the border area for illegal entrants, dragging the roads in the immediate vicinity of the border fence, then cutting these roads for sign of illegal entries. I began to be assigned to various operational duties away from the immediate border area, such as the city patrol. This consisted of plainclothes work in San Diego, checking the transportation centers such as bus stations, train stations, airports, etc. Farm and ranch check meant checking farm workers and farm- and ranch-related industries as far north as Los Angeles and Riverside. Back country sign cutting was another regular operation to which several officers were assigned each day. These officers, in groups of four or five, would begin sign cutting operations at daylight in areas north of those regularly worked by the line watch units. When they cut sign on the system of dirt roads and paths crisscrossing the hills and brush lands, they would begin a tracking operation in which they followed the sign until they caught the individuals. These units worked together with the line units to ensure that very few illegal entrants got away. When one or more did get beyond the line watch area of operations or eluded their efforts, they reported these as "got-a-ways" to a special unit known as the sign cutters.

I rotated through each of these operations except sign cutting, the one operation I most wanted to get involved in. I had learned to follow sign by that time by watching and listening to more experienced officers. All Border Patrolmen could track. It was expected of them. Some did it better than others, but all followed sign to some extent. The better trackers—about one out of every fifty PIs who most often found the people they were tracking—became regulars on the back country sign cut crew. The permanent sign cutters were a very select group of PIs, recognized as having exceptional tracking skills. Tracking was all they did and they were revered by fellow PIs and other law enforcement personnel.

The "got-a-ways" were often the guides, or mules, smuggling drugs and/or people across the border. The border units made detailed descriptions of the footprints of these persons and turned those descriptions over to the sign cut unit, which took the descriptions, found and followed the tracks until they found the individuals. They worked the real back country—the mountainous areas north and east of the line watch areas that the "got-a-ways" disappeared into. I was intrigued by the sign cutters' ability to come back with the subject who had made the tracks; I didn't know anyone else who could do this. During this time I was working smuggling operations and

Apprehended alien group tracked 125 air miles in 5 days by El Cajon Sign Cutters

making daily referrals to the sign cut crew and had become fairly well acquainted with several of the members. The general character of these specialists, I had discovered, was much the same. Most were quiet, guarded in their conversations and generally didn't socialize much with the other officers. They were loners who stuck together because of their unique aptitude for tracking.

One of these officers was Albert "Ab" Taylor, who was a talkative exception. When I met him, Ab Taylor was just under 40 years old, a dark-haired, sparkling-eyed character whose charismatic personality charmed everyone and radiated an infectious excitement. His ready smile seemed a promise to include you in a joke, a story or an ever-likely practical joke on someone. Ab was a tireless worker who shunned slackers and always gave credit to others where credit was due. He came from Alpine, Texas, a boy of the World War II era. With more mischief than could be contained in Texas, he lied about his age and went to England at 17 to fly for the RAF. Successful at that, he had found the way to make things happen, and he wasn't afraid to tackle anything. He was also smart enough to know when to step aside. He returned to Texas from Europe after the war old enough and with a reputation and lifestyle well suited for the Border Patrol, and they needed a few good men. Ab reached the esteemed supervisory level of Senior Patrol Inspector due almost totally to his boundless initiative and ability to motivate others, and despite his disdain for administrative paperwork and personnel issues. Ingenuity in getting a job done was Abs' trademark and sign cutting his forte. Ab enjoyed life, people, and himself and wasn't hesitant to teach others what he understood about his exceptional natural tracking skills. He was highly respected, even though he was by far the youngest of the "old sign cut crew," and he remains so to this day.

Whenever I had an opportunity, I talked at length with Ab regarding several of the more sophisticated smuggling operations. These operations involved taking the smuggled aliens several miles into and through the mountains, often two or three days' travel from the border. Together we schemed and plotted to capture these operators using the sign cut crew and my own unit. Then one day, Ab asked if I'd be interested in trying my hand on the sign cut crew. It was what I'd been waiting for, and I eagerly agreed to give it a shot.

I went through the new-recruit drill any trainee suffered. I washed the sign cutters' jeeps, made their coffee, drove around the mountain to pick them up, and jumped out to open all the gates. All of these initiation rites assured the other sign cutters that the tenderfoot was worthy of their attention. In a month or so, through my instigation, my regular partner, J.D. Burns, was invited to join in this venture. Together we learned how and when to talk with the sign cutters as they followed the sign. We watched everything they did, and now and then someone other than Ab would show us what he was seeing and what it meant. J.D. and I spent most of the next year working with the sign cut crew, soaking up everything they did and said and learning the full extent of the Chula Vista Sector. I fondly remember one summer day when I was working with Ab and Dana Ellsworth on a particularly difficult track. We had crawled around for two hours, and I found the missing piece of the sign puzzle. Dana turned to Ab and commented loud enough for me to hear. "I think you're going to make a sign cutter of this one."

Sometime during that year, exactly when we weren't sure, we were accepted as sign cutters. We felt honored, since we were immediately accorded the respect and responsibility that went along with being members of this elite unit. Assistant Chief Dale Swancutt sent us together "on detail" for two weeks, which in this case meant we were to take an alien transport bus and a van and head north of Los Angeles outside the Sector area to find and apprehend illegals. It had been more than 20 years since the last such detail had been sent from Chula Vista. We were entrusted to travel anywhere in California that we could apprehend illegals and to handle whatever situations might arise. We were afforded the opportunity to work on a wide variety of operations and we gained a great deal of experience not available to most other officers.

Along with the steady increase in illegal entries alien smuggling became the big problem. The Border Patrol in the Chula Vista sector was now apprehending more persons in one week than the entire Patrol had apprehended in our first year. New trainees had now become a regular part of the personnel at nearly all sector stations. Many of the old hands were retiring. The new influx of trainees, the new programs, and the new processing procedures that were brought in to manage this silent invasion were more than many of them could handle. Some decided to retire rather than adjust. The older trainees, such as J.D. and I, were quickly becoming the seasoned journeymen who shouldered the bulk of daily operations. I thought it was a great time to be a part of the Border Patrol. Our trainee class in Aril of 1965 was only the second class to graduate in the previous ten years and we were in the right place at the right time, riding the wave of the new tide of change. This was a different Border Patrol. Completely new methods and operations were necessary in order to cope with the constant influx of illegals along the border. J.D. and I loved it.

The changes affected the sign cut unit as well. The old crew fell apart as the new operations broke down their established routines. Over the next year, most retired and a couple transferred to smaller stations to prepare for retirement. Soon Ab Taylor was the only "old head" who remained, having been the youngest member of the elite crew. He was much too young and full of spirit to think of retirement. J.D. and I, as the newest members blessed by the old crew, were assigned to Ab to carry out whatever tracking operations there were.

Not long afterward, big things began to happen. Alien smuggling was quickly becoming a lucrative financial business for organized crime. Beginning in the Chula Vista sector, alien-smuggling operations soon took precedent over other operations. These were the days when alien smuggling involved important political figures, such as San Diego City councilmen and other well-known and respected members of society. Our pressure and direct involvement, the arrest and prosecution of several prominent figures, and the resulting media attention combined to cause these organizations to move out of our area and continue their operations elsewhere.

El Cajon was the "elsewhere" that many of the organizations ended up moving to. This station was immediately east of Chula Vista and was ideal for the smugglers, since they were still close enough to Tijuana to use their established resources. El Cajon was a five-man station struggling with some internal problems and was unable to cope with the tremendously increased pressure. Assistant Chief Swancutt asked J.D. and me if we would transfer to El Cajon late in 1968. We did, and Ab Taylor followed a year later as the station supervisor. J.D. and I had an advantage in that we were familiar with many of the smugglers. We knew their vehicles, their guides and their methods of operation. Our methods of dealing with these organizations quickly became the standard for the Border Patrol and we were amazingly successful.

Farms, ranches and some rolling, brush-covered hills characterized the Chula Vista station area. In comparison, the El Cajon area was rugged and mountainous. It was in the heart of the Laguna Mountains and contained some of the most beautiful waterfalls and granite cliffs I've ever seen. It was an area of stark contrast. The Carizzo Gorge one of the deepest canyons in the western hemisphere with shoulders to more than 3,000 feet was in some places below sea level beginning just south of interstate #80 east of El Cajon running south and emptying out into Mexico. Mount Laguna some sixty miles north of interstate #8 rose to over 6,000 feet and was smack in the middle of it all. Often illegal aliens would cross the fence in the mountains east of San Diego and continue to walk north through the mountains for many days. The officers at El Cajon station would often cut the sign in the valleys or canyons along the border at or below sea level in the early morning and then follow the sign through the mountains up to 5,000 or 6,000 feet before noon.

Tracking was the daily routine and a necessary part of all Border Patrol operations at El Cajon. California Highway 94 wound its way east from Chula Vista, more or less following the old stage route parallel to the border through the mountains to Yuma, Arizona. This highway came within 8 to 10 miles of the border fence and met the access highway to the Port of Entry at Tecate, then went east through the Campo Station area and intersected with Interstate #8, which paralleled highway #94 to San Diego. El Cajon's area was funnel shaped, with the tube of the funnel a narrow valley hidden from the highway by high mountains. Maroon Valley was part of a cattle ranch and was guarded by an iron gate that barred public entry to the single-lane road blasted in the rocky side of a narrow, steep canyon. The El Cajon PIs had keys for access through all ranch gates in their area.

The remote mountainous area of Maroon Valley became a focal point for major smuggling operations. The entry point and travel routes of illegal entrant alien groups were shadowed from observers to the prearranged pickup staging areas along the highways to the north. These pickup points could be along Highway 94 or further north on Interstate #8, or any of the many secondary roads through the mountains in between. Groups could travel a few days or more to arrive and wait for a load car or truck to come to get them. Sometimes the load vehicle would break down, get lost or picked off by patrol units, miss the pickup point, or simply not show because the smuggler took off with his money.

Many would travel on toward the closest town or city; some people died in the mountains. Daily the Sign Cutters would cut for sign on the game and

L-R – Lauria "PeeWee" LaGrasse, James Dorcy and Jack Kearney, with false deck smuggling truck and aliens.

cattle trails, along the creek bottoms, valley and mountainsides north from the border. Every group had to be tracked to determine its pickup point, to identify the guides and to establish pattern, route and entry point. For J.D. and me, any intrusion into our area was a personal challenge and we often worked several days and nights without stopping, scarcely eating or sleeping until the case was closed. J.D. became the best and most persistent sign cutter I ever worked with.

The Newton-Azrak Murders

I would be remiss if I didn't mention of the murders of two trainee Border Patrol agents from the Temecula, California, station in 1969. I'm ashamed to say that I've long ago misplaced or lost the newspaper accounts and all official correspondence that relates to this incident. While I was directly involved in the investigation subsequent to the disappearance of the two officers, so were a hundred or so other Border Patrol agents. I'll tell the story as best I remember it, but bear with me while I provide some background.

As I have related in this chapter, everything was changing rapidly in the Border Patrol between 1965 and 1975. It was not possible to secure the southern border with the Border Patrol capability we had at that time. The news media carried daily accounts of the effects that the illegal entrant migration was having on schools, social services, hospitals, working conditions, wages, the national economy and a lot more. Everyone knew that even though the Border Patrol along the southern border was catching an unprecedented number of illegal entrants daily, up to fifty times that number were eluding capture and going on north into the U.S. The service was hiring new officers as quickly as possible, or trying to. Political pressure was constant to increase the manpower allotments in an attempt to cope with the invasion, but money to pay and equip new personnel was much slower in coming.

My trainee class in April of 1965 was only the second group of new agents hired in the previous seven years; the class prior to ours was hired in October of 1964. Both of these trainee classes were comparatively small, only 30 or 40 officers. Nearly half of these were let go before completing their first year. The next class of trainees was hired in 1965, but didn't report for duty until late in 1966 and then had to go to the Academy for four months before being able to participate with the work force. Then began an endless succession of training classes, with new officers assigned to all duty stations to augment journeyman-level staffing. This often resulted in more new officers at different stages of post-Academy training on duty at any given station than journeyman officers to supervise and train them. There was more work than could be done and we had a cascade of daily changes in rules, regulations and procedures. The numbers we had to apprehend and the changing character of the people who were being handled were driving operations out of control. Among the illegal entrants, there was a big rise in disrespect of authority and officers found their work increasingly difficult. Arresting encounters with illegals steadily became more confrontational and dangerous. Encounters with weapons, once very rare, became an everyday occurrence, and we saw a big rise in professional drug and alien smuggling in a larger slice of the world where human values were very cheap.

Temecula, California, was a small town 100 miles north of the border and adjacent to Interstate 395, that runs from the Mexican border to the Canadian border. Both Interstate 395 at Temecula and U.S. 101 near San Clemente, California, had been at that time established as Border Patrol checkpoints. Patrol units from both of these stations manned these checkpoint operations around the clock as manpower permitted. The checkpoints were essentially a second border stop on the major north-south highways between Tijuana and the Los Angeles area. Tijuana was in that era the greatest gathering area for peoples from all over the world preparing to attempt illegal entry into the U.S. The checkpoint at San

Clemente was well established on the four-lane freeway, with vehicles and overhead freeway signage in place to effect a stop-and-check for all vehicle traffic. The checkpoint at Temecula was more of a roving effort on the smaller two-lane highways and consisted of one or more chase cars and a van with flashing red lights mounted on the rear and a portable stop sign that was rolled onto the center of the road. This equipment could be moved to the center line of the highway by two or three men wherever officers wanted to set it up. This permitted officers to move the checkpoint up and down the highway or even onto any of several interconnecting roads used by smugglers to avoid being stopped. Temecula was a smaller station with limited manpower, so the checkpoint was posted intermittently and wherever the officers believed it would be most effective.

The Temecula station had its fair share of trainee officers without sufficient supervisory officers during regular duty hours. Trainees who were into the second phase of the initial year's training were often assigned duty shifts working with other trainees. Thus one night's duty shift had two young trainees, Theodore L. Newton and George F. Azrak, assigned to take the checkpoint vehicle and a chase car and set up to check traffic on the two-lane Highway 79, a few miles east of U.S. 395. Highway 79 connects with the border highway system coming north through the Laguna Mountains and to the greater East Los Angeles area. It was a favorite smugglers' route to circumvent the Temecula checkpoint.

Newton and Azrak arrived near the tiny community of Oak Grove at about midnight where the checkpoint had been set previously. They rolled the stop sign into the middle of the highway to stop and check all vehicular traffic. There were very few travelers on this highway during the night until dawn brought the morning's work traffic. They radioed to the Temecula station and checked in as set up and operating and they were to call each hour as a safety measure. I don't recall if they checked in at 2 or 3 a.m., but by 4 a.m., a Temecula unit was at the checkpoint and found that the stop sign had been removed from the highway and the two officers and their chase car were gone.

A highway search began first with Temecula units being acti-
vated. Before dawn phone calls roused both J.D. and me from our
beds. A number of other officers were called into action, and everyone suspected foul play. By midday a full-scale search was underway
from Oak Grove north to Los Angeles and south to the border (and
unofficially south in Mexico as well). There was no way to know what
had happened though everyone wanted to believe that they had
jumped into the chase car to catch a vehicle that had run the checkpoint, a situation that commonly caused officers to abandon the
checkpoint. But they could have been anywhere. This was a back
country area with a few farms and ranches scattered between tiny
communities nestled in rolling hills and mountains. Highways
between these hamlets cut through huge cattle-grazing areas, grain
and hay fields, and hills of natural brush growth. They could have
been out of radio contact or their radio wasn't working. They could
have been involved in a high-speed chase and crashed and were dead
or injured and unable to use the radio. They could have chased a
vehicle up some tiny mountain road and their chase car had become
disabled or even worse—those they were chasing could have captured
them. Possibilities, at that point seemed endless.

Assistant chiefs began laying out a operation to systematically
check every mile of every road. Additionally, as required by regulations, they reported the disappearance of the two officers to the FBI,
the agency with jurisdiction for investigation of all such incidents
involving Federal officers. A political battle began as to who was in
charge and which agency's personnel did what. J.D. and I, in company
with dozens of other officers, went to the scene and began from there
checking every road and access that the chase car, a 1964 Plymouth
four-door sedan, could have traveled. The search continued throughout that day and night and stretched into the next several days and
nights. The Chula Vista station maintained a skeleton force of officers
on duty to keep the lid on in that area; everyone else was involved in
a search for our brother officers. J.D. and I had never met Newton or
Azrak, but that didn't matter—they were missing members of our

family. As the fruitless hours and days went by, we began to believe that when they were found, we would be attending funerals.

The FBI was firmly in control of the investigation and directing activities with a hundred agents on the case. We continued half-heartedly to check this and that as they directed us to, regardless of how many times it had been checked previously. The FBI ran TV and radio ads asking the public to help to find the two Border Patrol officers or their chase car. Newspapers carried reports that the FBI was offering a cash reward for information relating to the investigation and a huge amount of money for information linking anyone to the officers' disappearance. The FBI wanted a combined effort by their agents and Border Patrol officers to sweep-search miles of highway right-of-way north from Oak Grove toward Riverside and East Los Angeles. J.D. and I were part of this effort on a bright sunshiny day, walking abreast with others for miles along the highway hoping to find something that might be recognized as evidence. Border Patrol pilot Joe Page was flying overhead in his Piper Supercub searching for sign of something that wouldn't be seen from the ground.

We came to an area where there wasn't a right-of-way fence. A large barley field bordered directly on the roadway. Walking along, we saw where a vehicle had turned off the highway and driven into and through the barley field. J.D. and I began to follow the vehicle tracks through the barley field toward the foothills, curious to see what this vehicle was doing. We asked Joe to tell us where the tire tracks were going ahead of us through the field. He quickly found them and said the vehicle had driven through the field and into the foothills a short way to where an old cabin stood beneath some scrub oak trees. He saw that another vehicle had also driven through the field from the highway

to the cabin and returned to the highway some distance ahead of where the searching officers now were. Joe continued to circle the cabin area some distance ahead of us and soon said quietly on the radio that he had found the chase car near the cabin, well concealed with brush. We reported this to the FBI officer leading the search operation and waited for his arrival at our position in the middle of the barley field. We were told to sit under a tree while FBI agents approached the cabin and chase car and did a preliminary investigation. Newton and Azrak's bodies were in the old cabin. Later in the afternoon, we were allowed to approach the cabin and view the officers' bodies, still in uniform, lying on the floor. They were handcuffed together to the base of an old stove and each had been shot in the back of the head.

Nearly three weeks later, the offer of cold, hard reward money was too much for some people, and they reported information to the FBI that led to the arrest and conviction of two marijuana smugglers for the kidnapping and murder of the two Border Patrol officers. This wasn't the first such incident of violence, but it was the beginning of a swelling tide of border violence. Within the next few years, such incidents had become common.

Theodore Newton and George Azrak were the first Border Patrol officers killed in the line of duty in many years. The Immigration Service Border Patrol established a memorial award to be presented by the Commissioner of Immigration to an appropriate officer for service above and beyond the call of duty.

In 1980, I was privileged to be invited with my wife Janet as guests of the United States Department of Justice to Washington D.C. to be presented with this memorial award.

As the numbers of illegal entries increased, officers were discouraged from working the mountainous outback areas and directed to concentrate on the higher numbers of illegals entering and traveling to the metropolitan areas. Prior to 1969, rarely did any alien or drug-smuggling arrest incur physical violence of any sort. I was astounded to learn in my first year of duty that it mostly was like playing a game of tag—once an alien was physically touched, the game was over. Then the alien—man, woman or child—would follow, wait or do whatever was directed without comment, hesitation or refusal. It was rare to have to handcuff anyone. But by 1972, having some kind of violence erupt when stopping to interview or apprehend anyone became a daily occurrence. Drug smuggling's huge profits attracted very unsavory types, and each arrest of an illegal entrant might be a life-threatening situation.

We became aware that drug smugglers were more often armed and prone to extreme measures to evade capture. We were also noticing that illegal entrants and drug smugglers generally were younger than before, in their late teens, and they were equipped with better vehicles. These were not professional criminals, but streetwise, easy-money youths without maturity to have regard for anyone's life. We frequently followed them in long, high-speed chases, and watched them running through roadblocks and ramming cars. These heedless young men often injured or killed their human cargo. This was a rapidly changing time, and the rules regarding use of weapons were not applicable. The "bad" guys had no rules, and essentially we didn't

This smuggler was convicted when tracking proved prior arrangement and guide service to pickup point. The motorcycle was used as a scout vehicle on the highway, and as a guise for activities in the back country. L-R: Joel Hardin, Richard Lensink (on motorcycle) and Ab Taylor.

either. We did what was necessary at the time to protect each other and ourselves.

One day in the late spring of 1972, I awoke to the fact that I was just a player in this game, and I knew by then that if you played a game as dangerous as I did, sooner or later I'd make a mistake. Consequences of even a single mistake were not good. The next time I went to Sector Headquarters, I paid a visit to my old compadre, Assistant Chief Swancutt, and told him I was interested in transferring to a northern border station.

CHAPTER THREE

1971 Hot Pursuit
Officer Down!

I was used to calls in the middle of the night, so I was instantly awake when my phone rang at 4 a.m. Those early morning calls were usually routine when I was stationed at El Cajon, on the southern California border. Most often they entailed meeting another police agency to either pick up or track some "illegals." This call was different and I could sense it in the Border Patrol dispatcher's voice. Without formalities, he began telling me that an hour or more earlier, one of the Campo Station units had called and was "in pursuit," of a vehicle headed from Boulevard on Interstate 8 through a lonely stretch of the Laguna Mountains toward Pine Valley, California. Radio contact was intermittent at best in that area due to the mountains. The Chula Vista dispatcher had lost radio contact with the unit and too much time had passed. Something was wrong. The dispatcher had first called the other Campo unit as backup and was now calling El Cajon, the next closest unit west, to respond ASAP. The dispatcher hung up, knowing I'd be at the office and in the unit on the road in 15 minutes. He'd give me further information when I went in service, hitting the road headed east toward where the lost unit was last heard from.

When I got to the station, dispatch called saying that a concerned motorist had just called in on a Border Patrol radio with a disturbing report. He had passed by a Border Patrol vehicle stopped behind another car and had it's emergency overhead lights flashing. Seeing no one in either car, the concerned motorist had stopped, gotten out and found an officer lying in the ditch, bloodied and unconscious. Using the radio in the BP vehicle, this concerned individual had contacted dispatch, explained the situation and agreed to stand by until help arrived.

I was already headed east on the interstate at full speed by the time I had the full story. Dispatch advised that he had contacted a couple of the Campo Station units that would be responding, as well as my partner J.D., who would be a few minutes behind me. We were about an hour away so an ambulance from the Pine Valley Volunteer Fire Department would arrive before we did. The Campo units would arrive at about that same, nearly at daybreak. I was impatient as the freeway miles flew by. I saw little traffic in either direction, but kept a watchful eye for deer. I thought about the area, some 60 or 70 miles east of El Cajon in the Laguna Mountains. The area was typically scrub oak, buck brush and manzanita, interspersed with cactus, rattlesnakes and huge granite boulders. Steep and deep, the canyons were something to see. It got cold, down to near freezing at night, but it would be hot in the afternoon. Officer assaults were not yet common, so my adrenaline was flowing and time seemed to crawl. I tried to imagine what might have happened. This was something that we all thought about and knew could happen any time, any shift, working alone in single-man units, often without backup, in areas where radio contact was iffy at best. We anticipated when the "opposition" would actually plan to entrap an officer by inviting a stop on a section of the hundreds of miles of lonely mountain highways. Any time an officer is in trouble, we all feel a sense of great urgency because we are vividly aware that it can happen to any one of us.

Both the ambulance from Pine Valley and the Campo units arrived before J.D. and I did. The EMTs assured us that though our brother officer looked pretty bad, he would be O.K. His injuries were a broken nose, probably a broken rib or two, and some cuts and bruises caused by the struggle with the suspects. They had not used clubs or other weapons, thank God. J.D. and I did not know the officer well and left the close attendance to the Campo officers.

Upon their arrival, the Campo officers had found two illegals still at the suspect vehicle and took them into custody, talking briefly with them to determine the facts of the incident. The two were unable to provide much information, but they were willing to talk. They were brothers and had been under a blanket on the floor in the back seat area of the car. They didn't see what happened as they stayed under the blanket until they were told to get out of the car. Someone opened the door of the car and the trunk and told everyone to get out and run. They were told to run into the mountains and escape, but these two didn't even know which way to run, so they waited awhile then returned to the vehicle. They were being smuggled into the U.S. by two guides, sometimes called "coyotes" whom they described to us. They believed that one of them was driving the car, but they didn't know for sure, because they had been under the blanket. The smuggled group of ten people crossed the border fence and had walked all night and most of the next day through the mountains until almost evening when they came to a small dirt road where the guides told them to wait in the bushes. The guides left them there and returned after dark with a car. They were instructed with others to get into the back seat under a blanket and the rest to crowd into the trunk of the car.

The brothers heard the guides talking when the Border Patrol officer's car had come up behind them with the siren on. The officer had seen something suspicious, the smugglers didn't know what, but they didn't want to stop and talk about what to do. The two brothers knew that the car tried to outrun the *Patrulla* by going very fast, swerving from side to side. They heard the guides begin discussing how they could "catch" the patrolman. They would stop quickly, jump from the car and run for the brush along the highway. When the officer chased them they would turn and both would jump on him. Things had gone just as planned, at least so the interviewees thought. They had stayed in the car under the blanket with the other aliens and never looked to see what was happening. The car suddenly began to stop with tires squealing and sliding on the pavement, then the doors opened and the two jumped out. Then they could hear the officer yelling to the two to stop as he chased them. They then thought that they had heard the sounds of the beating, but they weren't sure. Still, they didn't look and no one moved. Then there was silence for a few minutes until the car door jerked open and the guides began yelling for them to get out and run into the mountains to hide. They hadn't gone far, because they were exhausted from being on the run for two days and nights already. They also stated that they didn't want anything to do with the beating of an officer. So they had returned to wait at the vehicle. They had seen the motorist stop and look around with a flashlight, then he found and checked the officer, and he didn't see them waiting by the bushes. The motorist had sat in the officer's car until the ambulance arrived.

J.D. and I began to cut for sign of the two smugglers. The two illegals in custody had no idea where the guides had gone or which direction they had run or why after disabling the officer they hadn't just driven off in the car. We guessed, based on experience, that the two smugglers wouldn't run the same path as the aliens. They would, in fact, probably run the opposite direction. The two brothers indicated that they had been directed to run to the brush on the same side of the highway as the cars were parked, which was the north side. We began a cut along the bank on the south side of the freeway. The two sets of tracks fleeing the scene were easy to find despite the dim predawn light. J.D. and I knew that we were a long way from anywhere here, and they would know this as well, so it was a pretty sure bet they had headed cross country south toward the border, which was 20 or 30 miles away. The sign was headed south through the brush at a fast clip, not running now, just traveling quickly without regard to keeping quiet or personal safety. This was going to be a race. The deck was stacked in our favor, since neither subject had planned for this. They would be tired, without food or water and moving through some pretty tough territory. When their adrenaline ran out, it would be tough going for them. Buck brush and the tough, ever-grabbing manzanita crowded each other for space intermixed with "jumping" cactus and scrub oaks. Big granite boulders, some the size of houses, dotted the landscape and poked through the brush and trees. Steep hillsides would funnel the travelers' route to either the ridge tops or the canyon bottoms. The canyon bottoms would prove to be nearly impassable with brush. These two would know this since they'd traveled across this type of country before, so if possible they'd stick to the ridges. We didn't know the territory but neither did they, so in that regard we were even.

Though we'd started out in darkness, very soon daylight began brightening the landscape, and the scrub oaks stood out in sharp relief. We put away our flashlights. Old Joe Page was already off the ground and on his way in the Piper Cub, but he'd be most of an hour getting to the area. I was guessing he would come in from the south and try to catch them out in the open or "brush them up." Often the Cub pilot could see aliens that were traveling as the sounds of their movement through the brush covered the sound of the small engine. Or the aliens would hear the sound of the  engine and hide in the brush unable to move about for fear that they would be seen. When the Cub came on scene and they had to hide, we would make up time quickly.

The sun was just over the horizon now, still in our eyes when looking toward the southeast. It was already warm and we could feel the heat that would come by noon. This was early in the season but 90 to 100 degrees was usual, making it stifling in the brush with no air stirring. It was even worse in the canyons. The sign went up and down the humps and hollows of the ridge, but we could tell they were try-ing to stay up high. This would help them watch their back-trail. The brothers had told us that one of the smugglers had a gun and we kept that in mind as we followed.

Following the sign proved to be pretty easy. They weren't trying to be clever, just heading for the fence as fast as they could. They took the easiest routes through the open, around most of the heavy brush, but pushing through it when necessary. In an hour we were a mile or more south of the highway, the last sounds of the big trucks long lost from hearing, now just the buzzing of an occasional bee or fly. The sign was telling us that they were beginning to get tired and probably thirsty. They had stopped and talked a couple of times, the stride length had shortened and here and there a toe drag and a stumble over a rock or limb.

 About 7 a.m., we heard the rush of air and then the roar of the engine and we ducked involuntarily as the Cub flew 100 feet over our heads toward the canyon bottom that still appeared dark and far ahead of us. Joe had been up high and was dropping down over the incident scene on the interstate. He was making his first pass down the ridge top trying to catch them in the open. The best of the best, J.D. and I always felt we had a ace in the hole with Joe flying overhead. This would "put them down or brush them up" and allow us to catch up. Joe would be down in the canyon bottoms and up above the ridges and silently dropping in upon you before you were aware he was around. He would be at tree top level one minute and the next riding a thermal to several thousand feet to see for many miles. The Cub drifted down the ridge and out of sight, headed south. He would be working his way back toward us, checking every little canyon and ridge off of this backbone. The little white plane glowed silver in the clear air with the reflection of the early morning sun. Out of nowhere I was struck by what a great job I had, being outside in beautiful desert back country, doing work I really enjoyed. But then my thoughts went back to the officer who had been beaten and wondered how he was doing.

By 9 a.m. we had been in pursuit for more than three hours and the two were showing signs of serious fatigue. We found a second place where they had stopped, the sign indicated that they had quickly ducked in under a small oak tree. We deduced that this was probably where they had been when they first heard the plane. We had talked to Joe on the radio explaining where we were, but he had seen us long before we had heard him. He had come back to talk with us over the outside speaker in a one-sided conversation with us, answering questions in one or two words on the radio. Now he was turning slow, low circles in the canyon below us. If Joe could have figured out a way to put a silencer and a noose on that Cub, he could have caught them all!

I checked the sign, trying to determine the age, when they had been here, before or after daylight. I couldn't find any conclusive indication of the exact age of the tracks. Often you can "age" them to within a few minutes of their actual passing, but this time there hadn't been any dew and the sunlight didn't reach the ground between all these trees, brush and boulders. The only thing I could determine for sure was that they had been here before the sun reached the grass because it was still cool and damp when stepped on, so probably about 7 or 7:30 a.m. We were about two hours behind them now and gaining some.

Suddenly the sign changed. It showed the subjects beginning to hide under or close to the trees. They headed into, instead of away from, the brush pockets and they skirted close to the boulders. It also appeared that they were trying to be careful with where they put their feet. All aliens were aware of the Patrol trackers, and the smugglers even more so. They would know we'd be following the sign trail and were trying to be careful while still traveling rapidly. They began taking advantage of the hard-packed dirt in the open areas, staying away from the grass and stepping over and through the brush instead of breaking it. It was no use, though. With two of them traveling together, they left a trail that J.D. and I could follow at a fast walk.

The sign showed that the subject pair had stopped again, this time under the shoulder of a large granite boulder. When they had started on again, they had split up. I looked at J.D., he shrugged and turned to follow the track to the left, leaving me the one to the right. J.D.'s track turned into a brush pocket and continued on and I stayed with the other one. It was six of one or a half dozen of the other since neither track seemed to indicate the leader. They had just been together up to this point. I followed the sign around boulders, under and through brush, in and out of gullies that were now beginning to mark the ridge. This guy's looking for a place to hole up, I thought, and said as much to J.D. with the walkie-talkie, knowing that Joe would be listening in the Cub. J.D. told Joe about the split-up and advised him that we were each taking a trail. Joe came back with some info on the terrain. "There's a deep canyon ahead of you about half a mile," Joe said. "It's deep and steep and looks to be choked with brush, it starts at the top of the ridge so unless one goes off of the west side, you'll both hit it. If they get that far it'll be a chore digging them out."

My guy was still moving pretty fast, trying to stay out of sight but not leave obvious sign. I picked up the pace, trying not to be careless as I did. I wanted to make up as much time as possible while Joe was still in a position to hold them both down. I noted that up here on the ridge the brush wasn't thick enough or the patches large enough for a person to hide very effectively. But that wouldn't be the case if he could make it to the next canyon. In a place like that a person could get down under the brush and crawl, unseen, for a mile or more.

Joe was circling over J.D. just level with the top of the ridge, indicating that the sign of J.D.'s suspect was beginning to side-hill downward. That also probably meant that he was getting into the heavy brush and Joe wanted to keep him in sight as well as watch ahead of him.

"This the canyon you were talking about?" I heard J.D. ask.

"Sure is," Joe replied, "and it looks like you're determined to get into it."

"Not me!" J.D. said, and I could tell he was grinning when he said it. "But if my friend wants to, then I suppose I don't have much choice!"

The Cub was working below me then in the canyon but I could hear the engine as Joe climbed to the top of the canyon for a look. I found where my guy had rested in the shade, squatting where he couldn't be seen, thinking, watching, and listening. He moved on and I could tell he was intending to make the border, which was probably about 20 miles away. He was in no hurry but traveling steadily, hoping to outdistance whoever was on the sign and trying to stay out of sight of the plane. The sign didn't tell me he could see or hear the plane, just that he knew it was watching. He leaned into the shadows, stayed hunched over while going under the brush and scrubby trees.

We continued moving while the sun got higher and hotter, the hunter and the hunted suffering equally. He decided the course and I followed. I was just the tail, but I knew where this snake was going. Every time I climbed to the top of one of these two-story boulders, I could easily see that he was headed straight south by the most direct route. Joe called to check on me, saying he wanted to stay with J.D. if I was still on the ridge top, which I was. I knew I would need Joe up ahead somewhere to help me put this guy down, or it would be a race to the fence, but I wasn't that close yet.

The ground surface of decomposed granite bounced the sun's glare back to me like a million tiny mirrors. J.D. would have his sunglasses on, but I had never  acquired that habit. I was wishing for a pair right then, though. Off we went around a boulder, through a narrow, shadowed hallway between two house-sized rocks, through another brush patch, under a scrub oak and up a loose-granite slope. He was leading me on a merry chase. The sign wasn't hard to follow, though he was trying not to be obvious. This area didn't accommodate too many attempts at concealing sign because there weren't many other human tracks, new or old. The ground surface was either the loose granite granules or soil with a high degree of clay or adobe that would hold a print for some time. The scrub brush held the evidence of "man" passage nearly until it was burned off.

Suddenly my subject's sign changed. He had been out in the open, crossing from a boulder to a large patch of brush, when he suddenly darted back into the shadow of the boulder. This clearly indicated to me that Joe had been scouting this area and that my subject had squatted here for some time—20 minutes maybe—quietly watching and listening to hear where the plane was going. The place he had squatted was in the blazing sun now, as it was nearing noon. At nine or ten in the morning, however, this place would have been hidden in deep shadow. That told me I was two or three hours behind and the fact that Joe had sent him into hiding for a while allowed me to make up some time on him. Not only had he lost distance, he had also lost momentum.

The sign went on but he was being far more careful, staying close to cover, hurrying across openings and going under the trees. That plane could slip up on you when you didn't know it was around and he was taking no chances. Several places showed where he had stood and waited, looking and listening and losing time. I also noticed that he was watching his back-trail now, choosing places to stop where the footprints indicated he was watching to see behind him. This slowed me down a little, forcing me to be more careful as well. This guy was demonstrating that he'd been out here before with trackers on his tail. Something about the sign looked familiar, but this was only one of many smugglers who knew their business and hoped you didn't.

The ridge that I was on was beginning to break downward toward a huge canyon, the opposite wall of which was a gray slope that promised cover. J.D. was down the canyon slope nearly to the bottom and from where I was I could see where this canyon ran into the larger one ahead of us. I saw that the brush got much thicker down below and I wasn't looking forward to tracking through it, having had it easier going on the ridge. The sign headed off down the ridge toward the bottom of the canyon and indicated that my subject was being even more careful. He was spooked for some reason and seemed to be expecting someone to step out in front of him at any moment. He was hiding more often and his stride was more hesitant. Whenever he had to cross an open patch, he hurried to the next bit of cover. We had his full attention.

An eerie, unintelligible voice floated up and over the rising air to me from wherever the Cub was in the canyon as Joe used the loud-speaker to talk to J.D. It always unnerved a run-ner to have Joe talking to the ground units about where the subject was hid-

ing and directing them to the position. Joe was good at making the rabbit think he knew exactly which bush he was under. I knew that if I could hear him, the guy in front of me was also hearing him from time to time and that was giving him something else to think about.

I knew we were getting close. J.D. was pushing his subject along parallel to the ridge slope quite far below me, but he wasn't that far behind. My subject was slowing down and I had a hunch that neither one of them had gotten to that canyon bottom. I called Joe on the radio and said, "When you can, drift down the canyon and around the end of this ridge. I think this guy's more than a little concerned that you've got someone ahead of him and I think he's holed up."

A short time later, Joe came back, telling me that he had flown down along the canyon ahead of me and that it looked pretty rough. "You O.K.?" he asked.

"Yeah, no problems," I answered. "The sign is telling me the trav-eler is getting concerned about who's ahead and where you are. Keep an eye out—I think they're close."

It was nearly 2 p.m. now and "hot" doesn't quite express it. No breeze was stirring and the sun was blazing so brightly no one could keep from squinting. We were probably about 8 to 10 miles from the highway. I stopped in the shade and waited for a couple minutes. Heck, I was getting tuckered myself! I had missed my morning coffee and donut. I looked ahead, my eye following the sign that led toward two huge boulders the size of small houses pitched together to form a dark shadowy void. Suddenly, as I watched, something moved in the shadows and a figure stepped into the sun, a man raised his hand and waved a slight greeting. As I walked forward I could see the embarrassed grin on his face. Bareheaded and empty-handed, he stepped forward to meet me. He was about my age, his appearance familiar, lightly dressed and obviously tired and spent. I knew he wouldn't be any problem from here on, he was caught.

"*Hola,*" he said, as I came forward. Then he touched the outside corner of his right eye with the tip of an index finger. "*Vio antes. Usted me conoce, verdad?* (I've seen you before. You know me, right?)," he added with a sly smile and continued in Spanish, "Remember one day you were with two others, Tejanos, and you found my track near the water tank to find me under the bush. Afterwards the dark one said you would become a tracker. I said for you to practice and one day we would try again. I think you are a tracker now, no? I waited for you here. There is nowhere to go."

It took me a minute as he talked, but finally I figured out that he was the "Chevron" from a couple of years before, when I was just learning to track. I had been working with Ab Taylor and Dana Ellsworth that day. I then recalled the incident clearly—that apprehension brought me the first acknowledgment by Ab that I had sign cutter potential. That day tracking had been a challenge and today the challenge had been met. I nodded.

"*Si, recuerdo.* (I remember)," I replied. "Where were you going?"

He turned and gestured toward the south. "I wanted to go home, but I think that won't be for some time now. I will go with you," he said, offering his hands for cuffing. I waved them away.

"I won't put cuffs on you," I said. "You need your hands free to walk out of here, but I will not look for you again. *Comprende?*"

"*Si, comprende* (yes, I understand)," he said, and I knew that he did. I radioed Joe that I had the guy and asked him the quickest way out of there. "Sit a bit," he said. "I think J.D. is about to nail his guy and then I'll come take a look."

I sat in the shade with the subject, whose name was Alfonso, and talked of life and nothing else specific. We spoke of the heat and he told me a story about horned toads as we watched one hiding itself in the hot sand. We did not talk of the incident on the highway, I wasn't in the mood, and this wasn't the time or place to take a statement or otherwise record anything that he might have to say. He knew it would be talked of but wasn't anxious for that to begin. Suddenly the Cub roared up over the canyon rim and wagged a wing at us. The loudspeaker crackled and Joe said, "J.D. is heading up over the ridge. Looks like your best way is right back the way you came."

It was harder going back up. We were tired, hot and now there wasn't any hurry. I hadn't realized we had come down the ridge so far, but it was 3 p.m. and we'd been following sign for eight hours. We plodded along generally following J.D.'s sign, but picked the easiest route. Finally we caught up to J.D. and the other desperado sitting under a scrub oak. J.D. was smoking his pipe and grinning. It had been a good day. He looked at the unlucky pair and said quietly, "We won't chase you again." They looked at each other and nodded in unison, saying they understood clearly. When we got back to the highway, several other agents were waiting and took our prisoners off our hands. They'd take the statements and do the paperwork.

"They give you any trouble?" they asked.

"Nope, neither one. They know where they're going. How's Bill?"

"He'll be fine," one agent said. "Knocked the bark off him. He'll be stiff and sore for a few days, but no real damage. Course he got a few new scars, but he was so darn ugly before it can't be anything but an improvement."

CHAPTER FOUR

Tracking Basics
Becoming Track Aware

Tracking must be one of the most misunderstood skills available to man. One of the first things a new tracker learns is that tracking, at least in the way in which we present and practice it, is certainly not what the general public thinks it is. There are no coonskin hats, no buckskin clothes, no mystical humming, drumming or chanting. In real-life situations, there is no special heritage needed. There are no born trackers. In fact, beginning trackers are eager people from all walks of life, with the interest and curiosity to find out more about what they think they may already know. The concept of tracking has been romanticized in books and movies, which for the most part come from the imagination of writers without much knowledge on the subject.

I'm just an average person who was fortunate to be in the right place at the right time with the right people to learn about tracking as they did it. That is not to say that it was necessarily the "right" way or the only way, but the men I learned from were very highly respected as being by far the most successful at what they did. I'm quite sure that these men didn't teach me all that they knew, but they did teach me the basics and time and practice taught me what I know today.

Before the days of electronic surveillance and infrared cameras, a Border Patrol tracker was pretty much on his own. His success in finding and apprehending "illegals" crossing the border was directly related to his ability to see, recognize or correctly interpret and follow a set of tracks. At times, in good conditions, a tracker could follow at a trot. The unstated goal among the men who did this work was to be able to follow the sign at least as quickly as it had been made. Some of the time however, things went at a much slower pace and sometimes, literally, at a crawl.

▷—◦—◦—◦—◁

So much has changed since I began my thirty-five year tracking career in 1965. It seems that there have been significant changes or major steps forward about every ten years. The first decade was the initial training and tracking period with the southern border experiences and adventures, and the beginning of tracking training for search and rescue and other law enforcement agencies. The second decade included my transfer to the northern border and a period of greatly varied adventures and travel representing the Border Patrol tracking and tracking training internationally. During this period a ten year association (1977 – 1990) was established with Frank Heyl and *Universal Training Systems* (UTS) of Lake Oswego, Oregon to formally promote tracking training for SAR and law enforcement. UTS provided the opportunity for my creation and production of formal training materials under that company name.

The third decade encompassed my retirement from the Border Patrol in October of 1990 to engage fulltime in tracking training and consultation services. May of 1991 brought the incorporation with some tracking colleagues to launch *Universal Tracking Services* (UTS) as my first formal program to teach tracking to law enforcement, military and search and rescue organizations. The "UTS" acronym had already gained international recognition as the emblem of formal tracking training and was retained with permission from Frank Heyl to identify the new corporation name.

December of 2003 brought my resignation from the UTS corporation and the founding of Joel Hardin Professional Tracking Services to permit my unlimited continuation of personal ideals, training goals and consultation services.

The training methods I promote today are not the same as were used by Border Patrol sign cutters when I began my training with them.

The Border Patrol didn't have a formal tracking or sign cutting training program. I recently talked to several individuals in the Patrol who were trying desperately to get some tracking training. The time of the "real" sign cutters has passed. When I began working with the sign-cut crew, which included Ab Taylor, Dana Ellsworth, Dan Danforth and others, the sign-cut training was "on the job training" or OJT. All Border Patrolmen in the early 1960s knew and understood tracking. It was a regular tool of the trade. Everyone tracked to some extent and many were very good trackers. The sign cutters were those select few who possessed special aptitude, temperament, interest, patience and persistence, which allowed them to continue to develop tracking skill. They were the best of the best. They took selected recruits into their confidence and slowly and carefully, in an unspoken and totally undocumented manner, developed their own successors. It was quite an honor to be selected to carry this particular torch.

Ab Taylor was the youngest and most receptive of the lot. He tried more than the others to teach what he knew and to help each novice to learn, to understand and to develop those techniques that would enable him to become successful at locating people who crossed the border illegally. As their sign cutting students, our job every day was to work sign. Ultimately this meant understanding that sign better than anyone else, following identified sign, and apprehending the persons creating the sign. There was practically no end to the trails left by the illegal aliens crossing over from Mexico. New sign lines (as we called the footprint trails they left behind) were created every day in a hundred places and the Border Patrol sign cutter had his work cut out for him.

Real sign cutting or tracking-training methods came from the Patrol with the advent of attempting (for humanitarian reasons) to teach tracking to other law enforcement and search and rescue volunteers. Ab's close association with San Diego Mountain Search and Rescue and sheriff's reserve components began when he successfully assisted in lost-child searches using his tracking skills. Search and Rescue officials quickly recognized that if their personnel could learn tracking, they would have a more successful and beneficial search resource. They officially requested permission to train with El Cajon Border Patrol trackers to learn these skills and were greatly surprised to learn that the Patrol had no such training program. They persisted in their desire to learn tracking skills and were given permission to accompany Border Patrol sign cutters as they went about their daily routine and could thereby learn by the OJT method. Word quickly spread, and we gained so many recruits from the SAR volunteers that soon the students far outnumbered the sign cutters. Ab knew there had to be a better way.

One day I returned to the station office late in the afternoon, having completed a long day of tracking. Ab informed me that there was going to be a gathering of SAR personnel that next weekend and told me to take another Border Patrolman with me and go give them a tracking class. "What do you want me to do?" I asked him. Ab said, "I don't rightly know, but you'll figure it out when you get there!" I guess I did, though I don't remember what I said or what we did. But on that day, the first Border Patrol SAR tracking class was born.

There was no plan, no procedure, no curriculum and no method of any kind. We gathered the people around in a group, talked to them about tracking, then walked off a short distance making tracks. Then we gathered them around and tried to show and tell them what we could see in each track. As I think back on it, they couldn't have learned much, but they surely were enthusiastic! We demonstrated and they cheered. It was more of a circus than a training class, but it was a beginning. Our "success" brought more demand, and soon tracking training was a regular activity for the sign cutters, in addition to our other duties. Not all sign cutters wanted to participate in this training, as it wasn't a part of regular duties, and they rightfully believed there was no way you could teach SAR volunteers to be trackers in a couple weekend-long training sessions. The program continued, however, with Ab loosely steering the effort. Jack Kearney, a college graduate, education major and an El Cajon tracker, helped greatly to give the classes some structure and format. Ab coined the "step-by-step" phrase, believing that SAR trackers could not save the life of a victim if they couldn't follow the sign every step of the way. It was critical that they not go beyond the last track they could see. Ab believed that to enable novice trackers to be a successful tracking resource for searching, they needed regimented procedures that minimized mistakes and maximized amateur efforts. The three-person team was identified as correct for the number of persons who could be in the right place to see the sign without causing each other problems. The triangle formation with the three trackers worked the best, with a point person and two flankers. SAR volunteers invented the tracking stick to enable students always to focus on the right place (termed the prime sign area) where the next footfall would be found.

Tracking Team

Areas of viewing responsibility
Indicate approximately 60° for each member

Prime Sign Area

Point Person

Left Flanker

Right Flanker

The flankers are in position to see any intersecting or contaminating sign which may enter the prime sign area from the side.

RJB

The question remained of how to teach novice trackers to see sign. I learned to study the tracking students. I noticed which ones learned and developed skills more quickly and which ones struggled to do so. I tried to analyze why some succeeded where others failed. Through this analysis, I became aware that we as tracking instructors didn't teach people to see sign at all. They could all see sign when we pointed it out to them. This meant that when we were successful with students, we hadn't taught them to find sign, only to be aware of what they could already see that related in any way to human footprints. We taught these students to focus on and literally "to be conscious of" all that was within their view and to recognize that which was human sign. This was a retraining of their conscious mind to recognize and properly analyze what is seen to associate it with footprint characteristics.

Most students of tracking from the start would like to be able to follow a trail as quickly as it was made. Even when the times and circumstances are right for that kind of tracking, however, it cannot be done with confidence until certain fundamentals are mastered. Just as the basketball player will spend hours working on dribbling, passing, jump shots and other fundamentals, a good tracker never wanders far from the basics. This is where patience comes in. To be a successful tracker, first you have to be patient and dedicated enough to learn these basics, rain or shine. So let's start at the beginning with the basics.

The First Step

No matter who or what you're tracking, you have to begin somewhere. It might surprise you to know, however, that the best place to start is not the first track. If you focus there first, you're only seeing a very small piece of what is usually a very complex puzzle. Begin, instead, with what you know or can find out about the conditions in which that first track was made. What are the natural elements? Has it been raining? Windy? Did the ground freeze last night? Has the sun been out? All of these questions, as you'll see, have a direct bearing on how the footprints themselves will appear. If you've been in the area, think back about what you remember about the conditions in the past few days. Otherwise, see what you can find out from people who have been in the vicinity. A more detailed discussion of this process will be found in Chapter 8 on aging sign. Suffice it to say, that the combination of natural elements and their continuing effects on the ground surface dictate the visual appearance of sign. Their predictable changes under various conditions enable trackers to conclude accurately when the sign was made.

Even after you've reviewed the recent weather conditions, you're still not ready for that first track. It's time now to examine the ground.

Stand back, look around, get an overview. Notice the color and even the texture of the dirt itself. Look at the vegetation and take note of the type, kind, the varying shades and textures of the foliage. If you can do it without compromising the trail you'll be following, make a few tracks of your own. See how resilient vegetation is, how soft the dirt is. Look closely at what your own shoes do to these surfaces and you'll have a rough idea of what you're looking for.

Patience is not only a virtue, it is an absolute essential in tracking. Take heart in knowing that if you'll make yourself spend the time learning these first steps, that time will easily be made up as you follow the trail. Remind yourself of that as you walk to the area's first track, because here is when patience will pay off in spades.

By the time you look for that first track, you should already know something about your subject. Interview roommates, spouses, friends or anyone who might have crucial information. Is your subject male or female? Small or large? Heavy or light? If you're lucky (or thorough) you'll know something about the subject's footgear. Maybe the subject's hunting partner can tell you what kind of boots he was wearing. In a search and rescue operation, perhaps a roommate or spouse can tell you which shoes are missing from the closet. Gather as much information as you can about the person you'll be looking for before you go looking. The tracks will tell you the rest.

Information gathered about the person you're tracking is invaluable. However, only use this information to help you narrow down your options—don't take it as fact. The roommate could be wrong, or your subject could have another pair of shoes in his or her pack. One near-tragic search for a missing boy in Oregon was thrown off for precious hours because his grandfather drew a detailed boot pattern that he insisted was his grandson's. The searchers took him at his word and dismissed many other potential trails because they didn't fit the profile. The boy was found suffering from exposure two days later several miles from the search area—and he was wearing sneakers.

Sometimes a person will step out of a car into a patch of gooey mud and make the perfect foot impression, right down to the insignia in the shoe's instep. If you're tracking animals, you'll see they will step firmly along a river bottom, and their tracks will be imprinted as clearly in your mind as they are on the sand. More often, however, the "first track" of the human will take some time to figure out. Once again, patience is the key. Rushing through this first part can easily take you on a merry chase that will waste hours. Clear tracks, easily read and leading in a likely direction are very tempting to follow simply because you can! I have always said that tracking is not just seeing the prints everyone else sees, but seeing the sign that most other people *don't* see.

If you start off on the wrong trail, chances are you'll stay on the wrong trail and no matter how good your tracking skills, you won't find your subject. Be as sure as you can that you're not just tracking well, but that you're on the right track. One way to do that is to pay enormous attention to detail.

Because this is a chapter on basics, I'm going to mention something that is so basic you may think it should go without saying: Don't touch the track. Don't breathe on the track. Don't even think about it! You'd be surprised how many beginning trackers, after a quick once over, will start immediately on a dissection that would rival a coroner's autopsy. This may be okay after a *thorough* examination, but it is a very bad idea at first. As soon as you change what's there, it's changed forever. You can never go back and double-check or confirm something. You can never show someone else this bit of pristine evidence. If this is a possible crime scene, this track could be valuable evidence that needs to be preserved. Since every minute detail of that track can tell you something, respect it. Even the disturbances that nature or weather has already created can help you age the trail, so by all means and at all costs, do the autopsy later!

When you're kneeling over the track you're relatively sure is the subject's, once again the devil is in the details. If you've come prepared for this, you'll have a pad and pencil with you. Artist or not, draw as detailed a sketch as you can of what you see. Count the number of lugs on a boot or the number of lines on an athletic shoe. Is there a well-defined heel or a gradual instep? Can you see lettering from a brand logo? Take your time and mark it all down. Especially if time is of the essence, you will be tempted to ignore this advice, but there are sound reasons for it. The main one is that this sketch will burn these details in your memory in a way that simply looking won't. Again, if the possibility of foul play is present, your sketch may become evidence. Many times I have gone into court as an expert witness having only my memory and that little sketch as evidence. You may go back and refer to this sketch along the trail, but ironically, the more time you spend on creating it, the less you'll actually have to look at it.

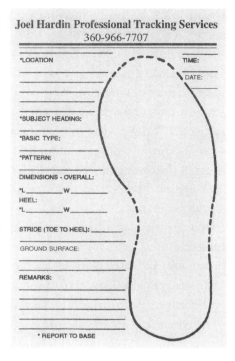

Footfall Sign Characteristics

Early on, tracking students become aware that it's usually footprint characteristics that first catch their attention. In class we spend quite a bit of time looking at footprints and noting how the different parts of the track are imprinted differently. The rear of the heel of most shoes, regardless of the style, size or purpose of the footgear, is curved. In a natural walking motion, all of the body's weight is on this portion of the heel for an instant before being transferred forward across the full heel, then across the instep and onto the ball of the foot, and finally stepping off of the tip of the toe of one foot the instant before the next heel strikes the surface. Walking in any direction, you must lift each foot from the ground surface momentarily, which means that the entire body weight is on the other foot during that moment. I spend a lot of time watching people walk, just observing how they carry their body weight in the complete stride. Under most conditions, the rear curved edge of the heel will leave a distinct mark on ground, floor or nearly any surface due to the body weight and impact of the forward movement. Similarly, the front edge of the heel will leave a straight or curved line, the edge of the ball of the foot will leave a noticeably long curved line, and the tip of the toe leaves marks that are round, pointed or square. Once a tracker's eye begins to associate such telltale characteristics to particular footgear, such sign becomes clear and distinct, though it often remains invisible to untrained persons. Students learn that all such marks are characteristics of human footwear and not made by any animals. Often people untrained or unacquainted with tracking believe that barefoot prints or moccasin prints are the most difficult to see, identify and follow. But tracking students quickly learn that these, too, leave very distinct impressions and compressions, which will remain visible for long periods of time, even when subject to extreme natural elements.

The Next Step

After you've drawn the track to the best of your ability, measure it. Use the following four measurements to help identify the print. Start with the length. Look closely at the toe and the heel to make sure you're seeing *all* the sign and including this in the length. Do the same with the width across the ball of the foot as well as across the heel. Also measure the length of the heel. If you don't have a tape measure, use whatever is at hand to get these measurements. If you carry a tracking stick, which will be addressed later, make the length of the foot your first mark and refer to it often.

Track Identification

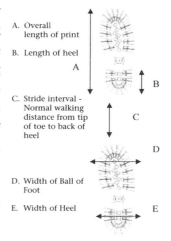

A. Overall length of print

B. Length of heel

A

B

C. Stride interval - Normal walking distance from tip of toe to back of heel

C

D

D. Width of Ball of Foot

E. Width of Heel

E

After you have documented everything you can about what you believe is the first track, you're ready to find the next one. Depending on what kind of terrain you're working with, this could mean anything from simply glancing ahead on the trail to a painstaking search. Remember to search with your eyes and move around as little as possible. If you're standing or kneeling on the next track, you're not likely to find it. As you look for the next track, be conscious of the last one. Stand or kneel to the side of the track so as not to destroy it.

Use the light to your advantage by putting the track between yourself and the light source, if possible. This will enhance the shadows and make the track more visible. Many tracks that are invisible from one angle will jump out at you from another. Putting your eye in the right position will improve its acuity. We teach student trackers in their first session to position themselves in relationship to the known or expected sign so as to take advantage of the "light angle." When trackers are following identified sign and it suddenly seems to disappear, they probably have lost the optimum light angle. This critical element is simply keeping the sign between you and the light source. This allows you to see impressions, compressed lines, and areas of contrasting light reflection or absorption better than looking straight down at them. Sounds easy, but there are many, many times when the sun doesn't cooperate with you. To take advantage of these light comparisons, you must try to position your eye so that the reflection, diffusion or absorption is most visible. This position varies with the sign line of the ground surface. Developing this skill takes good coaching and experience in the field because there is a lot of variation in eyesight. Some people perceive color or light reflection better than others.

If your light source is the sun, do the best you can, since it won't always be where you want it to be. Morning or evening tracking can be optimal times since the shadows are deepened and a track will show up well. At night you can create this effect by holding your light source down close to the ground and shining the beam in a 60-degree arc across the prime sign area.

As you search for the next track, look for anything that looks disturbed. You probably won't find an entire track, and even when you do, you probably won't see it all at once. Ignore nothing. Those few pieces of sand on that leaf or that tiny stick, freshly broken, may be major clues. The premise of optical illusions is that, at first glance, you see a vase or a bunch of random lines and patterns. But if you're able to shift your vision, or your expectation of what you're seeing, you can see the face or the dinosaur or the letters that spell a name. This is exactly what happens in tracking. It's often like that puzzle as you see tiny pieces of the track, a heel here, a lug there, suddenly come together and you "see" the track you've been scrutinizing for twenty minutes.

Once you've found the second track, it's time for another measurement—stride length. We measure this distance between the toe of one track and the heel of the next. Knowing a person's stride length can give skilled trackers a wealth of information about the person they're following. Stride length provides clues about how sure the sign maker is of his direction and his state of mind, as well as his physical size, condition and more. Probably the most useful information it can provide, however, is simply where to begin looking for the next track.

The Tracking Stick

The tracking stick is one of the most useful tools you can have while tracking. Its primary purpose is to measure and keep track of stride length and foot size. A tracking stick can be as simple as a broken branch found on the ground or it can be a golf club or ski pole. We use a fold-down version developed for convenience, but any long, thin object will do. Once the subject's track and stride length are determined, two O rings— rubber bands or notches—are used to mark these measurements.   Usually I mark the footprint measurement between the first two O rings on the tracking stick, and the stride length as the distance between the front O ring and tip of the stick. This measurement is the distance from the toe of one track to the heel of the next.

The tracking stick is a reference tool. If you find a great footprint,

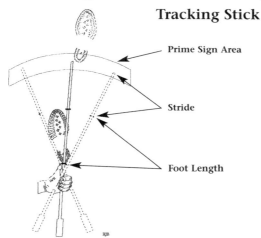

Tracking Stick

Prime Sign Area

Stride

Foot Length

but you're not sure if it's the right one, compare it with the track measurement on your stick. If you lose the trail and can't seem to go on, go back to the last clear track, place the stride-length O ring at the front of the last track, and the stick will show you where the next track is most likely to be. The tip should be pointing to the "prime sign area" where the next print should be. Keeping the O ring at the toe of the clear track, point the stick and sweep it in a 60-degree arc, looking for any small disturbance. Keep the stick as close to the ground as possible, but high enough to be sure not to create sign by disturbing the ground or the foliage beneath the stick. Since your next clue may be as little as dirt on a leaf or some tangled grass, leaving the area undisturbed is crucial.

Stride length may vary by a few inches based on several factors. Your subject may be tiring and shortening stride. Uphill travel tends to shorten the stride and downhill travel will lengthen it. The person may be traveling through rough terrain and adjusting stride to avoid or step over obstacles. If unsure of the direction or if traveling at night, a person tends to take uneven strides, so the stride length may vary considerably from one track to another. An average middle-age adult's walking stride on firm level ground is generally somewhere between 14 and 22 inches. The tracking stick will give you a good starting point to begin looking for the next track, but take these variables into account as you look.

One tendency I've observed when students are tracking through tall vegetation is to use the stick to move the foliage out of the way, giving them a better look at the ground. This habit is almost as bad as dissecting the track before you've fully examined it. The ground cover vegetation can give the tracker valuable clues as to the direction of travel. Grass and leaves will tangle and turn in the direction of travel and disturbing these before examining them can destroy valuable sign. When tracking through vegetation that obscures or hides the track on the ground, first examine the vegetation. If you have to move this ground cover to examine the track on the ground, do so only after you've given it a thorough examination to see what it can tell you.

The tracking stick can literally keep you "on track." When you've gotten stuck and can't seem to go on, go back to the stick. Put it on the toe of the last clear track you have and let it tell you where to look for the next track. Remember, unless your subject can fly or has been kidnapped by aliens, the next track *is there*! It's simply a matter of knowing what to look for and where.

Step by Step

The tracking method we use is called the "step-by-step" method. This means that the goal is to find every track and avoid skipping ahead. As your tracking training, knowledge and experience advances, we will discuss other tracking techniques such as sign cutting, but these techniques are reserved for advanced trackers. The primary reason for finding every track is to be sure you're following the same person you started with and to ensure that you do not lose the sign line. Skipping ahead to a clear track may be tempting, but it takes a skilled tracker to make a positive identification on that track, and to insure that you're still with the same subject. With so many similar sole patterns in the shoe market today, the only sure way to guarantee you're on the right person is to "connect the dots," finding every track. This may not seem practical if time is of the essence, but getting sloppy will most often lose time rather than gain it, since the chances are good that the track that you think you see ten steps ahead was made by someone else or isn't a footprint at all. If you jump ahead to examine it, you've also created sign and contaminated the area. This can have a devastating effect on your confidence if it turns out to be the wrong track or something else entirely. Sticking with your subject step by step is the only way to assure that you will stay on track.

Ten Signs of Passing

Everything that moves across the ground leaves some sign that it has been there. Even on hard ground or rock, there will be small, sometimes infinitesimal, clues. The following are some of the signs of passing a tracker might encounter.

1. **Rolled rocks.** Small rocks, helped by natural elements of wind, rain and the earth's vibration, will settle themselves into slight depressions in the dirt. Look for rocks that have been moved, rolled or mashed into the ground surface during the making of a print, or the tiny craters where they once were. Keep an eye out for small rocks sitting on top of the dirt when most others are settled in. They have probably been recently disturbed.

2. **Dirt transfer.** If you could watch a track being made in slow motion, you would see tiny avalanches, rock slides and flying debris. When the dust settles, so to speak, there is much for the tracker to see. Depending on the ground cover, tiny particles of dirt will often be visible if you look closely enough. Soil will often cling to the bottom of the sole and will be carried forward to the next track surface. Closely examine grass, leaves and other green

foliage for signs of fresh dirt on top. Check rocks and pebbles for smudges of dirt on them and compare them to other rocks in the area. Especially if the others have been cleaned off by rain, wind or dew, this can be a very valuable clue.

3. **Bruised foliage.** Slight discolorations in the leaves, grass and other foliation will often appear when they are kicked, struck or stepped on. Especially if the track is made with Vibram boot soles or other distinctive tread patterns. Leaves or blades of grass will often fold over on themselves. This will leave bruising in the creases. Check for smaller leaves or stems that have been bent or broken off and are lying in or near the track. Also carefully check the undersides of leaves, even if they are still attached. On many types of plants and ground cover vegetation, the bottom side of the leaf is a lighter shade of green and will show bruising much more clearly than the top side. Often human passage will turn up the underside of leaves.

4. **Broken sticks.** A freshly broken twig will often jump out at you because of the bright color of the damaged end. Older breaks are usually quite a bit more drab in color and can be eliminated. Break a twig yourself to get an idea what a fresh break will look like and use it as a reference. If you find a broken twig, look around for both halves. If this is an older break or if it has fallen or blown into the track, you won't find its mate. If it was stepped on and broken, however, a little searching will usually turn up the other part of the broken twig.

5. **Shine.** Shine is usually noticed on grassy areas, but can be seen even in heavily forested cover. When the conditions are right, the track will seem to have a shiny surface. This effect is created from the uniform level of compressed vegetation or dirt reflecting the available light. Even when other more obvious signs are absent, a track will often "shine" if seen from the right angle.

Shine is usually most visible in open areas. Shine allows us to see a footprint on wet pavement from a distance when close examination shows nothing at all.

6. **Flagging.** Leaves or grass turned in the direction of travel is the condition we call "flagging." Normally the underside of leaves, blades of grass or stems of vegetation are lighter in color due to being sheltered from the sun. Flagging can often be seen from a distance and in thick foliage or vegetation is one of the best indicators of passage. Over time these "flags" will spring back up to their original position, but unless the conditions are extreme, will remain for several days, or even weeks.

7. **Ground color.** Ground, dirt, soil color is slightly different from shine. A freshly disturbed surface will usually have a different color than the surrounding area. Normally this will be indicated by a slightly darker appearance, but in dry conditions, it will sometimes be lighter. Use ground color to help you pick up potential sign from your subject, then examine each footfall area carefully.

8. **Compressed areas.** Compression of dirt or sand indicates human sign. Look for rocks or pebbles that have been uniformly pressed into the dirt or simply places where the earth has been evenly compressed.

9. **Straight lines**, curves, parallel lines or marks. Ground-surface scuffs, scrapes and other marks that are not related to ground-surface debris or resident animal sign tend to have been created by human footprints.

10. **Litter**, discarded clothing, feces, etc. Other signs of human passage might not be in the track itself. Look for these more obvious clues to help you stay on your subject's sign.

Track Awareness

In tracking training, the first step or objective is to convince students that they can actually see, identify and follow the sign. Having this conviction is a fundamental part of becoming "aware of tracks." I have found that it takes an average of forty training hours to convince someone of these basic truths. Students who come to a weekend tracking course or a single 24-hour class and believe that they will go away trackers, are mistaken. It just doesn't happen. Once students understand and believe the basic tenet that all persons leave sign of their presence and passage and gain some awareness of their ability to find, identify and follow that sign, they are ready to begin learning about tracking.

I've said this before, but the most important characteristic of successful tracking students is patience. Additionally, they need persistence, plus a good attitude for learning, which usually means a willingness to unlearn habits and to give up misconceptions. One of the most common misconceptions held by untrained persons is that tracking is so slow it could never be successfully used to find a lost person alive or to capture a bad guy. This misconception is often gained while observing students in a training course or class—the students are moving very slowly, often on their hands and knees, spending an hour or more in following sign for perhaps only 20 to 30 steps. But in a training environment, students learn by concentrating on detail and minute footprint evidence that might be overlooked in a real mission. This type of training is teaching the student's conscious mind to be totally aware of what the eye is seeing and to recognize all of the footprint sign that is there.

So how much do you need to know about tracking to be effective—what level of the tracking training do you have to reach to really do something? I'm often asked this question by training officers, management personnel and tracking students alike. In answer, let me tell you an account of a missing-person incident that has been duplicated many times by students of formal tracking training. The College of the

Siskiyous at Weed, California, has sponsored a basic tracking program for several years, primarily due to the efforts of Bill Balfrey. Bill is a professor at the college and he instructs several wilderness and out-of-doors courses. He is a tracking enthusiast and participant in the tracking program.

At one of the training courses there were several members of a SAR unit from another California county. These were first-time tracking students and they had applied themselves in the training with diligence, interest and great enthusiasm. They were determined to be trackers! During the return drive home, they became aware of an ongoing search to which the other members of their unit had responded, and they chose to also report directly to the search scene. The search was for an elderly man with significant health issues who had been on a family outing earlier in the day. This was in late April in the mountains where spring flowers were in bloom and the early sun warmed the afternoon air temperature to about 75 degrees. However, that warm spring sun soon gave way to clouds of rain and sleet at sundown, and the temperature dropped to near freezing. Family members reported the elderly man missing when it got dark, after they had spent some time searching unsuccessfully for him themselves.

The new tracking students reported to the scene well after dark in heavy rain and sleet, with the temperature near freezing. Hope was slim of recovering the missing subject before he succumbed to the elements. Other searchers were already in the field. The search manager advised the novice trackers to wait until he could assign them to one of the ongoing operations with other searchers. They talked among themselves, got out their tracking sticks and decided to give the tracking training a try. They realized they actually knew little about tracking, but they knew enough to try to do something that was not being done. They asked for the physical description of the subject and his footwear. They learned that the family had gone for a hike early in the afternoon, leaving the grandfather at the site alone. Upon returning, the family had been unable to locate the man. They believed that he had attempted to follow the family up the hiking trail toward the top of the mountain, and the search was focused in this area. The new trackers looked at the area in which the family had chosen for the outing. There was a second option, an old grown-over road leading away from the outing site in the other direction. They began a thorough search for sign in this area and soon found several footprints which might match those of the described subject. They measured the prints, made quick sketches of what they could see and began to follow, step by step, as the sign line proceeded along the old roadway. Soon the old road left the ridge and began to descend into a drainage and the sign followed.

The fledgling trackers were excited by this time. There weren't any other tracks on the road, only the ones that seemed like they could match those of the missing man. The stride measurement on the stick was consistent, and in each successive prime sign area there appeared a smudge, slight compression, or mashed and bent grass, the mark of the heel or some other telltale sign—just as they had been seeing at the tracking class. They forgot the rain and sleet in the excitement of finding each new track. Before long they came to a sharp switch back in a steep portion of the old road, and there, sitting on the roadside partially hidden under a bush for protection from the cold downpour, was the grandfather. He was too cold to speak, but he assured them he was alive and glad to see them. They quickly radioed their success to the search base, and the recovery process immediately began. Had the old gentleman not been found before morning, he probably would not have survived the night.

Some of the tracking instructors, still on the long drive home in the early morning hours, received the good news via cell phone. "Tracking works! Our first find!" the new trackers crowed. "We're going to have more people at the next tracking class!"

Tracking students have on several occasions successfully located missing persons after going to only one or two tracking courses. However, these people are very well aware of how little they know about tracking, on which many lives may very well depend!

Confidence comes with experience. The more a person practices and the more successful experiences he or she has, the better equipped he or she will be to move through the levels of training. This means that reading any book will not, by itself, make you a tracker. It will only give you some tools, ideas, recommendations and experience of others to make yourself a better observer of the sign on the ground. Tracking experience is the only thing that will improve your tracking skills. As with any other skill, the key is supervised practice, more practice and more practice. Now that you have a grasp of the basics of tracking, what are you waiting for? Get started!

CHAPTER FIVE

Search and Rescue Tracking
Keeping Track of Lost People

Joe Page was flying slow circles in the air overhead while I was trudging through a huge southern California tomato field following sign. Joe had picked up the sign south and put me on it crossing the river bottom. It was good sign, but the sun was high overhead and hot, and I was questioning the wisdom of starting so far south on a trail this late in the day. All things considered, the trail makers we were pursuing should be some 15 or 20 miles north of the border by now, snoozing in the shade and waiting for evening to come so they could continue their journey. Flies buzzed and the Piper Cub's engine roared as I plodded through the dust halfheartedly and only half-conscious of the sign I was following.

The walkie-talkie jolted me out of my daydream, but I couldn't make out what was said. Someone who was just out of range had said something and all I got was noisy static. Then Joe spoke up, "Eight-twenty is trying to reach you," he said. The headquarters dispatch center's radio call sign was KAK820. "Want me to relay for you?"

I did and he soon called back to tell me that headquarters wanted to know if I could go on a lost child search up north.

"Where is north?" I asked.

"Close to Hemet," he replied. Hemet was a little town and community at the base of the San Jacinto Mountains about 150 miles north of us.

I took another look at the sign I was following and told Joe we were a long way behind these guys. I might as well see if I could help out if he could give me a ride. California Highway Patrol was furnishing a helicopter Joe told me as he looped around and set the plane down on the dirt road at the end of the field. He taxied toward me and I hurried over and soon we were headed north to Hemet to meet the chopper.

It was a hot lazy summer's day and the ride to Hemet was bumpy, just the way I like it. By now I had spent a great deal of time in the back seat of Joe's Cub, cutting for sign, following sign, and just plain looking at the countryside. Joe didn't like riders who got airsick. He was prone to flying the Cub like it was part of his body, turning and twisting, diving and scraping the ground, slipping and dipping, and endless turning on the wing tip while he was watching people on the ground through the Plexiglass® top of the cabin. Joe was exciting to fly with, but you had to have a strong stomach. Fortunately I did. We churned northward and finally Hemet came into view. Joe called flight control and slid onto the asphalt runway 200 feet from the waiting CHP chopper.

The pilot and copilot watched with amazed faces as the Cub rolled up quietly, dead prop, and turned neatly to allow me to exit nearly at their feet. They were gracious and obviously impressed at such a turn of events that had given them this opportunity to meet Joe, the slight old man of sixty some years whose reputation was very well known in aviation circles. The aviators compared notes, joked and talked. Both pilots were Vietnam vets and wanted to talk with one of the original World War II Flying Tigers. Then the chopper radio broke into the chatfest, calling the pilot. He grabbed the mic and told someone that I had just arrived and they'd be lifting off shortly. The two pilots jumped on this and insisted that Joe accompany us on the flight. I knew from previous back seat conversations that, while Joe would turn donuts in the air, he did not like the idea of helicopters, had never been in one, and surely didn't intend ever to fly in one. But with the insistence and reassurance from the two

CHP pilots, he finally gave in and agreed to come aboard, though he glared daggers at me. The two CHP pilots were as happy as two kids who'd just talked grandpa into taking them fishing. They helped Joe push the Cub to a parking spot and tie it down, then we got aboard, and Joe's first chopper flight began.

The flight was uneventful, with an easy liftoff and a steady climb from the airport to the mountain top destination. As we flew over the search scene which looked like a large campground with a circus midway, people milling about everywhere, small groups sheltered under trees in the shade, tents in every open space, red light emergency vehicles everywhere. Yep, this was a search scene all right. The pilots gave Joe and me a briefing of what they knew of the search operation so we could get the lay of the land from the air. As I looked down at the area, I was amazed. There were people everywhere, and not just associated with the search. Heck, this was a whole *city* full of people, along with vehicles of every make and description. As with most summers in California, everyone who could get away from the city was camping in the mountains. Tents, campers and motor homes were parked in every available space. Buses bringing kids from church camps and summer schools were circling the roads, some bringing kids in, others taking them back. We circled around and settled onto a chopper pad some distance from the search base. A vehicle was waiting to take me to the base camp, and I left Joe and the two pilots deeply engaged in aviation conversation.

Officials at the search base acquainted me with the facts, as they knew them to be. The lost boy was about four and a half years old and was last seen about 8:30 a.m. four days previously near a small pond of muddy water adjacent to the campground being used by the parents' camper. This was now established as the search base. I looked around and saw exhausted searchers piled in heaps under every tree. What a big bunch of people! Command said that there were between four and five hundred searchers signed in. He described to me the operation that had been conducted, every phase of which had been recorded and color-coded carefully on topographic maps. Dog teams had searched

and researched. They
had line searched,
grid searched, shot-
gun searched and
exhausted just about
every other type of
search they could
think of.

   This campground was perched near the edge of the mountaintop. The frog pond by which the boy was last seen was at the top of a
very steep drainage, which turned into a canyon running out to the
farmland in the valley below. Everything that they knew how to do had
been done, and the search managers were considering calling off the
search. They didn't know what else to do and, after four days, nearly all
the searchers were exhausted. A small crowd had gathered around during the briefing and now waited for me to say something profound. All
I could think to say was, "Well, I'll take a look around. Maybe I can see
something." I saw no looks of confidence in the group.

   I walked off toward the pond through all the people. I recognized
some of them from tracking classes and previous searches. The ground
was covered with tracks. With all the campgrounds filled with people
and all the media attention, onlookers, sympathizers and the curious,
there was no telling how many people had tromped through this area.
I finally got off by myself, thinking that this was as impossible a task as
I had ever gotten into and I was actually wishing I'd stayed on the trail
in the tomato field. I looked at the ground. The searchers had turned
over every rock, walked on every bush and barked up every tree. I don't
think they'd left any stone unturned, literally. I reached the pond and
slowly walked around it, trying to figure out just what I was going to
do. I needed to make it look like I was doing something useful before I
made some excuse that I hadn't thought of yet and got the heck out of
there, kid or no kid.

   A tired, dusty and bedraggled Explorer Scout approached and
spoke. "Hi, Joel. I was in one of your tracking classes-remember me?"

I did and said so. He told me that he and his unit had been some of the first searchers to arrive on the scene. They had been given about the same information that I had and were about to receive their assignments. He then spotted the missing boy's brother and asked him some questions before heading off on his assignment. "I remembered you telling us in the tracking class how important it was to have all the information before going off halfcocked," he said. He had struck up a conversation with the brother to see if he could get any more information.

The brother had told the scout that the morning the boy disappeared the two of them had gotten up early. Their parents were still sleeping in the camper, so the two boys had gotten dressed in shorts and T-shirts and gone out to play. The two had hiked, played cowboys and Indians and played in the pond, trying to catch frogs. They had gotten pretty dirty by the time they figured it was time for breakfast. They had turned and gone back to the camper. Their dad was up and awake when they got back and when he saw the wet and muddy boys, he came unglued. The boys had been told in no uncertain terms not to play in the pond. Their dad ranted and raved, grabbed the younger boy and kicked his fanny severely. He then told them to stay out of the camper and that he would call them when he needed them. The boys were both very upset. They felt they had been very considerate by getting up quietly and playing away from the camper so their parents could sleep. They left the camper and went to sit on a big rock to talk about the situation. The younger boy, still smarting from the kick he'd received from his father, headed off toward the pond, muttering something about not putting up with that kind of treatment any longer. "I'm not coming back," he had said to his brother. And, as it turned out, he didn't.

At the time, the older boy had believed that his brother was just going to play some more at the pond. He decided not to, fearing more trouble from their dad. He busied himself in the camping area until his mom poked her head out the camper door and announced that the two could come in to have breakfast. The older boy had called to his brother, then gone into the camper. The younger boy never showed up. After a while, the father began to get angry again and went to the camper door to call the boy. No answer. He then went looking for the boy, speaking to several other campers in the area, but no one had seen him. The parents began to get worried and both went out to search. As they looked, they talked to more campers and before long everyone was searching and calling the missing boy's name. Their mom had gotten frantic; their dad was running around, shouting and directing searchers here and there. Some were wading back and forth across the frog pond in case the boy had drowned.

The young scout went on to tell me that after he had talked to the brother, he had gone down toward the pond in the direction the brother had last seen the missing boy. Since he'd attended a recent tracking class, he was scanning the ground for tracks. There were so many prints he was unable to sort one from another, but he went on anyway. When he reached the pond he began looking around the banks. The pond was situated in a pothole with fairly smooth, steep banks surrounding it on all but one side. That side formed a natural spillway that started the downward plunge toward a canyon below. Several large boulders shouldered the pond banks and the spillway area, a natural place for youngsters to play. The scout came to the area above the spillway and had found a mark on the ground which he could not explain. He had used flagging tape secured with small rocks to ribbon off this mark. He went on to explain to me that this mark reminded him of the sliding imprint the back of a small barefoot heel would make. The mark was about 18 inches long, narrow and rounded in the bottom to form a type of groove in the dirt. Now he wondered if I would be interested in taking a look at the mark. He hadn't been back to visit the place and didn't know whether or not the print was still uncontaminated. "Let's go take a look," I said, and off we went.

As it turned out, the ribbons were still there. They marked off the only area that wasn't trampled by searchers' tracks. As I looked at the smudge in the dirt, I agreed with the boy's conclusion: a barefoot heel sliding down the bank could have made the mark. There were no other prints around to match it-no surprise with all the contamination. Since the mark was sliding downhill, however, I decided to take a look toward the bottom of the wash. We moved the ten feet or so to the bottom of the depression, which formed the top of the spillway. The bottom of the depression was filled with tracks, some from the searchers and some from other barefoot kids who had come to play around the pond. One set of these barefoot prints began to make their way down the watercourse. As we followed them 50 or 75 feet, we could see small hand prints and material impressions in the dirt as the little track-maker had lowered himself down over the lip to the next lower landing. They continued downward and I noticed there were no returning prints.

"You got contact with search base, son?" I asked, having noticed his radio earlier.

"Sure do," he grinned. "Do you think it's him?"

"Well, it sure looks like it. Better call base and tell them we're heading down the drainage into this canyon."

As the scout relayed the information, he was deluged with questions from base. How did we know this was the kid? Did we want the dog teams? Should they send more teams down the canyon? I told him to tell them to just give us a little time and we'd let them know what was happening.

A short while later we came to the point of no return for the little traveler. He had tumbled down over a lip of the drainage and, though he had clearly tried to make his way back up, the vertical banks of the wash had trapped him. At this point I was sure that this was our missing boy. I told the scout to call the search base and advise the SAR coordinator that the boy had headed downhill for sure. I suggested they start a search team from the bottom of the canyon and work it up the drainage toward our location. When the team started up the canyon, we cautioned them to be watching for the boy's sign and the scout and I continued down. The tracking wasn't nearly as difficult as the climb down. The going was slow and before long there was a shout from just below us that the subject had been found alive.

We learned later in the debriefing that the team below us had already been working their way up the drainage with our call. They had come quickly up the ravine, seeing from the terrain that anyone coming down would have only one path open to them. They had checked the bottom of the ravine several times and felt sure that the boy's sign wasn't there, figuring that the boy had to be above them somewhere. They had hurried on, calling his name every few dozen yards, but had gotten no response. Finally, when he was within arm's length of one of the shouting searchers, the boy had called out weakly and was found. He was huddled under a wash bank and had been there for a couple of nights. He had spent the first night somewhere up-canyon, under a similar bank. He was tired and hungry, but otherwise in fine condition. The journey down and out to a location where the chopper could pick him up took a couple of hours. Those hours allowed me to climb back up the ravine to the search base and, as the missing child was taken off in the helicopter to be returned to his parents, I climbed aboard the other bird with Joe and was returned to the waiting Cub at Hemet.

Tracking is an invaluable resource for searchers that has proven itself time and again. I was a bit embarrassed to get a lot of attention for the successful completion of this search, especially since the credit belonged to the Explorer Scout who had been observant. He had only been to one class and was not even certified Track Aware, but he had applied what little training that he had in a way that probably saved a young life.

Search and Rescue Tracking

As you can no doubt gather from the this story, one of the most rewarding applications of the art of tracking is successful missing person search tracking. To have some small part in finding a lost person, reuniting a family or preventing a tragedy is immensely gratifying. To a tracker able to use his or her skills to contribute to such a happy ending, all the hours of training become more than worthwhile.

On a search and rescue (SAR) mission, trackers are often not the ones who actually find the subject. That gratification usually goes to others after the trackers have ascertained the subject's direction and likely location. Trackers have the satisfaction of knowing, however, that without their efforts the search and the missing subject may have gone in entirely different directions. Trackers are first called on the scene to try and determine a direction of travel (DOT) from the place last seen (PLS). Once the direction of travel is established, search resources can be concentrated in a much smaller area, greatly increasing the chances of success.

There was a time when a Border Patrol tracker was called on to "save the day" when a search had seemed to fizzle out with no sign of the subject. Fortunately, that's exactly what we did in several instances. However, in a short while it became obvious that to have the spotlight, to be the savior, was a tough job. It's even more difficult when you know that much of the time you won't even be called to search; the responsibility will fall to volunteers in the field. The training program for SAR volunteers which began at the El Cajon Border Patrol station back in the late 1960s, began with the intention of equipping volunteers with enough expertise to accomplish a tracking operation on their own. We knew that this would greatly multiply our efforts and would put qualified people in the right places at the right time. I was a part of that education effort and the tracking-training program for which I am the chief instructor is devoted to that same principle. I've spent the past 33 years working with SAR volunteers from all over the world in my tracking classes. I've participated in numerous searches. I've also worked with the people responsible for designing, developing and producing SAR management-training programs. Together with the volunteers at all levels, the managers and the training development entities, we have come a long way toward creating a large corps of volunteer SAR professionals in the past 20 years. There's still a great deal we can do however, to ensure that in all missions we always do the very best that can be done.

No Time to Waste!

Early in my Border Patrol career, my partner J.D. and I responded to a search for a lost 12-year-old boy. He had been attending a youth camp at a semi-remote, mountainous area near Ramona, California. About 50 or 60 kids were there for a month-long camp and they were well into the second week of their stay. This particular boy, according to the counselors, had several medical problems and was a discipline problem to boot. He was supposed to take medication every three to four hours to prevent seizures and other possibly life-threatening problems. The afternoon that the boy was reported lost, the entire group of kids had been taken to a picnic area a little way from the camp itself. When it was time to return about 4 p.m., according to the counselors, the boy didn't want to go back and threw a royal tantrum about it. However, with a great deal of difficulty, the counselors managed to return him with the others in his group to the main camp and his dormitory.

The boy was missed when he did not show up at the dining hall for dinner, but the counselors were not concerned. After dinner, one of the counselors went to talk with the boy and was unable to locate him. The staff had begun a thorough search of the facility and notified the sheriff's office. It was well after dark when we arrived and since it had been several hours since the boy's medicine had been administered the counselors were beginning to get visibly upset. They were even more fearful of having to notify his well-to-do, influential parents. After talking things over with the counselors, our preliminary hunch was that the boy had waited until things calmed down after the dinner hour, then slipped back to the picnic area on his own.

Others last saw the boy in his cabin shortly after dinner, when he had been going through his things. There were a couple of obvious routes from the cabin into brushy areas adjacent to the facility clearing. We began sign cutting in those areas, looking for any sign heading in the general direction of the picnic area. We worked slowly and carefully, ever mindful of the potentially life-threatening situation. Our cuts turned up several tracks from kids in camp, but none fitting the right description.

Finally, we saw it! Right age, right size, and it was all by itself. We knew we had the sign. The track was crossing the edge of a wheat field and headed into the brush. The underbrush in that area was so thick that even the deer crawled on their bellies through little tunnels. Once in the brush, the boy was forced to crawl along through the same tunnels. Wildlife was abundant there. Deer, coyotes and rabbits all used these brushy areas. As we tracked, we could hear the animals moving around us. They had moved behind the boy, as well, smudging, covering and contaminating the boy's sign. It was slow going. The counselors brought coffee and sandwiches and we turned off our lights and closed our eyes as we ate. We were both tired from a long day of tracking illegals and the rest was welcome.

We were still on the sign when the stars began to fade and the first light began to brighten the tops of the trees. "We've got to get this done!" J.D. grinned. "It's nearly time to go to work!" I could see a big boulder up ahead and proposed that we get on it and see what we could see. It had been some time since either of us had stood up, so it would be another welcome break. We worked the sign toward the boulder, a granite rock as big as a house, when J.D. got a hunch. He quietly spoke the boy's name and then added, "We've got an extra sandwich here for you. Why don't you come over and help us eat it?" He continued to talk in the direction of the boulder. "Were you scared out here all night by yourself? Why don't you come out now?"

A quiet voice, quieter than J.D.'s, spoke from somewhere by the big boulder: "What's your name?"

J.D. told him and then reminded him of the sandwich and gently encouraged him to crawl over to us. Soon we heard the brush rustling and knew the boy was coming. J.D. grinned at me, then began to dig the promised sandwich from his knapsack. He apparently hadn't suffered any ill effects from missing his scheduled medication.

Looking back, that was a good tracking job. We listened carefully, looked at the overall picture, didn't get in a hurry, cut sign in the right area and worked the sign slowly and carefully. On the way back I asked J.D. how he knew the kid was there and he grinned again and said, "I didn't! Just had a feeling."

Tracking as a SAR Resource

The broad questions prompted by the apparent mystery of Search and Rescue tracking can only be answered with an understanding of tracking and its practical application. First we need to set reasonable parameters and understand basic guidelines from which we can reach reasonable conclusions as to the best use of tracking in a search situation.

Tracking can be defined as "the discoverable evidence of the presence or passing of a person or thing." Tracking is recognition of the physical evidence that a person or thing has passed. This evidence may vary as to its form, but must be of sufficient substance that it can be verified. Tracks may consist of many things. You will rarely see an entire track, perfect in every detail. "Tracks" can consist of reflection, absorption or the diffusion of light from footfall compressions on the ground surfaces, grass, leaves, vegetation or other surfaces such as building floors, wood, cement or rock. Trackers must be sufficiently knowledgeable and experienced to make judgments and reach conclusions as to the existence of footprint evidence. Untrained persons often fail to see anything other than the deeply imprinted tracks in mud, sand, dust or other substances which capture the entirety of the print to the extent that it can be cast, photographed or otherwise recorded. Trackers are trained to be aware of and examine footfall evidence that is not apparent to others. Our first broad parameter should be to allow a qualified, trained person to judge whether there is footprint evidence at an incident scene. Untrained SAR managers or field coordinators must not take it upon themselves to determine the possible existence of footprint evidence. Often the use of trackers is discounted because of some myths about the nature of tracks themselves. Some people believe that tracks disappear in the rain or in other types of inclement weather, that tracks get too old to follow and therefore it's too late for trackers, that the area has been too contaminated by other search efforts or participants at an incident scene. These misconceptions abound and are commonly held as fact. It sometimes keeps qualified trackers from being summoned in a timely manner.

Qualified trackers are the best resource to evaluate a scene for footprint evidence. For a serious search, not merely a training exercise, there needs to be a victim or subject of the search in the area in which the search takes place. The first task for trackers at an incident scene is to find hard evidence of the victim or subject in the area of the search. The simple fact is that without hard evidence, such as physical footprint evidence, that the person was at the place last seen (PLS) or otherwise in the area, there is little reason to conduct a search at all. Witness statements should be considered as only one component of information upon which to base a search.

SAR trackers should be adept at interviewing or interrogating witnesses. Trackers often must interview witnesses in order to make sense of sign at the incident scene, to eliminate some tracks and to identify others. The PLS is often easier to determine and the victim's track easier to identify when trackers are able to take a witness directly to the location. Without  this advantage, trackers often must search several rather large areas in which numerous people have already searched just to find, identify and isolate the victim's track. Many times witnesses describe areas in which the person or persons were last seen as "by the big stump on the trail," "in the picnic area," "near the lake," "in the backyard," or "going down the road." Each of these descriptions seem pretty exact until you begin to look for someone who isn't where they're supposed to be. This brings up another question often resolved through careful interviewing: Is the person lost to begin with?

The question I always keep in mind when talking with witnesses is "why is the person not where he or she is expected to be" or "why is the person lost?" This question is multifaceted. What was the person doing? What was his or her intention? Was he or she equipped to be doing what he or she was intending to do? Has he or she done this before? More often than not, persons being searched for are not lost at all. They simply aren't where someone else expects them to be. Examples abound, such as the child asleep in the closet, the hunter staying out all night with his kill or because he waited too long before starting back to his vehicle. Sometimes the "lost" person is someone just wanting to be alone for a while. There are always myriad reasons why a person isn't in the place that someone else expected him or her to be, and these must be explored before determining that the person is, in fact, lost.

Foul Play or Fooling Around?

I was called in to search for a man who had gone hiking and failed to return. The search was in its second day without success when I arrived at the search command center. I was briefed as to what the on-scene SAR manager knew of the incident, the victim and circumstances. The man was in his late thirties, a professional with a respectable job, good work ethic, family and friends. He apparently had no unusual financial difficulties, physical or mental problems. He was just your average middle-class, solid-citizen type. The man had decided, rather unexpectedly, to hike to the top of a nearby mountain to take pictures of the sunrise. His car was found at the trailhead parking lot. The story was that he had gone up the well-marked trail and failed to return. Search teams had hiked to the mountaintop and searched without success on the first day and now were being deployed along the slopes of the 5,000-foot peak. Friends and family members had given statements to assist in finding the subject, so when I arrived I reviewed these statements.

As I read, several questions came to mind. For instance, was he a hiker? It turned out that this hike was a first. In fact he wasn't physically active and didn't play sports. Then I wondered, was he a photographer? Again it turned out that he was not. Rarely did he take a picture, even of the family, and then it was with a small Instamatic they had. As I interviewed the witnesses, something just didn't sit right. When did this man decide to go on this hike? His wife said that they had been playing cards with friends the night before when he suddenly announced he must get home. When asked why, he said that he was going to get up in the morning, take this hike and get some good pictures of the sunrise. This came as a complete surprise to everyone, including his wife, but there was no doubt that he was very serious about doing this. When they got home he set the alarm for 4:00 a.m. and was up like a shot when it went off. The last she saw him was when he came in to tell her he was leaving.

Thinking back over the previous few days I seemed to remember that it had been raining most of the time. When asked, the wife said that it had been raining when they'd left their friends' house. The resident deputy confirmed that it had rained each night and morning for the past several days. This was normal for that area. Something about this story however, just didn't seem normal at all. For instance, taking a picture of the sunrise in the rain? Hmmm.? I spoke to the SAR coordinator privately and told him that I would proceed with a tracking operation in an attempt to find the victim's sign on the trail. I then told him that I didn't expect to find it and told him why. At my suggestion he then began an immediate background search on this individual.

I spent the day working the trail for sign in conjunction with the other trackers present. We found nothing, not a scrap of a print that matched that of the victim's shoes. Toward evening we headed in and the search was called off. When I arrived at base camp the coordinator confirmed my suspicions. A quick check had turned up the fact that our missing man had a girlfriend who was also missing. The victim's bank account had been emptied, along with his closets and other personal items. It turns out this guy was never "lost" at all...he just wasn't where he was expected to be!

A good tracker should never take a situation at face value! Instead he or she will always ask questions, carefully assess the answers and look for the unexpected. Just because everyone is panicking around you, worried about the "lost" person, you must keep your head. The pressure will sometimes be intense for a tracker to get going, to do something. Anything! The best thing to do, however, is to get all the information you can and proceed from there.

This story illustrates the principle that I constantly try to get across to my tracking students: first things first! We try to teach tracking students to stop, look, listen and see before they get the adrenaline pumping. I say, "Stop and examine the facts, the witness statements, the hard evidence of tracks on the ground. Try to match what you're seeing on the ground to what the witnesses have said." This will help you to weigh the veracity of what the witnesses have actually said and tell you how much stock to put into their statements.

The Start of the Tracking Operation

Once the tracker or trackers are sure that they have sufficient information to look for the physical evidence of the missing person at or near the PLS, they can begin the actual tracking operation. Locating the first identifiable print may take some looking, study, pondering and more looking. Most often this area has been somewhat contaminated by others who have learned of the missing person-friends, family members, team members and others. However, the one clue that trackers should use is the fact that everyone else is not missing and most often there are many of their footprints around to compare with. Identifying the print and establishing the direction of travel are the first, most important tasks of responding tracking resources. Therefore, all available well-trained and experienced tracking resources should be used immediately to assist in this chore. The track or sign line that seems to be leaving the area and not returning, doing whatever the witness reported, is of the right time frame and otherwise matches the description and information is probably the right one. Once this one is isolated, it can be followed to a point where it can be identified, the drawing made and measurements taken. Sometimes this may be some distance from the PLS, but it should be done with as much accuracy as possible and added to whenever a more clear footprint is found. If at

This drawing shows the distance a person can travel in any direction with time. Finding a direction of travel with tracking can cut down the search area. Most subjects are found within 10 miles from point last seen. 10 miles has a search area of 314 sq. miles. By establishing a direction of travel, the search area can be cut down to 26 sq. miles.

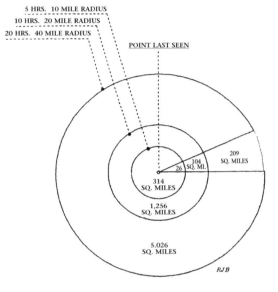

all possible, the tracking team working the sign should be made up of three trained, experienced persons and they become the Prime Sign Team. Once the print has been identified and a direction of travel established, this pertinent information should be relayed to the Incident Command System (ICS) or Managing the Search Organization (MSO) command and all other trained tracking personnel.

Tracking Operations Coordinator

Once a tracking operation is under way and it's appropriate to use multiple teams, one tracking-knowledgeable responder should be assigned to act as the Tracking Operations Coordinator (TOC). This person need not be the most skilled tracker, but instead should be the person best equipped with the people skills of tact, diplomacy and communication. The TOC's function will be to greet all tracking responders, insure they are signed in, assess their skill level and, in coordination with experienced trackers in the field, help organize them into tracking teams. The TOC will also show the responders the first known track and brief them about the nature of the operation. When appropriate, the TOC will update the search coordinator by giving current information about the progress of the tracking teams in the field, the route of the subject's travel and the physical condition of the subject as concluded from the sign the teams are following. The TOC should stay in close communication with the experienced trackers in the field in order to keep search officials updated on their progress.

This method of operation offers two distinct advantages. First, it greatly relieves the ICS or SAR coordinator of the moment-to-moment burden of recognizing, registering and assigning of tracking responders. It also helps the coordinator to assign tracking teams so that they are used with the most efficiency. Second, as a benefit to the tracking teams, it provides a two-way communicator between base camp and the field teams to minimize ineffective radio traffic. The TOC should be someone who is at least trained at a basic tracking level to better understand the tracking-team circumstances and situations in the field, and to assist them to get the immediate information needed for continuous operations.

In summary, the purpose of a tracking trained TOC is to communicate directly with trackers and the search IC or MSO coordinator. This insures that the right people are enabled to do what they have been trained to do. The on-scene tracking communicator is fully aware of other SAR resources being committed to the search. He is better able to advise the SAR coordinator in relation to the tracking operation and to assist in coordinating all resources being deployed.

One major concern to many SAR coordinators is the use of search-dog teams and tracking teams at the same time. Current SAR management texts and related instruction do a good job of explaining the use of both resources. However, SAR managers or coordinators without intimate knowledge or experience with one or the other or both resources are inclined to believe that all other resources should remain outside the search area until the teams have completed their assignments. This is due mainly to the misconception that search dogs and handlers are so undiscriminating that they cannot distinguish between searcher and victim. I'm certainly not a dog handler, but I'm assured by experienced people that this is a gross misconception and that dog teams are well trained and able to distinguish between individuals. Experienced canine handlers advise that if a handler wants the manager to keep everyone else out of the search area, the handler is in effect saying that the dog is not sufficiently trained to discriminate scents. It's similar to a tracker becoming ineffective if others are in the search field.

The same factors that interfere with dog-team efficiency interfere with trackers in that regard. The more people who have proceeded into the search area mean more tracks or individuals to eliminate as those not belonging to the victim. My training programs have always promoted the immediate deployment of both resources at the same time. Trackers will give way to the dog team to proceed from the PLS while the trackers are looking for and establishing the first track and determining a direction of travel. Most often the dog teams will travel at some distance downwind from the actual track itself, allowing the dog to "air scent." Even if the dog teams intersect the line of sign in front of the trackers, it is usually a fairly simple process to eliminate the dogs' and handlers' tracks and to proceed on the sign. I have yet to be engaged in a search in which search dogs and handlers have greatly hampered the effectiveness of trackers.

The greatest factor that inhibits most skilled trackers is what takes place in their own heads. It is easy to let yourself get discouraged when you are called two days late and when two hundred other searchers have preceded you to the area and contributed thousands of tracks to the scene, tromping down everything in sight. You may have it in the back of your mind that dog teams have searched and found nothing and that everyone is saying that the tracks are now too old to be followed. The trained tracker must be able to put all of these and other factors out of his or her mind and to have confidence in his or her ability to find and follow the subject's track. This is a state of mind, without which no tracker will be able to have the patience and persistence necessary to utilize the skill he or she has acquired.

One of the most common difficulties that trackers deal with is sign that has been trampled on by line or grid searchers. While neither method of searching will completely eliminate the subject's sign, it does add sufficiently confusing sign so as to make the work of the tracker very difficult. Again, the tracker's efficiency and ultimate success depends on keeping a positive outlook. Often trackers run into an area of sign put down by grid searchers and allow the numerous single lines of sign to frustrate their attempts to follow the primary sign line. When this happens, trackers must pause and let the dust settle a little. Once things have calmed down and the other searchers are out of the area, they must proceed with what they have been trained to do. Let's examine a recommended way to proceed when such a situation is encountered.

Assume that a tracking team has advanced the subject's line of sign to the point at which they encounter a great deal of contaminating sign. If this sign is from searchers, the sign will be fresher and will be characterized by thrashing around in the bushes, stomping, scuffing and kicking up the ground surface and tearing at the vegetation. Often this sign runs perpendicular to the victim's line of sign, but, in the case of a marked trail, may walk right on top of it. Let's also assume that, once the tracking team intercepts this activity, they have done as they have been instructed and trained to do. They have stopped, identified and marked their subject's last print and are now drawing a breath while examining and discussing the appearance of the intersecting sign line. The primary consideration at this point is how the prime sign contrasts with the contaminating sign. How does the age of the contaminating sign compare with the age of the primary track? Trackers should be noting differences in direction of travel, the sign maker's characteristics, such as stride length, etc. They should review the prime sign's direction, line of movement, and other distinctive characteristics unique to the track they're following. After doing this, they have the proper mindset to follow the subject's sign under, around or through the contaminated area.

Usually, a searcher's sign is fairly easy to distinguish from the subject's sign. The searcher has a particular mindset that is readable from the tracks. He's energized and motivated, usually moving along at a deliberate pace. His sign may go here and there, looking under trees, around bushes, etc. His sign almost shouts, "I'm a searcher! I'm here to find the victim!" The searcher's sign will usually be several hours fresher than the subject's sign. Trained trackers, working together and keeping the proper mental approach, can work the victim's sign under, around, over or through just about any contaminated area.

Working Sign with Multiple Teams

When sufficient numbers of trained and qualified responders report to a search scene, everyone should be used to make the parameter, or limiting, sign cuts. Once the initial print has been identified and the direction of travel established, the teams, properly coordinated, can work together to move the sign along very quickly. In its initial cuts, the sign-cutting team should be learning the physical layout of the area and the traffic patterns, aging the sign and establishing who else has been in the area, if possible. Thus, when updated victim information is forthcoming from the TOC, the teams have a running start. Often, the first sign-cut teams will be able to assist in determining the facts of the incident by comparing the results of their preliminary cuts with the information gathered from witnesses. Other teams might begin by sign cutting to establish outside perimeters. They should be cutting trails, roads, pathways, back alleys, neighbors' lawns, etc. One team could be assisting dog teams to get under way. Should the dogs identify a scent trail, this can be checked for footprint sign by the tracking team and verify whether or not the canine unit is on the correct trail.

Most SAR tracking programs provide training to equip tracking teams to work together in a coordinated effort that can move the sign along much faster than one team can by itself. This technique depends on accurate, disciplined and regimented application and takes a good deal of training to master. It also depends on the team's ability to cut sign. A cutting team working ahead of the prime sign team is a dangerous proposition if not strictly controlled and carefully carried out. The cutting team must work slowly and carefully, making a 100% cut, examining the *entire* area. This means that they have sufficient skill and have taken sufficient time to be able to say with absolute certainty whether or not the sign continues through the area they have cut. They can then relay their findings to the prime sign team, which is working the subject's sign step by step. If the cutting-team members come across sign and are comfortable that this is, in fact, the subject's sign, they can then call the prime team up to the next track, thus moving the operation ahead.

I cannot overemphasize that only qualified and experienced trackers should carry out cutting techniques. A tracking operation can easily grind to a halt when an inexperienced cutting team has cut ahead, missed the sign and contaminated the area. This not only serves to confuse trackers, but it can also destroy their confidence. It is much better to simply stay on the prime sign and forgo sign cutting if qualified people are not available to do the cutting.

Sign Cutting

Though the description of sign cutting seems simple, the actual application of it is far from easy. I recommend that two teams start out on the prime sign, and then when appropriate begin a single cutting-team operation. This system alternates teams between moving the prime sign and sign cutting oriented to the prime sign. The cutting team will survey the area of the predicted sign line, looking for natural terrain, vegetation or other environment that will permit footprint sign to show readily. This would include any area that may contain changes of vegetation, soil color or composition, terrain variances known as natural barriers. Once the two teams have agreed upon the operational plan, the cutting team turns and departs from the prime sign team at approximately a 90-degree angle, walking in single file and looking for sign evidence to a chosen point a few yards away. As a general rule, taking the natural cutting line into account, the cutting team will go out 6 to 8 steps. They will then pivot toward the predicted sign line and again, choosing a point to approach, continue the cut at

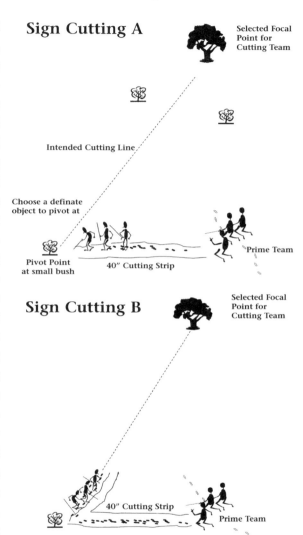

Sign Cutting A

Selected Focal Point for Cutting Team

Intended Cutting Line

Choose a definate object to pivot at

Pivot Point at small bush

40″ Cutting Strip

Prime Team

Sign Cutting B

Selected Focal Point for Cutting Team

40″ Cutting Strip

Prime Team

approximately a 45-degree angle to this predicted sign line. With their primary scrutiny focused on the prime sign, they should intersect the line of the subject's travel around 20 steps in front of the prime team. An important factor is communication. The two teams must always feel that they are working together. They should never be further apart than a normal speaking voice can carry and they should keep up a fairly constant dialogue regarding what they're seeing.

Sign cutting is fun. You're moving, you're searching and it's much less tedious than following the prime sign. This is why most tracking aspirants want to get to the point in their training where they can actually do sign cutting. The problem is that most people picture themselves casually walking through the brush, across the hillside or whatever, and picking up the victim's track fairly easily. Gosh, sometimes I picture myself doing that...then I wake up.

There are several cautions I give students. First, if you're unable to work or move prime sign, you are not tracking, and second, cutting sign is always more complex and difficult than moving or working the prime sign. It takes far more skill derived from supervised training and practical experience to cut sign successfully than it does to work the sign line step by step. This is the key principle upon which the entire modern tracking training program was devised.

Let's consider why there are so few recognized trackers. Are they the only people who want to be trackers? No. In fact many people see themselves as trackers and many more want to be trackers. They read books and attend courses and learn about tracking, but only a few make the grade to be recognized as skilled trackers. Tracking is a skill that requires considerable knowledge and experience. Everyone who pays attention can see footprints, or at least they can see *some* footprints. Usually the tracks that the inexperienced see are of less importance to trained trackers. These are the "gimmes," the ones that everyone sees and recognizes. These are the tracks in the sandbox, the mud, the molehill or the dust on the trail. From there, you need to be able to understand and explain who these tracks belong to, when they were made, which direction the subject was going and what he was doing. Until you can answer those questions, all you know is that somebody stepped in the mud. Trackers qualified to cut sign must be able to know and recognize that the track they see relates to the person they're looking for. They must be able to eliminate all the other damage they're seeing around them, made by nature, animals, insects or other people, and focus in on the sign characteristics of the subject under consideration. Anyone can get lucky and find a lone print somewhere on the trail or in the mud. Trackers can't depend on luck, though it's welcome when it comes. They must depend on the slow and arduous task of acquiring the skill and experience that will keep them on the subject's sign.

Sign cutting does not mean looking here and there, going from one track trap to another, hoping to find a print. Sign cutting is a specific tracking technique used successfully by experienced and skilled trackers. Most often the sign located using this tracking technique would only be associated with the evidence of human passage by a very experienced tracker. A novice tracker would most often overlook or misinterpret this sign. It might be seen, but not recognized as significant.

Multiple Teams

Another sign-cutting technique employed primarily in fairly open country is that of using multiple cutting teams. This is known as "double-team sign cutting" or to experienced sign cutters "braiding the sign." In this operation both cutting teams begin from the same prime sign position and, after making their plan, leave the prime sign in opposite directions, both cutting at a 90-degree angle. Keeping up a steady communication, they reach the first chosen point and pivot, each team now facing the predicted prime sign line at the 45-degree angle. Each team then chooses a point that will intersect the predicted sign line ahead of the prime team, just as a single cutting team operation would do. Ideally, they will intersect the sign line at exactly the same point.

This method has great potential for moving the sign along rapidly. Should the cutting teams fail to cut the sign where they should, they should re-cut the same cutting route back to the starting point. Three rules for deciding if a sign cutting operations are warranted: 1) sign cutting must expect to be 100 percent accurate; 2) sign cutting must be quicker or move the prime sign more rapidly than just working the prime sign; 3) sign cutting must be easier

on the sign-cut teams' eyes than working the prime sign. Single-
and double-cutting team operations are successful only when used
in direct relation to moving the prime sign from the known position. Therefore such operations depend always on having a prime
sign team. Sign cutting without direction and proper orientation to
a known point simply tires trackers' eyes, erodes confidence and
expends energies for nothing. Such random sign cutting efforts add
contamination through which the prime team must work the sign.
This is why sign cutting must be regimented, disciplined and always
expect to be 100% accurate. Inept sign cutting can be a great detriment to any tracking operation.

Two additional sign-cutting
techniques that are regularly used by
experienced trackers are known as
"natural and man-made barrier cutting" and "open-field cutting." A
barrier is a term that probably is mis-
leading to most. First of all, to sign
cutters a barrier is that area that for
whatever reason will cause any passing person to leave more or more
obvious sign or an area on which the
passing persons sign will show more
readily. Examples of man-made barriers are fence lines, roads or trails,
ditches, edges of yards, lots or fields, etc. Examples of natural barriers
would be creek banks, edges of wooded areas, changes of vegetation
such as meadow grass to high weeds, terrain changes such as banks,
slopes, humps, hollows and hills, etc. Therefore, sign cutting natural
or man-made barriers means for a sign-cutting team to work along
the edge of such an area looking for evidence of a passing person.

Open-field sign cutting is the term applied to an operation in
which sign cutting teams have no natural or man-made barriers
available in the route that they need to sign cut. In this instance sign

cutting teams may use a direct line of sight for the cut, or a compass heading. This operation is often used to eliminate large sections or areas from further search efforts through sign cut teams being able to state with confidence that no physical sign of the described subject appears in the sign line cut.

Current search management circles frequently refer to probability of detection (POD). This is the probability that the search subject will be found, under the given conditions and if the subject is actually in the search area. I tell trackers that there is no room for POD in tracking! If a sufficiently trained and experienced tracking team cuts an area for sign, the trackers should be 100% sure that the subject's sign either is or is not there. Search coordinators need someone on the search scene who can definitely say "the victim was not here" or "he was here and went there." Trackers with enough skill, training and experience can do exactly that.

Teamwork

Search and rescue tracking students are the best trained and most professional of all trackers as a class or grouping. Here and there you may find someone within another walk of life whose knowledge, experience and skills equal or surpass those of the SAR trackers, but very few will be found. The general public often wants to believe that military and law enforcement "trackers" are the best trained and most professional trackers. This is not so in my experience, but there is good reason for this public misconception. It would seem that both military and law enforcement needs would ensure training for specialists. Not so. In fact, most often with law enforcement, an agency or department can only spare an officer to attend one course or class. There is the mistaken belief that this person can learn everything needed in a single class or course. Military personnel are not much different. Neither entity has a training program with instructors that could equal in capability the professionalism of the average SAR volunteer who has been involved in a consistent training program for three or four years.

So what enables this SAR volunteer, in most instances paying for the training out of their own pocket, taking time from work, family and other interests to consistently attend training and achieve this level of expertise? The simple answer is motivation and teamwork. There are many different facets of teamwork and tracking depends on them all. Simple regimented tracking rules, procedures, practices and principles will keep individual, inexperienced trackers from taking options that are often unsuccessful. Three trackers in a team seeing everything that has the subject's sign characteristics, reasoning to agreement, and adhering to simple rules derived from experts' experience and knowledge. This is a system designed to produce successful results. Each student who wants to be successful must learn to concentrate on accuracy, patience and teamwork.

CHAPTER SIX

Tracks of Bigfoot
Fact or Fiction?

"...of all the implausible denizens of the Pacific Northwest, none has been seen more widely and often, advocated more eloquently, disputed more vigorously and rejected in the name of science more unscientifically than the Sasquatch, or Bigfoot, a race of giant and hairy man-apes who have been reported periodically...for a century. Over a thousand separate sightings have been documented and a disturbing majority seem to agree on several of the details." —LIFE

Bring up the topic of Bigfoot and you're sure to get an argument started. Here in the Pacific Northwest, it's worse than politics or religion. As with those two volatile topics, very few people ride the fence when it comes to the existence of the strange, manlike creature supposed to be living in the remotest regions of our wilderness areas. Stories describe a Bigfoot, or Sasquatch, as a very shy seven-foot forest dweller so it's very rarely ever seen by man. You encounter dyed-in-the-wool Bigfoot believers and jeering skeptics, but rarely is anyone without a definite opinion. I like to think of myself as an open-minded guy, but a practical one. As a law enforcement officer for 30 years, it's pretty hard for me to believe in anything without good, hard evidence to support it. The best evidence that Bigfoot believers have been able to come up with are footprints of the big guy. As a sign cutter for the Border Patrol, I have followed barefooted subjects on many occasions, so I am ready to look at any Bigfoot tracks with a practiced eye, but with a healthy dose of skepticism.

I was enjoying a second pot of coffee on a beautifully warm morning in June of 1982. The morning held the promise of a "too hot" afternoon. I was with my family on a couple weeks' vacation from busy Border Patrol activities to visit relatives in the Emmett Valley, of southern Idaho. My parents, wife and I were still sitting at the breakfast table in the kitchen as my daughters played. On her way outside to gather some vegetables from the garden, my mother asked if I'd seen the Bigfoot article in the *Idaho Statesman* that morning. When I said I hadn't, she paused to retrieve the Boise paper and found the small article buried on an inside page. I quickly read the short article that reported a Bigfoot sighting by a Forest Service employee in a closed area of the Mill Creek watershed drainage near Walla Walla, Washington, and laid the paper aside.

My father asked me if I'd ever seen any Bigfoot footprints during my travels around the country. I said no, and that began a conversation regarding the probability of such a creature roaming around the mountains. Though he was now retired from ranching and was doing the finish carpentry work that he favored, my father as a young man had spent considerable time in the back country mountain wilderness of the Oregon, Washington and Idaho mountains. He and a couple different partners had mined gold or fished nearly every lake and high mountain creek in all three states. Dad said he'd never caught sight, sound or stink of anything like a Bigfoot, as it was described in the article—a smelly, hairy seven-foot creature that walked on two legs and swung its arms as apes do. He did remember some unsavory characters who could probably pass as one after a couple months in the back country. This statement I recognized as a prologue to an interesting tale, but it was interrupted by the telephone ringing.

My mother, coming back into the house, answered and, to my surprise, she handed the phone to me. The man on the other end identified himself as the regional Forest Service Chief from the San

Francisco office. He asked, "Are you the Border Patrol tracker?" I was caught slightly off-guard because I didn't think anyone knew I was here, but I managed to mumble that I supposed that I was.

He apologized for calling me while I was on leave, but they were very pressed for time—they had kind of an emergency. He explained that the Forest Service was the agency responsible for the Walla Walla watershed near the town of the same name in southeast Washington. It had been a closed watershed for many years, which meant that public access was restricted or barred, including hunting and fishing. When I asked what it had to do with me, he finally got around to his problem.

He said that one of their employees had recently reported seeing a Bigfoot in the Mill Creek watershed. I wasn't sure if I should laugh or not, so I tried not to. My dad wasn't helping much, since he had grasped the gist of the conversation from the look on my face and was mouthing questions that I should ask. The Forest Service Chief added that somehow the three TV networks—ABC, NBC, CBS—had gotten wind of the Bigfoot sighting and had filed a court action in Washington to force the Forest Service to permit them access to this amazing discovery. The Forest Service had been given 48 hours to answer the injunction by coming up with evidence that the reported sighting was in fact a hoax. The chief paused, then asked if I thought I could look at the tracks and determine whether or not the prints were faked somehow.

I hesitated before offering that I couldn't tell anything at all about the prints without looking at them. If I saw them I probably could tell if they were faked or not. He asked if I was willing to go look at the prints now, to which I replied, "Sure, if you can get me there."

The chief asked for the location of the nearest airport and I told him of the small airport at Emmett, only 20 minutes away from me. He replied that unless he called back, I should be at the Emmett airport at 9:30 a.m. and he would have a plane there to take me to Walla Walla. The head ranger of the Walla Walla District would meet me there and take me to the footprints.

District Ranger Bruce Long met the plane as we taxied to a stop outside of the little terminal building at Walla Walla. It had been an uneventful 60-minute flight in a Piper twin-engine plane and I was delighted to get to view some territory that I had never seen from the air before. He advised the pilot that we'd no doubt be most of rest of the day if he wanted to wait, otherwise they'd get someone else to fly me back. The pilot said he'd wait. Long motioned for me to get into his Forest Service pickup for the ride to the Ranger Station. During the 20-minute drive we talked about Bigfoot, the sighting, and tracking. Bruce wanted to know what it was that I expected to see that he hadn't already seen. This inquiry kind of put me on the spot, so I just told him that I'd show him anything that I saw.

Bruce explained that the closed watershed contained several species of animals not generally seen elsewhere. The Forest Service cooperated with state and federal scientific studies to allow them to study the animals within the watershed. The Mi¹l Creek drainage had been closed to the public for more than 50 years, allowing the animals a protected and pristine natural habitat unlike any other in the Western United States or Canada. Therefore, anything and everything that was done in the watershed was supervised and monitored by numerous scientists. He would introduce me to several of them at the office and they would be accompanying us to see the footprints. The scientists had already been there but wanted to be able to see anything and everything that I saw in the footprints. They had made plaster casts of the prints and I would be able to see these at the office.

We arrived at the office and Ranger Long ushered me in and introduced me to several people. A couple were scientists of one type or another with "-ologist" ending their titles. Bruce came with a cup of coffee for me and led me into the back room to view the plaster casts. The plaster casts simply looked like big bare footprint casts. I couldn't see anything significant in them, and certainly didn't see anything that would make me think they weren't human, except the size. They were interesting enough to look at, but I could tell much more from tracks on the ground than from something like this. Since becoming a tracker, I have failed to see the value of plaster casts, regardless of the quality, and these weren't very good.

We laughed and talked while I finished my coffee and I definitely felt that these scientists seriously wanted validation of the existence of the creature, but not admission of the public to their private laboratory. Eventually we loaded up and began the 90-minute drive to the watershed. I understood that others would meet us at the "gate." Someone said that they were bringing a sandwich for me and we would picnic on the trail.

Walla Walla is a small town of great historical significance in the settlement of the Northwest Territory. It was the site of the U.S. Army's Fort Walla Walla and the Whitman Mission on the Lewis and Clark trail. It's nestled on the edge of the plain at the foothills of the Blue Mountains and located on the river by the same name. This river afforded natives, then the Lewis and Clark expedition and the following explorers and settlers of the Oregon Trail, relief from months of hazardous, dirty, dusty travel with a water passage to the Willamette Valley. The Walla Walla River is navigable by small boat and barge and flows directly into the Columbia River and eventually into the Pacific at Astoria, Oregon. The "Blues" form a dark and shadowy backdrop for the town with high peaked ridges of granite and slopes timbered with pine, larch, spruce, fir and hemlock.

We headed southeast out of town to the Mill Creek watershed, following county roads toward the dark slopes that gradually turned to forest green as scattered evergreens began to appear on the open foothills. We turned from the paved highway onto a wide dirt road leading directly toward the forested slopes that soon enveloped us on either side and along a smoothly flowing creek. Bruce nodded toward the creek and identified it as Mill Creek. We followed the creek upstream until we came upon a couple more green Forest Service vehicles parked where a white iron-bar gate closed the road. Evidence of vehicle traffic ended there, where the gateposts and a couple tree trunks were hung with large official signs warning that any entry by vehicle or on foot into the drainage was forbidden and punishable by law. A tidy little old log cabin with tubs of blossoming flowers sat on the other side of the gate and reminded me of the seven dwarfs' house in the Snow White story. The cabin, I was told, provided housing for a volunteer employee to guard the coming and going up the hiking trail that followed along side Mill Creek and was a historical site that had been left to the Forest Service.

We were joined by two additional Forest Service personnel and another very large man named Paul Freeman, who looked like a horse wrangler. They were waiting with a biologist, a botanist and a couple other "-ologist" titles that I wasn't familiar with at the gate. Another "closed area" warning sign adorned the head of the hiking trail that began in the old roadway past the cabin and continued onward along Mill Creek. The creek was flowing a pretty heavy stream of water here. It was probably 16 to 20 feet wide and nearly two feet deep in the middle. It looked like a great stream to fish. Everyone began gathering day packs, their lunches and various pieces of equipment—clipboards, charts and scientific equipment, the only item of which I recognized was a bag of dental powder for making casts. I was told the hike would take a couple hours to the area of the Bigfoot prints. A second set of prints was in a more distant location and would take several more hours of hiking to reach them.

The big wrangler Freeman wore a permanent scowl and I was sure I wasn't mistaking his glances of dislike. He didn't want to be a part of our little group of eight, or he didn't want to take this hike, or he didn't want something. Bruce told him to lead out up the trail, and the others fell in behind, leaving Bruce and me to bring up the rear of the string. I knew now through the combined conversations that the two rangers and the three scientists with us had all been up the trail a couple days before and had made the plaster casts that I had seen at the office. The scientists had tried to gather hair and anything else that might be attributed to the Bigfoot. Though I was going up the trail to determine if the tracks were a hoax, I gathered that they were going up the same trail to prove the creature had indeed walked there. It was a perfect day for a hike into a pristine wilderness, about 65 degrees in the open forest.

As we hiked up the trail, Bruce quietly filled me in further on the history of the watershed and the story of the Bigfoot sighting. He indicated that Freeman had reported seeing the Bigfoot about a week previously. This was the reported sighting that I had read about in the paper. Freeman was one of the part-time employee outriders hired by the Forest Service each summer to patrol the outer perimeter of the watershed. The outrider's job was to intercept or hunt down anyone who tried to get into the watershed—hunters, fishermen or just Joe Public who happened along. The watershed was surrounded on three sides by National Forest and the third side was private land, with its own entrance road that the riders paid close attention to. Once in a while, people would slip into the area, but they were usually found and brought in to face charges. Bruce described the outriders as competent men who had worked the watershed for several years. They were good trackers and very successful at detecting those who tried to surreptitiously enter the watershed through the back country.

We hiked steadily and talked, the ranger indicated that I might get to see some unusual animals that inhabited the watershed. He advised that some of the biggest trout imaginable lived right there in Mill Creek. To prove this, as we came to a creek crossing he pulled a sandwich from his day pack. Separating one of the slices of bread, he broke it into pieces and tossed it into the middle of the creek. Before the bread hit the water, the surface exploded with several large trout leaping to catch the bread. He laughed as we all watched with our mouths hanging open. It was a feeding frenzy as the huge trout—not one looked to be under five pounds—rolled and broke the surface, fighting with one another for the pieces of bread. I was reminded of professional basketball players under the hoop fighting for the best position to get the rebound. Several more sandwiches were broken out of day packs and fed to the frantic fish. We stood and talked of tossing a baited hook into this creek. None of the three rangers would admit ever having done so, though they had all been sorely tempted over the years. Bruce glanced around at the group and said quietly, "Keeping stories like this quiet is the only way to keep the public out." Almost miraculously, the rangers had been successful at this for the past 50 years.

I marveled at the unspoiled beauty. The scattered old-growth trees with their heads held high in the blue sky seemed to be of such immense proportions that they dwarfed the buck brush, huckleberry and heather that covered the ground at their feet. The high canopy filtered the bright sunlight, dappling and camouflaging all beneath. Springs oozed from mossy rocky outcroppings and trickled down and across the trail, feeding watercress-choked puddles and making rivulets into Mill Creek, which gurgled and splashed its way downhill. The hike was easy up the bottom of the drainage, with only a gradual but steady ascent toward the high country that guarded the origin of Mill Creek. This was a magnificent area, completely untouched by man. There weren't any of the usual signs of campgrounds or rest areas that you see in National Forest recreation areas, no sawn or chopped stumps, or rounds left to rot, or even the rusted metal parts and pieces that so often mark long-abandoned mining sites. This was just raw western mountain nature at its finest.

Around 2 p.m., we came to an area where the trail followed a small tributary to Mill Creek through a leprechaun-lover's glen dotted with the big trees sheltering a lush growth of some type of clover above a carpet of moss. On the right side of the trail, the ground rose steeply on a shoulder of granite hidden by the same carpet of lush moss and clover. Here and there small seeps of water flowed slowly from cracks in these rocks and onto and down the trail before finding a way down into the larger Mill Creek tributary. These seeps, or springs, soaked the trail's light-black, decomposed soil, which was churned by regular animal traffic into a loose soft mud that filled the trail's shallows and covered the granite crushed by years of wear.
Bruce and I came last into the glen and saw that the group was standing in a line, looking down at the trail. Everyone was looking at several large footprints in the trail. There was just enough of the light soft

mud in this area to leave perfectly
formed, shallow prints. I moved up close
to get a better view.

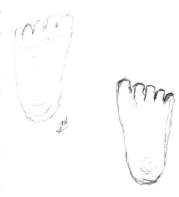

The prints weren't just easy to spot,
they jumped out at us! Huge barefoot
prints! Bare footprints in the mud that
nearly waved a flag and yelled, "Look at
me!" There were nearly a dozen of the
prints about a yard or more apart. Their
appearance was captivating—the size, the
perfection of each print, the placement right in the middle of the trail
in the mud. The seeping water had found ways around the prints without disturbing them, and now the top edges of the squashed mud were
beginning to dry slightly. I was a bit overwhelmed with the appearance
of the prints and walked behind the others, looking over their shoulders. I heard bits and pieces of conversation about the previous
examination of these prints and comparison with others where Bigfoot
was allegedly sighted.

The entire line of footprints was nearly 40 feet long. I reached the
beginning, where the first print entered the edge of the mud. The side
of the trail where everyone now squatted was heavily tromped, however the off side of the trail was close to the edge of the rocky ledge and
offered slight footing, therefore was virtually unspoiled. I took out pencil and paper and the measuring tape I had borrowed from my dad's
tool belt to begin making drawings and notes.

First, I looked at the overall appearance. I backed away to take in
the entire view, hoping the others wouldn't mess anything up as I took
my time. I peeled off my outside shirt and laid it across the trail just
behind the first print. The trail coming to this muddy section was basi-
cally on hard rock in the open, with a crumbling of crushed granite,
needles and light decomposed duff. I wanted to see just what this
Bigfoot would see as he walked down the trail toward the muddy section and began to work my way alongside the trail away from the
group. The trail continued in the open for probably twice as far as the

muddy strip was long before it faded into the shadow beneath another canopy of trees. On close examination, I could make out the hoof edges of deer, elk and horses or mules, with the scuff or compression of human footgear sign. I hadn't yet looked closely at the footprints in the mud and wondered if I should be seeing evidence of a hairy print, the smooth compression of tough leather, or just what. I wasn't seeing anything as I worked my way along the trail that would have been made by the huge feet that made the prints in the mud. The trail reappeared before I reached the canopy of trees and, though still quite rocky, there was some soil and debris that showed the animal prints quite definitely, but didn't show any indications of the Bigfoot prints.

I had gone into the next wooded section some 20 or 30 feet, and decided that was far enough. I began to work my way back toward the others, who were now beginning to gather together near where my shirt was laid. I was wondering where this Bigfoot had come from, as it didn't appear to me that he had been walking down the trail coming out of this section of woods. I walked slowly back toward the others, sign cutting both sides of the trail for any sign of huge footprint compressions smashing, crushing and otherwise damaging the lush, delicate ground coverings.

Bruce came to join me, with the others following, to ask if I could tell anything from the prints in the mud. I replied, "I think I can, but it'll probably take most of an hour to make a full examination." I asked him exactly when the prints had been made and he called to Freeman to come up and talk with us. Scowling while he talked, Freeman said he'd ridden up the trail with one pack animal three days before and gone all the way up to where he had seen the Bigfoot. The horses were pretty spooked up there and he didn't want to spend the night, so he had come back down the trail in the late afternoon and found these tracks right where his horses had walked going up. He had gone directly to the caretaker's cabin and called the Ranger Station and reported the tracks. So the tracks were three days old and with his estimated time frame made it sometime between 8 a.m. and 4 or 5 p.m. He hadn't seen anything around, but his horses were very spooked around here, as if they smelled something. I replied that I would begin doing an examination and walked back to where my shirt was lying across the trail.

I took in the entire setting again. I stood where everyone else had stood alongside the trail, then walked to the other end of the string of tracks. There were eight perfect prints. The entire party stood by my shirt as I looked at the tracks, watching and waiting to see what I would do. I looked, studied and tried to get a "feel" for what it was I was seeing while I slowly walked back to the first visible print. The first track began at the muddy area and the next seven continued through it, with number nine barely visible and seeming to disappear on the drier portion of the trail at the other end. I had looked at the trail closely on the upper end and found horse's hoof marks, so I went to the downhill end and studied the trail closely. There was sign of horse's hoofs reentering the trail just past where the last huge print was in the mud. It was strange that no deer, elk or other even little animals had walked through these prints, though I could readily see parts of animal sign on the trail between the huge footprints. Maybe the report of the stench of the Bigfoot was true.

I backtracked the trail a third time, coming back to where my shirt lay and looking closely at the prints and it suddenly came to me— these prints were far too perfect to be human or animal. From where my shirt lay, I began sign cutting the off side, or creek side, of the trail where no one had been. The vegetation was lush and long, impossible for even a squirrel to go across it without leaving an obvious print that would last for a month. I finished this cut down the trail through the lush vegetation to another place where there were several seeps and a strip of similar mud that ran for 10 or 12 feet and that had captured the horse tracks up and down the trail as well as all of ours. But no sign of Bigfoot prints. I returned to the shirt and began a cut in the opposite direction along the creek bank and the slope between the trail and the creek in a semicircle, well past the first of the wooded area up the trail. Definitely no Bigfoot—or even Littlefoot for that matter—had crossed to or from the trail in this area.

I ended up slightly further up the trail from where I had checked originally. I began a cut from the creek to the trail and continued to make another semicircular cut above the trail to completely encircle the muddy footprint area. In this manner I would be able to find where the Bigfoot had come onto and gone off of the trail.

It was nearly perfect sign cutting conditions, with the lush vegetation and good moisture seeping from the hillside in most places. Compared to the sign cutting conditions where I was working in southern California, where the soil was dry and powdery with sparse vegetation, this was a place for even beginners to see sign. How could anyone not be able to track here? The steep bank on the upper side of the trail would be very difficult for even an experienced tracker to cross without leaving obvious sign. The seeping water was keeping bare rocks damp whenever the sun wasn't bright on them. Everywhere in between was wet with plenty of mud and good lush grass. I would know without a doubt if anyone or anything had come through here. Nothing had.

I finished the cut and then re-cut a few areas. I was positive that this area would have shown any tracks going through it—in fact there were several small animal prints visible—but Mr. Bigfoot had not ventured this way. Nothing as large as a fox could have come through there in the several weeks previously without leaving obvious prints in the vegetation. When I finished the sign cutting, I again stood at the spot I'd left my shirt. I'd made a complete circle and found no sign larger than that of a deer entering or exiting the area from any point. All of the prints that this particular Bigfoot had made were contained within that small section. I counted the prints again: eight, well possibly nine, counting the scuff marks on the trail. If a Sasquatch had made these prints, it would have to have floated in, hit the ground walking for eight or nine steps, then floated away again.

Very skeptical at this point, I nevertheless began to measure and draw the prints, just as I would for any crime scene examination, noting in great detail everything I could see in the prints. I finished drawing the first print, a left foot, and measured the stride between it

Photo of Bigfoot print at Walla Walla site.

and the next, a right foot, then began the examination of the second print. One peculiarity I noticed was that the prints appeared to be laid out in a perfectly straight line. A string laid down on the center of the big toe of the first print ran to the exact center of the heel of the next and on through all the eight prints. This seven-foot creature would not only be able to walk a rail, he would be able to walk a tight wire! This was not only abnormal, but also almost impossible for a creature of this supposed size to do. Seldom does a person walk a perfectly straight line. Even when trying to do so, it's difficult and takes practice. Bipeds by nature have a hard time balancing themselves in such a way and their tracks are always offset by at least a few inches. Seldom will anyone walk with feet straight in line with the direction of travel. These prints were perfectly straight in line, not parallel, not naturally at a slight angle to the line of travel, but the last print in the line was straight as a string in line with all other seven. Impossible!

Another peculiarity of this set of tracks was the stride length. Every single track was exactly the same distance apart from tip of big toe to the back of the next bare heel, not varying by more than a sixteenth of an inch. Again, when bipeds walk, even on level ground, their stride will vary by an inch or two. When walking through squishy mud such as this, and on this uneven trail surface, some of the strides should vary.

Next I studied the prints for minute physical detail and I noticed that these prints had some of the most perfect dermal ridges I had ever seen. Dermal ridges are those little lines that form fingerprints, palm prints and footprints. They're so distinctive that newborn babies are identified by their dermal ridges on their feet. The ridges on these prints were prominent and perfectly formed— so perfectly formed, in fact, that I could place the tip of my pen on one ridge and follow it all the way around the print. There were no tears, scars, calluses or any other indication of normal and natural wear or trauma to the foot. Many of the barefooted subjects I have followed have rarely worn shoes for most of their lives. The soles of their feet show clear evidence of the miles of barefoot travel, with hard calluses, cracks and scars clearly evident and their dermal ridges worn smooth and almost flat over the weight-bearing sur- faces of the heel and the ball of the foot. The toes of those peoples' feet were generally enlarged and marked with cracks and scars from traveling over rough country. This was supposed to be an adult crea- ture that walked barefoot for years on rocks and sticks, yet the prints showed no evidence of hard travel over rough ground. The feet that had made these isolated Bigfoot tracks seemed to have just stepped out of a J.C. Penney store.

I also noticed the lack of any evidence of the normal body move- ment necessary for bipeds to move. In a normal biped walking motion, the heel of the foot strikes the ground first. The heel hits hard first, and the push-off from the ball of the foot leaves significant, distinctive compression relative to the other parts of the foot in the resulting foot- print. These Bigfoot tracks were not walking; they showed no motion.

I finished my drawings and called District Ranger Long over. The others had drifted away and because we were alone, I pointed out to him each factor I had observed and explained why each one provided evidence supporting my conclusion that the prints were a hoax. My opinion was that these prints were the creation of someone who had wanted to cause others to pause and speculate. They were not from a live creature, Bigfoot or otherwise.

"Good enough for me," Bruce said. "Are you willing to swear to that?"

"You bet," I replied.

One of the other rangers came up just then with one of the scientists and they excitedly announced that additional Bigfoot tracks had just been found up the hill above us at the edge of the timber in an elk wallow. Bruce looked at me and I at him, I shrugged and said, "Well, let's go see 'em."

The two led the way away from the main trail up the hill following a slight animal trail that I had noticed when I was making the cut around the muddy footprint strip on the trail. A hundred feet or so brought us to a slight bench, or fairly level area, that permitted water from the numerous springs or seeps to collect and stand, encouraging the growth of bear grass and reeds and forming a muddy, spa-sized pond. Elk frequent these little ponds during the summer months to wallow and get a mud coating to discourage biting and stinging insects. Such wallowing tends to stir the mud and round out the puddle to a significant depth as a full-grown elk is nearly as large as a horse. This was a typical elk wallow, with a water puddle in the middle of an approximately six-by-eight-foot tub of mud that oozed tiny rivulets of clear water from the seeps. Along the left side of the wallow was a large old log about two to three feet in diameter. The other members of the group were standing on the log looking into the mud wallow. As we approached, they excitedly pointed into the wallow along the log and indicated that was where the tracks appeared.

I stepped onto the end of the log and walked on top of it to where they were standing and there I could clearly see in the more stable mud alongside the log, deep footprints that had gone straight down, with no indication of travel. In the bottom of the prints, about 12 to 20 inches down in the mud, I could barely make out the impression of the same type of dermal ridges that appeared in the prints on the muddy trail. There were four of these prints alongside the log, each about three feet from the next, the last print providing the impression that the Bigfoot was stepping out of the mud and onto a hard rock trail. The trail, like the main trail below, was covered with crumbled granite, tree needles and duff, along with some dried dirt which had come as mud from the wallow.

I walked back past the group on the log to the first track and began a verbal examination loud enough for all to hear. "You might notice that Bigfoot was apparently suspended in air when he made this first print because it's a left footprint. If he had stepped off of this log with the left foot, the other foot would have to appear somewhere close to this first one. Notice that this print goes perfectly straight down into the mud and comes back up the same way, showing no indication of fluctuation of the ankle or knee. It would be impossible for Bigfoot or any one of you to step off of this log into the mud and not put the other foot down. Likewise it would be impossible to push your foot straight down and pull it straight back up.

I turned to pluck a two-foot-long heavy stem of grass and stripped the blades from it. Getting on my knees on the log, I leaned out over the mud bath and poked the grass stem straight down into the mud bottom of the footprint—then poked it further down and further down, as though there was no bottom to the print.

"Notice," I said, looking up at them, "that Bigfoot was able to put all of his estimated 800 pounds on one foot in this mud and somehow not go down to firm footing. Notice that none of these prints go down to a firm bottom." I went to each of the other prints and thrust the grass stem several inches down in the mud bottom of the prints. "These are what we call 'post hole' tracks, like you make walking in snow that's a couple feet deep. Every one of these tracks goes straight down and straight back up. This is not possible for a two-legged animal when moving forward in a natural line of movement."

Then I got on my hands and knees and motioned for them to get close enough to see what I was pointing at on the hard rock trail. "See this print where Bigfoot supposedly steps out of the mud onto the trail? Notice these little ripples in the sand and needles? This is the result of the effort to make sure that someone can notice the print. When you want to make a print you're sure someone will see on a very hard surface, most people tend to push down hard and wiggle the shoe to make sure the impression shows." I demonstrated, planting my foot slightly ahead of the Bigfoot print and wiggling it to make a print. It created the same tiny ripples around the heel and ball of the foot, outlining my boot. From their faces, they looked like I had just told that that there wasn't any Santa Claus. "Guys, I'm sorry, but someone wanted us to find these prints and get real excited. Someone put these footprints here for us to find. No Sasquatch made these."

We gathered up our gear and made ready to head back to the gate. I asked about Freeman, who was absent from the group and Bruce said quietly that he'd already headed back. There was little talking and joking as we trudged back down the trail. I was feeling like I had popped the party balloon. No one said anything to me, and no one questioned me. I knew they were going over in their minds what I'd said and showed them about the tracks in the wallow. They could see and understand what I was telling them was true, but they didn't want to believe it. The scientists really wanted to have the big hairy creatures here to study.

We arrived at the entrance gate and found that Freeman's pickup was already gone. Bruce offered the ranger who'd driven out with him a ride back to the office with us. He asked if I could provide a statement about my findings with the tracks at the office, so he could fax it to the Forest Service Chief. Back in his office, he brought coffee and I typed up a report describing what I'd seen and stating my conclusion that the Bigfoot tracks were a hoax. Bruce immediately faxed the report to the regional Forest Service Chief for his referral on to the appropriate attorneys to be filed in federal court.

During the drive back to the airport, Bruce told me about Freeman reporting the original Bigfoot sighting the week before. Freeman had called in excitedly from the gatekeeper's house late in the afternoon reporting that he'd had an encounter with a Bigfoot and the incident had so unnerved him and spooked his horses that he had ridden in to make the report. Bruce advised him to come to the office so they could talk about the incident, thinking that Freeman had seen a bear or something understandable. When Freeman arrived, he was quite agitated and wanted people to go with him to see the creature,

even though it was at the top of the drainage, about five to six hours' ride by horseback. Bruce and other rangers tried to convince him that he'd had mistakenly seen some other animal, but Freeman was adamant and detailed in his description of what he had seen. He described the creature as seven feet tall, with a thick, heavy build and long arms, with long dark brown and black hair all over the body and a very foul smell. Freeman said he was riding the top trail on the outside ridge of the drainage, trailing a packhorse. Suddenly, just ahead of him, the Bigfoot came walking out of a small stand of trees and walked across an open area and off around a slight bend behind some other trees out of sight. Freeman said that the Bigfoot stopped and turned and looked right at him, the hair on the back of its head standing up in some type of fan, and then it slowly turned away and walked out of his sight. His horses were totally spooked and nearly uncontrollable. Freeman had sat at the desk and written a report of the sighting and told the scientists about it. The next day Freeman had taken several people up to the sighting area and they had found Bigfoot prints, from which they made the plaster casts that I had seen at the office.

Bruce admitted that he hadn't believed the Freeman story and had just put the report in the desk without saying anything to anyone about it. But two days later, calls began coming from local and regional news media, and on the third day the major networks were on the story and the petition was filed in court for access to the Mill Creek watershed with a copy of the "official" Bigfoot sighting report that Freeman had written. Bruce had no idea how the media had gotten the copy or who had let the story out. He had been called on the carpet by the chief to explain the story and how it had turned into a little circus. He thanked me for my assistance and waved goodbye as I crawled into the Piper Twin for the return flight to Emmett.

Later, I learned a great deal more about this particular Bigfoot sighting incident, both through articles in the newspaper that followed the court's denial of the media's petition for admission into the Mill Creek watershed and a couple phone calls to Ranger Long. Bruce learned, subsequent to my involvement, that someone from the Walla Walla Forest Service office had placed phone calls to national newspapers and television networks, advising them of the original Bigfoot sighting.

The scientists I'd hiked up there with weren't satisfied with the results of my examination of the footprints and submitted their plaster casts to Dr. Grover Kranz, dean of Anthropology at Washington State University at Pullman, Washington. Dr. Krantz was a Bigfoot enthusiast and a member of the International Bigfoot Society and specialist in cryptozoology. He examined the plaster casts and, after several months of research, declared them to be casts of authentic Bigfoot footprints, primarily based on the fact that the dermal ridge impressions didn't match any known species, present or past. Dr. Krantz announced his findings at the annual Bigfoot conference, which created quite a stir among the members and executive research board that found his reasoning to be flawed. Dr. Krantz authored and published several scientific papers referring to the Freeman sighting casts in support of his position on authenticity.

Later on, the Bigfoot Society contacted me and requested a conference regarding the Freeman sighting and the plaster casts. Bigfoot Society President René Dahinden came from his residence in Langley, British Columbia, bringing pictures, casts and a copy of the original home movie of the Bigfoot taken in northern California in 1967 by Roger Patterson and Robert Grimlin. I was asked to examine everything and render conclusions and opinions of each. It was a long evening and in the end I couldn't tell anything about any of the items. Pictures can be faked, movies are seldom real, and plaster casts are not footprints. Dahinden was sincerely motivated to disprove every hoax that was reported in order to validate any credible evidence of existence of the creature. I agreed to assist him.

Several times between the 1982 sighting in the Mill Creek watershed and 1994, Paul Freeman was involved in other Bigfoot sightings, including one in which he reported having seen a family of the creatures, including a male, female and offspring. Local sheriff's deputies, searching the scene of the sighting, discredited this report and confronted Freeman. He admitted to authorities that he had not only made up the story but had constructed some "feet" to make tracks as evidence to validate his sighting and had done so in previous events.

René Dahinden died in 2000 and Grover Krantz died in 2002, having never settled their argument regarding the Freeman Blue Mountain sighting.

These episodes created for me a whole new awareness of the Bigfoot phenomena. I still haven't seen Bigfoot footprints that I believed were real, though I have to date looked at a number of very, very good hoaxes. Universal Tracking Services was contacted by Peter Byrne of the Bigfoot Research Project in Hood River, Oregon. This was a research group funded by the Academy of Applied Sciences to locate and secure evidence of the existence of such creatures in the areas where reported sightings were most numerous. I, in company with other UTS instructors, accompanied research personnel on several excursions to look for and examine prints found at reported sightings. This research project ended in 1998 without finding evidence of the existence of Sasquatch or validity to any alleged Bigfoot footprints or any reported sighting of the creature.

To date I have not seen any prints that I believe are authentic. Does the big creature of myth and legend exist? Could it be roaming the remote wilderness? Some believe it to be so. Some reject it outright. As I said, I like to think of myself as open-minded, but practical by nature. I'll believe it when I see it.

December 2003. Portland Oregonian

Families of Roger Patterson have come forward upon his death this month and announced with his permission that the film made in 1967 purporting to show a Sasquatch or Bigfoot walking swiftly away from the camera was faked. That Roger and Robert Grimlin planned and orchestrated filming Patterson's wife dressed in a gorilla costume and walking away from the camera. They furthered this hoax by constructing wooden feet made of alder and Patterson's wife wore the wooden feet to make the Bigfoot footprints found at the scene.

January 2003, New York Times

"...ask people here about the existence of a camera-resistant, grooming-challenged, upright biped known as Bigfoot or Sasquatch and the true believers shout to the misty heavens in affirmation. So it came as a considerable blow when the children of Ray L. Wallace announced that their prank-loving pop had created the modern myth of Bigfoot when he used a pair of carved wooden feet to stomp a track of oversized prints in a Northern California logging camp in 1958. Mr. Wallace, 84, died on Nov. 26 at a nursing home in Centralia, Wash.

CHAPTER SEVEN

Advanced Training
Beyond the Basics

I've mentioned in another chapter that it takes about 75 hours of classroom and field experience to grasp the basic techniques and gain enough experience to be considered a basic tracker. Most of those who go on to achieve a journeyman level of tracking spend another 165 to 200 hours in formal training and a like number of hours in practice and participation in tracking missions. For many, much of the advanced training work is a matter of nuance that is best experienced with an instructor in the field where people live and travel. It's difficult to adequately describe with words that which is more quickly and more completely understood by seeing it. Only through many hours of looking *at* sign and looking *for* sign can you develop the "eye" for the tiniest change or damage to the ground cover. Only by spending many training days in the field can you learn the difference between two-day-old sign in cut grass and four-day-old sign in the same cut grass. Only after many miles of tracking practice can you develop the knowledge to accurately interpret what the subject was thinking when he passed through a particular area. Good instruction however, provides the opportunity to learn these "advanced" tracking aspects without having to spend ten or more years in constant study trying to learn it all by yourself.

So, how do we get from "basic tracking" where we make a few tracks and meticulously study and draw them, learning to see all there is in each footprint, to the accomplished tracker stage? We already know it takes practice, practice, practice, but there must be more to it than that. Well yes there is, actually much more. First, let's understand that "advanced tracking" includes anything and everything in additional to basic tracking. Technically, "advanced tracking" includes the defined training levels of "Apprentice, Journeyman and Master or Sign Cutter. I define the Apprentice training level as that stage or period of learning to adapt or use tracking fundamentals in a practical application. The Journeyman training level is defined as the proficient use of all tracking techniques and procedures to effect a high rate of mission success. Master or Sign Cutter is the title identifying a near expert tracker who exhibits a near intuitional or clarvoyant application of techniques that nearly defy common sence of the untrained and only understood by experienced Journeyman level trackers. The term "expert" itself is reserved for those properly examined by legal authority and found to meet a level of expertise relative to time and place.

For some, tracking itself is success and fully satisfying. Persons in this category are quite content to identify a sign line and follow it until they cannot see the next track and then begin again wherever another or some other print is visible. To them, this is tracking. To others and I count myself among this group, success means being able to find and identify a specific track then follow that sign line to the end and correctly interpret all of the sign story along the way. It's much the same with crime scene examination, to some just being there is sufficient; to others there must be a practical element of relating footprint evidence to persons at the scene for understanding. I don't count tracking as successful unless you produce an accurate interpretation and solution that is understandable and undeniable to the untrained.

The mere act of finding and following sign is not in and of itself success in my book. Successful tracking operations involve a great deal of advanced training that many people don't believe has anything to do with tracking. For instance, let's suppose you're the best tracker in the world. Who says so? Who knows of you and of what you can do? What type of situations do you or will you work on? Superman in his blue suit with his red cape and the red S on his chest, this guy we know!

There is instant recognition and acceptance of his total abilities, knowledge and skills! But how do you know a tracker? What do they look like? Coonskin cap and buckskins? Not hardly! I learned some years ago that trackers did not get called to incidents or properly used when they were called because often no one knew who they were or what they were capable of doing. I learned that we need to teach trackers how to properly represent themselves to the SAR manager or official in charge at the search scene. They need to make these responsible persons aware of their special skills so they will get called when actually needed. This training isn't on the dirt and some say it isn't tracking at all, but if it gets you used as a tracker, then you have the opportunity to demonstrate that you are a tracker. If you're not called, you have no opportunity to exhibit who you are or what you can do and you must be content with self-confidence and self-examination of ability. So, what's my point? Well simply this: advanced tracking involves a great deal more than just working sign on the ground! To insure tracking success there is much you need to know, and a good part of that is to intelligently explain to other people what you know how to do.

I know of several instances in which trained trackers reported to search scenes and were immediately assigned to ongoing search activities, such as line or grid searching. Afterward they complained that the search manager had not even given them a chance to do any tracking. In talking with them, they and I agreed that in all probability these search managers didn't know they were tracking trained. In other instances, the search manager didn't know how to employ tracking resources correctly and the trackers didn't take the initiative to inform him or suggest their best use. When trackers don't properly introduce or represent themselves, they are partially responsible if search managers are not made aware of their skills or the proper use of tracking. Unfortunately this is the situation in a great many unsuccessful searches each year. Trackers who practice and train without ever being called on an actual mission soon lose interest and quit. They would rather do something else for which they get recognized and are needed.

On one occasion I was called by a search manager on the fifth or sixth day of a search when they were considering termination factors. The search manager described the missing-person incident information to me over the telephone and asked for my thoughts and opinion as to any overlooked options. I was familiar with the search area and the SAR units that would probably be on scene, I asked which units were there and learned that a couple very skilled tracking-trained people were on site. I asked to speak with one of them. When that person came on the phone, he told me that both of the trackers had arrived on the first day of the search. While yet unassigned to a specific search activity, he had taken the liberty of "looking around" for sign that fit the missing-person report. When I asked specific questions, he readily admitted that they had concluded that there wasn't sufficient evidence to substantiate the missing-person report before they first went into the field. There was sign of the person, but the sign story didn't match what was reported or believed to have taken place. I asked if they had advised the search manager of this, and he replied no, that no one had asked them. I got the search manager back on the phone and told him of these two persons' background in tracking and that they had sign-cut the area upon arrival and didn't find evidence to match the report. In short, they believed this was a contrived incident made to look like a missing-person incident. The search manager then talked with the two trackers and called off the search. The "missing person" was located three days later in Mexico. If their skills and opinion regarding the physical evidence had been communicated to the search manager, the search probably would have been called off much sooner.

Basic Tracker

Basic tracking training courses generally start students with a beginning or first identifiable print, from which they make their drawing and measurements. Thus, every line of sign found during class field work begins with the study and drawing, to ensure that students are learning to see all that there is to be seen in each print. Then we enhance this basic learning by following the sign line till the students come to the flag marking the end. This allows students to gain a feel for following the sign line. It motivates them by building their interest, while providing a tremendous variety of sign along the way. This greatly adds to their knowledge and experience. For the most part this basic learning takes place with students on hands and knees, getting close enough to the ground surface to see and identify the minutiae that is sign. Once students handle the basics comfortably and almost unconsciously, step by step and never proceeding beyond the next track that they can see, they're ready to take the first step up to the next level. That step depends, incorporates and builds upon all they've learned so far. Now they're ready for getting to their feet and learning to see the same sign detail from a standing position. They will begin to walk the sign line. As they begin to develop a reasonable degree of comfort and accuracy reading sign from a standing position, other techniques are introduced and added that most would readily recognize as practical tracking.

Apprentice Tracker

After having attended an average of 48 to 72 hours of professional tracking training at the beginner level, students enter the **apprentice training level**. Some students are comfortable and confident at seeing sign close up and have reservations about their ability to see the same detail while standing. At this stage of the training, they've already experienced losing the sign line several times and the idea of getting up and walking the sign is intimating. They know if they use their tracking stick and go slowly, step by step, they'll finish with success, so they're hesitant to change from a known successful method. Developing the confidence to make this change usually takes two or three 24-hour training courses, while also incorporating several other advanced techniques. Students will usually attend an average of 150 hours of formal training at this apprentice level. When they have completed this level, they can see sign, know what they are seeing and have begun to interpret simple sign-maker characteristics and aging factors. At this stage they competently see a track that their best friends would never believe is a footprint.

"Walking sign" means that you study and describe the intimate details of the footprint evidence from the standing position. Does this mean that you never again have to get back down on your hands and knees? No! All trackers will stoop and drop to a knee to examine minute sign detail from as close as possible, sometimes just to make sure of what they think they're seeing, other times because it's impossible to see such detail without getting very close to it. Occasionally some trackers may even apply a magnifying glass to the area, though I have never used one other than during forensic crime scene examinations. Some trackers include this item of equipment in their "tracking pack" along with their three-D-cell flashlight, measuring tape, extra tracking ID cards, pens and pencils, note pad, reflective mirror and tracking stick. This might give rise to question about trackers who wear eyeglasses, though this is usually a question asked by beginning trackers. Working with hundreds of tracking students over the years has taught me that corrective lens, either eyeglasses or contacts, have little or no bearing on the tracker's ability to see and correctly interpret sign. I now wear eyeglasses to accurately see the details of sign that I follow.

In the training process and at this level and after students begin to gain a measure of comfort and accuracy at walking the sign line, we begin to introduce what they've heard about and always wanted to do—"cut sign." Cutting sign simply means to walk carefully through an area and see the physical evidence of every footfall in the area. To make this technique successful a tracker must incorporate numerous factors and sign cutting fundamentals of learning how, why and where to look. There are several different Sign Cutting techniques referred to as "single and double team cutting, perimeter cutting, natural and manmade barrier cutting and open field cutting operations. These are journeyman-level aspects of tracking that must be introduced at the apprentice-training level to provide as much "time in practical application under supervision" as possible, which equates to experience. One method of introducing this technique is to not tell students where the sign line starts, but instead simply describe the print in general terms and indicate a general area where the print will be found. The instructor first makes up a story about the subject and lays out a sign line that corresponds to that story or scenario. Instructors must remember that they can't hide the sign of who, when, where, why, even from students at the apprentice level. Practice scenarios must be realistic and factual. The student sign cutting team must then search for a track that fits the description and information to recognize a sign line that matches the provided scenario. Once the print is located and identified, students make the drawing, take the measurements and establish the direction of travel. Often this print is in an area where they will see several other prints and they must separate or distinguish between several that are similar in age, size and style to select the described print. Repetition of this instructional technique helps students learn to associate specific prints with the "reporting party" information, such as when the prints were made, what the subject was doing, how they were prepared, and their knowledge or comfort in the area.

A "single cutting team operation" is used in a disciplined and regimented operation when two tracking teams are working together to move the "last known point" more rapidly. Large areas of search possibility are eliminated when no evidence of the subject is found by tracking teams using "perimeter or barrier" sign cutting methods along natural and man-made barriers. In instances in which there is significant contamination by other footprints trampling the ground surface, a sign cutting operation is used to locate the sign of the missing person on the outside of the central trafficked area. Sign cutting operations are used to determine when and why persons have been in an area or to locate the entry and exit routes to crime scenes and illegal wilderness-farming operations, sign of fish and game poachers, cattle rustling and many other such instances.

Team Tracking

Most civilian search and rescue responders, including tracking trainers, are part-time volunteers. Tracking depends on the complex dynamic of teamwork to be successful in saving lives in the shortest time possible. When Border Patrolmen first began to train search volunteers, we learned that a three-person team worked most efficiently, with a point person and two flanking trackers in a triangle formation. We quickly learned that a crucial factor to learning to see sign and tracking success was teaching team members to communicate with each other. We encouraged free discussion among all team members to talk about what they were seeing or not seeing. Comparatively, students learned three times as much in the same time period as when there was little or no discussion. Team trackers can work sign longer with a far greater efficiency in covering more of the search area. When apprentice level students are required to use the same discussion practices as they do in beginning courses, that is to put into words what they see or don't see, or do not understand, listening instructors are better able to coach or offer help. Student descriptions of what they believe they are seeing and their reasoning provides clarity and merit for everyone. Describing something to a teammate makes it real, so from the initial footprint that students draw, measure and identify, we insist that they freely discuss what they're seeing and understanding.

Tracking operations related to search missions should incorporate as many tracking teams as possible, especially if the subject may be in immediate danger. Therefore, learning all of the aspects of working in a coordinated, cooperative and compatible manner with other tracking teams is very important. First, you must learn to enhance the proficiency of your own team by being fully aware of interpersonal relationships, team leadership and the decision-making aspects of working closely in a three-person team. Right away many tracking students say, "What? All I want to do is track—I don't care about the rest of that stuff." Well, how successful do you want to be? One person can build an airplane, but several people all working together with proper planning and management can build several airplanes in less time. One tracker can resolve a tracking mission, but several trackers can reduce the amount of necessary time to a fraction of what one person would need.

I found that it was very rewarding to tracking students and productive to tracking missions to spend class time involving them in learning about their own personalities and thus better understand each other. Team building, team leader training and decision-making classes greatly enhance tracking team effectiveness when dealing with difficult and stressful search situations. Trackers are a unique, dependable and self-reliant resource. The search and rescue operations manual states that "only a tracker should decide if tracking is an appropriate resource for a particular mission." Similarly, only a tracker should decide when, where and how tracking should be used in a particular situation because only trained persons "see" what trackers see. Trackers therefore need to have proper training to equip themselves to handle even the most complex and difficult situation with whatever other persons are at hand.

Trackers need to be familiar with and prepared in all aspects of search and rescue and law enforcement work, and some aspects don't involve tracking. Tracking training lectures indicate the content and subject matter of a number of these "non-tracking" aspects: Interview and Interrogation Techniques, Evidence Preservation, Court Presentation of Evidence, Leadership, Decision Making, Team Building Techniques, Report Writing, Finding the Place Last Seen, Getting the First Print Started, and Proper Tracking Team Protocol. All of these topics serve to prepare and equip trackers to go anywhere, anytime and work with anyone to accomplish a successful tracking mission.

Let's get back to tracking! We're at the apprentice training level and applying the basics to practical use training. We're up and walking sign. Well, let's not walk too fast—we must adhere to the step-by-step principles. People so often ask, "You don't actually go step by step when you're tracking, do you?" The answer is yes, I do. I tell tracking students to pull their cap bill or hat down closer over their eyes so that they don't have the tendency to look ahead more than the next track. It saves frustrating hours of mistakes and retracing steps along the sign line to find where you've gone wrong.

There are many additional techniques to introduce at this level. A couple I've already talked about, such as locating the place last seen (PLS) and sign cutting, but other formal classroom and field instruction time covers getting the first track started, proper tracking team protocol, team work and decision making principles, search management concepts, multiple team operations, sign cutting operations, aging sign—gosh, is that enough? These all help tracking efficiency. It takes several training sessions for students to absorb, learn and gain practical use experience in all these techniques.

In each apprentice level course instructors incorporate two or more of these training elements that seem to be most appropriate for that particular course. For example, while we're encouraging each team at this level to stand and examine the sign, we stress teamwork, decision-making techniques and communication between team members and between teams. As we're following an identified line of sign, we also teach "reading" of sign characteristics, aging, identification and comparison to other sign encountered along the sign line. We begin to help teams to understand the concept of cutting for sign, plus when, where and how to recognize natural and man-made barriers which will show sign more effectively.

This is a delicate, sometimes difficult training stage for instructors. Students want to use the new, more exciting techniques and they must be continually reminded and encouraged to practice and develop their tracking fundamentals. The problem arises at this stage in that students are not sufficiently aware that all advanced techniques depend entirely on the subconscious, consistent, accurate and integral use of the fundamentals. Sign cutting is a great tool, but if you are unable to see, follow and read the sign you cut, you cannot make practical use of this technique! Therefore instructors introduce the new techniques while insisting students realize that their practice of the fundamentals is integral to successful use of the new technique.

They must allow students sufficient liberty to make mistakes, to get off the sign line and lose the sign entirely. Mistakes at this stage promote learning—they build necessary experience and help to insure adherence to principles.

Experienced apprentice level students, when asked what their most difficult task is, will most often reply, "Getting the first track started." This is the most difficult task for nearly all tracking missions, no matter the level of the tracker. Most apprentice level students working in a compatible team can follow confusing, contradictory and complex sign lines if given a definite starting point. Therefore training at this level, while involving teamwork, communication, multiple team operations, and elementary sign cutting, must give guidance and set principles for getting that first track started. I like to introduce this topic in a lecture class to help students better understand their role in a search situation. The same problem issues are a part of nearly all tracking situations regardless of the environment, military, law enforcement, missing person searching, or industrial-installation security. SAR managers or others requesting tracking assistance but without knowledge or experience in the application of tracking as an information-gathering resource, are unable to manage the resource well. Most often operational managers who request trackers will attempt to explain what is to be found and where, instead of allowing the trackers to provide information based on the physical evidence they discover.

Journeyman Tracker Techniques

Trackers must be trained to hear the manager's directions and based on the facts of the issue, decide how best to carry out their operation without being prejudiced by the instructions of non-trackers. Of course this must be done in a tactful, diplomatic fashion to produce what is desired but by using proper tracking methods and techniques. Often this isn't accomplished easily. Sometimes trackers get so carried away wanting to get to the task that they rush off to carry out the misdirection of well-intentioned, but untrained and unknowledgeable managers. It takes presence of mind and dedication to listen to what is being said, sorting and relating the information to find the facts, then to take actions based on those facts. I find that trackers are better able to accomplish this if they can clearly see themselves and their expertise in relation to the entire task at hand.

A good part of the initial application of tracking experience might seem to some observers as merely "standing around." I advise experienced trackers to have in mind a gimmick to use upon arriving on the scene that will enable them to ensure they proceed in an organized manner. I like to ask the SAR manager for a cup of coffee. For me, starting this way prompts my mind to set up the examination in an orderly progression starting with the inquiry and a comparison of information with physical evidence to provide clues to the next step. I take note of other responders and their activities, and I ask what has already been done and what has not, who has already looked where and where no one has looked, and I mentally note to look for sign of both. This is "hearing" what is being said, sorting and relating information to the physical facts. It's a crucial part of being an advanced tracker and getting the first track started.

Knowing where to look for sign isn't so much from instinct as from experience—experience gained from looking at sign and watching people and their actions, mannerisms, emotions, body language and positioning. Knowing where to look for sign is this knowledge coupled with observation of the surrounding area and information relating to the incident and the subject. Where would this person go and why? Often experienced trackers have difficulty explaining why they looked where they found the sign; this is due to the quick synthesis of all available information.

Learning What the Landscape Is Telling You

Natural and man-made barriers are very important to trackers. A road through the wilderness is a man-made barrier to trackers. The term "barrier" is a misnomer, in that the road and other objects that we will discuss are not in fact barriers at all, but areas in which footprints or sign evidence is more apt to be seen. Fence lines, ditches, edges of fields, lawns and gardens and jogging paths—all are man-made track-traps, or barriers for trackers. When persons traveling afoot encounter these obstacles and either alter their previous direction or cross the barrier, their physical actions cause additional or exceptional sign evidence of their travel. Often this sign gives clear indication of the traveler's awareness, knowledge and comfort in dealing with such obstacles. This is shown, for example, in how they cross the fence, where they jump or otherwise cross the ditch, or their hesitation upon entering the garden or leaving the lawn area.

Natural barriers for sign cutters are often more difficult to discern and this is where experience really counts. A creek is a recognized natural barrier, as is a cliff or cut bank. Trackers sometimes fail to recognize that the subtle differences in natural vegetation growth also represent natural barriers. Wooded areas bounded by meadows or open areas of contrasting vegetation form natural barriers. Cultivated areas contrasting with bordering or  adjacent natural growth form barriers. The edge of a slope, the top of a ridge, an old overgrown roadway or trail path bordered by a thicker or heavier growth of vegetation, brush or grasses, all act to some degree to channel traffic patterns of people and animals through the area. Sometimes the variations in natural light during different times of the day will provide the impression of a natural barrier. Some sign cutters are more naturally adept at cutting relatively open areas, and others are drawn to areas of dense vegetation. Others unconsciously seek areas in which there is subtle soil color or texture changes that, coupled with light availability, will show minute sign indications. All of these factors are part and parcel to the term "advanced tracking." As tracking students are often heard to mutter, "There's sure a lot more to this than just seeing sign!"

Reminds me of March 1983, when I was in Sitka, Alaska, at the State Police Academy to give a presentation to recruit law enforcement officers from all over the state. The director of the Police Academy realized the importance of officers being made more aware of what was around them and this was part of an ongoing program to provide introductory tracking awareness to new officers. The Border Patrol was graciously responding to official requests for this type of training. Who would think of doing a tracking class in Alaska in March! When I lived in southern California, within smelling distance of the salt water, I visualized Canada as a mostly white, frozen land that would be a formidable challenge to tracking. When I transferred to Washington State near the Canadian border, I found that the winters were quite mild, the grass was green year round, and the snow was rare except when you drove up the mountain to it. My image of Alaska was still of ice and snow until I went there and then I quickly found out that the southern coastal areas of Alaska are canopied by rain forest. Rain is measured in feet there each year, while the Washington coast gets only inches. The coastal areas there are characterized by heavy brush, cedar and fir trees in abundance, with moss-covered ground surfaces. Perhaps for some it is a less-than-ideal tracking environment, but it is certainly better than many others in which I've worked sign.

I learned, along with one of these Sitka Police Academy classes, that heavy rain does not necessarily wash out or otherwise destroy sign. When it rains there, it rains one, two or more inches per day, and often four or five inches per day for several days in succession. I'm not used to that much rain, even in Western Washington. That morning I made the usual classroom presentation as the rain fell. I dismissed the students for the lunch hour and went out looking for somewhere suitable to do the afternoon and evening field practice. Sitka isn't large. It's a relatively small land shelf area at the foot of steep mountains along the coast line and natural harbor. The entire area that is accessible by paved road in Sitka is very small. There isn't a great deal of flat ground around that doesn't have someone's house or business on it. The other areas are drainages and heavy brush—really unsuitable for a tracking class of two dozen students. I drove back and forth and inspected numerous areas, finally I talked to the owner of a construction/heavy equipment operation. He had a large open gravel parking lot, about the size of a football field and we were welcome to use it.

The parking lot looked like a shallow lake with one to two inches of water covering it. I walked out across the end of the lake in a slow circle and returned to the starting point. I knelt and examined the gravel surface beneath the water, sure enough, there was sediment, rolled rocks, compression and even variations of light reflections that were clearly discernible to show each footfall. We could track this! At 1 p.m. I gathered the class at the edge of the lake, having already laid numerous lines of sign across the parking lot. Each line was clearly flagged at the beginning and, to the extent possible, with prints which the students could measure and draw. I assigned the students into three-person tracking teams and they began following classroom instructions, though with doubt and reservations. Once the students became aware they could actually see the impressions of the "identifiable print," they began to gain enthusiasm. We worked all afternoon, each of us more amazed with each passing hour and each successive footfall that the steady rain on the shallow lake didn't seem to affect the prints in the slightest. The same basic tracking principles that they would employ on dry ground surfaces enabled them to see, define and identify each step across a surface covered by water. By dinner break that evening, they were believers! Though it continued to rain heavily, they were having fun, slapping each other on the back and joking—this was great, totally unbelievable that they could see, identify and follow tracks under these conditions. Perhaps the most fun they had was trying to explain to townspeople who chanced by what they were doing and why.

We continued with the sign lines in the lake during night tracking that evening with the use of flashlights as the rain continued a steady downpour. The next morning we finished up lines of sign and "graduated" to moving sign lines through the heavy brush and marsh areas using the knowledge and experience gained in the lake. It was a great tracking class, both for the students and for me. Never doubt the ability of students to adapt to situations and never doubt the possibility of sign evidence! I use this illustration to make students more confident when teaching them during inclement weather.

Night Tracking

When you're tracking a subject, the situation may dictate that you continue even when the sun goes down, so it's important to be as successful tracking at night as during daylight. Trackers on scene are the best judge of whether it's practical to start, continue or curtail tracking operations during hours of darkness. While I feel quite comfortable working with a flashlight for illumination of the prime sign area, I've had more practice and experience than most people. Certainly missing-person tracking can be as effective and in many cases more effective during the hours of darkness when search commotion tends to die down. There is usually less confusion and fewer distractions.

The proper flashlight for night tracking provides about the right amount of light and, because it's movable, the light can be directed at just the right angle to show the sign well. The fact that in darkness trackers can see only what is in the flashlight beam tends to help them to stay focused on the prime sign area and not become distracted by other sign. The drawback is that they may well overlook other important sign along the sign line which is not illuminated by the narrow focus of the flashlight beam. Experience is the best measure of who, what and how much to do. I'm well known for exhorting students to push themselves well into darkness without the use of the flashlight in order to experience their natural sight capabilities.

Students in Journeyman level tracking need to explore, experiment and experience the fact that they *can* track at night when appropriate to do so. A three-D-cell flashlight has a mellow yellow light of the right intensity to illuminate the prime sign and cause shadowing that is easily seen. The mistake most people make in night tracking is to use a flashlight that lights up a large area some distance from the holder. These flashlights are generally too bright and provide too much light. Hand lights with the newer neon, halogen or other bulbs, which provide an extremely bright, white and focused light beam, are very hard on the eyes and simply drown out the tracks. Head lamps work for tracking only when they are held in the hand. Coleman camp lanterns should be in camp and are a detriment to effective tracking. Little flashlights such as Mini-Mags with tiny beams of light quickly strain the eyes and therefore are not good for tracking; similarly, weak flashlight beams strain the eyes and are not good for tracking. The new LED lights do not have a directional light beam and like fluorescent lights, are not good for extended periods of tracking. While nearly everything has been tried, including infrared, black lights, blue lights and other colored lenses and night-vision equipment, the simplest is the best—a good three-D-cell flashlight without shadow, spot or rings in the beam.

The flashlight should be held nearly horizontal to the ground surface to cause as much shadowing and reflection from areas of compression as possible, these factors being the first and easiest for the eye to see. Holding the flashlight upright and pointing the beam directly down on the prime sign area tends to cause the light to hit the ground surface and "splash" in all directions, making it very difficult to see sign. These and more factors are discussed with the students before they go into the field for night tracking.

Night tracking has the potential for being more tiring on the eyes, but eyestrain is a common result of an extended search. Tired eyes tend to start seeing what isn't there and not seeing what is. It's easy to make mistakes. The best measure to tell when a tracker's eyes are beginning to "burn out" is his or her fellow team members. When you can no longer see what the others do, or you begin to see things the others do not, have an honest discussion with the team. Most often the one with tired eyes is not yet aware of their failure to see correctly and unless honest discussion by teammates causes the search to halt, the tired person may well lead the team astray. So what do you do when your eyes burn out? Rest your eyes! Take a break! Go get a cup of coffee and a sandwich and close your eyes for a while. If available, a relief team can take over the prime sign for an hour or so. Remember, it's teamwork that makes success and that means using more than one team if available. Often trackers will stop and "flag" the prime sign, back off a few steps and take a break by looking at other things for a short period. Such breaks bring temporary relief and generally will permit the tired trackers to continue, until the team is so tired that more time is spent resting than in following the sign line.

Aging Sign

Aging of sign, or determining how long since the sign evidence was created, is a fundamental part of advanced tracking. This topic is so important and complex that I've devoted a separate chapter to it. Let me say again—tracking is the matter of correctly seeing and interpreting physical evidence of human presence or passage. There is nothing spiritual or clairvoyant in reading sign, and aging sign is simply a basic component of reading sign. All physical evidence disturbance created by the presence or passage of humans is affected by the natural elements to which it's subjected. Aging sign is a practical matter of the tracker learning what footprint damage looks like when it's made on any and all ground surfaces and vegetation. Sometime afterward when the tracker observes the footprint damage the visual appearance comparison in consideration of all natural element effects permits an accurate reasoning of the time lapse since the print was originally made. This is one of the advanced training aspects that generally necessitates a good deal of knowledgeable instructor time that pays great future dividends. Usually crime scene examination has as much to do with the forensics of sign aging as it does with the identification of the visible sign. Read the Aging Sign chapter for more detailed information.

Advanced Students Go Live

Once we were teaching a tracking class at the U.S. Forest Service work camp facility at Rock Springs near Wamic, Oregon. This was a class of mixed students, some novice and beginning, others with a good deal of experience and working at the advanced tracker training level. Weather was great and the course was going very well. We had finished lunch, critiqued the morning's work and returned to sign lines under the scrub oak trees. About three in the afternoon a local county sheriff's sergeant roared up in a cloud of dust. "I need some trackers," he informed me with a grin.

"What's going on?" I asked.

He said that over in another valley about 15 miles away an 11-year-old boy was missing. "The boy is a little mentally deficient, perhaps some would say slow—I'm not sure what the real diagnosis is, but suffice it to say the boy has some mental problems. In addition to that he's physically handicapped—he has one leg that doesn't function properly. He's on medication and needs treatment every four hours. He was last seen about 10 a.m. when he had an argument with his mother. Boy just took off. It's all ranch and some dry farm country over there, lots of draws and brush. I knew of the tracking class here and thought perhaps you'd spare us some trackers to help locate the boy before it gets dark."

Marvin Martin, an old Eastern Oregon cowboy and tracking instructor, was listening to the request. I turned to him and said, "Well?" This wasn't the first time such a thing had interrupted our tracking class. There was the time the Oregon State Police was chasing the stolen car and it wrecked around the bend and down the road from the course. Marv had taken a few trackers and gone to assist on that case and turned in another successful mission, students grinning ear to ear! Marv knew I couldn't very well leave the students in the field. He said, "Who and how many do you want me to take?"

"Well, take eleven—that way you'll have an even four teams," I said. He began to call the students, and within 20 minutes they departed for the lost boy's house. Amid the disappointed grumbling of the remaining students, we re-formed teams and turned back to work lines of sign while the other got to go work on a "live" case.

Later, we were looking at our watches creeping toward 5 p.m. and considering whether to quit for dinner when the two vehicles came rolling back in. Beaming with accomplishment, the students piled out and we clustered around to hear the story, which went something like this: Upon arrival at the house, the trackers learned that the boy had probably gone out back and up the draw behind the barn. Someone had said that he was going to "run away to California." The teams were quickly made up and Marv directed the cutting of natural and man-made barriers to locate the boy's sign leaving the area. One of the teams was directed to begin cutting up the draw behind the barn; Gordon Byrnes was a member of this team. As he began walking out to the barn behind the other two team members, a little girl of about six or seven came along behind him. Gordon remembered the opening discussion of the course in the classroom, focused on gathering *all* of the information before getting into the field. He stopped and introduced himself to the little girl and asked her name. She became an instant "Miss Chatty," telling Gordon all about the family. Gordon directed the conversation to the missing boy as they began again to walk out to where the other two team members had already begun a cut.

Little Miss Chatty said that her brother was always running away, but he was always back by supper time. "Where does he go when he runs away?" Gordon asked.

"Oh, just up there," she said, pointing across the fields toward a brush-lined draw some distance away. Gordon asked how he got there.

"He just goes right up this fence and there's a hole in the fence near that corner up there that he crawls through," she said, pointing. Gordon asked her to show him and she began to run up the fence line.

Gordon quickly noted footprints in the dust along the fence that matched the missing boy's prints found in the yard.

"Come on!" yelled the little girl. Gordon called to his two teammates and filled them in. At the hole in the fence, sure enough, there was the boy's sign going through the fence and continuing toward the brushy draw. Gordon called Marv on the radio and informed him they had a route director who seemed pretty sure of her facts. They followed the little girl as she ran across the hill and toward the brushy draw, calling for them, "Come on!"

Other tracking teams converged on the draw and began to sign cut barriers to find the boy's sign leaving this area. A couple deputies watched and waited along the dirt road a short distance away. Gordon's tracking team entered the brush, advising the little girl to wait outside. They worked the sign, which was easy to follow as the boy would crawl under and through the brush, leaving good sign. Before long, they spotted the boy as he darted from one brush clump to another, hiding from the trackers who were getting ever closer. Gordon radioed Marv, advising him that they'd seen the boy and that he was hiding and running from them, trying to stay hidden from them in the brush. Marv and the two deputies converged and with the help of the other tracking teams soon had the boy surrounded. The tracking team worked its way through the brush and came up behind the boy, scaring him into an opening between two clumps of brush and right into the arms of a deputy. "Gotcha, boy!" The boy was grinning too. This was to him obviously a game and he had gotten some unexpected attention. Here was a fine example of applying information presented in the lecture class to interview and interrogation techniques. The entire class went in to dinner rejoicing in the success of the missing person search and the overall success of the day's tracking class.

That evening, after a short lecture period, with flashlights in hand the students were ready to return to the sign lines for night tracking. We took the class out to the field. This was going to be a great evening for tracking—it was warm and had the promise of a good moon to help light the area. The students were enthusiastic and their

good humor was infectious as we returned to continuation of the afternoon's projects. All went well and by 11 p.m. the students were
beginning to reach burnout, that period in which students' eyes just
refuse to recognize and correctly interpret sign easily seen only a few
steps before. Time to call a halt for the night. When the majority of students have reached this burnout stage, it's time to retire from the field
before they begin to lose confidence in themselves and each other. We
gathered back at the campground around the bonfire ring in which
someone had already started a fire. Time to sit back, relax and tell tracking stories. We had just begun to discuss different tracking episodes
when the local sheriff's sergeant roared in again. He came to me and
said, "We've got another search! A 14-year-old boy is missing over here
in another canyon. Father and two sons went for a day hike today, got
separated earlier this afternoon and when the father and one son
returned to the vehicle the older son was not there. The father and
younger son did some looking around, and at dark started a fire to help
signal the older boy, they've called, whistled and such, no sign of him.
We wondered if you guys would be up to helping on this one?"

I looked across the fire at Marv. Some of the students were already
heading out to gather gear, others were choosing up sides to see who
would get to go on this one. Marv said, "I'll take the same people I had
this afternoon, the same teams. They worked very well together."
Within 15 minutes they were headed out into the night. The rest of us
settled back around the fire, far quieter now. Some were secretly wishing they had been chosen to go, some, just as secretly, were glad they
had been left behind. We talked tracking for an hour and retired for the
night, mindful of those who would be out on the sign while we slept.

I woke easily when I heard vehicles approaching and glanced at
my watch—it was 4 a.m. The two vehicles rolled in quietly and I could
hear mumbled good nights and the trackers separated to their cabins.
Marv came in quietly and prepared for bed in the darkness. "Find
him?" I asked quietly.

"Yes, we found him. Absolutely perfect tracking operation. Found
his tracks around the camp where the father and other kid were. They

headed us up the trail where the three had gone hiking and told us about where they had split up. We all headed up the trail and found the lost kid's tracks coming and going on the trail on top of the father and other son's where they had walked out. Backtracked the kid up the trail for a couple miles and found him under a big pine tree with a small fire going. He was in good shape and was set for the night, just really unsure whether he was on the right trail or not, so had gone down the trail and back up to the big tree he recognized. He'd probably have walked out this morning, but he's safe and sound now. The father and other son will spend a much better night. The students did good! Great experience for them, couldn't of planned a class better, but let's get some sleep now."

Two successful tracking operations in one day—not bad, not bad at all!

Unsuccessful Missions

Not all tracking missions are successful, even for advanced trackers. I surely don't like to say that, but it's a fact. Why not? If no one walks anywhere without leaving sign, as I say, then why isn't tracking always a successful resource? There is a variety of reasons, but for the most part it's because trackers are only human and not infalable. Sometimes it's because trackers aren't working in the right place. Sometimes trackers just don't get the correct information to determine where to look and what to look for. Sometimes trackers see the sign, but fail to recognize it due to misinformation or misinterpretation of sign. Sometimes the conclusions or opinions of others lead trackers to find what is desired and not what else is there. Sometimes it's due to trackers not doing what they should do, or it's due to over-anxiousness, mismanagement or sometimes just simply missing the sign!

I've undoubtedly been guilty of this last reason myself! There are tracking missions I have participated in that I will never forget because I was unsuccessful. I didn't find what I was looking for, what I thought I should find. I will second-guess my misjudgments and wrong interpretation of mission information to the end of my days. Equally though, there are some missions that I have worked in which I felt quite successful, though the parties for whom I was working didn't feel that I had contributed significantly. The Green River serial murder cases fit that category. Lacking other specific information relating to a particular suspect, I feel the tracking information I was able to contribute from the body-find sites wasn't given much value. I felt and still feel that I contributed more positive information relating to a specific person than the files contained otherwise.

I've been asked to examine numerous homicide scenes and have been able to contribute a good deal of information relating to the "sign story" of what actually happened at the time of the homicide: who the participants were, what their actions were, what mental state they were in at the time of the incident, and what actions and decisions were made afterward. Often this information is far more important to the prosecution of a case than to the investigation because a suspect is in custody. Often investigators fail to complete a diligent and comprehensive investigation of a crime scene if a suspect somehow is arrested while the investigation is ongoing. These circumstances quite often place an undue burden or even limit the prosecutorial options available when the case is presented to court. Often prosecutors themselves are not experienced in criminal investigation resources or methods and are just not aware that there was or is the possibility of presenting more or additional evidence. Unfortunately, both criminal investigators and prosecutors in today's society are overwhelmed to the extent that in all probability both have limited experience.

This situation is not limited to the prosecutorial side of the aisle. Often the defense attorneys are no more experienced and, while some would say this makes things even, I firmly believe that the true measure of justice is when each side is totally knowledgeable. I've always advised trackers that the one way I'm always sure of my testimony is to help the defense attorney to become as educated about tracking as possible. I want the defense attorney to ask reasonable and knowledgeable questions of me concerning my testimony. I want the judge and jury to be fully convinced, that the evidence, my testimony, is beyond doubt. I have testified as an expert tracking witness more often than anyone else that I'm aware of and I've not had to go to court often. Most cases are resolved prior to court through plea bargaining. Such court procedures, while often leaving witnesses, victims and family members feeling cheated of revenge or justice, save the overloaded court systems money and time.

Shasta County Homicide

Advanced tracking is not limited to work in the field. A trained tracker can make valuable judgments on evidence that is recorded in detectives' notes or in photos. I received a request from a knowledgeable sheriff's detective to examine evidence pictures taken at a California crime scene. The pictures showed a dilapidated carport attached to an old house via a breezeway. There were two wooden steps leading from the dirt floor of the carport to the breezeway floor, which led to the rear door of the dwelling. Several footprints were marked by crime-scene tape and identification tabs in the photos. The photos gave the wide view of the entire carport and house. There were several close-ups of the identified footprints. The prints had all been identified. Detectives knew to whom they belonged and when they had been made—all except the suspect's prints. A suspect was in custody and he had admitted making the footprints in question, but not during the time the homicide was committed. Detectives and prosecutors asked me if it were possible to determine within an eight-day period when the suspect's prints were made.

I studied the photos and advised the detectives that there were several facts I'd need to know to permit me to compare the time frame of the known prints with the suspect's prints. First, I'd need the weather reports from the immediate area for a ten-day or two-week period, several days prior to and after the suspect time frame. And I'd need to know when each of the identified prints had been made.

The detective soon provided me with U.S. Weather Bureau reports and a statement as to when the identified prints were made. I compared the appearance of the known prints with the weather reports, then the known prints with the suspect prints and the weather charts. I was able to discern several factors which would allow me to conclude definitively when the suspect's prints were made. I wrote my report, explaining my reasoning and setting the age of the suspect print within a six- to eight-hour time period.

The prosecutor called me with questions about my report, wanting to know more about how I was able to see in the photos what I was stating to be fact. I began to educate the prosecutor with enough fundamental tracking information for him to understand how such conclusions were possible. The prosecutor and lead detective traveled to Oregon and attended a tracking class to broaden their understanding and acceptance of my ability to age the prints in question. The case would hinge on my testimony that the suspect's footprints had in fact been made during the time period between when the victim was last seen alive and when he was found deceased. The investigation had developed other significant evidence which pointed to the defendant, but putting his admitted footprints at the scene at the right time would be crucial.

Nearly five years later, the case came to court. I testified to the reports that I had submitted and was questioned by the defense. The jury was out for 45 minutes and returned a guilty verdict—the footprints were accepted as made at the time of the murder.

Advanced Training Never Ends

As it's difficult to define the term "advanced tracking," it's equally difficult to define or describe all that might contribute to this definition. Tracking may well be an old and somewhat natural skill, but tracking changes and what I include in an advanced tracking class changes. Heck, I don't know it all. Some people might say that I don't know anything. But what I do know is that while tracking basics are fairly well defined within the nature of learning to "see that which others look at and don't see," everything else fits into the description of "advanced" tracking. As I work on training sessions and tracking missions in an ever widening arena, I find the need to examine, learn and include new and additional items, techniques and teaching in advanced tracking.

The more that I learn about people, the changes in characteristics, motivations and mixes of humanity itself, I recognize the need to tell students to focus on integral aspects of tracking that may occur outside the action of following sign. Changes and development of outdoor gear, footwear, electronic gear, survival training and tests, recreational opportunities of all types, and different kinds of people doing more in the great out-of-doors—all these factors call for new lines of study in advanced tracking.

These sign-maker characteristics that are constantly changing are only a sample of all that is written in the sign line for the advanced tracker to read. I'm still occasionally finding something I've not encountered before in tracking. The learning never ends, as long as people continue to make tracks to follow.

>─┼─◆>─○─<◆─┼─<

CHAPTER EIGHT

Aging Sign
The Critical Skill in Tracking

On an October Friday, I was at my home near Everson, Washington. Rain began gently during the night. I awoke at 3:00 a.m. and heard the trickle of water in the gutter drains. I listened for awhile. I could hear the dripping in the woods and could easily imagine the glisten and sparkle of wetness on the leaves, twigs, and branches, and moisture appearing on the ground surfaces beneath. I arose at 6:00 and, with coffee cup in hand, went out to the deck and sank into the steamy water of my hot tub. In the stillness I could hear the rain falling in a fine mist and feel its cool touch on my shoulders. I looked across the lawn in the early morning dimness and could see the light reflection of footfalls in the grass. The footprints were mine and those of two of my grandkids. Wednesday had been a day of warm sunshine with a temperature of about 68 degrees. I had mowed the lawn about ten days prior. The grass had grown and was again in need of being mowed; though not unsightly in the growing light, it appeared smooth and freshly green and lush.

Wednesday, the girls had arrived shortly after midday and we played on the lawn after our lunch. I had observed the next day how well the footprints told the story of an afternoon of fun and games. A careful observer could see where three-year-old Morgan had gone to look, to see this and that, to investigate everything and show PaPa how fast she could run. Among these playful footprints were the more direct, purposeful footprints of her five-year-old sister, McKenzie, going to the canoe to play, visiting the bird feeder and coming back to the picnic table. Morgan's erratic, hither-and-thither footprint trails easily and clearly contrasted the purposed footfall trails of her older sister with a longer, more stable focus and concentration. I had carried some items from the woodshed to the storage shed, pulled some weeds in the flower bed, clipped some roses, and had been engaged with the girls in their activities at the same time.

By 9:00 a.m., and it had been raining heavily for more than an hour, the lack of wind allowed the rain to come straight down in large heavy drops. Water beat on the patio, rushed and chorused through the gutters and gushed in the down spouts. Everything in sight was soaked through and through.

By then I was on my third or fourth cup of coffee and I looked out across the patio at the lawn. There, glistening and shining in the dim light of the rainy morning, were the footprints in the grass. I clearly saw the prints of Morgan and McKenzie, and other smaller ones that belonged to the raccoons that came to check the patio for food. My prints, large and heavy with the rain, remained for some time, probably as clear and distinct as they were in the rain until I mowed again. Seeing all these prints made me think about trying to educate students about sign aging. How is it that others don't see these as clearly as I do? Or do they, and not know what it is they see, or have no confidence to believe in what they are seeing? Those prints, then three days old and subjected to the heavy rain that most would swear would erase all footprint evidence, remained virtually as evident as they were that day until the lawnmower carried them away.

Those prints would remain, easily seen by anyone who looked, long into the fall and early winter due to the conditions or natural elements present when the footfalls were made. The grass was growing late in that season, the mowing prompted it to mature and try to make seed before winter or the end of the growing season. The days had high humidity, early nightfall, cooling the day and bringing heavy dew, which nurtured the grass. The midday sun, though short, was warm, but not so hot so as to wilt and damage the grass. The conditions were those I and nearly all others so enjoy in the Indian summer, early fall—calm, warm days with cool nights. Those footprints looked the way they did that day because of the conditions at the time of day on the day that they were made. This is the essence of the tracking term "aging."

The aging of sign is a primary and necessary element of tracking. Anyone can find a track. But for that track to become a usable piece of information, we must identify it and relate it by certain other factors to a particular person or incident. One of the most crucial skills a tracker can acquire is the ability to determine the age, or time that the print was made. There are about as many factors to consider in determining the age of a print as there are hairs on a dog. But let's try to describe some basic characteristics which may help the reader or beginning tracker to understand how complex this subject is. First, it's important to understand that many or most of the aspects discussed here are automatically or subconsciously taken into consideration by the journeyman tracker within the totality of the appearance of the sign. That is to say, taken into full consideration of the whole, and not item by item or aspect by aspect. Only when it's necessary to explain the age of a track to someone, such as a jury, would most journeymen trackers consider each of these elements separately.

Both Jack Kearney and Ab Taylor do a fair job of describing the sign-aging process in their own books.[1] I'm not going to attempt to improve on either book but will try to offer a different perspective that will give the student further insight into this difficult subject. I often hesitate to make a beginning of something to which there is no real end, and make no mistake, sign aging is a large, complex and often controversial subject. With that disclaimer, allow me to launch out into the deep.

"Aging" is a term used to describe the change that takes place in the appearance of sign over a period of time. When we speak of "sign" we must remember that this is not limited to the footfall area—it also

[1] *Tracking, A Blueprint for Learning How* by Jack Kearney, Pathways Press 1978; *Fundamentals of Mantracking,* by Ab Taylor & Don Cooper, Emergency Response Institute 1990.

encompasses any and all areas contacted or damaged by the presence or passage of the person making the sign. Natural elements cause various changes of appearance to inanimate objects such as plain old dirt. To simplify discussions we can describe ground surfaces which would be damaged by footfalls in three categories: 1) soil, 2) vegetation, and 3) all others. All three surfaces are affected by the natural elements, such as sun, wind, rain, humidity, and air temperature, as well as by humans, animals, or insects. The tracker must consider the extremely variable nature of each element.

Sun has a great influence on sign. Compare the effect on everything, including sign, of a bright midday Arizona sun with a bright midday Seattle sun. The sunbather at Lake Havasu will surely blister without some type of protection, though a sunbather on the beach at Lake Washington near Seattle would not suffer nearly the same amount of skin damage during the same time period. A potted flower on the beach at Lake Havasu would be totally cooked in one afternoon. At Lake Washington, the same potted flower might wilt but would easily revive in the usually cool and humid nighttime. These kinds of differences in intensity will greatly affect at what rate a track ages in these different climates.

Wind is another factor that has varying degrees of impact on a track. If someone says, "It's been windy today," are we talking about a steady light breeze of four to five miles an hour? Or slight gusting breezes caused by temporary temperature changes? Or gusting summer breezes of anywhere from five miles to twenty miles an hour? There is quite a difference, depending on the individual conception of the term "wind."

Rain can vary greatly. There is light rain, steady, heavy rain, mist, intermittent showers. Comparing Tucson rain with Seattle rain may be comparing apples and oranges. The amount and intensity of the precipitation may greatly differ and so will the effects on the sign you're seeing on the ground.

So, to understand sign aging we must keep the variation among these elements in mind. One variable deals with different

understandings of the words we use to describe the aging factors themselves—what is your idea of light rain? Another variable deals with the
detectable differences of each variable element and how they impact
the track itself. We must also keep in mind that the sign-aging characteristics are physical changes and must be visually or physically
apparent to the tracker to be considered. At times trackers are aware
that sign for some reason looks different, but they don't know why, nor
are they able to explain what that discernible difference is.

Additionally, trackers, with rare exception, do not generally identify brown by the shades of greens and reds that it takes to make up
that particular color. To me, brown is brown, like brown shoe polish,
and may be somewhat differentiated by saying light brown, medium
brown, dark brown, or something in between. If you look at what I'm
looking at, you'll see what I mean when I say brown. Green, for most
trackers, when applied to sign, describes light green, medium green, or
dark green. Seldom do trackers describe vegetation as teal, lime, aqua,
or for heaven's sake viridian! Each person and therefore each tracker
describes the color and texture of what he/she sees using those word
phrases that have meaning to him/her. You and I may see the same
color or texture, but we may describe it differently. It's also possible we
don't see the same colors in the same way, given differences in our per-
ception of color. It's not unusual to find in a tracking team working
closely together, one member seeing shades of red as green, and
another not seeing the shades of brown at all. In terms of texture, some
may see smooth and others only see flat.

Another term artists use is "value," referring to shadowing, light
and dark changes, and it's used in a manner that I don't understand at
all. However, some trackers, usually those with some measure of color
blindness, may describe sign as being light or dark or medium. As
many variations as there are in the physical sign caused by all of the
elemental changes and effects, there are even more possibilities in
which the physical sign is seen and described. One factor can eliminate all of this confusion. When you and I both look at the same sign,
we see the same thing and we can talk about it, and we can agree on

the sign age due to the physical color and texture, no matter what it is or how we see it.

Keeping all of these factors with near-limitless variation in mind, here's an illustration which might confront a tracker and through which, together, we can visualize the natural element effects which will indicate the sign age. The task for the reader will be to use the imagination to try to visualize this print location, the natural element factors presented, the print itself, and how the physical appearance relates to the sequence of natural element changes.

This will be one of those hypothetical cases, which are always somewhat suspect. When instructing students on issues pertinent to crime scene investigations, evidence preparation, and presentation in court, I delight in telling them of an axiom learned many years ago from a seasoned veteran of many court examinations: When asked in court proceedings to speculate as to some hypothetical situation the attorney has created as an example for the court, make sure you reply, "I'll answer your hypothetical situation with an equally hypothetical answer."

The Hypothetical Example

Imagine long, slow grassy sea waves sprinkled liberally with wild flower blooms, a slight wind, just enough to roll the long grasses just beginning to form seed heads, enough to lift a kite but not enough to carry it to the heights of the hazy blue sky. The horizons seem far away and are hidden here and there by strings of brush, willows and some large trees. Those familiar with the region would recognize the brushy tree line as a creek bottom running through the low rolling hills to a river somewhere further off.

This represents a typical day at this time of year—warm sunshine, blue skies, air temperature is 84 degrees at 1:00 p.m., air humidity about 40 percent. The temperature was 55 degrees last night, reaching dew point at 2:00 a.m. with air humidity of 57 percent. This is typical for this time of year and has been fairly constant for the past five days.

In the previous five days, there were three days of partly cloudy skies, scattered showers and some light rain with cool temperatures.

A total of .9 inches of rain fell in the area during the three days, enough that most local gardeners and farmers with growing crops were pleased with the moisture. Those with hay down were strongly perturbed with the deterioration of the crop.

These are factors that a tracker would be considering as he approached the area in which a subject's sign was expected to be found. These are the "first things first" for trackers, putting them in the "right" mental state, alerting all senses. Taking into account everything from the soil, vegetation, weather, humidity, soil moisture, and the weather conditions of the recent past. Experienced trackers will question residents of the area as to the past conditions in order to add to and confirm what is seen.

There is a little-used trail that comes into the wooded area. It is shouldered by strongly growing grasses and weeds. Most of these are midway to their maturity at 18 inches to two feet high. Long, long ago this area was the bottom of an immense lake and even now  curious anthropologists will recover some fossilized evidence of the aquatic creatures that once inhabited the area. The soil is a fertile mixture of silt, good humus and some clay, a light soil which the locals describe as "good to grow anything." A young lad's shoe print appears in a relatively open patch of the trail. The print is that of a 12-year-old wearing a court shoe on his way with rod and worm in hand to catch a fish in the creek. Our job is to make a determination as to when the boy traveled this trail, make a written report and articulate the pertinent factors used to make that judgment. We'll make four sample aging examinations of the print at sequential intervals. I'll try to describe the natural element factors and resultant sequential changes, both visual and physical, that would be apparent if we were actually kneeling in examination of the prints. I hope this illustration will assist the reader to better understand the simplicity of complex procedures and factors in sign aging which we all see about us every day. A tracker's most technical equipment is always carried with him. They are his five senses (eyes, ears, nose, tongue, touch) and—perhaps most important of all—COMMON SENSE, to enable the proper use of the previous five.

Now, I'll describe the print as I see it. The trail itself, running through the meadow, grasslands and into the woods, has open dirt surfaces interspersed with tufts of grasses, hardy broadleaf weed plants like dandelion, buckhorn and white clover. The open dirt areas are mostly characterized by a fine covering of silt over darker and harder clay. The print is easily seen as we walk the trail. An irregular, somewhat open area surrounds the print. A second print succeeding the first is seen partially on vegetation. These will be the two prints on which we concentrate and to which the discussion generally applies. The soil surface of the trail within these irregular open areas is a light sandy gray/tan color on the very surface and a light to darker brown soil color beneath. There are places on the trail in which the soil appears much darker brown or lightly black in color. The print itself, at first glance, is quite clear in detail. From a standing position we can see lines, or bars, and circles, and get a definite impression of the geometric pattern of the shoe sole.

To see detail more closely, to take measurements and to insure we're not missing anything in the print, we have to get closer. We need to get down on our hands and knees. We have to get our eye close to the print. Then we're able to see the fine detail in the print, which gives us the information upon which to reach conclusions, form opinions and make decisions. From this position, this is what we see: We see a large, heavy bar of a horseshoe shape, paralleling the outline of the heel, but within the heel from the outside edge by measurement exactly 1/2 inch. This bar is 1/4 inch wide, square across the top and approximately 1/8 inch deep. This bar extends toward the instep of the shoe about 1-1/2 inches further on the inside of the print than it does on the outside. On the outside of the print, this bar flares out and tapers to a point as it ends at the outside of the heel, about where an ordinary heel would be on this shoe, or by measurement from a center point of the heel, 3-3/8 inches. From the same measuring point, the opposite side of the this bar on the instep side exits the print similarly at 4-7/8 inches. Within this horseshoe bar and at the center of the heel appears an oval shape formed by a similar-width bar.

Very fine lines run diagonally across the heel both within and without this horseshoe and to the edge of the print. The fine lines are on the print, and the horseshoe bar and oval are imprinted into the fine lines. These lines appear to be the width of the edge of a flat toothpick, about 1/32 inch deep and square across the top. The print itself has picked up and carried forward some parts of these fine lines, breaking and tearing the soil surface, which was forced into the grooves between the lines. The sole portion of the print has similar geometric patterning, with the same bar widths, a series of seven ovals about the size of dimes in the center of the sole, and the same

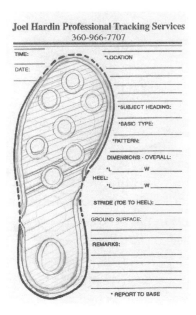

fine lines running diagonally across the entire print. The fine lines are the consistent pattern that covers the entire print, with the heavier bars and ovals seeming to overlay or be imprinted into the fine lines. Two bars run diagonally across the sole of the shoe in the instep area, each intersecting with one of the dime-sized circles. Another horseshoe-shaped configuration encircles the sole 1/2 inch from the edge, beginning about where the one from the heel ends. You might try drawing what you perceive the print to look like at this point.

EXAMPLE A, Day One

The First Print

We must decide when this print was made in relation to the present time, taking into consideration all of the factors previously discussed, and put the opinion factors into words that everyone else can understand. We arrive at 10:00 am to look at the prints.

> 1) When we examine the large horseshoe bar in the heel and sole, it appears on the top surface to be a light tan/grayish color, very similar to the undisturbed soil surface of the trail surrounding the print. It gets darker in color toward the bottom of the bar, (into the soil surface). The surface of the bar is square, flat and reflects all light changes. This appears to be a "fresh" or newly made print based on these primary factors, to ensure or confirm our first impression we should examine further.

Light changes are made simply by using a hand or hat to shadow or shade the area then removing, raising and lowering to adjust the darkness of the shadow. We'll use this same technique throughout our examination of these prints. Trackers learn that light is a primary factor to enable seeing difficult sign. Light reacts primarily in one of three ways to the disturbance or compression resulting from a footfall.

Reflection: Light is reflected from the compression of the ground surfaces. This includes surfaces that may be covered with loose debris of one type or another, grass and vegetation, rough soil types and rocky surfaces. Light reflection is the factor which allows the eye to see footprints on such surfaces as rain-slick blacktop or concrete sidewalks, across short lawn grass, kitchen tile, hardwood flooring, or household carpeting.

Absorption: Light may be absorbed by footprint distrubance of the ground surface in contrast to the area immediately surrounding the footprint. This contrast often shows as a slight contrast of color, shadow or lighting of just the right size and shape.

Diffusion: Light may be scattered by the footprint pattern or ground surface distrubance. The trained eye can see the footprint due to seemingly minute light diffusion in contrast to the surrounding area.

You may see trackers using a flashlight in the open on a clear day to cause one or more of these light changes, creating contrasts to assist the eye in seeing or examining a footfall area. Often trackers will use the flashlight when working sign under the canopy of trees or in heavy brush even though it may seem there is sufficient light to see. Or you may see them shading the print from light to cause a lighting contrast to help the trained eye to see what otherwise could not be seen.

A question often debated among trackers is whether tracking is an art or a science. The fact is, it's a little bit of both. Trackers may not realize the significance of physics, chemistry, biology, botany, and other scientific studies they automatically take into consideration to see sign and to determine aging factors. In this example, whether we're aware of it or not, we consider many scientific factors. The moisture that has fallen in the past week is retained and evident in the darker subsurface soil, and in the bright green grasses and weeds. The drier air constantly tries to pull moisture from the soil and vegetation to fill the void. Have you ever walked out onto a heavily grassed area when the summer sun was hot, and noticed the steam bath effect? Try it. This effect is caused by the comparative humidity or moisture difference between the air and the grasses and soil in which they are growing. Soil surface gives up its moisture more slowly when it's protected from direct sun and breeze by vegetation, whether grasses or trees. We all easily notice how dry, hard, and crusted open ground surfaces become because they are subject to the full effects of the natural elements. The soil type and consistency have a great deal to do with it but equal is the effect of the air humidity and that is affected by the turn of day and night and the hours and intensity of the sun. We know and understand the concept behind drying clothes. Dump them wet in a corner and they'll mold before all the moisture escapes. Hang them on a clothesline and they'll dry, and even more quickly if the sun is shining, the humidity is low, and a breeze is blowing. It's the same with moisture in the soil and vegetation. All of these factors must be taken into account when trying to age a track.

The fact that our trail at this imaginary location is bordered by the tall grasses and weeds has helped to retain surface moisture by protecting it from both light breezes and the sun. The light sandy topsoil surface is actually soil of the same type and consistency as that of the subsurface. The difference here in texture and appearance is that the very top surface has dried or given up the moisture to the drier air. When the top surface is disturbed it allows subsoil moisture to escape through that disturbance and, as it does so, the texture and appearance of those areas change. A footprint on this surface is a disturbance. Therefore the surface of this footprint or disturbed area will visually and physically be different from the other surfaces immediately surrounding it. This physical difference usually appearing as color and texture change, is that which is most visible to a tracker.

2) The edges of the top surface of the bars are formed of dust-like particles troweled to a smooth squareness. This effect is caused by footfall pressure and the slight moisture that is passing through this fine dust like top-surface soil. Another indication this is a new or fresh print.

3) The fine diagonal lines within the print are clear and distinct. Some have torn away and parts of the line or ridge are gone or loose and lying elsewhere on the print. The fact that some small pieces of these lines have torn away shows us that there is moisture in this top surface soil, allowing it to hold together under pressure. The fact that we can clearly see the torn edges with tiny particles of soil clinging to the edges and sticking out into the air, other torn pieces easily identified as to their origins in the smallest detail further indicates a new or fresh print.

4) Look closely at the torn pieces of the soil which are lying about. They're intact, compacted together and easily identified

even though their edges are rough and the jagged. Tiny grains of sand or particles of dirt hang loosely and form the irregular edges of the tear. Again such compacted pieces of material show the moisture contained in the dry-appearing soil surface. The fact that there is no evidence of erosion of these jagged edges is evidence that the sign is fresh, new.

5) The print itself has an overall clean and neat appearance.

6) The deepest portions of the shoe imprint are darker and shadowy and subsurface soil moisture is evident. This darker color fades from bottom to top of the geometric patterning and blends to the light tan/gray color which dominates the top surface of the print. This factor tells us that the print has not been subject to the elements for any significant time period or the bottom of the pattern imprint would have the same dry appearance as the top surface.

7) The large horseshoe ridge in the sole shows a slightly deeper imprinting toward the ball of the foot and toe areas. These areas also show a slight lifting and pulling or tearing of the bottom of the ridge from the soil surface beneath. The bar on the inside of the ball of the foot appears to be slightly deeper than on the outside, and the outside appears to have a little more of the lifting or tearing. These facts again indicate that this is a fresh print. With time, these geometric shoe-pattern areas that show the lifting and pulling or tearing away will settle back down, close the cracks and dry into the cracked surfaces.

7a) The two diagonal bars which each intersect with circles have the same appearance as the large horseshoe ridge or bar. Each shows a slight lifting of the heel side and depressing of the toe side of the bar, with a very slight twisting motion evident toward the inside of the print, indicating a forward walking motion.

8) The ovals in the ball of the foot show a slightly deeper indenting or imprinting of each toward the toe. The rear or heel side of each shows the slight lifting and tearing of the deepest soil surface comparable to that of the heavy horseshoe bar, supporting the conclusion that the boy knew where he was going and was eager to get there.

8a) The fine diagonal lines are more uniformly disturbed through the ball of the foot and toe sections. Within the ball of the foot, toward the inside they appear to be twisted slightly forward on the right and rearward on the left side. On the outside of the ball of the foot they appear to be uniformly pushed slightly backward. The toe of the print shows the body's forward movement in the slight rearward thrust of these fine lines. Tiny particles of soil cling here and there to the edges of the bars and fine lines. The tearing, lifting and twisting of the geometric patterning within this footfall shows that at this point the boy was in good spirits. He is not hurried, but walking along quickly, nearly hip-hopping, almost bouncing or springing with each step. That physical action gives extra thrust to the ball of the foot and results in this tearing, lifting and twisting that we observe in this print. A tracker examining this sign might describe the track maker as light spirited, purposed, and looking forward to catching a fish, and at this location, without cares or concerns and expecting a wonderful day.

9) There are no marks or evidence of outside contributors to the sign, such as bugs, worms, or other such creatures. There are no bird tracks, no blowing weeds or grasses sweeping across the sign. As noted in item #5, the sign appears clean, clear and unblemished. This further supports our opinion that this is a new or fresh print.

With the trail being the only open area within this section of the meadow or grassland, this area will be subjected to insect, animal and bird activity throughout day and night. This "natural creature" activity will show clearly on or in the prints. Such natural creature activity will provide clues with which to age sign. Various animals and insects are nocturnal, and their sign will appear after their activity at night. Equally, some animals and insects will only be about during day, again an aging clue. Birds, generally, are only out and on the ground during hours of daylight. The activities of all of these creatures will be greatly affected by the other natural elements. The breeze or wind often blows loose debris, weeds, grasses and other items over and through sign, causing additional marks or indications of that particular time element. Each and all of these factors become an automatic time clock indication to the tracker as to when the prints were made.

We're using this hypothetical situation to illustrate many of the various factors that trackers use to determine sign age. However, I want to caution readers that this illustration fails in nearly all instances to cover or address all of the aging factors applicable to any particular situation. To totally address and explain all aging factors of every situation would necessitate volumes, and even they would fail to do so adequately.

The Second Print

The next footfall is equally easy to see. This print is partially on vegetation and partially on open soil surface. A small tuft of grass is in the middle of the print. The soil surface impacted by the footfall appears much the same as in the first print. The diagonal lines of the shoe sole have impacted a broadleaf plant and several grass stems and blades. These compressed plant leaves and grass blades, when examined closely are kinked and bruised with the same sequential pattern as the diagonal lines in the soil surface.

The portion of the footprint that has impacted the small tuft of grass has depressed those grass blades and small stems in the same direction of travel as the footfalls. The grass blades show they have been damaged. They've been pushed forward and pressed by the foot-fall weight onto the trail surface. This is not the same type or kind of grass as that growing on either side of the trail. When looking closely we'll see that the grass blades are of a different shape and size and the small stems that will eventually become seed stalks are of a different nature. This grass tuft has grown *in* the trail, and not alongside or in the open field. This trail is traveled by animals, birds, insects and peo-ple, and in all probability has been here for hundreds of years. This tuft of grass will not react to this footfall damage the same as the beautiful tall grasses growing alongside the trail.

> 1) The blades of this grass, when examined closely, are kinked and bruised. These areas appear dark, either dark green or black and give the impression of being slightly moist—they have a freshly damaged appearance, like a fresh scrape, or cut on your finger or arm. The damaged surface is wet with the juices of the freshly broken tissue. A slight bleeding of plant sap appears on one grass stem.

> 2) On the broadleaf plant, faint parallel lines about a quarter inch apart appear slightly tan or light-colored can be seen across the leaf, evidence of the heavy bar in the shoe sole. These lines are similar to what your arm looks like when you press a wire coat hanger across it. That presses the blood and tissue fluids from the skin surface. Such pressure applied to a plant crushes the life as well as moisture from the cells of the leaf or stem and causes a permanent scar.

> 3) The underside of the broadleaf plant shows a few fine grains of sand imbedded in the leaf, with dark and moist bruised areas around the tiny stones.[2] Similar dark, bruised and moist areas

[2] Examination of the underside of a leaf, as with any physical disturbance of the sign, should only be made after a thorough examination has been made of the immediately visible elements of the track.

appear with indications where the underside of the leaf was mashed onto other tiny rocks and surface debris. This is a definite indication that this sign has been made within the hour, given the weather conditions we've already described. If it were much more than an hour old, on most all damaged vegetation the oozing of plant juices would have stopped, dried on the surface and began to heal.

Here we again delve into the "science" aspect of tracking. I tell students in basic tracking classes that plant leaves, branches and stems can be likened to your finger or arm. The plant lives through a process of chemically changing food sources through the roots with water or moisture into a circulatory system of veins and capillaries. The plant's circulatory system is similar to ours in that it carries life-sustaining fluids and chemicals to every area of the organism. Plant surfaces contain microscopic chemical cells which convert the plant fluids, sunlight and carbon dioxide from the air to make plant food—this process is called photosynthesis. What's important to trackers is the fact that each tiny leaf, stem, branch or part of a plant is living tissue. The entire plant is a living, breathing organism. When it's broken, bruised, cut, or torn, it reflects physiological damage evidence very similar to that on the human body.

When you injure your skin surface, what happens? How long does it take a cut finger to stop bleeding? On a nice warm day, the blood clots rather quickly, and the body immediately begins to heal itself—to repair the damage. The same cut on a warm rainy day would take much longer to clot and on a cold day less time. Plants are much the same. How do you learn how long it takes for a particular plant under certain conditions to stop bleeding and begin healing or to appear bruised? You observe damaged plants. You step on vegetation, you observe others stepping on any and all types of vegetation, you look at the damage now and at intervals thereafter, taking note of the natural conditions and the physical changes. This manner of learning is the most practical and effective since every plant and soil type has its own peculiarities affected differently by varying natural conditions. This method has allowed me to be able to age vegetation and people-damaged soil with exceptional accuracy.

Now back to examination of the footprint:

4) Fine dust particles cling to the underside of the leaf.

5) A very slight, fine grayish-tan residue can be seen on some of the same grass blades and stems, and somewhat on the broadleaf plant, a dusty transfer of very light soil by the shoe sole from the previous footfall.

6) Three small pieces of compacted material easily identified as portions of the torn lines from the prior footfall are seen in the grass. It appears as though it would be fairly easy to fit these back into the line from which they were torn—these have fallen loose from the other shoe as the foot came forward, making the next step.

Seem complicated? We're applying science and reasoning in order to age what we see on the ground surfaces that even sophisticated and highly advanced cameras are unable to distinguish. I provided the information at the beginning of this chapter in order to layer on additional factors which are unconsciously taken into consideration by trackers. How many variations of dirt combinations would you guess that there are? Each one would have a slightly different appearance when subjected to footfall pressures. We begin to address these differences in classroom presentations to stimulate students' imaginations and help them to understand the variables.

Another factor even more difficult for me to describe in print is the variation in the appearance of vegetation sign due to the moisture content or the life stage of the plant. Moisture content is the amount of moisture or water that a plant is getting to grow and how much it contains in leaves and stems at the particular moment. The life stage is the particular moment in the plant's life at which the damage occurs.

When plants are young, they are more resilient, recover from damage more quickly and continue their development (just like people). A plant's only purpose in life is to stay alive and make seed. That being its only objective, it will do that or die trying. Step on them, bend them, break them, blacktop over them—somehow they will do as nature has designed them to do and keep on growing. Some are hardier than others. Some manage to grow and thrive where humans would not believe possible. Some are lush and full of plant fluid; some are coarse, hard and tough. There are as many variations as there are plants and differences of environments in which they grow. Each of these variations reacts in its own particular way when we walk on them. Native plants and grasses act and react differently than do most hybrid vegetation. A good example is the native grasses that grow along the road and the rolling hills of our illustration. The native grasses have not been altered by man. Wherever they are found their purpose is to grow to maturity and produce seed to continue the species. Compare these wild grasses with the grass of your lawn, the golf course or the high school football field. They are genetically altered by man to resist human damage, never get tough and coarse—and NEVER SHOW A FOOTPRINT.

I don't want to lose the reader with endless discussion of each plant that I've had experience with. That would take another volume all by itself. Instead let's look at the grasses of the rolling hills that we describe in this illustration. Think of springtime when the tender grass shoots are pushing through the wet ground surface covered with what's left of last fall's weeds and grasses. These tender grass shoots are soft and light green, lush with moisture and weak from lack of the sunlight. Step on these today at noon and they bend, bruise and break easily. Look at them tomorrow at noon and they're almost standing straight again, or at least they're trying to. The broken ones have healed and repaired the damage made by the footfall. The bruises are nearly faded and with each hour of sun they grow. At this stage, the grasses know they've got a long way to go and they want to get there.

Time passes, let's say a month, and now these grasses are half grown. Now they're long enough that when they're stepped on, many are bent and broken near the ground, with some bent much higher up the stem and some near the tops. When the footfall occurs at noon today, it shows plainly, shimmering in the sun. The primary reason that anyone and everyone can see this print is that the grasses are long and, once stepped on, are laid out at length, shinning as they reflect the light. In May the late-spring sun is out, moisture isn't as plentiful as it was four weeks ago and these grasses wilt in the afternoon heat. They lie there like they'll never recover. But evening and then nighttime comes and with it the coolness that brings higher humidity and eventually dew. When the cool of the evening begins, the grasses begin to recover. The long grasses bent at the tops recover more quickly and as they try to straighten they help to lift up others bent and broken further down the stem. These in turn help to lift others. As the ground surface cools, it restores strength to the shorter grasses and those bent and broken nearer the ground. These grasses are going to fulfill their destiny, that of producing seed.

At noon the day after the footfall, the print in the grass is still quite evident. It still shines in the sun, but much of the grass has recovered at least part of the way. The breaks have begun to heal. Those grasses broken near the ground will never stand straight again, but look closely and you'll see that they will continue to grow. Those grasses bent higher but not broken will  return and become nearly straight again in a couple more days. The fact that most of the grasses will never fully recover, but all will continue to grow means that looking carefully the tracker can still see this print in November, long after all have died and turned gray and brown.

A month later, in June, most of the grasses have formed early green seed heads. They stand tall and wave in the noonday breeze. The color of the stem or stalks has changed slightly. Now they're a lighter green with a dried leaf blade here and there. One is yellowed and another has lost color and is whitish. They've grown tough, stringy and coarse. As we walk through it now, the grasses splash down in great splatters of sign and only with concentration can we determine the exact size and shape of the shoe creating this damage. The damaged grasses wilt and droop down flat in the afternoon sun. Again, the evening coolness and nighttime humidity and dew have a refreshing and restoring effect on the damaged grasses, but this time, they do not regain much of their vertical position. Instead they remain bent to the contour of the earth. One or two days or even a week later, they will remain in that position until they die and grow stiff and brown. These grasses are now at a stage in their life when they've almost got the job done—just a little more time and the seed heads will be mature. They "know" that it's far more important to produce mature seed than to stand tall and maybe only have immature seeds. Therefore they concentrate their energy in remaining healthy and producing the mature seed heads, even if they are bent low to the ground. The late-June tracks will show these particular characteristics until destroyed by animals or winter weather. The tracks that survive the animals and natural elements will show these footprints made at this stage of growth well into the next year and after the new spring grasses have begun the process all over again.

Three different times of the year, three different appearances of the sign on the same grass surfaces. The difference has more to do with the stage of the life of the grasses than all of the other elements. Trackers must be cognizant of each of these factors to become accurate in judging the age of sign.

Go hiking up the mountain and reach alpine meadows that see little sunlight without their blanket of snow until the middle of June. The plants have begun to grow as soon as the snow melt begins to run beneath that cold white blanket. These plants have about 90 days to go from first unobstructed light to mature seed heads if they want to produce for the next year. These plants do not have the luxury of lying around on the ground after being stepped on. They begin immediately to repair the damage, to try to stand up again, stanch the flow of plant "blood" and get on with growing to maturity. What does this mean? A footprint on foliage in an alpine meadow will recover much more quickly and look much older than prints on foliage at the 3,000-, 4,000- or 5,000-foot levels. Vegetation with short growing seasons and subjected to extreme natural elements are more hardy than elsewhere. These plants generally do not suffer damage from footfalls to the same extent as others. Similarly, most vegetation that grows in desert areas having a short growing season are hardy and resistant to damage such as footfalls. Trackers must be able to look at vegetation and recognize the particular types and characteristics, then determine what human sign will look like when damaging these plants.

The tracker's stock in trade is not in knowing every plant that grows, but just in "knowing"—knowing the natural elements and observing which of those are pertinent in examining a particular plant in question and reasoning the whys and wherefores of the sign. This knowing is gained through education, training and practical tracking applications to gain experience. Scarcely described and meagerly explained, this knowledge is not contained sufficiently in this or other written works, but in the minds of those who've been on the trail.

EXAMPLE B, Day 2

The First Print

At 10:00 a.m., the sign is now 24 hours older than when we first examined it. Let's take another look and see if we can distinguish the changes and understand them so we learn what effect each of the natural elements caused.

First, as we trudge out to the area of the prints, we recollect the prints as they appeared yesterday and try to project how they would appear now due to the natural element factors. Let's again begin with examination of the heavy bars configuration of the print. These heavy bars have created the most dramatic disturbance to the ground surface, and they attract the eye. They also are most subject to effects of the elements. They sink deepest into the soil and draw the most moisture from below. The tall square corners of the ribs are constantly subject to the wind, sun, and air humidity.

As we approach the site of the first track, we begin to observe the trail surface more closely and to compare with what we've been seeing as we were walking out here. We look to see other sign that has appeared since we were here yesterday. We look for the sign of animals, insects, birds and people. Such sign will also appear and be part of the examination and aging of the tracks we found yesterday. Let's look at the tracks. Remember that footfall pressure and soil surface moisture formed the natural soil into concrete like shapes. However, this is not concrete and color tone and texture changes are evidence of even slight natural element effects.

1) The top surface of the bars is slightly lighter in color when compared to undisturbed soil surface. The bottom of the square bar impression is dark but now showing through is a slight dry-gray shadowing—the gray-tan color has crept downward on the walls of the bar impression. The subsoil moisture is coming through the deepest bottom of the rib indention but the drier daytime air is slowly turning the entire surface to the color tone and texture of the surface soil. The sun's brightness has bleached the undisturbed surface soil uniformly, giving it the light tan color.

2) The top surface of the bar still appears smooth and flat, but has slightly fuzzy edges. Reflected light changes are subtle and the flat surface looks flat or dull instead of bright and fresh. The sun has bleached and dried the dirt and nighttime humidity has caused the dust particles to curl and separate, leaving a microscopically rough surface dulling the bright shine of yesterday. That rougher surface, fails to reflect the light as it did yesterday.

3) The fine diagonal lines are clear and distinct. The edges of the torn areas from which portions are gone are all dry. Small particles of material have fallen away from the torn edge and, while once compacted together, now are beginning to fall apart. When we look closely, we see that the edges of lines are slightly fuzzy— some cracks appear here and there and have dried into the center of the lines. We are able to see clearly the effects of the sun, air temperature, humidity and breeze.

4) The scattered, torn pieces of compacted line material are gray/tan in color. They are completely dry. The edges show where small particles have fallen away and are separating from each other. The torn edges are distinct and firm with the same type fuzzy appearance as seen on the bars.

5) The deepest portions of the impression are dark but have a distinct overcast or shadow of dry-gray appearing surface. The walls of the impression are all dry and a tan-gray in color.
6) Notice the deeper bar impression in the ball of the foot and the toe area where we noticed a lifting and tearing away of the compacted material. The edges of these tears are now dry and gray-tan in color. Some small particles have fallen loose from the edges of the bars and lines. These conditions are more evident on the outside of the impression, showing the effects of the drying conditions.

6) Note the ball of the foot ovals, which were showing a similar tearing away of the compacted materials. Again the tear cracks and jagged edges show small particles of material have fallen away from both edges. These edges remain clear and distinct, firm almost to the point of looking cemented. They are now dry and hard, showing the effects of the sun, wind and humidity.

7) The evidence of the forward walking motion, the thrust resulting in rearward push of compacted material is evident but not as dramatic as yesterday.

8) There are very light sweeping scratches across the first print, the evidence that a weed now tangled in the trailside grass has been dragged by the breeze across the print.

The Second Print

The soil surface disturbed by the footprint appears about the same as factors noted in the other footfall. Let's see what we can determine by examining the vegetation damage. First, the little tuft of grass:

1) The kinked and bruised areas that were dark green or black and moist-appearing yesterday now appear tan and brown in color. The damage that was moist yesterday is dry in appearance and to the touch as we examine blades and touch the leaves with our fingers. The footfall damage to a couple blades of grass has become almost clear or transparent. The grass blades are dry and have cured damage areas surrounded by tan-colored areas that appear to be healing.

2) All of the damaged areas are dry in appearance.

The broadleaf plant:

1) The parallel damage lines on the leaf are tan in color and clearly run perpendicular to the normal leaf veins. This is sign of fresh healing, like new scar tissue, showing little or no evidence of being subject to the sun and air.

2) The underside of the broadleaf shows fresh healing and scarring that appears as tan-colored areas in which some grains of sand are still imbedded. In other such areas the grains of imbedded sand that we noted yesterday have fallen loose and several of

these deeply impacted areas are beginning to develop a transparent appearance.

3) Some fine dust residue clings to the underside of the leaf and appears to be more of a color contrast than dust, but is easily rubbed off with a fingertip.

4) A gray-tan stain is evident on some grass blades and stems, and we see that this is dust transfer evidence that appears at first glance more as a color change or contrast.

5) The torn pieces of compacted lines carried forward by the shoe from the previous footfall that we saw lying on or about this print yesterday appear dry and crusted today, and the edges are somewhat fuzzy. Small particles have fallen loose—the pieces are beginning to lose their definition and do not readily appear to fit into the previous print.

Aging factors in this second footfall that allow us to determine that this print is now two days old:

• The soil residue appears to only be dust on the blades of grass. The torn pieces of diagonal line have dried completely and the edges have began to crumble. Grains of soil are lying separately— the pieces appear very dry and gray in color

• The grass blades are bent at about a 30- to 45-degree angle in the direction of travel.

• The damaged area of the broadleaf plant has dried in the center to a light tan color. The outside of the bruise remains dark but is now dry.

• The edge of the print is quite gray/tan and drier looking and does not stand out. We have to look more closely to identify individual diagonal lines.

EXAMPLE C, Day Three

The sign is now 72 hours old. We begin our walk out to the area where we will again look at the prints, anticipating what we will find. Today we have the experience of two days' observation, so we know it's important to see what we can determine that has changed from yesterday and the day before. It's important to be in the right frame of mind when we approach a tracking situation, to be thinking "tracking." Consciously, as we walk and talk, we mentally compare the visual effect of the natural elements changes and their expected effect on the sign since we were here yesterday. The natural elements on these days have remained virtually the same in all aspects.

Our tracks from the first day are in the grasses and on the trail, and our tracks from yesterday are here also. Today they suddenly become very obvious. Yesterday we saw them, but our focus and concentration was only on the two prints in question. During the examination yesterday we learned, gaining both knowledge and experience. Aging sign is an inherent element of "tracking." Now we might see and recognize that our tracks and those we came to examine, form a type of "story stick" that tells us factual information and in turn could tell others of our activities, what we looked at, why we were looking and when. No one moves about on foot without leaving sign, and that sign can be seen and read by a tracker. Another factor that should be apparent is the complexity of learning to age sign. Begin with one or two tracks the first day. Make sure the sign is open to the elements, then study them at every possible opportunity. Always look at the sequential sign trips that you make each time you go. This is a near ideal training aid, it provides the constant change of elements and the equally constant evolution of soil and vegetation through their normal cycles.

We've learned what fresh sign looks like and today we can see animal sign in the grasses and along the trail that was not there yesterday. Some of it looks like we should have noticed it the day before. We automatically observe our own tracks as we walk to the area, comparing them to those of rabbit, cat, coyote, bug and bird, both the ones on top of ours and others that we stepped on. We try to identify and distinguish one from another, questioning ourselves: Which was first? Which ones were made in the afternoon? Which were made in the evening and the nighttime?

The First Print

1) The horseshoe bar in the heel and sole of the print is about the same color and texture of the surrounding soil surface. Today there is little color contrast. The entirety of the square bar is gray-tan in color. The bottom of the groove is also gray-tan in color, the dark shadowing in the bottom from yesterday has faded into an even gray/tan color, possibly a little darker than the top surface of the print, but perhaps that is just because of the depth of the depression and the light.

2) The top surface of the square bar remains flat, but now an obvious roughness is visible. In a few places the edges of the bar are beginning to crack and break off, with tiny portions falling into the depressions. The flat surface is almost fuzzy and looks more like the edges appeared yesterday, and it does not reflect the light well instead seeming to absorb it. Some of the edges that were the fuzziest yesterday are beginning to lose their sharpness and are becoming slightly rounded off.

3) The fine diagonal lines are disintegrating, have become blurred and are not clear or distinct. Portions seem to just be settling out or flattening down. Areas from which portions have been torn away are becoming rounded and somewhat indistinct—the delicate edges and firm, distinct shapes are slipping away. Loose material that has fallen away from all of these parts litters the grooves and some portions of the fine lines have separated and crumbled away.

4) The small lumps of soil debris, "soil transfer" from the print, are also beginning to fall apart. They are cracked and broken and much of the detail has been lost.

5) All portions of the print impression are the same color, approximating the surrounding soil surface. All of the print impression is dry in appearance and faded by the sun's heat and brightness.

6) The cracked and torn areas of the sole pattern in ball of foot and toe areas, that gave us the obvious indications of the walking motion, are completely dry in color and texture, and the lifted areas have settled back, closing the cracks. A good deal of material has fallen loose. Corners and edges are deteriorating and becoming rounded. Tiny, crumbling lumps of compacted ridges, bars and lines show the print is losing its clear, clean definition.

7) The ovals in the ball of the foot area have cracked and began to fall away breaking up the oval in places, and showing us stresses which we failed to note in day one or two. The flat surfaces of the bars are now fuzzy and the edges are losing their sharp shapes. They are cracking and crumbling in places and there is definite indications of rounding off.

8) The forward walking motion is still quite evident, though bars and ovals have settled back, closing all cracks, but perhaps that's because we've seen it when it was well defined. We realize others might doubt what we see and understand. The impression is still clear to us indicated by the amount of disturbed geometric pattern and compacted soil which is beginning to crumble and break up.

9) There is some evidence of insect damage to the print impression, which has helped the erosion of some small portions of the diagonal lines and the ovals. A bird track shows that some little

wren or such has hopped along the trail onto and through the print. The bird tracks have helped to erode and break away some of the parts of the diagonal lines and the bars. In one place the morning and evening breeze has caused long bent grasses from the trail side to sweep back and forth leaving circular sweeping damage to an area of the print and further eroding and helping to confuse the appearance.

It's not surprising or unusual that we might see in this print the evidence that others might doubt because we have studied this print on two prior occasions and know the effects to be there. Trackers quite often look at sign and believe they see certain indications in the sign which are not visible to anyone else. Most often this is due to experience. The tracker has seen something similar before, sometime, someplace, and somewhere in the brain the information is stored. You'll find it hard to convince someone you know that rain is coming because you can smell the humidity change in the air if they don't smell anything.

The Second Print

1) The kinked and bruised areas on grass blades appear to be completely healed. The fresh scar tissue that formed and looked very new and fresh yesterday now appears dry, healed and like a natural part of the plant.

2) The parallel damage lines are beginning to show white, clear or nearly transparent; other sections have developed a brown/tan coloring, dry and healed-looking. These would appear to the untrained as a normal or natural occurance on the leaf.

3) Some small tan-brown colored damage areas are becoming scars, showing regeneration of material all around the damaged area. A few grass blade tips are totally dead.

4) A slight stain indicates where soil and dust transfer existed on grass leaves and stems. It does not seem to rub off, but in fact seems as though the other portions of the blades and stems have taken on a darker and more lively color.

5) The small lumps of compacted diagonal line material are all cracking and falling apart. It's hard to visualize just how they went together. Some very small parts have fallen apart and become simply loose grains of soil. We recognize these as portions of the previous print, but could we convince others of what we know to be true? Few recognizable characteristics remain in most of these particles.

EXAMPLE D, Day Five

Five-day-old sign! What will it look like? How have the elements affected it, what damage have the insects, animals and others done to our prints! Today as we walk out to the trail area, we mentally review the image of what the sign looked like, not just the last time we saw it, but actually how it has changed from day one to now, and we begin to visualize what effects we *expect* to see. We know what the natural elements have been during the past five days, we have the experience of the aging effects of the first three days, and we reason the further effects and anticipate what we should be seeing.

The First Print

1) The shoe imprint is clear and easy to see. It's distinct and obvious, but obviously not fresh—the color of the print surface is definitely the same as the surrounding soil, bleached and dry to a uniform light sandy color indistinguishable from the surrounding soil. However, we see it easily, in detail. The shadowing is there showing the bars and the impression of the fine diagonal lines, the circles, the thrust of force from the ball of the foot and the toe. There just isn't that dramatic difference

of color or texture contrast and detail that was present the first three days.

2) On the outside rib bar, some places and pieces are still solidly intact, but in many places the edges have begun to break loose. There are dry cracks everywhere, and in places pieces have fallen into the bottom of the impression. Some of these have broken down further and are tiny piles of dust particles. The edges and flat surfaces show many cracks and breaks. The smooth surfaces generally have a definite rough and granular appearance and we can see them returning to a sameness with the surrounding soil.

3) Our eyes see the fine diagonal lines throughout the print, but when we kneel to examine them more closely, they become less distinct. They've begun to settle and to disintegrate. At this point we would have a difficult time convincing the unknowing of the definition we could clearly see three days ago.

4) Small areas of soil appear counter or crosswise to the diagonal-line impression. This adds to the eye's confusion in close examination. The destruction of the print by insects, birds and other creatures becomes more apparent and more confusing. The sweeping of the blowing grass stems and another weed having blown down the trail are evidence that there has been a good breeze blowing over the prints.

5) When we stand and look again, the overall print is easy to see, but it's now indistinct, fuzzy and all same color throughout. The heavy bars, circles, lines and edges are rounding, smoothing out, leaving sufficient areas intact so that we "see" the entire print. But would anyone else? Would unknowing persons even notice this print?

6) The bottoms of the rib impressions are essentially the same color as the top surfaces with considerable top surface soil having sifted into these depths. The general deterioration, erosion and sifting of loose soil has hidden, eroded, and disintegrated much of the fine detail features.

7) The aging of the ovals in the ball of the shoe print appear to be consistent with the other similar patterning in the print. They look more like round humps now than the original empty ovals.

8) The small particles of compacted soil that were torn away and carried forward then dropped off of the shoe have all but disintegrated into tiny dirt clods. The few remaining compacted particles are rough in appearance—fuzzy, with few straight edges or flat surfaces.

The Second Print

1) The print on the soil appears much as the first one described. The damaged areas on the plant leaves have all completely healed and now appear as tan or transparent scar tissue, the center section of irregularly shaped damaged spots is gone, leaving a jagged hole, the edges of the hole are tan, transparent, light brown, tissue-like and crispy dry.

2) The blades and stems of the tuft of grass are all nearly vertical once more, the damage showing as stripes or ribbons slanting across the upright growth.

3) The broadleaf plant's damage is cured, tan to light brown in color. Some places that remained black have begun to fall apart, leaving some open dry and healed scars.

There are constant changes as the sign ages further, which I'll simplify here. I can't emphasize enough that the best training is observing selected sign regularly over a long period of time.

Day Ten

> • The edge of the footprint shows the heavy rib, but more the impression than the actual and definable shape, size and characteristic of the rib itself.

> • The fine lines appear and disappear as the viewer's eye changes position, even when they seem to be there, they are indistinct, more impressionistic than realistic.

> • There is a definite impression of circles within the center of the shoe sole, they can be counted, but again they are illusinary.

> • The definite toe-dig, body-thrust appearance is accentuated by the somewhat ribbed and a general humped appearance of dirt material within the ball of the foot area.

> • The small particles of compacted soil have become dirt spots or clods and have no form or shape related to the shoe pattern.

> • All soil particles are the same color as trail surfaces.

> • The damaged areas on the plant leaves have all completely healed and now appear as tan or transparent scar tissue.

> • The center section of irregularly shaped damaged spots is gone, leaving jagged holes. The edges of the holes are tan, transparent, light brown, tissue-like and crispy dry.

Week Three

Three weeks have gone by with no human sign to disturb our two tracks, so let's see what they look like now. We come to the area where the tracks are and we can see the first print on the trail. The first print still appears obvious; however when we pause to look, the detail seems unclear.

- The heavy horseshoe bar is distinguishable but appears mostly as a cord or small rope-type geometric pattern.

- There are only a few indications of square-corner edges. They seem inconsistent with the rounded shape of the rest of the pattern.

- There are some flat areas, obvious pieces of a pattern, that appear to be cement hard, rough surfaced, thoroughly dry and inconsistent with the appearance of adjoining materials.

- The footfall disturbance with the lines and groves, shapes and shadows collects the light and makes the track appear somewhat darker than the undisturbed surrounding trail area. This factor is what makes the print easy for the eye to notice.

- When we look more closely at the print, the tracker's eye has the impression of fine diagonal lines throughout the print, but only by changing the light reflections and eye position in small areas, the lines seem individually identifiable. Moving the viewer's eye tends to make the lines appear only as a ribbed or ruffled area without separate or distinct lines. Considerable top surface soil has sifted into and nearly filled the grooves, making all of the surface the same color;

- Here and there, pieces and portions of the lines in a compacted form remain, but they are broken and separated from each other, making reconstruction with the eye quite difficult.

- Ovals in the ball of the imprint appear as raised circles of dirt without clear distinction as to detail but are consistent with similar patterning in the print.

• All color and the texture of the uncompacted material within the print is the same as the surrounding soil.

• Insects, birds and possibly a rodent have assisted wind erosion in nature's alteration of the imprint.

• A humping or very slight lifting of soil in the ball of foot/toe areas indicate walking motions and accentuates the toe-dig depression.

• Some small lumps of soil could match time/age/type character-istics to be associated as soil transfers.

Aging sign is a fundamental and critical element of tracking. With concentration and good coaching from instructors, most students readily learn to distinguish sign that is a matter of one, two or three days old. I hope the examples of the two footprints on the trail to the old fishing hole have provided readers with some realistic understanding of what trackers look for and take into consideration in aging prints over a period of time. I've been involved in tracking for more than 30 years and I am unaware of any other written materials developed to assist trackers to learn to age sign. This is one element of tracking that most trackers are reluctant to discuss in detail, let alone put their thoughts and opinions into print.

SNOW TRACKING

Aging Tracks in the Snow

I get many questions each year about tracking and aging tracks in the snow. I'm certainly no expert on the subject but I've had some experience finding and following sign in the snow and in attempting to age sign in the snow. similarities to tracking on dirt outnumber the differences.

One Sunday afternoon in late fall, I finished a tracking course with Ab Taylor in southeastern Oregon at about 2 p.m. When I arrived at my home in Everson, Washington, about 11 p.m., I was advised that Skagit County SAR had an ongoing search for a young hunter. I dumped the tracking course paraphernalia and picked up my SAR mission pack and headed for Rockport, Washington, a small village on the Skagit River where search base was set up and about a two-hour drive away. When I arrived, I was escorted to the place where the victim was last seen. The 22-year-old missing hunter had been let off by his father along a logging road at about 6 a.m. the previous morning. Snow had been falling for about an hour and was about two inches deep as the father drove off. The victim was to hunt along a ridge and return to the drop-off point by 4 p.m., but he failed to return. The father had driven the roads, honked the horn and such until well after dark, then drove to Rockport and reported the son missing. The Skagit SAR unit had responded, getting set up at about 10 p.m. They had expanded the search area and were still busy running the roads when I arrived around 1 a.m.

When I arrived at the PLS there were five SAR members there waiting. They asked me about looking for and working sign in the snow and were anxious to get started. We had nearly an exact starting point. There was now about five inches of snow on the ground. The father said that as near as he could remember there was about an inch or two when the victim started out. We got organized into two three-person teams and began feeling and brushing the snow with our hands. Within a few steps of the road we found packed snow and ice footprints hidden beneath two or three inches of snow. We quickly managed to put several prints together and establish the sign line and we were off and running. The sign line was following a faint trail or pathway through the woods along the ridge top. We formed teams and began to check the trail at intervals, using our bare hands and fir boughs to scrape and brush the snow until we found the tracks. It was slow business, but probably faster than if the ground surface had been bare and wet. We had gone a quarter of a mile or so when I decided that the day was beginning to get pretty long and if I was going to follow this sign all the next day, I'd better get some sleep.

We called the command post and told them that we were going to get a few hours of sleep and start again in the morning. Facilities were limited and we ended up making space and throwing sleeping bags on the floor of the Forest Service storage shed. Sleep was sound and refreshing, the three hours went quickly and we rolled out to the promise of broken clouds and, we hoped, some air-search possibilities. We had established a solid direction of travel giving a good indication of where to concentrate other operations. We grabbed some "gorp" and a cup of hot coffee and headed back up the mountain to where we had left the sign.

We resumed where we had left off the sign and had gone another quarter mile, pushing the sign rather rapidly now. We were really getting the hang of where to look and how to find the prints under the snow, when we heard the wop-wop of the search chopper. We kept at our job. Soon we heard the chopper circling in the canyon bottom a mile or so below us. Within minutes, the call came on the radio that they had picked up the victim down below near the river.

Often tracks in the snow take on many of the same characteristics as tracks in loose, dry sand. This happens when the snow is dry and great for skiing. When the snow is powder dry, it rolls and sifts and reacts to footfall depressions about the same as loose sand does. When snow is dry and blows easily, it doesn't pack together—you can't make snowballs very well because there isn't enough moisture to hold the snow together, and it doesn't hold the characteristics of a shoe, either.

Imagine tracks in three to five inches of snow. What is the difference between tracks in the three to five inches of snow and on the bare ground where only trained persons are apt to see them? Simple— the mere fact that the snow covers nearly all of the ground surface and eliminates nearly all possible eye and mind confusion. The ground is white, the color not as important as the fact that there is little or no contrast. All complexities have been eliminated, so any mark or track stands out to the eye.

Suppose there are fifty kids playing on the unrestricted playground for two hours and you're looking for the sign or tracks of one particular child. The playground is covered with tracks in the snow—it's difficult to sort one track from another, there are so many one on top of another. Now let's visualize this scene: the playground brand new, a clean-graded dirt surface without even one footfall, then turn the fifty kids loose for the same two hours of unrestricted play. Visualize one, then the other, and both side by side. What's the difference? The greatest difference is creation of false impressions. The first one is that most people think that finding and following tracks in three to five inches of snow is easy; the second one is that finding one child's tracks in a mass of footprints poses an impossible task.

We can complicate this picture equally by saying that the snow and the soil surface are both very dry and the wind is blowing. The footprints will blow, blowing material will cover others, and the wind itself will erode and destroy some of the prints, but the effect will be about the same relative to both the snow and the open dirt. Moisture content of both substances is the key.

Suppose it's snowing when the fifty kids go out to play, and during the two hours they're out there it snows two inches, and after the kids leave it's two hours before you get the call to go look for the missing child. So you have four or five inches of snow on top of the kids' tracks—how do you track now? Well, let's make this parallel—suppose that when the kids go out to play that the playground isn't finished yet, and the contractor comes back and dumps and spreads four or five inches more dirt on top of the kids' tracks before you get the call. Now what are you going to do? I'd have to do the same thing in both cases—forget about looking for the prints on the playground and hidden under the snow or new soil. Possibly I'd have a break with the dirt problem, the chance that the missing child was on the playground and not be seen would be slim to none, meaning the tracks would go somewhere else and could be found. The snow would probably cover all areas where the child would have traveled, hiding the tracks from sight.

In snow two feet deep the elk hunter heads off into the wilderness and doesn't come back. Can we track him? Yes, the tracks will be clearly visible until and unless they're covered by more snow or the snow melts because the tracks are actually "in" the snow. Now when it begins to snow again and begins to fill and cover the tracks, those tracks are in snow that's two feet deep. Ever try to walk in snow two feet deep? You leave big tracks and big drag marks between the tracks. It's darn hard to walk very far and keep lifting your feet up and out of the snow for every step. Therefore, if we find the first track and get started, it's going to take a considerable amount of snow to fill and cover the sign of a man wallowing along in two feet of snow. We're going to be able to follow the man's sign probably until another foot of snow falls. Now in many places that will be the first night out and, if so, we probably won't be able to find the first track. Suppose he starts out when the weather is clearing and just going to get cold for a few days. The clear cold will encase the tracks in heavy crusting of the snow and possibly ice if the sun shines just right. Come another foot of fairly light or dry snow, we probably could find and follow those tracks under the new snow because they've crusted so hard in the snow.

Tracks in the snow age rather quickly sometimes. Other times they become frozen within minutes and remain virtually unchanged for days or weeks. Tracks in foot-deep snow that are subject to direct sunshine during the middle of the day when the temperature gets up to 30 degrees or so age quickly. The footfall depressions seem to collect the sun's heat and melt more than the surrounding snow. They quickly lose all footfall characteristics and take on the same deep, nondescript look as two-day-old tracks in deep, loose sand.

New tracks in the snow have the same fresh, neat and polished look as those in clean, fresh dirt. They reflect light in much the same way, the sharpness of detail is as clear and well defined, the tiny particles of snow hang and cling about the same as with compacted soil particles. The new snow prints seem to lose their crisp shine and freshness, subject to natural elements, about the same as dirt prints do. The second day there is a noticeable change in the color and texture of the snow print. Depending on the elements, after about the third day, I have a hard time aging snow prints. I can use reason to judge the amount of sun melt, disfiguring due to freezing and moisture loss, and general erosion of fine detail, but these judgments are not based on the same experience studies that I've done with tracks on soil surfaces.

I've been asked about aging ski tracks when there were missing skiers on the mountain, and whether I could age the ski marks to try to identify those of the missing skiers. It's possible, if I were looking at the tracks and talking with others who have intimate knowledge of the mountain and the elements consistent with the time frame of the missing skiers. Ski patrol personnel and others who have been there every day might have as good an opinion as mine.

CHAPTER NINE

Trailing the Elk
Hoofprints in the Forest

What would a book about tracking be without addressing animal tracking? I am *not* an animal tracker but I'm often asked about the tracking of animals because most people think tracking is only used in following animals. Some of these are hunters, some are environmentalists, some are conservationists and scientists, and many are just lovers of the outdoors. Tracking people and tracking animals are very closely related skills. Both skills call on the same aspects of learning to see that which others look at and do not see. The baseline for tracking is the same whatever the interest, objective and purpose. Animal tracking or human tracking utilizes the same basic factors to recognize sign, identify and age sign. The great difference between animal and human tracking is that the one animal, Homo sapiens, is like none other on the face of the earth. Now I'm not going to get into a debate comparing the foot or hand prints of the ape species with humans, or discussing prints purported to be "near human." The fact is that none of the ape species very closely resemble the human characteristics of walking any more than any other two or four-legged animal does. The term "characteristics" is a key to tracking of both kinds of animals.

A major factor in tracking humans is to know the human animal. In the beginning of my tracking education and career, I quickly learned to see the different characteristics   in the sign line story between the people I was tracking. These differences included their thought processes, objectives, intentions and purposes. For example, a fleeing man's sign appears differently than that of a tired, stealthy or lost man. Those sign-story characteristics are important factors in determining which sign to follow and what to expect when encountering those being followed. I learned that the best way to learn these characteristics was by studying people. Knowing these distinctions took on greater importance as I became more involved in forensic crime-scene examination and in studying how to teach trackers to be more successful. Accurate "reading" of the story in the sign line requires understanding people and their motives, ambitions, education, body English, mannerisms, habits, mental and physical state.

Good or great animal trackers must make the same study of animals and learn their characteristics, habits, mannerisms and motivations—in other words, their mental and physical state. The intimate knowledge of a particular animal enables the animal tracker to readily recognize and identify its sign and to understand what the animal was doing and why. Fortunately for animals their lives are generally a bit less complicated than humans have made theirs. Animals are motivated by hunger, thirst, desire for suitable bedding areas, resting, getting away from or getting close to humans, mating or gathering with others of kind, etc. In short, the more the animal tracker knows about the animal being tracked the greater the success in following and reading the animals' sign story.

I observe animal tracks wherever they appear as part and parcel of seeing all that is on the ground surface. Animal sign often contributes to the interpretation of the human sign that I observe. But I have found that most notable trackers fall into one of the two camps. They are either animal trackers or human trackers. There simply isn't sufficient number of days in a lifetime to become proficient at both. For those most interested in tracking animals, I encourage you to access the International Association of Professional Trackers, whose membership is made up primarily of animal trackers.

Sit back now and let me incorporate this prelude into an amimal tracking story about the elk that has become a part of the family. He spends all his time here, near where I sit and he is always attentive, his soft brown eyes indicating his pleasant and understanding nature. He proves this almost daily by listening with great care when I speak, no matter the topic, never interrupting and willing to endure even the longest conversation. I think it is a virtue that he is able to hold his tongue so well while others, needing to speak their innermost turmoil, go on and on. His only comment, spoken so softly you must read it in his eyes, is to say, "Be thankful you have this day." It reminds me that there are many who would be grateful to take all my problems just to have the privilege of enjoying today.

Without making prior arrangements, the elk came to stay with us a few years ago. I had been invited to go with several dear friends to spend a few days at a cabin in the mountains of eastern Oregon. The stated objective was to go elk hunting, but as all hunters know, the hunting is really secondary to just being together to laugh and talk and just relax. Life is stressful after all, and, well what better way to relieve stress than to get away for a few days in the beautiful creation God placed here for just such a purpose? I sometimes think that trappers and "mountain men," or maybe even prehistoric hunters, dreamed up the concept of stress as an excuse to roam around for awhile, free of the burdens of civilization. But back to the elk...

The gang—Dean Fitzwater, Gale Goyins, John Flinger, Dick Woodfin, Frank Heyl and I—had gathered at the cabin the night before the elk season opened. The evening was filled with a comfortable mixture of "stress relief" in the form of good-natured ribbing, laughter and not a few trips down memory lane. Most of these began with "Hey, remember the time..." and ended with uproarious laughter, whether or not the story was really funny. It's my theory that deer and elk don't really have current copies of the hunting regulations, as some ardently believe. Instead they simply post scouts to report the silly goings-on at various hunting cabins like ours. When the good times begin, hunting season is soon to follow.

The opening morning plan was laid out for us by the old master, Dean. It was his cabin, so he always got to lay out the plan because he did, in fact, know the most about the area and the best way to hunt it.

John, Dean decided, would climb up the mountain from this direction, Gale from another. Dick would go up the middle ridge, Dean and Frank would go up kind of in the middle, and I was to go all the way up the hiking trail that followed Sullivan creek to the creek junction, then hunt along following the left fork or Sawbar creek upstream.

I was unfamiliar with the area as this was the first of what has now become nearly 20 years of late-fall elk hunting in eastern Oregon. I was able to figure out the lay of the land and where I was to go from the map on the wall. On it were the names of old gold mines and their long-dead miners, mixed liberally with landmark names written in pencil, Pothole, Baldy, Sheep Camp, Little Kettle, Twin Canyon and one fork called the Little Twin. Each place had its own story, the telling of which was necessary (or at least, that's what the guys insisted on) to fully comprehend the origin of the name. Over the years I came to feel comfortable when I reached the "Old Jeep Trail," "Sawbar," "The Slide," "Dick's Knob" and other increasingly familiar places. Fact is, I added several names to the map over time and I'm proud to say they're still marked on the map-on-the-wall in fading pencil.

We started at daylight, not quite soon enough for Dick, who was up at 4 a.m., but it suited me. Up the trail, one by one, we were each dropped off at the starting point of our assigned routes. I soon learned that to be "dropped off," meant you were about to go climbing. The cabin was at the base of Sullivan Mountain, so anywhere you went from there was up. None of those flatland elk for us, no sir-reee. When you come home from a week of hunting, you want to know you've been somewhere and done something, and my aching muscles usually tell me that tale quite adequately.

I hiked slowly up the trail along the main creek, watching for game and waiting for the day to bring full daylight. Eventually I came to the fork in the creek I'd been told about. The joining of Sawbar creek with Sullivan creek formed a small basin and was fairly flat, with big timber in the bottom along the trail. It sure looked like good elk country to me. This smaller fork joining the main creek came in from the left and I knew it to be the one Dean had said to go up. He'd said it would take me past the Slide and into the Sawbar where we would meet for lunch. Sawbar, he'd explained, was a small basin or "saddle" area between two peaks where other hunters many years before had made a semi-permanent camp. It took its name from the three-foot long saw blade someone had stuck into the top of a stump. "Can't miss it," he said. I hate it when somebody says that, because that usually means I can miss it. Luckily, I wasn't a complete greenhorn and had been given directions like that before and knew to take them with a grain of salt.

I looked up the creek. It appeared to be a very narrow canyon that certainly was uphill with numerous little waterfalls and with walls that seemed to be as tightly clasped together as a child's hands playing "church and steeple." The canyon ran generally northeast so the sun that was coming would warm the left side of the canyon and melt the frost more quickly. Well, I usually hunt slowly and carefully anyway, so I thought this would force me to do just that. I began to work my way up the creek and at the same time to climb the side of the main ridge that formed the left wall of the canyon. Dean had advised that this ridge would lead up nearly to the summit of Sullivan. I wanted to try and get to a position high enough that I could actually see the creek bottom as well as the other side of the canyon that looked to be choked with thick timber and allow the sun to find me. I worked my way along, keeping an eye on the opposite side of the canyon. Suddenly, something over there caught my attention and I stopped to see what had drawn my eye. What I'd seen was a long skid mark of a large animal slipping and sliding while making its way down the steep slope, sometimes walking, sometimes sliding.

I found a place that suited my behind and settled while getting out my binoculars. Looking through the lenses, I could tell that it was fresh elk sign, and it had been coming down toward the creek through an area not usually traveled by large animals. No other tracks or animal trails traversed the slope in that area and I knew right away that this was was sign of an elk that walked where he wanted, when he wanted! That's got to be a bull, I thought. A cow would pick her way more carefully and wouldn't just head hell-for-leather down the side of this killer slope unless something was chasing and that wasn't the case; this animal was walking where it could. Something about this track told me this guy wasn't running from anything, just coming down the hill with an attitude.

Nothing gets a person in trouble faster than having an attitude I've found, so I hoped I'd be the one bringing on the trouble. I worked my way slowly uphill onto a knife-edge bare-rock ridge where I could see what the elk had done when he got to the creek. With the binoculars I could follow the obvious sign of hoof marks and skid trail down to the water, which then went across the creek onto my side of the canyon. Here he had melted into the brush and big trees on the sloping bench along the creek bottom and I couldn't see any more sign. I thought to myself that he would be coming down to water to drink, then look for some comfortable place to take a nap until the sun got high and heated up the creek bottom. I was guessing at some of this because from where I was I could only see 40 or 50 feet into the trees, the little ridge I was on was blocking my sight of the bottom immediately below.

I worked my way along the slope, careful to be quiet, across a slide area and up the shoulder of another little ridge running up to the top of the main ridge I was on. When I got to the top of this ridge I could see another small gentle slope with some scattered trees, brush clumps and good grass that looked like an ideal spot for Mr. Bull to spend the day. I looked it over with the binoculars. Not much moving except a couple of squirrels and a bird here and there. The sun was walking slowly down the side of the mountain now and was going to be warming where I was sitting pretty soon. It wasn't really cold but got chilly when I stopped moving. There was a good frost in the bottoms of the little draws that I was crossing. It was colder up here on the mountain than it had been down at the cabin. If I could stay up on this steeper hillside at this level above most of the brush and scattered timber, I knew I could work my way along pretty quietly. The noise of the creek below would cover most of the noise I might make for anyone that was listening down below. I picked out a route suited to afford some cover yet still give me a good vantage from which to see down into the small ravines below.

I studied the creek edge with the binoculars before moving, the dark shadows were disappearing quickly now with the coming sunshine. I thought that I could make out the animal's sign as he came up out of the creek and meandered into the brush. Good, just what I thought he might do. He had come down the hill at daylight or before to water and should be lying now chewing and getting sleepy. My tracking experience allowed me to follow this sign with the binoculars without moving. This wasn't the first time I'd used binoculars in this way, just the first time that I was trying to follow animal sign instead of people sign!

I thought about how so many things are the same or very similar to what I'd been doing for what now seemed all of my life, the knowing what you're seeing, understanding the sign story and understanding the character and motives of the sign maker. I'd spent far more time in the past several years learning to know people than I had big game—that might give the elk the advantage this time.

I was getting chilled sitting and thinking while watching the sun work its way down the hillside toward me. It was time to move. One more quick look with the glasses and I started out. I moved slowly, watching everything below me. Then without warning something moved. I wasn't sure what it was, just that something had definitely caught my eye. I froze in mid-step and slowly scanned the same bit of brush and timber that I'd been looking into for the past 30 minutes, but this time I saw something else. Branches of a big brush clump in the timber below seemed to have moved. I was sure they had moved, just slightly, but they definitely moved and now they moved again. I squatted down and brought up the glasses and looking at the bush, I quickly realized some of those weren't branches, but antlers! I kept watching, but even with the glasses I could only make out the antlers when they moved. Otherwise everything just looked like branches of the brush. I knew this bull had to be lying in close to that brush clump and about 150 yards away. There were two problems with this situation: one was getting in some position where I could see him clearly enough to shoot, and the other was keeping him from hearing me roll some little rock while I was moving around. I was almost in the open and one rolling rock would tell him I was there.

I settled down onto the ground watching the clump of brush. Nothing got up or moved. Carefully I slipped out of the shoulder straps of my pack and let it lay back on the rocks. Then, without taking my eyes from the brush ahead and below, I began to work my way forward and downward. I could see that to get to where I would have an angle and possibility of seeing the animal I was going to have to travel a bit of a distance. I hunched down and took advantage of some small bushes, rocks and a stump to help hide me while I continued to watch the bush. He still hadn't heard me moving. I

worked my way toward an old downed log and snuggled up to it and peeked over at the bush. I studied and brought up the binoculars and, resting them on the log, studied the bush carefully. Then his head moved and I could distinguish his antlers and then the position of his head. Now I could see about six inches of his neck clearly, the bottom of the right ear and down for about six inches, so I waited and watched. Not a bad shot, really, as long as I didn't clip the log that was on my side of the bush that he was lying by, or hit one of the branches. I knew the shot couldn't be more than an inch or two off center or I'd just burn his neck and lose him for good. I would have a better position if I moved up the hill slightly and back from the log. I carefully inched myself into position and sat, then found a comfortable rest on my knees. When the cross hairs were where I wanted, I took a breath, held it and squeezed off the shot.

The guys talked me into bringing him home. I had never considered taking a head mount, but according to Dean, the chance of getting another one like this was pretty slim. Dean had numerous big game head mounts that I admired a good deal. This was a perfect six point, beautifully symmetrical with a respectable thickness. I gave in, packed him up and gave him a long ride back home.

It's been several years since that hunt and in that time I've had many long talks with Elk. He's a favorite with the grandkids and is as patient with their chatter as with my long-winded philosophizing. I realize that I interrupted a perfectly good nap on carefree day, but he doesn't seem to mind that. He just quietly reminds me that none of us live forever and that I should enjoy the day I've been given.

⊷⊶⊙⊷⊶

CHAPTER TEN

Law Enforcement Tracking
Thinking Like the Bad Guys

Stop—Look—See

Having been a law enforcement officer for 30 years, I've been present at all types of crime scenes—scenes of burglaries, homicides, assaults, criminal trespass and nearly everything else that constitutes a violation of the law. I've also participated in local, state and federal crime scene investigations of all types, though I focused primarily on capital crimes. I've arrived on the scene while the initial investigation was taking place, I've been called several days after the scene was investigated, and I've even been called several years after the crime. It's almost universal that investigating officers are prone to rush into the center of a a scene prematurely. The best position from which to observe the scene of any crime is from outside the incident area. Of course, there are situations that call for immediate action on the part of the officer. For example, the officer can't be worried about preserving the crime scene, while a crime is still in progress, or a life is in danger. Even in situations like this, however, the officer who pauses to actually see what is happening (e.g., who is doing what, what are the positions of the participants and other officers) is better equipped to take the appropriate action. The officer who does this may seem to act immediately, with no hesitation, but a careful study will reveal that he has paused in his mind to see, hear and analyze the pieces of information that will help him to act in the appropriate way.

Tracking is most often utilized in historical crime scenes. That is to say that most crime scenes may be considered "historical" in the sense that the criminal action is over and the perpetrators have gone. It is important, therefore, to observe and record history accurately, leaving out nothing. What we do from the instant we arrive on the scene will directly influence the possibility of a successful criminal prosecution. There are very few crime scenes in which tracking could not play a role simply because in most cases the criminals are on foot at least part of the time. Wherever people walk they leave some sign of their passing. Since this is true, most crime scenes contain footprint evidence. This evidence may verify witness statements, prove which actions relate to the suspects and which to the victims, and possibly identify the suspect or suspects.

Unfortunately, while footprint evidence may be common, and one of the most numerous clues, it often is also the most overlooked, misinterpreted or ignored evidence. This one universal factor is due in large part to a lack of education concerning footprint evidence. Crime scene investigators, for the most part, are not trained to be track aware. They may be very capable at preserving (for example, by casting) the obvious tracks that exist, but they are not trained to see the tracks that are not obvious. Most scenes offer a few complete, distinct, clearly visible footprints and they grab attention. However, bloody footprints on a clean floor or a boot print in the mud outside the bedroom window are the exception at a crime scene rather than the rule. Education and training are the key to finding the obscure footprint evidence that exists at practically every crime scene.

If tracking is to be used effectively in law enforcement applications, it must be treated the same way as any other specialty. The apprentice tracker must be given sufficient instruction, plus time and on-the-job training to become proficient. OJT is a great way for a young officer to learn, as long as he is working with someone with sufficient expertise and experience. A trainee working with someone who has no more knowledge or field experience than he has contributes to the decline of professionalism and expertise. Tracking is a very valuable resource for any police agency as almost every crime scene (if not every one) will have hard evidence in the form of footprints.

One of the benefits of basic tracking training is that it teaches officers to be more aware of all potential evidence at any crime scene. One incident that exemplifies this track-awareness benefit took place when a local police department called me to assist at the scene in which a woman was found dead at a motel. I had worked with this department many times and all of their officers were quite familiar with appropriate tracking procedures at crime scenes.

A single woman had rented a room at a small motel. The maid had opened the door in the morning when there  was no response to her knock and immediately noticed that the room smelled of smoke and the walls appeared to be blackened with soot. She saw a naked woman lying prone on the bed with a small kitten perched on top of her. She then realized that this woman appeared to be dead, she carefully closed the door and called the police. The first officer to arrive listened carefully to the maid's story, then opened the door and without entering the room, visually examined it. A second officer also peered in. They observed that soot covered everything and the room smelled of burned plastic. They also noted that there were kitten tracks in the heavy soot on nearly everything in the room.

When I arrived at the scene there were several officers there, as well as the county coroner, all of whom were waiting outside the room. No one had entered or contaminated the scene. The detective took me aside and said simply that he needed me to visually examine the scene and tell him whatever I could before they began their examination. He asked that I determine if possible how many people had been there, what they had been doing and whatever else I could conclude. I opened the door to look inside. Beginning at the threshold, I made a careful examination of the floor. The single main room was carpeted and I could see that the bathroom had a tile floor surface of some kind.

As I made my way slowly and carefully into the room I was able to see that there were footprints of two different shoe types as well as barefoot prints on the carpet in the room. The prints were all the same size, and when we checked we found that both shoe types matched shoes in the woman's luggage. The barefoot prints were matched to the body. Within 15 minutes I was able to tell the detectives that there had been no one but the dead woman in the room since the maid had cleaned it the day before.

Based on this information, the detectives were able to figure out quickly that the woman had passed out on the bed from drinking an excessive amount of alcohol. The fire had started in the plastic trash can beside the bed, where a cigarette had evidently fallen and ignited some paper that slowly smoldered until the trash can was melted. The fire had died without igniting anything else, but by that time it had been too late. A subsequent autopsy verified that the woman had died of smoke inhalation.

The case was solved quickly because these officers understood the value and significance of footprint evidence. Had they walked back and forth through the scene, as is so often the case, it would have been more difficult to unravel. The two hours invested in waiting for my arrival and use of the proper tool—tracking—at best estimates saved the department one week of investigative man-days.

The method used in this situation is important for every tracker:

1. Obtain the best information from the best sources.

2. Decide what operation will be used to gather evidence.

3. Work the area completely in an organized and methodical process. Determine to the best of your ability exactly what happened based on the footprint evidence. This may or may not match up with the other information you've received, but this is your evidence.

In dealing with law enforcement, this method of operation becomes even more crucial. William Bodziak, Supervisory Special Agent, Laboratory Division of the Federal Bureau of Investigation, writes in *Footwear Impression Evidence*: "Crimes involve people and places. Persons committing a crime leave footwear impressions en route to, at, and exiting the crime scene."[1] I couldn't say it better nor more clearly. Bodziak was the FBI's leading footprint specialist until his retirement in 1994. He adds, "Footwear impression evidence unfortunately has been neglected to the extent that it is used in only a small percentage of cases. Neglect of this evidence is not forgivable, but there are some reasons that may help account for it" (p.2).

Bodziak points out that such evidence has been undervalued by investigators, attorneys, and the courts due to their limited knowledge of it. He asserts further that such treatment and general misunderstanding of footprint evidence has been a major reason that crime scene investigators don't look for it. He adds that because much footprint evidence is latent or nearly invisible, the crime scene technician may erroneously feel that it is not present or by not thoroughly looking, he may rationalize that it doesn't exist. I have been called by a variety of local, state and federal agencies to assist in various criminal and crime scene investigations. Several have involved the complex examination of footprint evidence to render an opinion or conclusion as to facts. Most investigations, however, have involved rather simple tracking operations which astounded and mystified observing officers. The production of most common footprint evidence is generally incomprehensible to even seasoned crime scene technicians.

"Before beginning the crime scene search," Bodziak notes, "careful thought should be given to what occurred at the crime scene, how footwear impression evidence could contribute to the proof of facts, and what areas of the crime scene might contain footwear impression evidence. Then the footwear impressions should be looked for aggressively and carefully. What is not looked for will not be found!" (p. 2).

---

[1] *Practical Aspects of Criminal and Forensic Investigations*, New York: Elsevier Science Publishing, 1990, p. 1.

Trackers know that wherever people walk they leave sign. A tracker's skill is in finding, identifying and correctly interpreting what story the sign tells. A tracker therefore, approaches every incident involving people, knowing that there is footprint evidence that tells who, what, when, where, how and sometimes why. He stops before he enters the scene and decides how best to approach based on information available. Then he proceeds, reading all of the footprint story as he goes.

Track-aware officers know that if they preserve incident areas until they can be examined by tracking-trained persons, it will not only save their agencies many thousands of investigative hours, but also the dollars those hours cost. If all basic police training academies or schools presented to trainees an appropriate introduction to track awareness— how, why, when and where it's appropriate—this awareness would result in tremendous savings of man hours and successful prosecutions over the course of those trainees' police careers. Officers from each trainee class over the course of their introduction and education into police work could be selected for further tracking training to ensure sufficient personnel were trained to a journeyman-tracker level. These journeyman trackers would be called to an incident scene much the same as other police specialists are called to incident scenes needing their specialty. For nearly all agencies, no matter the size, location or jurisdiction, just one or two incidents in which track awareness is the right tool would more than pay for all of the training for officers. The motel case was solved so quickly because these officers understood the value and significance of footprint evidence and didn't contaminate it by walking back and forth through the scene.

A Quick Mission

Many tracking missions are handled seemingly quite easily and quickly. One such mission involved the discovery of a body which had been dumped a short distance off of a paved road in a rural area of Whatcom County, Washington. There was an old dirt roadway going a short distance into the woods. The body was lying in a small ravine or creek bottom about 20 feet from this old roadway. Sheriff's deputies were standing by at the entrance to the old roadway upon my arrival. My task at their request was to tell them anything I could regarding the body. I could see tire tracks on the old roadway, which was covered by loose forest debris, grasses and leaves. The tire tracks indicated that a vehicle had backed into the roadway from the pavement then had driven out again. I followed the tracks, cutting for sign of persons exiting the vehicle. There was sign of one person walking along the old roadway in and out; those prints were identified as the sign of the person who had found the body. I worked quickly to where tire impressions indicated the vehicle had stopped.

There I could see footprint sign; marks, scrapes, freshly turned and mashed old leaves, a straight-line impression on others, the clear impression of footsteps, which was the evidence of someone getting out of the vehicle. The sign was of a footprint pivoting, turning toward the rear of the vehicle, the other foot fully impacting the ground and touching the tire print. These prints were indications of someone getting out of a higher vehicle, such as a van or pickup, rather than a car. Similar sign appeared on the other side of the tire impressions where the passenger had exited the vehicle. This sign confirmed that the vehicle was higher than the usual auto. The footprint sign on both sides walked to the rear center of the vehicle tracks and stood facing the vehicle. There was considerable scuffing, scraping and marking of the ground surface here; the two people were engaged in doing something together. Then the sign walked away from the vehicle and toward the dry creek bed. One set of sign followed the other; the person in front walked mostly backward, watchful to step over and around brush and obstacles. The two were walking close together and were struggling with something between them—the body obviously. They came to and went down into the ditch of the creek bottom and dropped the body face down. Then both climbed out of the ditch and returned to the vehicle, the passenger stopping to close the rear doors of the vehicle. This had to be a double-rear-door van of some type. The driver was wearing heavy lugged boots with a high instep, something like a "Packer" boot with a Vibram-type tread pattern on the sole and heel. I was able to get good measurements and make a drawing of this print in the creek bottom near the head and shoulders of the body. The second track was a smaller print, with fine lines running completely across the sole and heel; it was flat, like a tennis shoe. This print was smaller and narrower and resembled that of the less expensive pointed-toe canvas tennis shoes sold at most discount houses and typically worn by women.

I carefully made drawings of both prints, took the measurements and made notes for my report. When detectives arrived on the scene, I filled them in on what I'd learned about the suspects: there were two persons, probably a male and a female, and I gave appropriate general physical descriptions. They were familiar with this old roadway because they did not look it over before backing the vehicle into the woods; they already knew where it was and that the old creek bottom was at the end of it. The victim was dead prior to arrival and had been loaded into the rear of a double-rear-door van. The two dumped the body quickly, but without panic, during daylight hours. I departed the scene, having spent less than two hours in the examination.

Later I was informed by the sheriff's office that once the identity of the victim had been established, officers quickly arrested two persons who lived in the victim's house for the murder. These two matched the descriptions I had provided from the sign characteristics and the victim owned a blue Ford Econoline van that was found parked in the garage. They both summarily entered plea agreements and were sentenced to serve long prison terms.

Every Picture Tells a Story

Another incident that illustrates the use and value of tracking in a crime scene investigation was a case in which my assistance was requested by the Washington State Attorney General's Office of Special Investigations. The case involved the accidental death of a young woman several years previously. Some family members had never believed that her death was accidental. Her sister believed strongly that the dead woman's husband had somehow contributed to her death. The sister came to the Office of Special Investigations when she heard that the husband had bragged to a friend that he had killed his wife and gotten away with it. The chief investigator reviewed the original case file; along with the hearsay evidence, he found sufficient cause to reopen the investigation.

The original story goes something like this: The woman and her husband, a young couple, were living in a small house on some acreage which had a small barn and a three-sided open horse stable out back. One side of the stable was the wall of the barn in which she kept hay and tack for her horse. A salt box with a salt block sat in the middle of the 12 x 12-foot stable. The incident happened in January and there were about three to five inches of snow on the ground, which appeared from the pictures to have fallen several days before.

The husband explained that, having gone somewhere in the early morning, he had returned home midmorning and found his wife lying on the ground inside the stable. He stated that he could see blood on her head and a large splash of blood on the timbers of the barn wall. He immediately called the sheriff's office and an officer responded, but did not move or examine the body. While waiting for the medical examiner and the detectives to arrive, the deputy took pictures of the scene and made some notes. The conclusion of the investigation was that the woman had been working with the horse and had been kicked in the head. The force of the kick had thrown her against the wall, splashing blood there, the body had rebounded from the wall and fallen on the ground as it was found.

Seven years had now passed since the initial investigation. The body was exhumed and reexamined and the skull was retained for further forensic tests. The only other remaining evidence were the photos taken by the deputy and the original reports filed by the detectives. The pictures gave a good impression of the death scene and position of the body, including the entrance and exit to the stable. However, the pictures were taken with a small Instamatic-type camera and were less than ideal.

The chief investigator completed a preliminary fact-finding investigation and called three experts—a forensic pathologist, a blood-splatter expert, and me. Of the pathologist he asked for an examination of the skull and his conclusion as to the cause of death. The blood-splatter expert was to examine the photos showing the blood on the timbers of the wall and render his opinion as to the how events might have unfolded for it to be there. I was to study photos from the file, enlarging them if necessary, and see what I could determine regarding the footprint evidence.

The photos captured the tragic scene. There lay a young woman whose life had been cut short either by a horrible accident or a horrendous act of malice. Like suspended animation, she lay in the same position that she had seven years before, looking uncomfortable, as if in the throes of a restless night's sleep. Her legs were drawn up and her torso was twisted. The stable floor made a makeshift mattress of dirty straw and manure. Long, dark hair spilled over her shoulders and I allowed myself to think of how beautiful she must have been on that crisp winter morning. But now it was time for business and I pushed sentiment to the side to let the analytical mind have center stage.

I selected and grouped the photos that would show me 1) the trail in the snow that ran from the house to the stable, 2) the stable floor and 3) the open side of the stable. I asked to have them blown up in three different sizes, the largest being 8x10 inches. When the enlargements came back from the State photography lab, I was eager to get started. Using a large, lighted magnifying glass obtained for just this type of examination, I began to go over the photos. It was slow, painstaking work. First I would look at the photo, trying to make sure I was fully aware of everything my eyes were seeing in each photo. I would then close my eyes and visualize it in detail, then look over it again. At first I wasn't looking for details, but doing an overview, making sure I was completely familiar with the entire scene. Then, after resting my eyes awhile, I placed a clear quarter-inch graph sheet over the photo and began looking for details.

I began with the photos showing the path in the snow coming into the stable area from the house. There were numerous footprints evident in the snow, though none that were identifiable. I could see where people had walked up, stood talking, rested briefcases in the snow, etc. A couple furniture pads and a blanket were dumped in the corner of the stable entrance and snow outlined one footprint on the blanket corner. Very few prints were outside of the trail. I could see packed prints in the snow, presumably those of the investigators, who had walked around the stable area. Packed snow clumps from the horse's hooves also dotted the stable floor.

In one of the pictures someone's shoes and pant cuffs were visible as he tried unsuccessfully to stand out of the way of the photographer. It was helpful, though, because I could see snow clinging to the sides of the individual's shoes. This, along with the packed snow prints, told me that the temperature at the time of the photos was just above freezing. That sparked a memory and I knew I had something. I remembered clearly that there was no snow at all on the bottom of the victim's boot soles. That was shown on another photo, but I didn't even have to look, I knew that the bottoms of her boots were absolutely dry.

Of course, it was possible that the boot soles had dried out before the photos were taken, but there was another clue that substantiated my initial feeling. On the bottom of one of the heels of her crosshatched soles was a white residue. On closer examination, it became obvious that this residue was not snow. It seemed to be a powder of some kind, and it was packed into the depressions of the tiny crisscrossed lines that made up the pattern on the bottom of her boot. This dry powder would have been quickly removed by the snow had the victim walked in those boots, and this was proof positive that she had not walked to her present position.

As I studied every aspect of the photos, I came across another footprint in an unlikely place. In the center of the stable was a salt box, in which blocks of salt and minerals were placed for the horse to nibble on. The impressions on the ground showed that this box had been moved to one side, ostensibly by the force of the woman's body as she was knocked to the ground. As I examined the scene, however, I noticed the faint impression of a boot-print on the side of the box, exactly where you would expect it to be had the box been kicked out of the way. As the clues came together I became more and more sure that someone had created a scene meant to throw everyone off his or her trail.

I gathered my conclusions and presented them to the chief investigator. Shortly afterwards he went to the victim's husband with this evidence, along with that of the pathologist and the blood-spatter expert. In a matter of minutes, he broke down and confessed. He said that he and his wife had had an argument that morning. They'd gone for a drive and just as they pulled back into their driveway, he had "lost it," striking her on the head with a hammer he kept in the truck. Realizing that this had been a fatal blow, he decided to make it look like an accident involving the horse. She was wearing tennis shoes at the time of her death but, had she been feeding the horse, she would have been wearing her boots. He retrieved them from the back porch, placed them on her feet and carried her to the barn. He then kicked the salt box out of the way to help form the illusion that the horse had been out of control, and threw her body onto the floor.

As he talked, he also cleared up the mystery of the dry residue that I had seen on the bottom of the victim's boot. It was grain dust that had gathered on the back porch where he hung his work clothes. Since he worked in a granary, his clothes were always covered with the dry, flour-like grain dust that proved to be his undoing. This man was brought to trial and is currently serving a life sentence for murder.

When officers are trained to stop before they enter an incident scene, look to see the entirety of what is there and then to actually *see* what it is that they are looking at, they secure hard evidence in a great many more incidents than previously and that evidence assists in successfully prosecuting criminals.

Alaskan Fugitive

I was presenting a training course in Sitka, Alaska. I had arrived at the Police Academy early in the morning and was to begin the tracking course presentation the next day. A trooper came to the instructor's quarters and asked me to come downstairs and talk with the director, who informed me that a prisoner had escaped from the jail in Juneau. There was an ongoing police search with the possibility that the escapee was in the woods, and he asked if I would join the effort to recapture him. I was there to assist the State Police, so I agreed to do whatever I could. They began to make arrangements to get me from Sitka to Juneau. There were no commercial flights available, and due to weather no charter flights would be able to make the trip. The character of the escapee caused State Police authorities to believe there was danger to the general public, and that he might well take a hostage to effect his escape from the Juneau area. They contacted the U.S. Coast Guard, and I was to get my first U.S. Coast Guard helicopter flight!

I arrived in Juneau and was whisked away by State Police to the search area at the rear of the jail. Here an eyewitness had seen the escapee running along the bank of a creek that formed a deep ravine and dropping from sight into the creek bottom. The escapee had run through the back gate as a vehicle was exiting at about 4:30 p.m. the previous day. It was now about 1 p.m., so he'd been gone nearly 24 hours. Troopers and other local law enforcement were searching the neighborhoods. They had already used search dogs, starting on the sign line in the creek bottom almost immediately after the escape. Based on bits and pieces of conversation from other prisoners and some written evidence, someone suggested that the subject was going to attempt to go afoot out of the Juneau area to another settlement about 100 miles to the northeast. This routing would take him over what was referred to as the Lemon Glacier, which didn't mean much to me at the time, except that officers believed he was still in the woods going high into the mountains. First Sergeant John Murphy of the Alaska State Troopers was in charge of the search operation. He assigned three officers to accompany me to the embankment where the subject was last seen.

From the footprints, it seemed that everyone had been to and had gone down the embankment. I was told that the rushing, milky, turquoise-colored creek was the drainage from the Lemon Glacier and ran a good stream of water year round. The stream banks were nearly 20 feet high, with scattered tree stumps, broken limbs and debris washed downstream from the steep hillside. I looked for the subject's sign, but there was such a jumble of tracks at the bank and down into the creek that picking out just one was an effort. Each searcher had been seeking secure footing and his own path up the creek. I checked each line and picked up one that seemed to have been walked on by nearly everyone else, so it must have been first up the creek bottom. I had been given a verbal description of the escapee's footgear by Sgt. Murphy and it seemed to match this line—it was about the right size, shape, composition and age. A really big plus was that it was running pell mell away from the jail area and up the creek bottom. All of the other tracks were walking, stopping, standing, looking and continuing. The tracks of the search dog marked the handler's sign clearly. Yep, this was our guy, all right. As I usually do in this type of situation, I called to the three officers accompanying me and showed them the tracks, explaining and pointing out the characteristics which identified our escapee subject from all of the others.

Even persons without formal tracking knowledge or training can clearly see sign when a tracker points it out and shows it to them. Involving accompanying officers in the tracking operation, showing and explaining significant evidence to them in a manner that they can see and understand what they are seeing, helps to ensure their acceptance and help. Trackers must always remember to keep things simple for untrained people, and that untrained people should be able to see and understand any footprint evidence that you might bring into court as evidence.

We began to work the sign up the creek bottom in, out and among the other tracks. It appeared that the dog was in fact following the subject's scent as the dog tracks were often in those of the escapee. Here and there the sign was greatly confused and lost in areas of driftwood piles and debris hang-ups where the searchers' tracks were funneled into the same narrow passageway as the subject's. We pushed on, actually traveling at a fairly good pace. The creek bottom was getting steeper as it approached the edge of the wooded mountains farther from the cleared areas behind housing, businesses and the jail. We were able to see the treetops beginning to appear as we worked upstream. As the creek got more shallow, the banks were closer and lower. We stopped to catch our breath and look back at the top roof line of the jail, now in the distance, with its antennas and transmitter towers showing. I observed that at this point our fugitive in the creek bottom would still be out of sight of anyone watching or looking for him unless they were up on the creek bank itself. I had a feeling the subject was fully aware of where he was in respect to where people would be, calculating the time and distance he'd need to disappear into the woods. He continued on, running where possible, up the drainage and we followed the sign. He rounded a big old stump with debris clinging to the roots, and headed directly up the bank to the right and into the woods.

We followed through the slight fringe of small brush and trees into and under the canopy of forest. Our guy ran a few more steps, then dove in behind an old rotted log and hid himself, raising to peer over the log and through the wooded fringe back toward the jail area. Copying what the sign told us he'd done, we got down on hands and knees and looked over the log in the same position. We could see the cyclone fence and gate at the back of the jail, more than a quarter mile away. At this point he would be able to see whatever efforts were being made to pursue him. I estimated that he spent 15 to 20 minutes in this position before bolting and running wherever possible through the woods and further away from the jail and the creek. The sign, dramatically different in the woods, was more difficult to follow with his jumping over logs and dodging to avoid limbs and branches. We followed, the three officers getting an education as I tried to tell them everything I was seeing along the sign line. Here and there the runner would stop and rest behind a stump or bush, watching his back trail.

By 3 p.m. we had covered the fugitive's routing pretty quickly though not as quickly as he would have done. Considering the time he spent resting and watching the back trail, I figured we were about where he would have been at dark. I told the officers that the sign line had slightly changed directions and was now traveling almost parallel to the coast line. One of the officers informed Sgt. Murphy our direction and approximate location as best we could judge. We were deep in the woods at this time and unable to determine how far it was to the cleared areas. Then we reached a small area of big timber and huge old downed logs covered with moss and scattered small new trees. I wouldn't have been surprised if a family of trolls came out from a home under one of the big old stumps. Here the sign went into one of the thickets of little trees between two old downed logs and here the guy rested. He had laid down, sat, got up and looked around and went back and sat and probably slept for a short time. Then he traveled again.

The direction of travel changed again; our guy was heading back toward the cleared areas bordering the highway and industrial areas. Now he traveled more slowly and carefully, almost tree to tree or bush to tree, and I noted that the sign was stumbling over deadfalls, branches and stepping into holes in the brush, this indicated to me that it was now dark when he was here. Soon we were able to hear the sounds of traffic on the highway, then we could see through the trees here and there and know that we were approaching the cleared area. He would have been able to see lights of cars and buildings. We followed the sign out to the fringe area of the woods, where it turned and traveled inside the wood line but parallel to it. He stumbled and fell, tripped and stepped in holes—all indications not only that was it dark, but also that he was trying to keep watch into the cleared area. Our location was radioed to Sgt. Murphy. I found a couple places where our fugitive came out into the clearing behind bushes or large stumps and studied the landscape toward civilization. He seemed to be looking for something that he might see at night. Then he would turn and head back into the woods, continuing south within the wood line. Soon we came to an area in which he would stand and study the landscape, then go a few steps and study more. We stood in the same places and looked as the sign was telling us he had done. We could barely see the highway and some buildings, and out across some open water there was a big island which appeared to be heavily forested. "What's that?" I asked the officers, pointing to the island. One said it was Douglas Island and he pointed out a bridge farther south that connected the mainland to the island.

I was beginning to have an idea, and we pushed the sign a little further, following it along the fringe of the woods. The escapee began to go from stump to bush, venturing out into the cleared area. Now it was nearing 5 p.m. I said to the officers, "I think that this guy knows where he's at and knows where he's going, based on the manner in which he's been looking and has circled around from the jail. Now I think it's about two or three in the morning for him and he can see the lights of cars crossing the bridge onto Douglas Island. Where can you go from Douglas Island?"

One of the officers laughed. "You don't know much about Juneau, do you?" he asked. I said I'd never been here before, and he replied, "Well, you can't go anywhere from Juneau unless you go by boat, plane or on foot. Douglas Island is just that, an island. He wouldn't be anywhere if he was over there, he'd be better off here on the mainland. This is where there's access to the outside."

"Well, guys, the sign is telling me that he's wanting to get to the island for some reason. Any chance he knows someone there?"

Our communicator called Sgt. Murphy. "Hardin says the sign is telling him that this guy is going to Douglas Island—he probably knows someone over there."

"Give me a minute," was the reply. We continued the sign line and in a few minutes there came a reply that our fugitive had a girl-friend who lived on Douglas Island and surveillance cars were on the way. The sign was now definitely headed out across the cleared areas toward the intersection of the highway and the bridge to the island. We broke off the chase, marking the last tracks, and within the hour the subject was located at his girlfriend's apartment and back in custody.

Putting a Suspect at the Scene

Early one July morning I was called by the Whatcom County (Washington) Sheriff's Office and requested to respond to the scene of a shooting homicide. I arrived on scene at about 8:00 a.m. of a beauti-ful sunny day. The temperature was about 60 degrees with the promise of the high 70s by midday. The night had been fairly cool with a heavy dew fall beginning about midnight. Upon arrival, I was informed that officers had a suspect in custody and he had been identified by wit-nesses as the shooter. However they needed evidence to place this individual at the scene of the crime, which was a rural apartment com-plex formed in a large circle with a common area inside the circle. The complex was surrounded on two sides by cultivated raspberry fields and on the other two sides by woods, brush and creek bottom areas. The apartments themselves were duplex and triplex single-story units constructed to serve low-income migrant families. Information was that in one apartment there was a gathering of several persons in the middle of the night. Suddenly the front door burst open and a lone gunman entered, firing a rifle indiscriminately around the living room. Persons ran screaming to other rooms and hid behind furniture as the bullets sprayed around the room. The gunman was wearing a ski mask and gloves. He fired numerous rounds then fled out the door and into the night. One man who had hidden inside a closet at the side of the living room was struck and killed by a bullet penetrating the closet door. No one else was injured.

Occupants of the apartment had immediately called 911 and reported the shooting. Responding officers secured the area with a roadblock on the single entrance/exit lane and held all persons within and without the apartment complex. During their investigation, a vehicle approached the officer stationed at the roadway close to the apartment. As the officer was questioning the lone male occupant of the vehicle to establish his identity and place of residence, one of the women who lived in the apartment was watching from a window and suddenly rushed outside, shouting to the deputy that this was the shooter. The deputy immediately placed the subject in the back seat of his patrol vehicle until this new information could be evaluated. The suspect had already aroused the deputies' suspicion when he asked if anyone was killed in the shooting, but wouldn't explain how he knew about the incident. Soon deputies learned from other apartment residents that the suspect had recently been the boyfriend of one of the young ladies living in the apartment and that the man who was killed was the new boyfriend. The deputies believed they had the shooter in custody all right, but had no evidence to tie him to the incident. No one in the apartment could identify the individual due his wearing to the ski mask and the fact that he'd not said anything during the shooting incident.

Deputies provided the suspect's shoes for me to look at in an attempt to match them with footprints in the area. Witnesses reported that they had not heard a vehicle approach prior to the shooting nor had they heard one leave after the shooter left the scene. I called a member of the Pacific Northwest Trackers Association who lived in the area and he joined me to assist as we began cutting sign adjacent to the paved roadway and apartment walkways. It was now nine o'clock and the dew had gone. With the rising temperature and humidity, it was going to be a very nice day. We knew the time of the shooting and the time that the shooter had run from the apartment. We could reason what sign would look like made after the cool of the evening as dew would begin to form on the grass and other ground cover. Soon we located a line of prints that were identical in print pattern and measurement to the suspect's shoes. The tracks were approaching the apartment complex from the wooded creek-bottom area and parallel to this sign line we found indications that the same prints were returning in great haste via the same route. We separated the sign lines in the brush and reeds surrounding the marsh and began to follow the sign line leaving the apartment complex. This sign line plunged into the muck and mire of the swampy area in the creek bottom, sure indication of nighttime travel and near-panic flight. In comparison, the approaching sign line worked its way carefully around the mud and water areas. We worked the sign, which went in a circular route that returned to the entrance roadway and crossed into the berry fields, still traveling away from the complex. The sign left the berry field and climbed over the fence into a horse pasture where tracking was extremely difficult. Our progress, which had been quite rapid, slowed to a snail's pace, we were following step by step on our hands and knees. This is one of the situations that we always tell beginning trackers about, the necessity of getting down to find the evidence of each footprint. We moved across the horse pasture at the rate of less than 100 yards in an hour, but we were still on the sign. The sign bypassed a horse barn and continued in the general direction of other migrant housing, where we were informed by accompanying deputies that the suspect lived.

We continued with the sign and were nearing the edge of another horse pasture when we came to a small pine tree under which the horses sheltered from the sun and rain. The sign traveled under the tree and we paused, looking around the tree for where the sign exited, when there on the ground we saw .22-caliber ammunition. We involuntarily looked up in the tree, as the shells appeared to have fallen onto the ground around the tree trunk.

There in the branches were a rifle and other items above our heads! We stood and examined the items more closely, there were black gloves, the rifle, a ski mask and other items. We called to waiting deputies, informing them of the find. While waiting for them to take custody of the items in the tree, we located and moved the sign following the suspect's exiting sign line onward from the tree toward the fence line.

The sign crossed the fence and entered another field behind the other migrant housing area. Then suddenly we found, intertwined with the sign we were following, identical prints coming toward us. The subject had at this point come and gone via this same route. We were able to follow both sign lines to a hole in the fence behind a cabin and continuing around the corner and to a front door. Deputies approached the cabin from the roadway and identified it as the one in which the suspect lived. They began the formal process of requesting a search warrant and we requested a ride back to our vehicle, it was nearly one o-clock and time for lunch. Another successful tracking mission was completed, except for the paperwork. Lunchtime would give us the opportunity to get our notes together and do a drawing of the tracking operation. Every mission requires a comprehensive written report to be complete, and this one was no different.

Matching a Pair of Shoes

Sometimes an important case is resolved by a tracker, but not by sign cutting. I received a request from San Francisco Police Homicide Squad asking if I could identify the shoe print found at a homicide on the victim's bedspread. The print looked familiar, but it was a little different from any others I'd seen. I looked through my reference materials. The homicide squad had  already checked all law enforcement footprint research indexes, but hadn't been able to make a match. I pondered the print in question for a couple months, checking first one source then another.

I decided one day that the way to find out what type of shoe had made this print was through basic, boring, old-fashioned police work. I began at the Canadian border and headed south, systematically checking each different shoe retail outlet along Interstate 5. There were a bunch and I didn't get it all done in a day. In fact, each of the many times I traveled south from Bellingham I continued the systematic checking of retail outlets, questioning the persons who ordered shoes, but going along the racks of shoes and personally checking each shoe sole and heel. The greater Seattle area took nearly a week to check, then I worked my way south. During this time, I was investigating two major smuggling cases which involved moving people and drugs between borders along the I-5 corridor. I spent a considerable amount of time driving I-5 between San Francisco and Vancouver, Canada, and I had the opportunity to check a lot of shoe shops.

My search had gotten to the greater Portland area shoe shops and I was methodically going from shop to shop in the Clackamas Town Center, at that time one of the largest shopping malls in the northwest. I would enter the shoe shop and quickly go down the shelves and displays of shoes, turning each shoe and looking at the sole pattern, then replacing it. I had already checked several shops when halfway through another I picked up a loafer-type shoe and bingo!—there was the pattern I was looking for. I took the shoe to the store manager and explained what I was doing and requested the name of the particular distributor and manufacturer.

Armed with the proper information I wrote to the manufacturer and to the distributor advising them of the purpose and need for the information; both responded promptly. The shoes were a model designed specifically for marketing to a particular age and financial status. This shoe was marketed by a major distributor, but due to the narrow customers target range, it was distributed to only a few stores for test marketing. The distributor listed the west coast retail outlets to which the shoes had been shipped. With the print dimensions, they also furnished the size of the shoe that made the print. I forwarded the information to the San Francisco Police Department. Later I received a reply from the homicide squad reporting that the information had been used to help identify a suspect in the case. The suspect had confessed to the murder and was awaiting trial.

The Mandy Stavic Homicide

An unsuccessful tracking mission that haunts me is the murder of a vivacious young lady who lived not far from Everson, Washington. Outgoing and personable, Mandy Stavic had graduated from high school, distinguishing herself both academically and athletically, and had gone on to Central Washington State University. She'd returned home with friends for the Thanksgiving holidays. The Friday after Thanksgiving, she decided to go for a run, which was consistent with her old habits and current college athletic interests. About 3 p.m. Mandy set out with the family dog. Her usual route was down the lane on which they lived and across open fields owned by neighbors onto adjacent gravel roadways, which would eventually lead her back to the highway and to the lane where she started.

Mandy didn't return from this run. The dog was seen much later—wet, muddy and tired—trotting along the the road leading back to the house. A call to the sheriff's office resulted in an organized search, which continued for several days. It was quite clear to everyone after the first couple hours of looking that Mandy had been abducted. By whom, where and when? Search efforts after the first 12 hours were aimed at finding a body, but where? This is a rural area characterized by small farms and a nearby community store that has been in operation since early in the century. A state highway runs through the valley and Mandy would have run along this highway for about two miles before turning onto another paved road leading back to her lane. The highway isn't heavily traveled by people not living in the small valley, though this was a holiday weekend and there was more daily traffic than usual.

It had rained heavily Friday night and the temperature was near freezing. My services were requested and I, with two other trackers,

Jerry Darkis and Alan Pratt, reported to the search scene at midmorning on Saturday, the second day of the search. We gathered the information and began a sign-cutting operation of the areas around the Stavic house and adjacent houses. No one had seen Mandy from the time she had gone out the door of the house. Neighbors had already been questioned by deputies, and vehicles that had been seen in the area were being checked out. We were unable to locate any sign to match Mandy's running shoes. We sign cut along the lane in the direction she was believed to have gone from the house. This lane was paved and only traveled by persons coming or going from two or three houses, and she would have run on the pavement. We approached and passed through the gate that she would have used entering the open fields, and here we found sign—running footfalls and with a dog alongside. Midway across an 80-acre hay field, I found diamond-patterned shapes imprinted on red clover leaves—this was Mandy's running-shoe sign line without doubt. The line continued across the field and out through an open barbed-wire field gate and onto the gravel road.

At this point Mandy could have gone the direction she usually ran, back towards the highway about a mile away, or parallel to the highway and into a dead-end area of brush and briars in the middle of an old overgrown Christmas tree farm. We worked both roadway areas. Both had already been searched and driven by dozens of searchers in the first hours of the search. We were unable to find even one partial print which matched that of the running shoes in either direction. The sign just ended on the roadway near the gate. Mandy would normally run in the light gravel-sandy road as it was seldom traveled by anything but farm equipment coming or going from the fields. It was possible that her prints had been run over by the searching vehicles, as she would normally run in the tire-track portion of the road. Vehicle traffic on roads such as this tends to eject the rocks that aren't impressed into the road surface, leaving a pathway relatively free of the loose rocks that might cause injury to a runner.

The two sign cutters and I worked the roadsides in both directions, first one to the dead-end and on, and then back to the highway. No sign of the running shoes, not even a single "maybe". We continued to cut sign here and there in response to whatever other searchers found, but still we were unable to come up with anything that made sense. I concluded she had encountered someone almost immediately after coming onto the road from the hay field and had been abducted in a vehicle.

On the fourth or fifth day of the search, Mandy's body was found in the river upstream a couple miles from the search area. The body, naked except for her running shoes, was hung up on an old stump in the middle of the shallow river. We waited for the coroner's report to give us additional information as to where to look for whatever evidence. Later that day we got the report, but no additional information. It said the cause of death was not immediately determinable, and it offered little else of value except that her arms and legs were badly cut and scratched by briars.

We decided to try to learn where and how the body had gotten into the river. We went to the river bridge a couple miles upriver from where the body was found and began sign cutting. We located sign on the bridge itself that looked suspicious, possible evidence that the body had been dumped into the river from the middle of the bridge. However, we couldn't confirm this information. We began to sign cut the bank of the river and worked our way downstream to where the body had been located. Then we sign cut the bank on the other side of the river. This process took most of three days, but in the end we were convinced that no one had walked or carried Mandy to the river between the bridge and where her body was found. A rumor was around that Mandy had somehow managed to escape her abductor and had run through briars into the river and drowned. Not true. There was no sign of anyone going into the river between the bridge and the body find—Mandy or anyone else—that we could not explain.

The pathologist's report later on stated that Mandy had died of drowning, though there was only a very minimal amount of fluid in her lungs. She had large and significant bruising on the rear of her head, but not sufficient to have killed her. The case remains open, unexplained and unanswered. I will always feel that I missed something, somewhere. Possibly someday, I'll get another chance to deal with the culprit somewhere else down the line, and I'll not miss the sign!

Kittitas County Body Parts

To me, a successful tracking operation is not only when the sign is found, but also when it is correctly interpreted. Sometimes what you find on the ground doesn't add up, and the advanced tracker has to formulate a plausible theory for the evidence he sees. One spring day I got a call from the Kittitas County (Washington) Sheriff's Office. The officer identified himself as someone who had been in a tracking class that Ab Taylor and I had conducted many years previously. He was now a detective with the sheriff's department and was assisting in a homicide investigation. He filled me in on the case.

State highway maintenance workers gathering trash had discovered a black plastic garbage bag stuffed under a large sage brush along the roadway at one of the viewpoints on Interstate 82 in Kittitas County. One of them gingerly poked a hole in the bag and discovered that it contained a human body or at least parts of one. The workers had called the sheriff's office without disturbing the bag or body further or otherwise contaminating the evidence. The sheriff's office detectives who arrived on scene made a thorough examination finding the garbage bag contained the torso of a female body. The limbs and head were not in the bag, and as it had apparently been tied shut, they were somewhere else. During the next couple days detectives completed a crime scene investigation of the area and removed the bag and body. During their examination of the scene they had observed dried footprints in the mud between the guard rail and the sage brush. They were unable to determine if these footprints were associated with the deposit of the body or not. This officer thought that with my tracking knowledge and experience I might be able to make such a determination for them. Well, can't say without seeing, I told him, but I was willing to drive over there the next day and take a look. Which I did.

I arrived at the sheriff's office at 9 a.m. and met with the officer. He, busy with many things to do, called one of the "road" deputies to accompany me to the scene of the body find. Taking a mug of coffee, we headed out and arrived 20 minutes later at the viewpoint location. The deputy directed me to the large sage brush adjacent to a section of guard rail along the viewpoint drive. He pointed out the foot-prints outside the guard rail. I looked at them and immediately recognized them as the prints of an artificial-turf soccer or football shoe. They had been in the mud for some time, probably since the previous fall's early rains. The prints were stepping over the guard rail and taking one step to stand close to and partly turned toward the bush, his back quartering to the pavement, directly away from any approaching traffic. It looked to me like a man stepping over the guard rail and taking one step to stand close to the sage brush and urinate with his back to any approaching vehicles. He then took one step back across the guard rail. The prints certainly didn't go on around the bush in either direction; they would have been just as evident in that soft mud as where they were plainly showing. Nope, not related to the body find.

I'm as curious as anyone else, maybe more so. I eased around the bush observing the sign of the investigating officers. The backside view of the sage revealed where the garbage bag had been placed, as well as the knee and toe prints of the investigators scuffing and turning up the dry soil surface as they crawled and knelt, then poked and toyed with the bag. They had eventually pulled the bag out from under the bush and removed it from the area. There appeared to be four investigators' tracks, in addition to the highway department person's tracks. I had been asked to attempt to determine, if possible, when the bag had been placed under the bush. I had gained considerable experience doing this type of aging analysis during my examination of Green River serial murder body-find areas around Seattle. I knelt and studied the ground surface, now exposed where the body bag had lain. It was late March and the new year's grass had started to grow beneath the bag, but it was weak and very pale yellowish-green, nearly white. Stunted and gnarled beneath the bag, it was now beginning to straighten out in just the couple days and it would soon green up like the other grasses around the area. Other indicators in the surrounding soil surface area told me that the bag had been placed under the bush after the last snow had left this area. The bag had protected the ground surface from the effects of surface moisture freezing and thawing and rains, which were evident all around it.

The deputy, replying to my inquiry, said that the snow would probably have been gone from this area in the middle to end of February. That would make the timing about right—the bag was probably placed there about the end of February. The time frame could be pinned down more accurately by checking with the highway maintenance people; they'd be aware of when the snow melted around the viewpoint.

I was studying the ground surface around the bush and where the detectives had walked, knelt and placed equipment, where they'd scuffed and scraped the dry ground surface. I was looking for any evidence of a suspect's prints from both sides of the bush. I noticed a few black hairs mixed in with tufts of dry and wintered, but now greening grass, where the officers had been kneeling. I knelt and examined them closely. The hairs, probably four or five of them about an inch long, appeared to have been cut on both ends. I looked closer at other areas of the ground surface, and I could see other similar hairs—one here, two there. Most were mixed in with soil or grass tufts that had been beneath the officers' feet as they made their examination. I continued to look for hair and could find some further away from the bush, but not trampled upon, again caught up in the tufts of grass. Then I located a couple dark-colored, black, crusty and cinder-like clumps of material about the size of a marble or small rock. These appeared to me as though they could be clumps of coagulated blood that had dried and weathered but not completely eroded. I asked the deputy if the detectives had collected hair samples from this find. He had no idea of what they'd found, so I asked him to call the office on his radio and ask if they'd gotten all the hair samples that they needed. He went to the car radio and contacted the office.

"They want to know what hair samples you're talking about," the deputy called to me. Didn't they see this hair? Maybe not. I told the deputy to ask if they'd noticed and collected hair samples here at the scene. He was on the radio again. "They didn't see any hair," he replied. The deputy brought a dozen or so small evidence bags and tweezers from his car. I showed him the hairs in the tufts of grass and those mixed in with the dirt. "Let's get as much as possible," I told him. "It all appears to be the same." With his magnifying glass we determined that the hair all seemed to be the same color and definitely cut on both ends, all about an inch long. We put all we found into several small bags. We examined the two pieces of cinder-like material. Under the glass it appeared even more like clumps of dried blood. We also collected those and placed them in the bags.

While the deputy was busy carefully labeling and marking all the bags, I continued to examine the ground surfaces in the area of the bush. Some of the hairs were caught in tufts of grass 10 feet and more from the bush. In fact the hair seemed to be in a line from the bush, and a couple of the tufts of grass were bent downhill and away from the bush. I could see a slight mark or line that seemed to connect a couple of these tufts of grass to which one or two hairs were clinging. I looked a little further: the hairs were less frequent, but still I saw one here and there and a couple more of the cinder-like clumps about the size of a pea, and again here and there the tufts of grass were bent downhill in line with the hair and cindery material. This all belonged together somehow. The marks on the ground appeared here and there, not consistent, and differently in a place or two, but they were all related. I moved off a few steps and sat down to look at the whole scene and think. The deputy was now standing and watching me. "Whatcha finding now?" he asked.

"Well, I've found something, but can't figure out what it is."

He came to where I was sitting. I pointed out and explained what I'd found. "This all means something. I just haven't figured out what it is yet."

A second marked sheriff's car pulled up and stopped. The deputy got out and asked what we were doing. The deputy with me returned to the vehicles and they began looking at the sample bags we had filled. I continued to study the ground and the line of evidence. I went over and looked at the scrape marks on the ground between the bent grass tufts. Suddenly, I knew what it was! The head, it was the victim's head, in a garbage bag, that a coyote had bitten and torn open in places. The coyote had the bag in its mouth, trying to carry it away. The head was too heavy to be carried clear of the ground more than a few feet at a time, then it would hit the ground and be pulled along by the coyote for a few feet, until the coyote stopped to catch its breath. The hair and blood dribbled out through the holes where the coyote had bitten and torn the bag; the marks on the ground were where the head, in the bag, struck the ground and was pulled along for several feet by the coyote. The head was heavy enough to bend the tufts of grass over and cause the marks on the ground surface. There was an inconsistency because the coyote would then pick the head up and actually carry it above the ground surface for a few feet before it became too heavy and hit the ground again. I had it! If we could find the head, wherever the coyote had taken it, we'd have the body identified.

I called the deputies and explained my theory. "So how do we find the coyote?" one of them asked. The viewpoint was situated between the freeway a couple hundred yards away and the state right-of-way fence a hundred yards the opposite direction. The viewpoint exit and return to the freeway ran from our position parallel to the freeway and merged with it more than a quarter of a mile away. I said I'd continue to work the sign line where the coyote has dragged the head from this point; it seemed to be going downhill midway between the return road and the freeway.

"I don't think the coyote lives on the other side of the freeway when it's got thousands of acres on this side," I told them. "You guys go back to the roadway there and, one on each side, go along the base of the roadway. You need to be looking for a coyote run—the area will be a small trail used by rodents and other animals, and will resemble a miniature pathway or trail. The coyote will use a culvert or pipe under the road if it's large enough, so look for that, but there should be a definite trail on both sides of the roadway, so keep talking together, checking with each other about what you find. If one finds something that looks likely, the other should find something close to match it. The key will be to find a couple of the hairs. Look at the hair in the grass tufts again, so you'll both know what we're looking for. The holes in the bag should keep dribbling some of the blood and hairs here and there—they will be our clues."

We began. Now that I knew what I was looking for, the sign wasn't that hard to follow. The coyote was having quite a time getting the head through some of the sage brush clumps and down into a creek bottom and up the other side. The coyote run should be fairly clear and the deputies could find it if it in fact crossed over or under the roadway. I found a small tattered piece of black plastic clinging to the roots of a sage brush in the sign trail. A couple hairs appeared here and there. In a place or two I had to check out other intersecting animal trails, and the sign did get more difficult to follow—the cinder-like material failed to appear altogether, the hairs were found less frequently. Here and there I saw some mark—a hair, a bent tuft of grass or scrape on the bushes—so I thought I was still on it. From the top of a small ridge I could see the deputy on my side of the road working slowly and meticulously, now and then I could faintly hear him call out to the other deputy, who was out of sight on the other side of the roadway. An hour passed and well into another. My head was down and I was concentrating on following the sign line when I heard one of the deputies calling to me. "We've found it!" he shouted, obviously excited. "We found the hair going under the fence! Come on, we've found it!"

I joined them and walked along the roadway while they excitedly told me of finding the sign line just as I had described it to them. The coyote run did come through a large pipe under the roadway and had gone into the bottom of a small draw running under the right-of-way fence and off uphill some distance away. Either the highway crew or ranch owner of the adjoining property had fenced the bottom of the narrow draw with woven wire to prevent cattle from walking under the barbed-wire fence while in the ditch. The woven wire had proven too difficult for the coyote to get the head under. The coyote had dragged the head up the bank and under the barbed-wire fence before continuing on up the draw. We were on the sign line! We worked up the draw. It grew much steeper and branched several times, then near the top of the hill suddenly there was the human skull. It was lying where the coyotes had finished with it, in the open, on the grassy hillside near the top of the draw. One of the deputies had thoughtfully stuck a large plastic bag in his hip pocket and we placed the skull in it.

"Well, where's that coyote den that you said would be near?" one deputy asked. We looked around and, sure enough, about 50 feet further up the hillside there was an obvious coyote den under a large bush. We returned to the vehicles. The deputies, both grinning now, said, "Have we got it all now?" "I guess we have," I said, "Let's go."

Later a letter of thanks from the sheriff's office advised me that with the intact skull the state's pathologist was able to identify the body in the matter of a few days. The victim turned out to be a known prostitute reported missing the last week of February from Burian, Washington. The lady had been well known to local officers and the pimp for whom she worked was equally well known. Under questioning, the pimp had admitted the murder and was awaiting prosecution. The Kittitas County sheriff's office estimated the savings to their office because we'd located the victim's skull to enable identification at $200,000. Two hours of thoughtful tracking had done what conventional investigative methods might have taken two officers nearly a year to accomplish.

Professional Understanding of Tracking Techniques

Criminal prosecutions have generated many legal precedents in the past hundred years regarding footwear impression evidence and testimony. The precedents generally relate to matching footwear with an impression found at the scene of a crime and the resulting legal arguments regarding generation, production and admissibility of such evidence. Very, very few court cases have resulted in legal precedents regarding tracking evidence and testimony.

That difference between footwear-impression evidence and tracking evidence is what my career has been about. "Footwear impression" is the proper legal definition that refers to evidence collected at the scene, preserved and presented in these court proceedings. These impressions are usually clearly visible and obvious to all investigators, such as footwear impressions in blood on the floor, in the mud or dirt at the scene, in the snow, or in drywall or similar dust transfers. Crime scene investigators are trained to collect these clearly visible footwear impressions and preserve them as evidence. Typically they are preserved through photographs, casting or sometimes, actually preserving the section of flooring, wall, door, carpet or other such area containing the impression. Examiners analyze the footwear impression evidence when it comes into the laboratory. Prosecuting attorneys then present this physical evidence in court along with opinions and conclusions through the testimony of the police officers, crime scene investigators and laboratory examiners.

Trackers are also trained to locate, collect, preserve and present the same type of footwear-impression evidence that relates to a particular crime scene. The difference between the footprint evidence produced by a tracker and the footwear-impression evidence of the crime scene investigator is in the nature of the two closely related, but dramatically different, forensic examinations. Most often footwear-impression evidence relates to a laboratory application. Tracking evidence relates to a uniquely developed visual examination and recording of evidence that is most often otherwise overlooked. Trackers are specially trained to visually locate, collect, preserve and present latent footprint evidence that is not obvious, or clearly visible to experienced crime scene investigators. Inherent with tracking examinations is the training, experience and skill to accurately interpret the movement of persons, their physical and mental state, and individual characteristics from the footprint evidence.

Often crime scene investigators, prosecutors and courts lack expertise or experience in seeing or understanding tracking evidence. This lack of expertise and experience may result in questions of credibility in recognizing the expertise of trackers. These are reasonable, professional criminologists—and trackers ask them to believe something that directly relates to physical evidence that they look at but do not see! These professionals have even more difficulty accepting that experienced trackers in the proper setting have the ability to interpret the "sign story" and accurately determine personal characteristics of the sign maker. How can a tracker, looking at something other investigators can't see, determine a person's personality type; mental and physical state or condition; intent, purpose or objective; thought processes, whether panicked or rational; or level of familiarity, comfort or anxiety?

During my career, I've had the opportunity to examine, collect, preserve and testify about tracking evidence in several criminal court proceedings. The result has been legal precedents relating to tracking evidence.

⊱⊶⊙⊷⊰

At 8:00 a.m. on the bright Monday morning of June 1, 1981, the Whatcom County (Washington) Sheriff's Office requested my services as a tracker at the scene of a homicide. I responded directly from my home to the scene, a distance of about eight miles. In this instance I would be fully familiar with the necessary tracker's background information about the natural elements: humidity, temperature, dew point, wind, amount and intensity of sunlight, etc. The duty investigator on scene was Detective Sergeant Ron Peterson, who met me outside of the carport of the residence to brief me on what he knew of the incident.

An elderly lady had lived by herself in the two-story, single-family residence. Family members and friends had last seen her alive on Saturday. She was not seen on Sunday during the day and she did not answer telephone calls from other family members. Early Monday morning, her son came to the residence to check on her and found her dead. Preliminary investigation had determined that she had died of stab wounds. Within several rooms in the house were areas with significant blood on vinyl and carpeted floors. A preliminary search of the outskirts of the yard had located footprints that seemed to be exiting the lawn area and traveling into an adjoining plowed field. Peterson requested that I make determinations from the interior of the house, if possible, of 1) number of persons who may have participated in this crime; 2) possible identification of this person or persons; and 3) any other tangible, intangible or latent evidence that I might gather, conclude or form opinions about. This was a two-level house with a daylight-basement living area. We were to enter the house by the back door through a three-stall carport. This entrance opened into the second-story level of the house. There was one car parked in the center stall directly to the left of the door into the house.

As we walked past the parked car toward the door to the house, I noticed slight blood smears on the concrete floor of the carport. A soft, flat-soled shoe had stepped in or on a significant blood smear elsewhere and was leaving small blood transfers with each footstep. The marks indicated that someone making these blood-smudge transfers came from the house to the driver's door of the car, then had returned to the house. Smears on the door handle indicated that this person had used the driver's door to enter the car. The blood smudges were bright in color, and appeared to be fresh, but were completely dry.

I entered the house through the rear door into a long, vinyl-floored hallway from which there were doors to two bedrooms and a bathroom. Carpeted stairs led down to the living room, kitchen and other rooms. The central part of the hallway floor between the door of one bedroom, the bathroom and the stairs was a total smear of blood. The blood smear was pockmarked with many footwear impressions. A quick examination of these impressions clearly indicated a soft-composition, flat-soled shoe with distinctive geometric patterning. The entire blood smear with the impressions was firmly dry. This blood-smear area was approximately four feet in length and extended in all ways so that no one could have walked up or down the stairs or in or out of any of the upstairs rooms without stepping in the smear and leaving footwear impressions in the blood. I observed identical dry footwear impressions resulting from wet shoe soles on the vinyl hall-way floor entering the house via the back door. These impressions indicated that at the time the prints were made the person had been walking in the rain or through water immediately prior to entry into the house.

I examined blood footwear impressions on the carpeted stairs and in other rooms of the downstairs and each room upstairs. I determined that only one person had participated in this crime. That person had entered the house during a period when it was most likely raining outside. The same person had been in all rooms of the house—both wet footwear transfers and blood footwear transfers were clearly visible to me. I could discern no other footwear impressions of the same time frame. There were indications of barefoot prints in the carpeting and in the bedroom and bathroom. I was advised by Sgt. Peterson that the deceased lady had been barefoot. It would have been nearly impossible for more than the one person to have been involved in this crime without leaving footprint impressions in, or on, any of the bloody areas. I measured these footprints and made a drawing of the shoe, showing the geometric patterning.

Then I went outside to look at the sign that had been previously located by the outside-evidence search. Exiting the house via the same door as I had entered, I observed several large blood droplets that were in sequence leading to the left from the back door, across the carport and vehicle stall next to the one by which I had entered the house. These bloody droplets were splashed onto the concrete floor, showing rapid movement toward the open lawn area at the left corner of the carport. The droplets were not of the same full-blood consistency as those leading to the car; but instead appeared to be more watery, having blood mixed with clean water. Immediately adjacent to the corner of the concrete-pad carport, I could clearly see footprints in the grass that were different from those of investigating officers. These footprints indicated a soft, flat-soled shoe similar to that which had made the impressions on the hallway floor and in the blood smear. The footprints had been made when the grass was wet, probably when it was raining, within the same time frame as the matching footprints entering the house via the back door. I made notes of these particular characteristics.

As I lived in the area, I knew that the weather had been overcast the previous Thursday, Friday and Saturday, with intermittent rain showers. Early Saturday evening had been typical—wind and moderate to heavy rain that diminished, returning on Sunday as only slight intermittent showers. (If this were an area I was unfamiliar with, I'd need to consult someone to determine these factors.)

I explained what I was seeing to Detective Peterson and why I matched these footprints and their time frame to the footprints in the hallway. I followed this line of footprints, running in a controlled flight (which means fleeing in a controlled manner, in contrast to a panicked flight) across the lawn to a large, overgrown ditch. On the soft soil of the ditch bank, other searchers had located a deeply imbedded footwear impression. This footprint indicated a continued running stride jumping across the ditch, connecting with the running footsteps that I followed across the lawn from the carport. The deep footprint was slightly eroded by rainfall, but it still retained the general characteristics of the footwear impressions found in the hallway. Again I made notes of these particular characteristics.

The ditch-bank print led into a line of footprints across the plowed field. Other searchers were waiting patiently for me to approach their location at nine steps along this line, where they had located several small items taken from the house. I noted that the person had stepped into a hole in the uneven plowed ground and fallen, dropping a small knife, a little knob and a couple other items from both hands and leaving them where the hands had hit the ground. The person regained footing and continued in a controlled run—not panicked flight, but with direction and purpose to cross the open field as quickly as possible. I was able to find partial footprints with the same geometric patterning found in the blood smear in the hallway. The sign line continued diagonally across the field and crossed through a fence bordering a long driveway to a neighbor's residence situated in the middle of a large raspberry field. The sign line jogged down the drive-

way a short way, then crossed the opposite driveway fence into a pasture and continued running diagonally across this pasture and entered the raspberry field.

I stopped to look back along the sign line. I didn't know where this person was going, but it was obvious to me that the person knew the area and had a destination in mind. The jogging footprints went between two raspberry rows and slowed to a walking pace. The person continued walking between the rows of raspberries, then crossed through one row of berries to the right, walked a few steps between rows, then crossed another to the right and continued in this manner, systematically crossing toward the diagonal opposite corner of the field. Crossing through raspberry rows is not easy. The bushes are strung on two wires, one approximately knee high and the other at about four feet high. A person must duck and bend down to step between the two wires. In early June, the bushes are fully leafed out and new canes fill the open spaces between the older bushes. I had spent a good deal of time chasing undocumented raspberry workers through similar fields and knew well that only people who knew the manner in which these berries were pruned and tied could cross through the rows easily and with limited damage. This person crossed without tearing the bushes or breaking the canes or tripping over the wire and falling.

The sign crossing the center between two berry rows suddenly stopped and the person stood still, facing toward the owner's residence some distance away. From the opposite end and up the same alley between the rows toward the sign maker came prints of the owner's dog—stiff-legged pounces of an alerted guard animal barking and challenging this person found in his fields. Approximately 20 feet from the person, the dog stopped, and then the paw prints demonstrated an eager, fearless, bounding approach, with dancing movements around the person, who was probably petting and fondling him. This indicated to me that the dog recognized and was well acquainted with the subject. Then the dog turned abruptly and trotted  back toward the owner's house and the subject continued crawling through the berry rows.

I could see that a field-access road surrounded the entire berry field and crisscrossed through the center of it. The home, garage, machine sheds and other buildings and equipment were at the intersection, in the center of approximately 40 acres of berry rows. Our sign maker was intentionally avoiding the road around these fields and avoiding the possibility of being seen from the owner's home by making a diagonal crossing of the rectangular fields. I still didn't know where this person was going, but I knew the person had a destination in mind. The sign line continued toward the far corner of the field, crossing one or two berry rows, walking down a row then crossing another row or two, then down a few steps and across another row or two. Nearing the far corner of the field, the subject stopped and stood alongside the post supporting the tie wires. The subject leaned against the post, thinking and shuffling feet back and forth in the sandy dirt, at times standing on one foot then the other with the resting foot against the post or suspended by the berry tie wire. Turning, the person leaned with hands or forearms against the post and stood on one foot then the other, scuffing the ground with the free foot. I estimated the period of time the person spent leaning against the post to be about 20 minutes. This was probably a period of contemplation and consideration of the recent deed.

Then the subject resumed working the zigzag route across the berry rows to arrive at the end of the last berry row. I could see a small subdivision of houses that adjoined the corner of the berry fields. I was unfamiliar with this development of approximately 25 to 30 houses. The subject stood quietly at the last berry-row post securing the tie wire, then he walked quickly toward the corner of the woven-wire fence bordering the field. This point bordered the back yard of one residence. Tall grasses dominated this corner and almost hid a hole in the fence, probably made by neighborhood kids to gain access to the berries. The subject went almost to the hole, then turned abruptly in the grass and went along the barbed-wire fence toward an open field adjacent to the subdivision and behind the berry fields. Then the person stopped and climbed the barbed-wire fence and, striding through the tall grasses on the other side, walked directly to pavement that marked the end of the extended residential street. I was able to follow the footprints along the curb line of the street for approximately two blocks and past several houses until all of the moisture and field-soil transfers were lost.

At this point, the Sheriff's Chief Deputy Doug Gill approached in his car and stopped to ask for my thoughts. I told him what I'd concluded from reading the sign:

1) I believed this person was a young man (teens to mid-twenties), evidenced by the running manner, and most probably of Mexican descent, evidence by the comfort and familiarity in the berry field (and the fact that most berry-field workers in this area were Mexicans). From the damage to the berry bushes in crossing

through the rows and the depth and other disturbance of foot-falls, I estimated him to be about five feet, five inches to seven inches tall and weigh 140 to 160 pounds.

2) This was a person who lived in this subdivision.

3) This person was acquainted with the elderly lady and familiar with the interior of her home, as evidenced by the casual walking manner in the hallway after entry via the back door.

4) The homicide had occurred late Saturday night or in the early morning hours of Sunday and the person had departed the scene of the crime at or near daylight. The sign was made during and after a period of rain followed by clear sky and drying air and sunshine, elements that characterized Saturday night and Sunday morning. The appearance of the sign on the lawn and in the fields clearly showed Sunday's fair weather, indicating it was made after the heavy rain that occurred before midnight Saturday night and during the heavy dew period before the clearing, partially cloudy skies and fair weather of Sunday.

5) The person ran easily and comfortably from the house, having in mind a route to travel and conscious of the possibility of being seen crossing the open field areas. This was evidenced by his measured strides and each sequence of his travel furthering a straight line to the hole in the fence. Once reaching the relative cover of the berry rows, he immediately stopped running and began walking at a comfortable, unhurried pace.

6) The berry field owner's dog recognized this person and knew him to be friendly.

7) The subject knew that the dog would know him when it got close enough to hear his voice.

8) This person was fully familiar with the method in which raspberry bushes are pruned and tied to the supporting wires, and was very careful not to damage the bushes in going through the canes, evidence that this person had probably worked in the berry fields, helping to prune and tie the bushes.

9) This person was fully rational at the time of exiting the crime scene and thinking rationally during the entire exit routing to where I was presently standing. This was clear to me because at no time did the running sign indicate full flight, or panic flight, but rather steady, rapid crossing the exposed, open areas at a controlled running gait. The subject chose a route that led, in small zigzags, to the hole in the woven-wire fence at the corner of the berry field. Only someone living in the subdivision would know of this hole in the fence, obviously made and used by children, going to and from the berry field. This person didn't go through the hole in the fence as it opened directly into a back yard and he would have to pass alongside someone's house to the street in front. Instead he stopped and chose to cross the fence in the other direction so he could walk directly onto the dead-end street pavement hidden from sight in the tall grasses.

10) This person stopped before coming to the final corner of the berry field and spent an estimated 20 minutes in contemplation, as indicated by his actions while relaxing and leaning on the post.

Chief Gill said there was an individual who fit this description who lived with his family in the subdivision and who was known to the department. I asked if he'd like me to examine around the person's house and attempt to find matching prints after he obtained a search warrant. He agreed and I'd return to my office to prepare a report to be used as information to support the application for the search warrant.

Subsequently, a young Mexican male was arrested and held for trial, charged with first-degree murder. Probable cause was clearly established because when he was located, the suspect was wearing the shoes worn during the homicide. The suspect was well known to the victim and had visited in her home often. The suspect was seen in the area of the deceased's home at about midnight that Saturday night as he tried to gain entry to another residence during a period of heavy rain. These facts and other detail evidence seemed to establish beyond a reasonable doubt that this defendant had committed the crime. The suspect's shoes were taken into custody and examined. William Bodziak of the FBI was called to present the conclusive evidence of the shoes matching the footwear impressions found in the house. Traces of the victim's blood were found on the shoes. Defense attorneys, facing an overwhelming weight of evidence, pleaded their client not guilty, intending to argue a defense of diminished mental capacity. The defendant was known to have learning disabilities. My report and conclusions about the footwear impressions at the scene, along with the sign line and the sign story became crucial prosecution evidence to refute this defense tactic.

In laying the background for my courtroom testimony, prosecutors questioned when and how I had learned to interpret or "read" sign-maker information from the sign line. They asked me to explain in detail and give descriptive examples of sign aging, ability to determining height, weight and background of a subject, identifying fear, discomfort or irrational thinking, and how it's possible to see and understand physical evidence that other professional crime-scene investigators look at and do not see.

Defense attorneys conceded my ability to identify and follow a sign line from point A to point B, but objected to my ability to testify as an expert as to the personality and mental state of the subject. The judge decided to allow the testimony step by step and, based upon the testimony itself, made the decision to accept the testimony, overruling defense objections. During the summation of my testimony, the judge requested a conference in chambers with both attorneys and me. He discussed the presentation of my evidence with the defense attorneys who had objected on numerous occasions, laying the groundwork for a possible appeal should the defendant be convicted. The judge told the prosecuting attorney that he believed that my testimony had been fully sufficient in outlining my experience to accept that I had the experience, knowledge and skill to accurately interpret the mental state of the sign maker. However, he admonished the prosecutor that to have me testify about whether I could determine the sign maker's ethnic origin would open an unneeded and undesirable line of questioning and possible grounds for future appeals. The prosecutor conceded that this one point was not necessary for jurors to decide the guilt or innocence of the defendant and the question as to his mental state.

Subsequently the defendant was convicted of murder in the first degree. The jury concluded from the facts I had interpreted from the subject's sign line that the defendant did not have diminished mental capacity, and had been in fact, fully aware and cognizant of his actions during the commission of the crime and throughout his travel route immediately after exiting the crime scene.

Defense attorneys filed a mistrial appeal which was sustained and the case was subsequently remanded for retrial. The prosecution presented the same case and again I testified. We were successful again in convincing the court based on my testimony that the defendant was fully aware and cognizant during the commission of the crime. Defense attorneys then appealed to the State Supreme Court, which upheld the conviction, and the case was appealed to the federal level at the 9th Circuit Court of Appeals. The defense argument before the 9th Circuit Court focused on the ability of a tracker, as an expert, to interpret a person's state of mind, thought processing, intent, objective, comfort, etc. Ultimately the 9th Circuit, the most liberal of all federal court jurisdictions, sustained all points of the conviction based on the facts contained in the record.

I'll refer back to FBI footwear-impressions specialist William Bodziak, who makes the following statements in writing *Footwear Impression Evidence*:

Crimes involve people and places. Persons committing a crime leave footwear impressions en route to, at, and exiting the crime scene. Footwear impression evidence has been frequently undervalued by investigators, attorneys, and the courts due to their limited knowledge of it. What is not looked for will not be seen. (page 2)

Bodziak struggled for 20 years to educate crime-scene examiners, laboratory examiners and court systems in the use of footwear impressions. We share a camaraderie and common belief in that for the same 20 years I have struggled to educate the same people and systems in the use of tracking evidence. Well-trained trackers offer law enforcement another investigative technique that has been court proven. Legal precedents, that have been sustained by higher courts, now permit the admission of factual tracking evidence that is otherwise lost to criminal prosecutions. Trackers are specially trained to see that which others look at and do not see!

Fleeing Fugitive Incidents

Many people more readily relate their ideas or concepts of tracking operations to the incident of a fugitive fleeing from a crime scene or an escapee from an institution. However in only a very few instances do the circumstances provide this opportunity for professionally trained trackers. In this chapter I have related several instances in which my services were requested to assist with a crime scene examination or incident. These instances are a fair representation of when and how trackers generally assist law enforcement incidents. I have been fortunate to participate in several fleeing fugitive incidents such as that told in the stories "The Most Dangerous Prey, Hot Pursuit" and others included in this book. However such incidents are the exception and not the usual, normal utilization of tracking resources.

Anyone rushing or fleeing from an incident leaves sign more readily found and followed simply due to the characteristic that haste or flight generally precludes care and caution as to the sign line left behind. A person running or fleeing across or through an area doesn't have the opportunity to observe and select the avenue of escape or exit. The very act of running or fleeing is forceful, dynamic and creates more footprint damage or sign than the same person would if walking rapidly along the same route. Running footfalls strike the ground surface hard and the forward thrust from the ball of the foot is dramatic, both leaving obvious and definite sign. Running footfalls nearly destroy ground surface vegetation, rip, tear, bend and break brush or other vegetation from knee high to head high. Such sign is usually quite easily followed by anyone with moderate interest and using common sense. When the fleeing subject gets tired of running or out of breath and slows to a walk the untrained tracker is usually lost.

The possibility of fleeing fugitives being armed and a danger to the tracker is a concern for responsible law enforcement officials. However with only two exceptions, in my thirty years association with this vocation I have never known of any tracker being hurt or injured by a fleeing subject that was being tracked. One exception to this statement is the southern border trackers of border enforcement agencies however that's a special and exceptional environment. The second exception is the U.S. military presently in combat zones of the middle east and again theirs' is a special and exceptional environment. I encourage and caution tracking students that are comfortable and confident in undertaking fleeing fugitive requests to concentrate on the tracking, and let others provide whatever security is appropriate.

⊱┈✦┈◦┈✦┈⊰

CHAPTER ELEVEN

The Mountain Man
Tracking a Mystery Subject

I knew that I was listening too carefully and watching for something, anything to move—a branch, a shadow—anything. I drew a long breath realizing how tight I was. I was trying too hard, straining to see or hear something. I needed to relax some and glanced down at my feet. I closed my eyes for a moment and tried to think of something else. My boots were wet from the climbing through damp underbrush—heck, I was wringing wet all over! What the heck was I doing here? We had been climbing hard all morning cutting sign while trying not to miss anything. I glanced at my watch—almost two o'clock. We'd taken a break at the creek below while we were trying to find where the trail went from there, so it was a working break. I slowly drew another deep breath and glanced around at the rest of the team; we needed to stop for lunch and break this spell. The damp overcast dreariness made it seem even darker and more closed in than it was. We were now on a very steep wooded hillside of old down and dead timber with small living trees stunted and gnarled, we were spread apart so we could clearly see each other. The nature of this whole setting would tend to make anyone wary if not spooked. I knew the others were as tight as I was.

What were we doing here? This was New Year's Eve 1997. While most people were getting ready for a wild night on the town, here we were tiptoeing through a dense, rain-soaked Eastern Snohomish County wilderness of Western Washington's Cascade Mountains in search of a peculiar fugitive nicknamed "The Mountain Man." A midwinter hike like this was one of those ventures that some would excitingly plan for and I would shun as a mindless waste of energy without some practical reason for doing it. It wasn't really cold, maybe 45 to 50 degrees, but I knew everyone was as wet with sweat from the climbing and crawling through the brush as I was.

I glanced around at the two armed SWAT members, who were twenty steps or so behind me and to either side, carefully scrutinizing the hillside above and ahead of us. I glanced to the right, 20 yards or so away—Kathy Wilhelm, an experienced Snohomish County SAR tracker, had her head down and was busy studying the ground, while grasping a fir bough tip to keep her footing. To the left and a little further away but at about the same elevation was Phil Vining, another experienced Snohomish SAR tracker. I watched as Phil worked up an open incline through a broken and smashed old-growth's slick and slimy wreckage. I shivered involuntarily, I didn't like the "feel" of this situation. Sweat streamed down my face and back—no wonder my boots felt soaked inside and out. The slope we were on was steep, but it didn't seem so bad because we were moving slowly and for the most part with our heads down examining the ground, until we looked behind us and realized we weren't looking behind, we were looking DOWN! Any injury out here from a slip or fall would be serious because we were several miles from where we had left the vehicles at the end of the logging road below. We had begun from the end of the road before good light knowing the first section of the trail from the previous trips and wanting to get an early start. Dark would begin to come into the trees below shortly after 4 p.m. We were prepared to stay the night if necessary on the mountain, but sleeping out in the woods without a good reason wasn't in my play book.

This was one of those eerie situations that directors and set designers try to develop for the movies. The damp and dark drearily silent woods, stark and ghostly, blended with our overwhelming expectation of something, who knows what, but something happening just any second. We had resorted hours ago to whispers, staring to gain attention, and hand signals in order to not make any noise ourselves and to hear everything else. Every little noise—a bird calling, a squirrel chattering or jumping from tree to tree—caused us all to jump and turn, straining to see something. Any sudden loud voice would shake the trees and even the rocks themselves, and probably even draw live fire. I looked down at my feet again to hide a big grin just thinking how they'd jump if I suddenly clapped my hands together.

Tony Aston and Glenn Bergstrom, the two members of the Snohomish County SWAT were on edge even more than the tracking team, since it was their job to protect us as we worked. They were short one or two men today and this made them even more anxious and probably nervous but I'm sure they wouldn't admit that. They were trying to stay closely positioned somewhat between and slightly behind to cover all three trackers all of the time while not exposing themselves needlessly. Glenn was crouched against the trunk of a tree, now looking at me watching everyone else. Glenn sensed that I was thinking something—I could see the question on his face. Tony to the other side was watching Phil. I didn't really think that we were in danger of being attacked. But the atmosphere of the situation, coupled with the attitude and deep seriousness of the cover team slowly seeped into the team psyche. From what I knew of him from police reports, I suspected the Mountain Man was more likely to run away from us than toward us. My real fear was that he would hear us, see us or otherwise know that we were coming and slip away deeper into the mountains. The only way that he would likely endanger one of us was if we cornered him or we came upon him unexpectedly and someone got hurt in his trying to escape. We knew he was armed, but being armed for defense didn't mean he was prone to attacking anyone. Glenn, in on all the law enforcement discussions, agreed but wasn't about to take chances.

The Mountain Man was the local nickname given to a mysterious, reclusive Bulgarian freedom fighter who had somehow managed to live for almost thirteen years in the deep wilderness of state and national forest areas of Eastern Snohomish County in Western Washington. Barely 100 miles from Seattle, this was more like a novel or movie script than reality. When and how he entered the United

States as an escapee from a Bulgarian prison was as much a mystery as how he was mistakenly released from custody after being charged in a neighboring county with attempted homicide. He was now being pursued as a fleeing felon by Snohomish sheriff's personnel. Having tried every conventional method of apprehending the elusive nocturnal burglar who seemed almost to be more a figment of folklore than reality, authorities finally thought that tracking might be the answer. That was why I was there, sweating, tired and responsible for the tracking team. A couple things became very clear as we searched for sign of him: he was not a normal person, and he did *not* want to be found.

I turned and looked toward Kathy again. As if she felt my eyes, she looked up and I motioned for her to come to me. I looked toward Phil, who was almost out of sight around some stumps and brush. When I got his attention, I motioned for him to move across the hill toward me. I had last seen sign of the trail just to my left and moved carefully over toward Glenn, who had been watching my hand signals to Phil and Kath, and he signaled to Tony to join us. I found a place where a couple of trees formed a small, somewhat level spot big enough for the five of us to gather. Glenn and Tony were moving slowly, all the while keeping an eye open uphill and down. When we all got close together, I said softly, "Lunchtime." No one argued, not even Phil, who was like a hound on a trail when he got going.

Everyone was glad for a few minutes' break. I remained standing, leaning against a tree, and said just loud enough for all to hear clearly, "You guys are too quiet. Relax—you're beginning to make me spooky!" That broke the spell and everyone began to relax. We slid off our packs and opened up eats. Glenn began to lay out an elaborate picnic from a military MRE packet, though his attention wasn't so diverted that he didn't keep watch all around us. Phil stepped around the tree I was leaning on to relieve himself and emerged holding up an empty 7-Up can that he had found tucked tightly against the base of the tree trunk. "Yeah, we're right on the sign line here," I said softly.

Kathy remarked that she had just marked some sign when I signaled her to come over. She said there seemed to be a great deal of sign, coming and going, back and forth, but not in any one definable trail like we were looking for. Phil said he too had found a good deal of older sign in the area he had been working. We ate and softly talked about the sign line, age, condition and characteristics. The tracks returning home had just disappeared down below at the last landing area where the creek began. The creek began as an overflow from a small lake formed in the pocket of the saddle between a little hump and this main mountain ridge. Obviously that was an area in which the Mountain Man spent considerable time and wasn't concerned about being found or seen. His sign, from a week to several years old, could be seen nearly everywhere. This was the difficulty. We could find the sign, but finding where it came from and where it went to that would lead us to where he was living, that was the problem. We didn't want to encounter him while he was out strolling around; we wanted to find him at home and in his bed, if possible. Keeping track of the trail here on this hillside was a real tracking chore. Simply finding sign was easy once you knew what to look for, but determining his road home took experience and tracking skill. Our tracking team needed to be able to "read" the sign they were seeing, to see and disregard the sign of aimless wandering, to look for things like specific rocks, pieces of wood or brush, and to be able to distinguish purposeful coming-and-going footprints. Both Kathy and Phil were good trackers, always learning, asking questions, and comparing sign aging and characteristics.

Glenn and Tony mostly listened as we watched Glenn prepare and begin to eat his four- or five-course meal. They asked about the bright shining nails that we'd seen pounded into the base of some of the trees, and wondered about the possibility of trip wires. Trip wires didn't seem likely, I speculated aloud. There wasn't any other contributing evidence, no wire or line of any kind for one thing, and no evidence on the nails that there had been. I had to admit, however, that I didn't have any other explanation.

Booby-trapping must have been the purpose, but if so, the traps had yet to be completed. These were bright nails, either stainless steel or polished aluminum, and they didn't look like aluminum. Most of

them had been there awhile—two, three or four years.There wasn't
anything fresh. They were Forest Service nails all right, but I sure
didn't think this was a Forest Service project. There just wasn't any
other reasonable explanation except trip wires. If these were in fact
tripwire setups, then we were a lot closer than I had thought we would
be. That was one of the factors that had gotten everyone so uptight—
we all sensed somehow that we might be close to the heart of the
Mountain Man's domain. This was certainly a good place to have a
hideout if you could find a place level enough to do more than stand
up. Lots of old-growth trees, both fir and cedar, that hadn't been logged
since the first cut at the turn of the century, had fallen down now and
would provide wood for fires as well as building. Huge trees lay splintered and broken here and there all over the hillside. The hillside was
so steep anyone perched above would be able to see and hear approaching visitors quite easily, and even the strongest Olympic sprinter wasn't
going to run up this hill and catch anyone!

As we rested, I was listening more than watching. This wasn't a
very good place to watch anything unless it was something downhill.
I'd have to depend on my feelings, studying the sign, and my ears. I
knew the others were waiting for me to say something, to explain why
I had decided to call a halt here and now. I slid down the tree trunk
and sat quietly trying to put all of my thoughts together, sift them
down and shake them out. Something was nagging just on the edge of
my consciousness. Just what *did* I have in my mind? I glanced at my
watch and saw that it was 2:45 p.m. Here we were, the five of us, high
on the side of a steep hillside on an overcast, gloomy day that would
suddenly grow pitch black by five o'clock. We were at best, two hours
from the vehicles, and that would mean some real humping, heading
downhill on steep, slippery, and rugged terrain. Dark would come later
this high on the mountain, ensuring that once dusk came, it would be
midnight black below us. We would have an hour and a half at the
most before dark. This wasn't the place to be after dark, Mountain
Man or no Mountain Man. I looked up again. The hill was so steep
that, while it seemed that I could see the top not very far above us, it

very easily could be a bench on the mountainside and there could be several more benches between us and the top. I asked Phil how high we were. He rubbed his chin and squinted uphill, then looked down, then around and grinned. "Well," he said in his customary slow thoughtful drawl, "depends if you're looking up or down."

Kathy broke out her altimeter and Phil the map. They discussed our position and with input from Glenn, generally agreed that we must be at about 2,500 feet, and the top of this ridge was 2,700 feet, according to the map. All of us could look up and see that the top was more than 200 feet further up. Phil studied the map; he was more familiar with the mountain than any of us and said, "The microwave relay station is at 2,700 feet, but we may not be where we think we are on the mountain. It could be quite a bit farther than it looks like from the map." He threw in the comment that he was very surprised that we had not hit snow already. When you live in a region of 10,000- and 12,000-foot mountains, 2,700 feet doesn't really sound like much, but when you begin at near sea level in the valley floor, every step upward is earned.

Glenn was clearing away his banquet, quietly replacing his gear. "Whatcha thinking?" he asked. I responded, intentionally talking softly. None of us had to think about being quiet. There was just something about the "feel" in the thick, damp air that had for the past couple hours permeated all of us. We weren't spooked, just wary, and even when we were more relaxed we still had the feeling we were being watched, something like stepping into the dark, expecting at any minute to bump into or maybe be touched by something.

"I don't like the feel of this," I said. "We're at best an hour and a half from dark, we're on the 'good' sign line. This is the route he used in and out the last time. I don't think we're very far away from where he lives. I'd rather not arrive on his doorstep right at dark. That gives him all of the advantage, especially if the house is somewhere on this side-hill. We're not prepared for a couple days on his sign should he spot us and run. We could do it, but we really didn't come prepared for this. I think we're too close to go further unless we want to figure on being able to stay with it till we get him."

"You think he knows we're here?" Glenn asked.

"No, I don't think so, but I wouldn't be at all surprised. I think we increase that possibility with every step uphill, though."

Tony asked, "Do you see anything different in the sign?"

"No, the sign is still just coming down the mountain and going back home, though he's been all over this hillside in the past three or four years. Kath, Phil, any other ideas?" I asked, looking from one to the other. Kathy offered that she hadn't seen anything to indicate he was aware that anyone might be around. In fact, all of the sign she was seeing was older, a month or more, some several months. Phil agreed that the sign he was seeing was older too. We were seeing a great deal of sign, but no fresh sign and little evidence even of any main trail.

"Well, guys," I said, taking another look around, "we can pack up and hit the back-trail, hump right along and we'll just make the vehicles before it gets too dark to see. We wait another thirty minutes and the last mile will be by feel. So it's either go on up and stay the night, and maybe a couple more on the trail, or head out now. I vote for heading out now. I'd rather come back prepared to stay until we get him. We know the trail to here and can get to this spot in a couple hours, then have the most of the day to do whatever we have to do. I think that by continuing on now, we hand the advantage to him. I still think we can run him down, but I'd rather do it the easy way if possible. Why make it an outright challenge."

Glenn, who was in charge of the operation, looked around at each of them. "This is a good place to start next time and push to the finish," he said.

The going down was more hazardous than going up. We were slipping and sliding, trying not to create unusual sign and trying to be as quiet as possible. I was trying to see whatever we had missed on the way up. "Carrying sign", a term trackers use to mean they have the sign line as if they were following a string line, sometimes causes you to become so focused that you tend to miss some obvious things along the way. We had worked back and forth across the sign line trying to be sure that we were seeing everything that was important. Here and there, the Mountain Man had taken side trips to somewhere or would reenter the main routing from somewhere and each side excursion had to be checked out. Here and there we would find areas that he obviously liked and would spend time. We were trying to be careful to not leave an obvious trail that he might notice and that would indicate our team's pursuit of him. I wanted to mark several areas to spend more time checking around on my return, but didn't dare use any type of marking that he would notice or that would be noticed by someone else. I made mental notes of reference for each location. A tree here, a stump there, the way a sapling was bent or leaning.

This would be a New Year's Eve to tell the grandkids about. If only we'd had a couple more hours, I would have felt differently about turning around up there. Phil was sure that the Bulgarian's home was across the valley from the ridge that we were on, but the sign sure didn't say so. It looked to me like we had been within shouting distance of the hideout when we stopped. Phil was a local. He lived in the Darrington Valley and had been working this guy's sign for three or four years, off and on. He had found sign that he believed was the Bulgarian's much further back in the mountains. This guy had covered a good deal of the mountainside in his travels. Some of the sign was fairly recent, some of it was two or three years old, and some was even older—the guy had been here for 13 years or so. But to me the scattered sign going uphill the last 200 or 300 yards sure looked like a direct climb to the house. This guy was a real study that was sure.

We came out to the vehicles after dark. Our eyes had adjusted as the light left us and we could see reasonably well, but we were relieved when we finally came to the edge of the timber where the land had already been logged. We were tired, wet with sweat, and it had taken nearly two hours to come down, with only one five-minute rest—we'd humped some. It would take a good two and a half hours to re-climb the same route. Working the sign in we had taken our time. That and the side-trail examinations had taken time, so it wasn't as though we were climbing all of the time.

We unloaded at the vehicles and Glenn came to talk. "How close do you think we were?"

"I think we were as close as we dared get unless we were prepared and willing to do whatever was necessary to get him."

Glenn scratched his head, glancing up the mountain. "Think he could see or hear us? Has he been watching us?" he asked.

"No, I didn't see or hear anything that would make me think that," I said. "I just have a feeling. The sign looks to me like we were within striking distance. The problem is that we're all tired. We've put in a hell of a day. We've been working since six thirty this morning without a stop until we got together up there. Remember, when we started this morning we didn't have any real hope of getting close. We just wanted to work out the sign on that first hillside and make sure we had a route going somewhere." We didn't get that cautious up there for nothing, we were close." I leaned up against the truck as I changed out of my hiking boots. "We did that and more. I've learned to be sensitive to what the sign is telling me, and it was telling me that we'd better either stop where we were or figure that we were going to jump him."

Kath and Phil had come up close and were listening. "So what's next?" Kath asked.

I suggested that we return, head right back to where we had quit today and begin again, with the intention of staying on the trail until we got our man. I told them that I was sure we were on his main route and were pushing the sign uphill pretty well.

Glenn spoke again, "Whatcha think, provisions for overnight? Maybe two or three days?"

I looked at Kathy and Phil, "Yeah, I think that would do it. If we play our cards right we won't have to chase him anyway. We can get close if we read the sign well enough, keep doing what we were doing this afternoon."

"Might be snow up there soon," drawled Phil, "should be two or three feet of snow up there right now, so something to think about."

"He'll be coming out again for provisions in a couple weeks, so we want to go in before that or after. I don't want to be going in looking for his sign when he's headed down the mountain, he'd spot us long before we saw him."

"Right," Glenn said, "I'll get with Danny and bring him up to speed. He'll give everyone a call when we go again."

Kathy and I had ridden from I-5 together and on the 30-minute drive back to her vehicle we talked the sign and characteristics from the day's work and put that together with the previous several days we had spent sign cutting the area. We were still speculating when I dropped her off and headed on north. I still had another hour's drive home and I was beat.

I began to go over the entire project in my mind. I thought about the Bulgarian and the job ahead. We had been lucky so far, especially with the weather. It had rained most of the half dozen or so days we had been out sign cutting for the main trail. But it hadn't been cold and nasty, except for one day. That one day when we headed for the vehicles at dark we were spattered with a wet blinding snow. For the most part it had been just light rain and not cold, and if that held for one more trip we'd have it done.

Phil's knees had been really bothering him today; it wouldn't have been good to spend the night on the mountain. I was trying to recall, was it three years ago or four that Phil had first asked for ideas as to how he might trap the Bulgarian burglar? We'd been at a tracking course, I remembered that for sure. I had known Phil for 15 years or more. Phil had come to his first tracking class with a dedicated interest in learning all he could from me. He already knew about tracking but wanted formal training to enable him to do even more. He lived near Darrington, within shouting distance of where we had been working and between two of the resort communities most often frequented by the Bulgarian. Phil was well known in the Darrington Valley. He'd been a search and rescue responder for many years and was a responsible participant in community affairs. Phil spends a good deal of time thinking about what he wants to say before he says it. In reply to the questions that I asked, Phil told me in his own way what he knew about the Bulgarian.

The Bulgarian had come to the Darrington Valley a dozen or more years ago. He lived like a hermit in the mountains. Many, including Phil, figured he made his home somewhere behind  White Horse Mountain, the most notorious if not the most prominent peak in this section of the Cascades. The peak is claimed by both Arlington and Darrington Valley residents as theirs. The guy would come down out of the mountains and burglarize summer homes weekend cabins and ever more frequently now, the local resident homes. For the most part the guy only took food or other smaller items obviously needed for his existence in the woods. This had been going on for more than ten years and most of the early incidents went unreported. When the burglaries were reported to the sheriff's office they were seldom given much importance, investigation or attention due to the value of items taken. Often owners didn't even know when the burglary took place due to the infrequency of their own visiting on weekends, holidays or vacation periods. Residents often couldn't accurately remember what had been there and couldn't specifically detail what items might be missing. But over the years, the stories accumulated, and local residents began to get increasingly upset about having a burglar who was always lurking around in the woods behind their houses and couldn't be caught.

Before that, people had always felt quite secure in the Darrington Valley, leaving their houses unlocked, keys in the car. Kids played outside and on the street with little parental concern. This certainly wasn't Seattle. This was a small rural community where everyone knew everyone else, with the exception of the tourists that traveled through. Now however with the increase of violence seemingly everywhere, locals began to complain about this burglar who skulked around their houses at night, waiting and watching where and when to enter and take whatever he wanted. People began to pressure the sheriff's office to do something about this violation of their space and privacy. Investigating officers asked more questions, filed more reports and poked around the neighborhood, looking for evidence of the burglar. In 1995 the Snohomish County Sheriff's Office had made a serious attempt to capture the man. They researched case files and made up flyers that were distributed throughout the county. They responded to burglary reports and used surveillance and police dogs in attempts to locate the subject. All efforts were fruitless, the burglaries continued, and deputies got frustrated and found other things to do.

Phil was a Boeing aircraft engineer. Catching the Bulgarian burglar was a challenge, not because he was doing any real harm but because it was a challenge. Phil wanted to learn tracking to be a better resource for lost person search and rescue operations. He well knew that "tracking" was a resource that could not only identify the burglar but in fact follow his sign trail to wherever he lived in the mountains. Phil made it known to resident deputies who initially responded to burglary reports that he was interested in attempting to track this culprit. He responded to the burglary scene when notified and identified footprints of the burglar by measuring and drawing the description of the tracks. Phil then worked the sign whenever possible, usually on his days off, backtracking and following and learning the habits and characteristics of the individual as he'd learned to do in the tracking classes. Phil had amassed a good deal of information about this person, had felt he had gotten close a couple times, but had been unable to actually   follow the sign trail back into the mountains. When Phil went into the mountains sign cutting for the individual, he found sign—lots of sign—but sorting the trails out and determining which was the one that went to where the guy was living seemed an impossible task.

We had consulted, Phil and I. He continued to work the case as he had time available. I had gone to Darrington on one occasion and spent the afternoon with Phil going over the information he had gathered and looking over the areas in which he had found sign. He discussed the case with other Snohomish County SAR trackers and together they spent time helping Phil to cut for sign, locate and follow various trails and gather information.

My part in this episode began in late fall of 1997, when I was contacted by the Snohomish County SAR coordinator, John Taylor. John and I had been professional colleagues and personal friends for more than 20 years. He was one of the most respected SAR coordinators in Washington State, having been in the position for more than 20 years. John was known as a proficient and notorious procurer of government surplus equipment for SAR use. A respected helicopter pilot, he had procured several surplus helicopters for Snohomish County and now had the largest fleet of air worthy "birds" operated by any county in the northwest. Within Snohomish and adjoining counties, John was very respected for his intimate knowledge of the relatively uninhabited mountainous areas of state, federal and private forest lands in Snohomish County.

John quickly explained to me that he was making contact for the Snohomish County SWAT sergeant, Danny Wickstrom. He said Danny needed to talk with me about the Bulgarian in Darrington. John went on to briefly explain that Sgt Wickstrom had been assigned to apprehend the Bulgarian and wanted my input as to how to go about the project. He added that he had told Danny that I was the best tracker around and it was his opinion that tracking was the only practical method of finding the subject. The next day I introduced myself by phone to Sgt. Danny Wickstrom. He asked what and how much I knew about the Bulgarian case. I replied that I knew of the case, but actually knew very little factual information about it, or about the subject. We arranged a meeting for the following week. Danny explained that he had been assigned as the new SAR coordinator since John Taylor was retiring. The Snohomish County Sheriff's Department had determined that this case should be the responsibility of the SWAT sergeant and SAR coordinator. After all, this guy did live in the woods like a hermit. Danny was concerned that I fully understand the case and the possibilities before I gave assurance that I would be interested in assisting or contributing to the case. Equally, he wanted me to understand that he was new to working in the woods, didn't have a SAR background, wasn't a survivalist, and most of all, had no preconceived notions as to how to go about getting this guy. While many people had opinions about how to accomplish the arrest, few of them intended to be involved in their own schemes. Danny had an open mind and wanted realistic ideas and consultation. The sheriff was serious about getting this guy into custody and had confidence that Danny could do the job when others had failed.

Shortly afterward, a meeting was held at a substation of the Snohomish County Sheriff's Office near Snohomish, Washington. Coffee was poured and introductions were made. The cast of characters around the planning table included the detective sergeant, two of the "upriver" deputies, Danny and me. I wanted to know all that they knew about this guy and his manner and method of operations. The detective sergeant had the paper file and quickly went through it. The file consisted mainly of burglary reports from the past three or four years, all with little or no follow up, all referencing the Bulgarian. Some reports referred to entry by kicking the door in, others by cutting a hole in the door and reaching in to unlock it, still others described entry through a window. Most of the reports came from homeowners returning to their property after an absence of a week or longer and therefore the exact time of entry was difficult to determine. Most of the burglaries seemed to fall into a well-defined pattern of activity. I quickly leafed through the reports and sorted them into two piles, those that fit the profile and those that reflected a different manner of entry or items taken.

I quickly sifted through the pile of Bulgarian burglaries, noting the dates of the reports. The reports related to activity occurring along nearly a 10-mile strip of summer homes, cabins and residences bordered by the Stillaguamish River, an old railroad right of way, and state highway 530. The railroad tracks had been removed and now a hiking and jogging trail afforded access along the entire area using the track bed. During the previous couple years sheriff's deputies answering such calls in the area had called Phil to come when he could, to look for sign around the burglary scene. Phil had told me of finding sign of the Bulgarian walking and crossing this access route. I had advised him to make "track traps", small areas raked clean to capture footprints in strategic locations to determine time, date and direction of travel of the intruder. Phil had been able to gather some information from these track traps and other areas that readily captured the footfall of this individual.

Slowly Phil began to build a knowledge base of the activities of this person—his routing, manner of travel, and personal characteristics. Actually Phil probably knew this individual better than anyone else now, and certainly knew more about his habits and mannerisms. This information would become of vital importance if we were ever able to talk face to face with this guy.

The talk went on around me at the table. But for the obvious physical evidence of the break-in and resulting damage, nearly every event could be attributed to people's imagination stimulated by stories of the same substance as Big Foot and the Loch Ness monster. People of the Darrington Valley believed the stories that grew with each telling and over time losing facts and gaining imaginary substance. There were the reported "sightings" of this shadowy individual in back yards and through the trees on a dark night, crossing the highway in car lights, much the same as with the notorious Big Foot. The deputies who responded gave such calls the same amount of validity, no matter the indignation of reporting parties who "knew what they saw."

I was methodically going through the reports, looking for and sorting papers as to various similarities, times of year, locations, booty taken, time lapse during which there had been no one at the residence, etc. I made several piles of the three dozen or so reports. A couple things became clear to me: One, most of the reports had been taken rather superficially, without much diligence since it was supposed that the burglary was the work of the Bulgarian. No one expected to catch the Bulgarian because no one had. And two, he seemed more a figment of the imagination than real, and not a high priority on the rating system of criminals.

"Okay," I said to all at the table. "First, we need to have someone pull all of the incident reports for the past ten years that might seem to relate to or fit into this MO. It's obvious that there are some that are not in this file. Second, when we have the entire pile of those, we need to have someone go through them one by one and separate them into categories. First eliminate those that don't fit the characteristics, either by time and place, items taken, or manner of entry and damages, as I've done with these. Then, we need to make a pin map of the area to show where the burglaries took place and during what month of the year. Then we can begin to actually do some sign cutting."

Danny looked puzzled. "Why do we need to do all that?" he asked.

"Well for one thing," I replied, "we think these burglaries only take place along a strip about 10 or 12 miles long, and at all times of the year, right?" He nodded. "But Danny, do you really know that? Does anyone here at this table actually know that?"

Everyone looked at each other, and one of the deputies answered, "Well, all of the burglaries take place in the Darrington Valley along the river."

"Yes, but what about over the hill in Skagit County? Do they have similar burglaries in similar areas? And what about down river toward Arlington?" I continued. "Are there break-ins with similarities down that way that would fit the same characteristics?" No one answered.

"Let's back up and begin at the beginning. First of all, I'm invited to this meeting because for the first time in years someone is serious about taking this guy into custody, right?" Nods all around. "Over the past several years, it has become common knowledge that this guy lives in the Darrington Valley and he burglarizes homes, but no one knows who he is or where he lives and no one has actually seen him, right?" All were listening and their silence confirmed what I was saying. These were good, experienced law enforcement officers building a mental image of the scene as I laid it out. I was helping them to see what I could see and hoping to ensure that they also would be able to see what I didn't see—the holes, the facts that were not in evidence.

"Let me ask this question of you," I said. "Does anyone at this table actually know why we're calling this suspect the Bulgarian? Is he actually from Bulgaria, or does he speak with an accent or look like what someone thinks a Bulgarian looks like, or what? Where and when did the title or term Bulgarian come from? Do we have any information that this guy is actually dangerous or violent, other than the fact that he does the burglaries?"

They looked from one to another. Danny cleared his throat and looked at them each one. Finally Glenn, the upriver deputy who lived in the Darrington Valley and had been with the sheriff's office for several years in the back country, spoke up: "The guy *is* from Bulgaria. I remember a few years ago, a real effort was made to get this guy. A *real* effort. We had units that sat up there night after night watching for him. Took the dogs into the woods where we thought he was and even found some kind of brush huts, camping sites and such where we thought he was living. During that time we were all pretty much aware of the information relating to this guy. He's from Bulgaria, all right. He was arrested in King or Pierce County and they turned him loose and that's when he came up here. I think they still have a warrant for him for arson or something else. It seems like they did at that time, anyway. That's where we got most of the information on him. In some of the burglaries there were fingerprints taken that were good, from the windows or glass items that he fiddled with in the house during the burglary and the fingerprints matched. That's how we knew it was the Bulgarian.

"As to him being dangerous, a few years ago one of the Forest Service timber cruisers was working or marking a timber sale over on the side of Three Fingers Mountain. He was going through the woods approaching a big old cedar stump when a guy jumped up on the top of the stump and started waving around a big pistol. He yelled for the cruiser to get out of there or he'd get shot. The cruiser thought that this was the Mountain Man, and he retreated and got out of there. There have been other incidents over the years when people have encountered a man in the woods with pretty much the same description who had the same type of reaction. We know that he has taken weapons several times in burglaries, so we know he has access to weapons. I'd consider him dangerous till I found out otherwise."

"Okay, that's a start then," I said. "But if he's a Bulgarian, where was he born? When did he come to the U.S. and what else do we know for sure about him?" All of us at the table were looking at Glenn. Obviously they were hearing this information for the first time.

"Well," Glenn said, "I don't really know all that. What I remember hearing was that he was some type of immigrant from Bulgaria. He came to this area about the same time as the body of that other Bulgarian who was found in the plastic bag floating in the river."

"What's that story?" I asked. Glenn was now on guard, aware that I wanted to know hard information and not general rumor, supposition, or conjecture.

"I'd need to go back to some old reports to remember for sure," he replied. "As I remember, it turned out not to be related to this guy anyway. But someone found the dismembered body of another Bulgarian immigrant along the river. Apparently there wasn't any connection between these two. They had just come to the U.S. about the same time."

I looked around the table. "How many of the rest of you know anything factual about this guy?" I asked. They looked at each other and all looked at Glenn. It was obvious there wasn't any more information forthcoming. "Okay, we need to get whatever information is available on this guy. If King or Pierce counties have a file on him, let's get a copy. Find out if there is still a warrant for him and what the facts were of the incident for which he was originally arrested. When and why he came to Snohomish County. Let's nail down everything that we really know about this guy."

Danny spoke up almost sheepishly. "Will this help us find him?"

I smiled. "Well, Danny, do we really know if this guy goes back to Bulgaria to visit family at Christmas, takes the winter months off and goes south, has a family, what his immigration status is, such things as that? There's one very important factor missing from this operation before you find him, let alone before you begin to arrest him." Everyone looked at me in silence, waiting. "How do you know that Glenn doesn't see this guy on the street every time he goes to Darrington? You don't have a picture of him. You don't have a reliable witness to point him out. If you see some guy walking along the jogging path in the middle of the night, minding his own business, what are you going to arrest him for? How are you going to know that it's really the Bulgarian? Because he talks funny, looks funny or looks like he's living in the woods near Darrington? Heck, Danny, that's half of the Darrington Valley population! Unless you catch him in the act, you don't have much to hold him on until you can even get his fingerprints to match him to one of the past burglaries."

"So," Danny said to the detective sergeant, "you'll pull all of the reports for the past ten years and get some people to sort through them and make up the pin map?"

She nodded, making some notes, then added, "I'll get someone to do the King and Pierce County files search and see what we can find."

Danny looked at Glenn and said, "And you'll go back through whatever we've got in the files and see what you can find on the effort that was made to get this guy before." Glenn nodded.

I said to Danny, "The immigration thing is a question, it would be good to have someone check on that."

"How would that help?" Danny asked.

"Well, if this guy was actually an immigrant, maybe the arrest and criminal actions in King or Pierce counties would make him deportable. Immigrants can't own or possess firearms, which provides cause for stop and question him, if you know him to be an immigrant and have reason to believe he may be carrying a firearm. Also, the term immigrant is used to refer to people that come here from a foreign country. When the term is used by other than an immigration officer, it seldom refers to the legal status of that person. Depending on what status the person was in when he arrived and what has transpired since, he may be subject to arrest without warrant for violation of immigration law. That would go a long way to provide probable cause for questioning when encountering someone in the woods near Darrington, if you believed that the person was in an illegal immigration status."

"Okay, gotcha," Danny said. "I'll get hold of immigration and see what I can find out. So," he looked around the table, "we meet again in two weeks?"

Two weeks later we were again around the table at the substation. Fewer people this time—we were down to the get-it-done boys. The reports had been rounded up, sorted and complied and the pin map made up. Glenn and Danny had gathered the rest of the known information on the Bulgarian. Glenn provided a copy of a Snohomish County wanted-person poster dated 1995. He explained that the posters were made up the time before when they tried to catch this guy. The posters showed a mug shot of the Bulgarian at the time he was booked by Pierce County, and contained the name and other identifying data relating to the subject. The name was Mincio Vasilev Donciev, born July 3, 1930, in Bulgaria. Glenn also produced a copy of a report taken by Pierce County in relation to an arson and possible attempted homicide which resulted in the arrest of Donciev. This arrest produced the identity and relating evidence.

Essentially, the report told of Donciev arriving in the U.S. as a refugee from Bulgaria in August 1982. I quickly reverted to my previous Border Patrol manner and asked the why, how, where, and when questions regarding his immigration record and status. There was a definite lack of specific information regarding his legal immigration status. Glenn had been told previously that this guy was a legal resident alien. If the rest of the information was correct about his criminal record, to have gained such status it would appear that his arrival and adjustment to legal status would have been facilitated by a U.S. governmental agency in the interest of the U.S. I had found several such cases during my years as a immigration officer. Glenn related that this guy claimed to have been a police officer in Bulgaria. He had been involved in two different criminal matters resulting in someone's death. He was convicted of murder for one of these and sentenced to life in prison. He escaped from prison and somehow, not too long afterward, got into the U.S. There was some additional unsubstantiated information about the Bulgarian government wanting to get their hands on him again for political reasons.

After arrival in the U.S., Donciev had traveled to the greater Seattle area where he took up residence. In 1983 or 1984 he became acquainted with a woman who befriended him. During a short, platonic relationship, during which he did work around the woman's home, Donciev became very possessive, to the extent of resenting visits even from her parents and good friends. During this time the pair visited the woman's relatives who lived in the Darrington Valley. During several visits he would spend time alone walking in the woods. The possessive relationship grew worse and the woman finally advised Donciev that he would have to leave her property and end the friendship. He procrastinated and showed no signs of leaving. She set a deadline for him to be gone. Then one day the woman and a male friend returned to her home unexpectedly and found her house wired with gasoline bombs set to explode when the lights were turned on. Donciev was arrested for the attempted arson and booked by Pierce County.

There was an arrest report with the preliminary investigative report attached. There was no information that told what happened after Donciev was arrested. Glenn told us that due to some type of mix-up, Donciev was released on bond awaiting trial or was mistakenly released from jail prior to trial. Glenn said that no one seemed to have the facts as to that particular part of the story. But what was known and put together from different people and reported by the relatives of the woman was this: The woman's car was stolen. Shortly thereafter a man fitting Donciev's description was seen by one of her relatives, a neighbor whom he had visited in the Darrington Valley. Then the woman's car was discovered later stuck in the mud on a back road. There was meat and bread in the car and evidence that someone had been sleeping in it. Soon thereafter the thefts began, first at the relatives' residences and then the neighbor's. Usually items taken were food, items for shelter, clothing and such so it generally became accepted that the thief was only taking what was needed to survive in a camping environment. It was also accepted that the thief was Donciev and that he was not violent, careful to make sure no one was home, and clean and neat during the burglaries, causing little or no damage. The Darrington Valley came to understand that they had their own real-live hermit living in the woods somewhere. He didn't bother anyone, just stole foodstuffs, camping and survival items, all of which would have been given freely and gladly had he asked. Over time and with the telling and retelling of stories, all with varying degrees of accuracy, Mincio Donciev became a type of legend known as the Darrington "Mountain Man."

As time passed, more people discovered the Stillaguamish River and the Darrington Valley. More homes and summer cabins were built, as well as two resort developments. The amount of damage the Bulgarian caused, the items he took, and messes he made began to alarm people as time passed. Several burglaries involved the theft of firearms. The Stillaguamish river was recognized as a premier steelhead trout river and drew fishermen from far and wide all during the year. Occasionally a fisherman or hunter's vehicle would be broken into and weapons taken. It became known that the Mountain Man was armed.

Several years passed and the Mountain Man began to cut holes in the front doors of residences to gain entry. Now and then he would break a window or kick in the door, but the damage might go unnoticed for several days by absentee owners. Increasingly, evidence was discovered of the Mountain Man's presence in the outbuildings, woodsheds and backyards near active residences. He was gradually becoming more daring. It became evident that he was watching people in their houses from the surrounding woods, then coming into their homes immediately after they departed. He began to make seemingly deliberate messes in the houses, scattering foodstuffs on the floors and furniture, leaving filthy clothes where he stole others, and sleeping in their beds in muddy and stinking clothes. The legend of the Mountain Man was quickly losing its quaintness and the community's view of Donciev was quickly changing. As the "legend" became more daring, he also became more feared. Increasingly people began to "feel" the Mountain Man's presence in the surrounding woods when they walked, played or sat in their back yards. They knew he was around and increased community gossip made them even more fearful. The view of Donciev had changed from that of a charming oddity to a repellent outlaw who was feared and hated.

Darrington might be remote in Snohomish County, but residents paid their taxes and by golly they wanted to feel secure in their homes and in the woods they had previously explored unafraid. This culprit had gone unchallenged for more than 10 years. People said it was time the sheriff took them seriously and did something about this menace. So here we were in November 1997, starting a new search operation.

Sergeant Wickstrom, Glenn Bergstrom, two other detectives and I studied the pin map together. I could see that by putting the time frames together with the locations of the burglaries on the map, our subject was probably using different routing at different times of the year to enter the areas. During March, April and May, nearly all of the break-ins were in one location. In June, July, August, September and

October the break-ins were in another location. Then during November, December, January and February the break-ins were primarily in a third area. Each of these separate areas encompassed a couple square miles or so of residences, and each area was three or four miles from the others all along or between the highway and the Stillaguamish River. The suspect would often take an estimated 60 to 70 pounds of canned goods, foodstuffs and other items, sometimes breaking into two or more homes to get a full load.

I studied the map closely. This man was afoot. He had plenty of time but still he walked and carried all that he took. He might be a Mountain Man legend, but I figured he was probably more just a man. Hiking up these mountains with a 60- or 70-pound pack would not be an easy job for anyone, not even the Mountain Man, and I knew he wouldn't want to go farther than necessary. The pin map was indicating to me the probability that he lived in three different places determined by the time of year, possibly relating to who else was using the same wooded areas at that time. However, it didn't make sense that, during the winter months when the snow was often two to three feet deep in the mountains, he would carry what was taken even farther than during the spring and summer months. The days during winter would be shorter, colder and wetter.

The Darrington Valley is oriented primarily east and west, with high mountains on both sides. The terrain in the valley floor is relatively flat, and the valley floor from the river on the north side to the steep uplifting of the mountains on the south side was about a mile on average. Small farms and residences with a few cultivated but mostly pastured fields covered the valley floor. The wooded areas are now primarily along the steep and rushing creeks that cross the valley and bring fall salmon to spawning grounds in deep crevices in the steeply forested hillsides. The mountainsides were logged at the turn of the century and are now again being harvested of the marketable trees in many places. The 80- to 100-year-old logging-access roads are still there, though now overgrown in most places with 30- and 40 -year forest growth. This is an area of significant rainfall each year and relatively deep snows in winter. Huge ferns hide and protect the moss-covered rocks and deadfall debris that covers the hillsides. The forest—of fir, maple, alder and birch trees—typically provides a canopy that keeps significant direct sunlight from reaching the ground cover vegetation. During a couple summer months—the last of July, August, and maybe the first couple weeks of September—the woods become dry, but otherwise you'd better be wearing wet-weather gear for a walk in these woods. There are no bare or open hillsides here, even the huge house-sized rocks are hidden in the camouflage of trees and brushy growth that keeps Washington State green.

I didn't think this guy had been hiding out in the valley floor for ten years without someone knowing where he was living. So, I concluded, he was climbing the mountainside somewhere and I didn't think he was regularly carrying sixty to seventy pounds any further than he had to. Therefore based on a quick study of the topographic maps, he would almost surely have two or three principal places of abode, each as close as possible to the area that he was burglarizing. We were now into November and, looking at the map, I knew where we had to begin sign cutting to locate the route to and from his hideout. We'd start the operation the next week.

Unless we were very, very lucky and hit the sign right off, this operation would take several days of work looking along natural terrain barriers and through logged-off areas for not just Mountain Man sign, but sign that would lead us to where he was living. Finding the sign wasn't the hard task. Phil had told me he had often found the guy's sign here or there in the woods and on the hillsides during the previous couple years. This was reasonable—the guy didn't have to go to work every day like most of us; he just roamed around in the woods whenever he wanted, leaving his sign everywhere he went. The trouble was that we could spend days just following sign that didn't really go anywhere.

We launched our operation after Thanksgiving in November. I had contacted Kathy Wilhelm, a competent and compatible tracker whom I enjoyed working with from the Snohomish County SAR group. We were working virtually in Phil's backyard and this was "his" case, so naturally he was on the team. Kathy had already been on some of Phil's small-scale search operations for the Mountain Man, so she was familiar with the project. We met Danny, Glenn, and Tony, decked out in their typical SWAT black coverall uniforms and equipment. They and others of the SWAT alternately would furnish security and authority for our operation. First, we would explore and sign cut the area between the highway and the river and adjacent to the residential areas where burglaries took place in November, December, January, and February. This would be a strip about three to four miles long. I wanted to get a "feel" for the area, for possible entry and exit routing that provided access to the old railroad right-of-way jogging and hiking trail.

I figured Phil was right in knowing that our guy followed a route to the jogging trail, then walked it east and west to the residences he wanted to hit. This old railroad right-of-way was bordered closely with heavy brush and in places had been actually reduced to only a trail, which afforded easy cover to hide from anyone else traveling along the trail. Backyards bordered the jogging trail in places; in others there was only natural woods in which neighborhood children played and made tree houses, swings, and many, many trails to follow. We had lots of things to look at—some interesting, most just natural sign of local people doing what they do. We were primarily looking for year-old sign, made the November before. Here and there, though, we found obvious sign of "our guy." Old sign, man-sized, showed where someone had sat down, lain down, and almost always eaten and left behind the remains. For example, we found cottage cheese containers, frozen drink cans, plastic refrigerator dishes, Coke and 7-Up cans discarded the year previously and mixed in with last fall's leaves under

the crop from this year. By nightfall I thought I had gotten what I needed to begin looking on the mountainside of the highway.

We put in three more long, tiring days slogging through the woods in nearly constant light rain sign cutting the edge of the mountains. We found our subject's sign and followed it up hill and down, into and out of canyons and creek bottoms, climbing through over and under downed and dead trees and brush. We found a quick shelter patched into the brush. The SWAT members in full regalia worked along with us, covering us from behind a stump, then moving to a hump or behind another bush. They tried to flank our operations without interfering and helped whenever they could. While our heads were down, they kept theirs up and watched. My concern wasn't for our physical safety. I didn't think that the Mountain Man would suddenly jump up and start shooting at us. What I feared was that he would see us, then slip off and leave the country. We'd search and find and follow sign and follow sign and follow sign, and all the while he'd be cooling his heels 50 or 100 miles away somewhere. Catching this guy was a matter of gathering information and using that information to make the grab before he knew we were even interested in searching for him. Sometimes the sign was fairly fresh and clear, his footprints and actions obvious to us. But "fresh" is an arbitrary term, and none of the sign had been laid down within days, or even the past two or three weeks. The newest was perhaps a month old and ranged upward to more than a year. But nothing that we found seemed like it was coming or going to or from a residence. It was just sign that showed this man was simply exploring around in the woods.

On the fourth day of our sign cutting on the lower part of the mountain, we ventured at first daylight into dark, dank dripping woods clothed with a drifting mist. The rain was colder that day, with the promise of the season's first snow. I had invited another tracker along that day. Cindy Coker was a paramedic attached to the SWAT and a special friend of mine. I had met her many years before when she was a 15-year-old Explorer Scout and had joined me in a search for a missing hunter in Skagit County. That occasion provided the beginning of a long and close friendship that continues today. Cindy knew how to track and cut sign. The day wore on much the same as the ones previously. Phil and Kathy worked together, as did Cindy and I, with the SWAT guys trying to cover both teams. We found sign and worked it, found tin cans, some left behind by loggers and some by our guy. The difference was that nearly all of the ones left by our guy were of the same brand or type. The frozen-drink containers were a giveaway. Not many people will carry frozen grape, orange, apple juice into the woods and just sit down and eat the entire containers' contents. The Mountain Man always used a knife to cut open cans of food and he carelessly left this trademark wherever he stopped to eat.

We had worked our way over the mossy carpet lip of a bank and down a steep fern-covered ravine and across the creek, up the other side. On the ridge top there was almost a trail caused by the many trips of our guy back and forth to the point of the ridge that dropped off into a large, swift-running creek. The rain was steady and made the trail slick and slimy. The ferns hid branches and holes, making us occasionally trip or fall. It was obvious that our guy came here to fish in the creek. Here and there were obvious footprint pockets where he stood among the rocks near pools formed behind large boulders in the creek. He, had been there about three weeks previously, it appeared. We found a brush shelter, but no garbage. We worked the sign up the ridge and onto a large timbered area that suddenly dropped off in the other direction into another ravine. We found evidence of a campfire, some garbage buried in several layers of mosses. Some big trees were covered with moss nearly six inches deep, and the light, nearly noiseless rain, made the place seem almost spooky.

When it was time for lunch, we gathered for a quiet discussion of where we were and what we had found. As we broke open our packs, we talked quietly and laughed at each other's falls, slips and spills taken during the morning's work. We'd come a long way, but it was mostly in circles. We were following sign, but going nowhere. Somehow we had to find the outside of this circle. The guy came from somewhere and went somewhere; he visited now and again, possibly staying for a day or two, but he didn't live here, and he wasn't here now. I needed to try something different. I felt that we had to get outside of this area, but use this area as a pivot. We decided to re-cross the creek and work uphill or upstream from where we were. We all agreed that the guy lived somewhere above us, higher on the hill. We stuffed our packs again and set out, sign cutting our way into new territory on the uphill side of the creek.

Late in the afternoon, Cindy and I worked cutting the sides of a small steep creek bank that led to the bigger creek that we had started on. An old logging road crossed the small creek and ran to a dead end. Curiously someone had driven up this road and near the end had unloaded a couple cases of assorted canned goods, which were still there. The cans were in good condition, but more than a year old, weathered, but not bulged or giving sign of spoiled contents. Why would someone drive up here and leave two cases of canned goods? It seemed to us that there could only be one answer: Someone wanted to provide food for the Mountain Man. The problem with this was that obviously he either didn't trust the source of the food or had never found it. The cardboard boxes had begun to fall apart and some of the cans had fallen out and were scattered around by animals. I thought it was strange that some bear hadn't gotten into this pile and bitten open the cans, but there wasn't any evidence of this. A few of the cans had been rolled over the bank into the brush, with the labels still intact. It looked like there were at least two full boxes of cans there; surely not many had been taken away. We signcut back along the road to the little creek running under the road through a iron culvert. This was a natural place where animals and humans wanting to go uphill would leave the road and climb the creek bank onto the ridge top above.

Cindy began working uphill out of the creek on the left side of the creek and away from the road into the woods. I worked the right side, keeping an eye on her. She seemed to be working sign, finding one footprint then another, and another, as opposed to cutting sign or just looking for it. I called quietly to her asking what she had. She turned and said there was some recent foot traffic on an old animal trail, and motioned for me to join her. She had footprint sign of a lugged boot some two to three weeks old. We worked the sign along and into a more used trail further up the side of the ridge. Here there was more and fresher print sign. This was pretty good-looking sign—scuffs and tears in the moss, heel depressions and toe digs that barked the roots and bottom of the trail and marked the sides of the trail and cut the blades and stems of grass and plant leaves. This sign fit my "right size/right time/right place" qualification criteria. Here game animals used the trail and it was far more distinct. This trail through brushy areas displayed well-trod spaces of footprint size between the limbs and small tree roots telling me this was primarily a human footfall trail. A short way further, under the low boughs of a small cedar tree we found telltale sign of the Mountain Man—food cans crudely cut open with a large knife. We examined the site and found recently deposited trash mixed in with that from years of previous deposits. Cindy found a half dozen jars of different sizes with lids, clean, dry and cached under a log nearby. Another older footfall trail led to parts and pieces of a transistor radio, flashlights and other such items stuffed in under a rotten stump.

The trail led to the beginning of a steep slope and up through the waist-high ferns. We went slowly. The trail followed along a huge downed cedar tree and here and there, cached under the tree, were other bits of evidence: plastic containers, frozen juice containers, empty food cans, etc. We had finally found the trail exiting the valley and heading up the hill. This trail was leading home! We notified the other team members via radio and they joined us at the foot of the hill. They looked and questioned. Was I sure and how could I be sure? To Danny, Glenn, and Tony, the trail looked just the same as many others that we had already worked. But Phil and Kathy could see the freshness of the footfalls. Their questions had to do with my conviction that this was the trail to the house. My confidence was sufficient for them, they just wanted to understand what I couldn't quite explain.

It felt like a time for rejoicing, though quietly. Who knew if he were watching? Together we all began to work our way up the small ridge toward the steep fern-draped and timbered hillside. The trail seemed to grow more distinct and funneled by the downed timber and spaces to walk as it approached the hillside. There was lots of sign here. Obviously our guy relaxed here and put his pack down and wandered around some. He had reached the location where he felt quite safe from sight or discovery. What would a person think about in long, silent, wet days up in these mountains?

The trail worked itself uphill beside a huge old fir that had fallen some years before laying nearly straight down the hill, its top wedged between a couple small trees. Now it was a dark, ugly red strip of bark and wet rotted log with partially exposed limb spokes poking into the dense ferns, and here the Mountain Man sat to eat. Here and there were cans, bottles, plastic containers, a wrapper, frozen juice containers. Our guy took his time going up this mountainside, sitting on one or another of the limb spokes. He would stop and rest and when he stopped he ate, throwing or stuffing the debris under the log. In some places debris was covered with sections of the two-inch-thick bark, causing us to dig through every accumulation expecting to find something important.

The little creek was tumbling down the hill only a few yards away and there he went for water tromping through the ferns, tearing, turning and ruffling the moss. Here and there a small branch was broken. A couple empty cans and a jar turned upside down by a large boulder showed that he stopped here regularly to catch water to drink and perhaps fill containers. The creek was small here and in places nearly overgrown with the huge ferns and brush. This year's crop of maple leaves blanketed nearly everything. We found no evidence of a fire anywhere, so he didn't cook any of this stuff he ate.

Kathy checked her compass, conferred with Phil, and marked locations on the map. The sign was going almost due east and up along a little ridge top. I directed Phil to work the left, or north, side of the hillside in front of us, Kathy to work along the creek on the right. Cindy and I would work the center between and keep track of both Phil and Kath. Danny directed Tony to stick with Phil; he and Glenn would work back and forth between Kathy and the center, where Cindy and I would be. Everyone was very conscious that our guy could be watching us right now.

Much of the sign we worked was hidden from sight by the leaves and ferns. Here and there a trail through this covering indicated that our guy had frequented the area at various periods during the fall. The soft rain had subsided sometime while we worked and there was a lightness beginning to show through the overcast. We worked silently. Hand signals directed our search and confirmed sign trails as we mouthed "fresh" or "old" relating to a particular bit of evidence. Phil found a small pile of wood stacked neatly between two small trees that had grown since and pushed the pile to and fro. There was sufficient evidence to indicate that at one time someone had camped near the woodpile in a 10-by-10-foot, mostly flat spot. We estimated the wood had been cut and piled about four to five years previously.

Kathy called softly and I turned to see her beckoning. I worked my way back across the hillside to where she waited. She had discovered a place along the creek where the sign seemed to be coming to the creek from around the hill in the other direction. This sign was only a couple weeks old and we worked it together for fifty yards or so, Glenn and Danny on high alert. We were working the sign backwards as it was coming toward the creek and us. Abruptly we came to a small rocky bluff; the sign had climbed down from above this bluff so we worked our way around and up on top. There we could see where someone had spent some time, sitting, lying down and facing downhill back along the trail that we had followed. This guy was watching his back-trail.

Anywhere on this side-hill, as steep as it was, it was much easier to look down if you wanted to look at anything. It was nearly impossible in most areas to see very far uphill, and the trees and brush blocked the view in either direction around the hill. So it would be natural if you were just spending time sitting here on the side-hill to be watching downhill. However there were a couple other factors that entered into our contemplation. Why come over *here* to sit and look around? You had to climb through, over and up a steep bank and all you could really see was the area downhill along the old downed fir tree, where the trail was. The watcher had pulled up fern fronds and piled them to sit and lie on. This meant that at the time he was here it probably was-n't raining and the ground was dry. Picking through the pile of mashed fronds, we saw others in varying stages of decay. Our guy evidently came here every once in a while and watched his back-trail along the old fir tree, maybe every time he came up the hill. Danny and Glenn had moved over to us and took it all in without saying a word. I saw Danny signal to Tony to keep on the alert. We were approximately 75 yards from the main and obvious uphill trail and in a perfect location to depart this lookout position surreptitiously by going away from the main trail and downhill. The lookout would be able to see anyone com-ing up the main trail and watch them until they were on the same level and slip out the back door and be gone. Searchers would never know they had been seen.

This was what I was afraid we would find. This guy was no dummy. He wanted to know if someone followed him home. Now that we had found it, what to do about it? How do we contend with this situation? Nearly anywhere out here our guy had all of the advantages, every opportunity to see or hear us long before we knew we were even close to him!

I parted from Kathy and sign-cut my way back across the tinkling little creek toward Cindy. Most of the sign we were seeing was more than two months old, which we could tell because maple, birch, and alder leaves were in and on the sign. I saw some newer sign in the area of several large old cedar stumps. Working my way between them, I saw green fern fronds placed on top of one of the stumps. I got closer and looked and there, obviously, were the impressions of someone's hind end sitting on top of the stump on the ferns. This sign was fresh! I glanced around me and around the hillside. Phil was head-down, work-ing along another little seep that turned into a tiny creek further downhill. Tony, flanking and alert, was watching the north side of the wooded hillside. Glenn was closer and was watching me intently. Danny was over by Kathy who was almost hidden in some vine-maple clumps. There were some birds about, and everything seemed normal.

Cindy was still waiting, watching with a little grin that told me I had found what she could clearly see from where she was standing. I motioned for Glenn to join me at the stump and picked up a couple of the fern fronds and explained that the torn stems were not more than a day old. Our guy had been sitting right there yesterday, on top of this stump, in the afternoon, looking down the hill right where we had just climbed up. I wondered where he was right then. I glanced at my watch. It was 4:00 p.m. We had a little less than an hour of light left.

A low whistle brought me back from my reflections. Cindy had moved uphill and was pointing at one of the little cedar trees. I didn't see anything unusual from where I was, so I moved up toward her. There was something on the tree that she was pointing to. I moved up beside her and there it was, a sharp blaze cut in the bark of the tree. The bark had been cut at an angle with a sharp knife or hatchet and slivered downward leaving the white layer exposed about an inch wide and a foot long. She pointed to another tree and there again was a similar blaze, then another further along. The trail was marked! We worked our way to the second and the third blaze and, searching, found another and then another. The trail was going uphill but around the hill to the north where Phil was working.

Cindy was following an older side-trail back the other direction and, watching her, I suddenly became aware that I was seeing a camouflaged shelter, built out from the wall formed by an old, tipped-up root ball. Someone had placed small poles propped up on the root ball and covered the whole thing with branches and ferns. Over time, some of the ferns had taken root and grown and some had died; other grasses and moss had grown over to cause the roof of the shelter to appear much the same as all of the ground surfaces around it. There were a few of the crudely opened cans around in the bushes and ferns. Here and there we found other evidence of someone having spent some time there, but they were long gone now. The shelter hadn't been lived in for two or three years, but there was some recent footfall sign in the area and Cindy and I began to widen and explore further. Phil was still working uphill and hadn't reached the point where it looked like the blaze trail was going. Kathy was still working the small creek area that had gotten really steep and overgrown with vine maples and some devil's club. Cindy and I poked and looked and examined. I realized that it was getting harder to see as the overcast sky was growing darker and the day was slipping away. Decision time. I motioned to Glenn and told him to pass word to Tony to have Phil join us at the big "sitting stump." I waited and watched until I caught Danny's eye and motioned for him and Kathy to join us there.

Kathy and Phil both examined the blazes on the trees, and then went up to the shelter to look it over. We reconvened at the stump to talk. The trail was marked for some reason, and it wasn't a false trail, as the guy had walked it many times. I had discovered several other trees that had been blazed so long ago the blazes had healed over. That must be the reason for the new blazes. I pointed out to the team that the blazes were made in such a manner that unless you were in just the right position you couldn't see them. The blazes would permit a person to follow this portion of the trail at night with a flashlight because the blazes were all on cedar trees and were a bright white that would reflect light. So a person reaching the area of the big sitting stump could turn on a flashlight at night and easily follow this trail as the blazes would appear like reflector tape stitched on the trees. If someone came up the little ridge from below and started up the hill along the big old fir tree then came on straight up he would be able to come right to the sitting stump and from there to the blaze trail.

It was time to head back down the hill. We would just make it back to the vehicles before dark. I cautioned all to be conscious of creating sign that might be noticed and we headed out. We now knew where to find the trail and had a blazed trail to begin following when we came back. I felt good going out. Now we could actually begin to do something. We had found enough today to tell us where and how to go about finding this guy. He'd probably be watching, but if we were careful we'd have an even chance of getting him. I don't think the correct term would be jubilant, but surely we were in a good mood by the time we got to the vehicles.

Before parting company at the vehicles Danny wanted definitive answers to several questions to be prepared for what would surely be asked of him by superiors. How sure was I that this was the trail that we were looking for? Did I think the guy knew we were around? How much further to his dwelling place? These things I could only speculate about but I was sure this was the right trail—it looked right and felt right. I saw nothing that would indicate that he was aware that anyone was out looking for him such as trying to disguise or hide the trail. The two lookout positions had also been positions of rest and relaxing. The sign on the sitting stump was fresh, but there wasn't any sign that our guy heard or saw anything that caused him alarm. I had no idea how much further it was to where he was living. He had spent some time in the area of the sitting stump, but surely didn't live there. The blaze trail was a pretty good indication that we still had a way to go to get close to the end. There wouldn't be any blazes near where he was living. Danny would coordinate the team for another try.

After Christmas came a call from Sergeant Wickstrom—we had clearance to go up the hill one more time. We started out on New Year's Eve morning in a soft drizzle. Since the day we'd found the trail to where he lived, the Mountain Man had run out of provisions and had returned to the valley. He had struck two residences and gathered his usual 60 to 70 pounds of food, flashlight batteries, matches, a new Forester's all-weather coat, some wool pants, and other clothing items. This latest foray, however, provided fresh opportunities for investigators to search specifically for identifying evidence with which to prosecute the burglar once he was in custody. This coming and going provided for us new sign that was only about three weeks old. We discussed this additional factor in our favor. The guy either wasn't aware of our discovery of his homeward trail, or he didn't care. Either way, it made it easier for us, I hoped.

We had driven up the logging access road and parked in the woods while it was still dark. As quietly as possible we had donned our rain gear and slung on our packs. Danny was on another case today and unable to go with us and Cindy was on duty with Medic One and unable to be there. Being short two people had nearly caused another postponement, but finally Danny and Glenn had decided that we were to go and just be careful. We didn't expect to get to wherever the man lived anyway. We headed up the trail and by the time we could see in the gray light we were working our way up the little ridge toward the steep hillside. We reached the base of the hill where the trail started up alongside the old fir tree in 30 minutes and stopped to rest. From here I wanted to be very quiet and careful, though we had been since leaving the vehicles. We took a 10-minute break, then headed up the trail with me leading and cutting sign. The fresh footfall sign was pretty clear going up the trail along the big tree. We could easily see where he had stopped and had gone to the creek for water. The sign went on up toward the sitting stump, and so did we. There our guy had put his pack down and spent some time coming and going and looking around some, so it was daylight when he was here. We split up again, with Phil electing to go to the north side where he had worked before, so he would quickly recognize anything new, and Kathy heading the way where she had been before. I took the center to try to work all of the sign between. I wanted to read the sign on the blaze trail a little ahead of Kathy and Phil, just to make sure we would have a head start if he was waiting for us. Glenn would cover the one side and Tony the other.

The rain-wet blazes looked like white reflectors when we got in the right position. They suddenly appeared like highway markers when the headlights flash on them. The blazes had been done in the daylight, carefully planned and cut so only one could be seen at a time, and always a few steps past the last. The recent tracks appeared as ugly black blotches in the rotted leaves and compost that made up the ground surface. Color tone was certainly the aging characteristic that was prominent here. I wished that all my novice students could look at these as they'd readily see what I was trying to explain to them. Sure the ferns were bent here and there, or swept and tangled together, hinting of footfalls and direction of travel, speed of movement, and mind set, but the churning of the compost on the ground in the right size and shape cinched it. Here and there the heel corner or outside edge was still prominent and deeply impressed. The sign was good where the ground was this soft. Our guy had gone right along the blaze trail without hesitation, except for stopping to catch his breath every little bit. I paused far more often than he did, trying to allow the totality of my senses to operate.

Phil had moved along the same route he had taken before, going back to the area around the woodpile, cutting for sign. Kathy had moved back across the creek in the area of the lookout on the little rock cliff and sign-cutting all of the way, had come back to just this side of the creek. That left the entire area between us undisturbed, except for Glenn moving along slowly keeping watch on both Kathy and me. I was trying to keep a little ahead of both Phil and Kathy as I had done previously, keeping them both well in view. Dawn had brought heavier drizzle and a sort of eerie light that seemed very surreal. It would have been very easy to believe that we were dreaming instead of being awake. The sign was still going uphill, but up and around the hill also. I could now hear a creek that was running quite a volume of water and plunging down a steep channel. Phil was almost out of sight down over a gradual rise, which must be where the creek was. It was beginning to sound like a waterfall over there.

I looked up to see that Kathy was above me and working around the hill on about the same angle I was taking. She was just keeping the distance from me and paralleling me on the blaze trail. We worked on—watching, listening, looking, poking, and picking—hoping and trying to make sure we were reading the sign correctly and not missing anything. The sign went down into and up out of several large holes caused by root balls turned up years ago when trees went down; they had long ago rotted away. I followed over downed logs covered with ferns, tripped over limbs across the trail, and found one blaze after another cut the same in the small cedar trees. I stopped to examine the blazes and estimated that they had probably been cut in August or early September, as it appeared that the inside layers of bark were fairly dry at the time.

I could now see the woods over Phil's head and realized that the ground surface over there was lower. I was looking across a steep narrow, deep ravine where the creek was splashing. Kathy was angling down toward me now, coming around below another rocky cliff. This rocky outcropping was going to bring her around and probably intersecting with the uphill sign line angle that I was on. That made sense. This guy knew the area, and he had to go up across the hillside at this angle to get around that rocky outcropping, or find a way to climb over it. From where I was, the rocks were black and slimy with moss and mud. There was a vertical upward thrust of eight to ten feet most of the way and not anything easy-looking above it either. Phil was now working almost straight uphill, which would mean he was along the edge of the ravine and all three of us would almost come together 100 yards or so ahead. I continued to work my way to another blazed tree. I looked for the next tree. I could see the sign going onward, but I couldn't see another blaze.

I only found an old blaze on a fir tree long since healed over and barely noticeable. Kathy was coming across above me, obviously not seeing any sign up there and now I could see  Phil working his way along up the edge of the ravine. The splashing water bounding down over boulders drowned out any noise. We were coming together. I was still on the sign, but there weren't any more blazed trees. I searched around, thinking that maybe I'd missed one somewhere, I went back to the last one and tried to locate the next one as I'd done with the rest, but didn't see another one. I worked my way back to where Phil and Kathy had come to the sign line I was following. We could talk here because the creek alongside us was going to drown out any noise we made.

The sign turned before reaching the edge of the ravine and now was going right straight up the hill, so we followed. This was hand over hand in places, working from bush to little tree for handholds. I was trying to imagine this guy climbing up this hump with his 60 or 70 pounds of food and other gear. My feet were slipping and sliding, here and there churning two and three steps before gaining enough footing to lift myself up to the next step. The ground surface was black and damp, hidden by last year's maple and alder leaves entwined in the hip-deep ferns. The team was together here since it was too steep to spread out. The difficulty here wasn't in seeing the trail, it was in the going up it! The sign climbed up to a bit of a shoulder on the rim of the ravine. From here I could see the creek splashing and jumping down from one small waterfall to the next. I could also look across the narrow ravine and see a couple can lids at the base of a tree on the opposite creek bank. This was where our guy had turned and crossed the creek. I worked my way under one mossy log and up over the next, under a cedar limb and through some bushes and then was standing on a flat, rocky shelf that pooled the creek for the its next downward plunge. Here by walking carefully, crawling over one large mossy boulder and hanging onto the tips of a little fir tree, we were able to two-step across the creek itself and come out on the bank where the two can lids were. One by one we worked our way across the creek, with Glenn and Tony immediately dropping away from us on the other side.

High above we could see a 50-foot rock cliff that came around the hill and within 75 yards or so of the creek bank. Small firs and some cedars covered this hillside too, but here they had grown too thickly and many had died and fallen, littering the steep hillside. Moss covered everything. A basin bottom lay to our left as we looked upstream and was littered with the splintered and broken slabs of large old-growth firs and cedars that had fallen and slid down the hill. Big rocks squatted like trolls along this hillside, some as large as cars. There was footfall evidence, trails and such everywhere we looked. This side of the creek seemed to have completely different vegetation and appearance from the fern-covered slope we had just crossed. We could see the ground surface almost everywhere here. Moss covered nearly everything, broken where it had been scuffed or scraped off, leaving wet dark-brown, red, and black splotches.

This place looked creepy! I stood leaning against a tree and just looked. This side of the creek would allow someone to see pursuers clear across the basin. On the side that we had come up and across, you'd have to be within 25 or 50 yards to see anyone. I could see clear across the basin, all the way to the rim above. I could easily see several places that looked like old man-made shelters. Huge boulders had broken away from the rocky ledge and cliff above and ran down the hill to the basin bottom 100 years or more ago. These were now just a jumble strung out up the hill with trees growing among the brush here and there, hiding the corners and edges making the whole thing seem like a carefully planned camouflage design.

Phil was poking around, looking at the trash and garbage found strewn randomly, some at the base of trees, some in between big rocks or against a stump. Obviously our guy moved quickly from that first steep climb to here. Then he plopped down the pack and ate again. I guess this would lighten the pack some for the further climb. The old sign here looked good until we really looked at it closely. Here and there moss had been knocked off of a rock, limb, or stump, not cushioned here by three or four inches of compost. Here the moss was a half-inch-thick outdoor carpet over most of the rocks. Fir needles covered the ground, but they tended to blend with the moss and didn't offer the ground surface much protection either.

This would be a windfall area except that no significant wind could blow down this hillside, so everything that died just fell crisscrossed and every which-a-way. Throw a few big boulders into this jumble and put that all on a sixty percent grade, then cover everything with moss and send almost constant rain on it. Now you've got an idea of the hillside. Our guy had climbed over, through and under this mess on many occasions, his sign showed it. Once up and away from the creek crossing, the going got easier, the sign plainer, the hill steeper. Tony and Glenn didn't lapse in their vigilance, staying with us around the boulders and downfalls.

We slowly worked our way uphill. The sign was fairly easy to see and was contained within a fairly narrow corridor, zigzagging more or less straight up the hill. This guy must be part mountain goat! He didn't take advantage of differing terrain features to work his way upward, he just went straight up. We could now clearly see the face of the cliff ahead and to our left a fairly narrow passageway with trees closer to the creek going up onto what appeared to be the rocky knob on top of the hill. We pushed the sign upward. Now Phil and I were together, with Kathy still along the creek. We climbed and stopped to rest, watching around us, looking at the sign and realizing how vulnerable we were on this hillside. Here and there on the climb we would find a can, wrapper, piece of plastic or other evidence that our guy stopped once in awhile also, and when he stopped he usually ate something. I think that gave us encouragement. At least he had to stop and get his breath also. I looked back at Glenn and Tony, who were sweating like they were in a steam bath. The temperature was about 45 degrees, I guessed, and the humidity at 90 percent. Nice day for a hike on a steep hillside.

Phil and I came to a pile of big old trees that had fallen together at the foot of the rocks. The trail went up and over the logs and so did we. We gained the rocks on the other side and looked down to find under the first old log a whole pile of trash—cans, paper and plastic containers. Garbage piles usually mean people are living close by. We squatted, waiting for Kathy and the cover team to climb up over the logjam. Ahead the woods were thicker, the top was rounded and humped in places, the creek drifting between the humps and coming to the rim to our right to begin the spill downward. There was brush on the top. This would be the place to have a cabin. This could be the garbage dump if the cabin was close. The left side was bordered by the edge of the cliff so we didn't have to worry about that. We couldn't see what was on the other side of the knob top and it might well be far larger than we thought. Now we could partially see to the right back across the creek and higher, another equally steep hillside, the continuation of the first one we had climbed up and across. From where we were it was impossible to determine the expanse to the top. Heck, we couldn't even see a top! In fact, across the creek because of the trees, ferns, and brush, we couldn't see more than 100 yards or so. It bothered me that I was unable to visualize that hillside. I didn't understand the flow from where we had been down below to the level where we were now. Well, maybe it would make sense later.

We could see that along the creek and to the right there was a considerable area that appeared to be relatively level and just sloping to the creek. It seemed to consist of lots of brush, berries, fir and cedar trees, along with a few big maples. To the left, the rocky knob was covered with berries and brush and a few smaller fir trees. Certainly enough there to hide a small cabin and close enough to dump the garbage in this hole under the logs. We had gathered and everyone was looking and pondering with their own thoughts. It was time for an action plan.

"Okay, Kath," I started, "stick with the creek, work your way across into that brush and hopefully out the other side so you can see what you're doing. Phil, work your way around this edge to the left and see if you can get clear around to the backside of this knob. But don't go on forever. If this knob connects to another hill, cut back across the top in this direction. This garbage dump may well mean that the cabin is here on this hump or somewhere right here along this creek in the brush. Go slow, be careful, look for sign made the last day or two, or maybe even today. Keep your eyes wide open. This is the closest we've gotten. It might not be here, but this looks pretty good to me. Tony, you stick with Phil. I'm going to work this bottom, but very slowly, trying to give you two the pincers around the outside. If someone is watching, maybe they'll keep their eyes on me till you get around behind."

Everyone took a deep breath and moved out. I went slowly, making sure that my movements would be noticed by anyone watching. There was plenty of sign to look at, though not really what I was expecting or wanting to find. Mostly just foot traffic, indicating travel. There were a couple man/animal trails here in the woods on the top, some small humps and bumps with little fir trees so thick I couldn't see through them and could barely walk through them. No sign of anything that would cause me to believe that the guy was living here—no trees chopped down, no other piles of garbage or human junk, nothing. I spotted Phil working toward me, He had been able to work around the knob and was now coming back toward the center line that I was working. Suddenly there was a pond on my right, a couple hundred feet across each way and with dead trees and brush covering the edges. My centerline trail was now quickly running out of sign. Phil was now working the top of the knob where in many places there were open granite patches of rock. This wasn't it; the guy didn't live here. I turned and worked back around the edge of the pond to the beginning of the creek. Kathy was now along the creek and working toward me. We worked toward each other until we met. Kathy shrugged her shoulders. She had found sign in several places, but nothing significant. I hadn't found where the guy went from here and I didn't think Phil was going to find it up on top unless he was crawling into a hole in the rock. Where the heck was he and where was the trail from the top?

Phil wandered down to where Kathy and I were talking with Glenn. "We didn't find it, Phil," I said.

He looked pained and said he hadn't found anything either. Some old sign, but nothing to get excited about. We went back to the rock outcrop above the logjam. The trail was plain to this point, then the guy went into the edge of the wooded area and to the creek. Kathy had found tracks in the marshy creek bottom. Where the heck did he go from there? I began a cut starting low on the right side and working my way over to the creek. I crossed the creek and began working up the other side through heavy brush, downed logs and debris that had long ago been washed downhill and piled up at the top of this ravine. I was working a circle further out than Kathy had, and suddenly I found it! The trail marked by a few scuffs and broken stems was coming through the brush and out on this side of the creek and headed toward the dark, steep hillside above us. Rotten leaves and duff was marked slightly here and there with heel depressions, ball-of-the-foot compressions and edge cuts and marks. The prints were coming and going to and from the hillside. I went back and retrieved the rest of the team. I had marked the trail out far enough to know the direction and to know this was going to be different than the other two steep inclines we had worked the sign up.

This hillside was nearly bare of moss or ferns and ground growth. It swept up from the creek bottom for 100 yards or so that we could see, gradually increasing its steep angle. Two hundred yards from the creek, the hill was practically straight up and down. The ground surface was covered with small branches, twigs and debris that had fallen from the thick growth of the mostly fir canopy. The lower portions of the hillside were fairly open with scattered bigger trees. As the incline got steeper, the number of trees increased and the size decreased. It felt increasingly dark and gloomy. There were three or four little ground-water seeps visible on this hillside—a couple trickled down into this side of the pond and a couple more disappeared over the lip of the hill to my right. One such seep ran almost straight ahead of us, right up the center of the hillside. That's where our sign went. Here and there we could find a partial print in the mud of the seep.

Above the seep the sign seemed to disappear. The ground surface was hard, covered with twigs and needles, dark colored and wet. It had stopped drizzling while we were coming up the other hill, but now we were under the dense fir canopy and it was dark and the air was thick and almost foul with days of rain. We split up in what had become the usual form, Phil on the left and Kathy on the right. We had again cautioned about noise, given the possibility of our guy taking a walk and discovering us, or just hearing or seeing something, then slipping off into nothing and disappearing. That would be just the same as a miss! We might well never even know that we had been seen. That was my idea of what this guy would do. I didn't really think he was going to attack or fire on us as long as he had an escape.

I picked up another scuff and some old sign going on up the hill and motioned to Phil and Kath that I had the sign. We slowly worked across the gradual incline and began to work up the steep slope. A step at a time, an occasional scuff or scrape, rolled rocks impressed to flatness at one time, the tip of a broken stick impacted into the ground surface. The sign was there, but just didn't look like much.

Kathy indicated she was finding a little sign over on her side and Phil also did on his side. I thought the sign line I was on was the freshest and stuck with it, seeing offshoot trails here and there, much the same as down on the hillside below us. Suddenly I saw something bright and shining near the base of a tree on the uphill side. I moved over and knelt down looking closely at a bright nail driven into the trunk base of the tree about six inches off of the ground. Then spotted a similar nail in a tree between Kathy and me and set almost head high. I scanned the trees and toward Phil saw a nail near the ground in one and one nearly head high in another.

I waited until Kathy came up in line with me, then catching her eye, I reached down and touched the nail so she would see. She immediately began then to examine the trees close to her and found a nail in a tree close to her and then a couple more in trees between us. Glenn passed the word to Tony and Phil and they began to look for and find the nails. I looked for sign and found nothing unusual at any of the trees where I could find the nails. These nails had been in the trees for some time; the wounds in the trees had long ago healed. I looked carefully at the nails for evidence of wire or string ties or marks, none, but these were stainless nails and hard, not subject to rusting or corrosion. I looked from where Kathy had found her first nail and to where Phil had found his first nails. A string or wire tied between these nails would be at just the right height for a trip wire. The nails were driven at the right height in trees that would maintain a line at about six inches above the ground.

I waved everyone over to me, beckoning them in close so I could talk in a whisper. I gestured toward the nails. "These are Forest Service nails," I said. "See that little tag on that one over there?" I pointed to one at the base of a nearby tree. "But I doubt the Forest Service put them here. I don't think they would mark trees with nails driven so close to the ground. You'll notice that these are nearly in a line across from where Kathy found the first one to where Phil found the one over there. There are a few here and there driven higher in some trees. However, look at these trees that have the nails—some are old rotten trees, some young, some fir and some are not. Notice that all of the nails are on the uphill side of the tree bases. This doesn't look like any type of official marking." We stood awhile and contemplated, glancing around nervously. This was our first indication that this guy just might be laying traps and none of us liked the prospect.

"I doubt that this is some kind of booby-trap. If I was living up here on this hill and wanted to know if I was going to have unexpected callers for coffee, I might just string up a warning line. This line of nails could hold a trip wire that would be darn hard to see if you didn't know it was there going uphill like this the chances of stepping over it without tripping it are very slim. Looks to me like our guy may be much closer than we thought and there may be other devices to warn him of our arrival. Let's be very careful and quiet. This line would be guarding the avenue straight on up the hill to somewhere above here. I've got the last good sign right here, still going straight up the hill."

An hour later, I turned onto Mecklem Road and was home. I had gone over the whole story to date, and was almost laughing to myself at the image I had of the five of us huddled together that afternoon on the little flat spot on the mountainside. We were whispering because we were afraid to talk out loud, grown-ups as spooked as little kids in a cemetery at night.

Three weeks later, Danny Wickstrom was on the phone. "Well," he said, "things have taken a sudden turn and kind of gotten out of hand. Glenn came back from that last trip up the mountain and gave me the report, I wrote it up and sent it up the chain. Then the crap hit the fan. A couple members of the upper brass have gotten involved and now want to run the case themselves. They've pretty much taken it out of my hands. They think this is just too dangerous for us to handle and want to equip and train a squad of men to charge up the hill and bring the guy back."

"What are you talking about, Danny?" I asked, incredulously.

"Well they've had a couple meetings and one special member of the brass has convinced the staff that we are undermanned and ill equipped for this job. So it's looking like he's going to get approval to select a dozen men and equip them for this job. The SWAT team probably won't have any more to do with it."

"Equip them how?" I inquired.

"They're still planning and studying about what they need to do the job," he said. "But the equipment list includes full packs of survival gear, clothing, climbing gear and automatic weapons, plus a paramedic with drug-administering authorization."

"Danny, you know we can't go up that hill with a dozen men without alerting the whole countryside! The guy will know we're coming from the time the last vehicle door is slammed."

"I know, I know," Danny said tiredly. "I've tried to argue, plead, yell and calmly discuss this, all to no avail. They're going to do the BIG SHOW!"

"Holy cow, Danny, they were bitching about the cost of paying me to track this guy in the first place and the duty time it took off of the job for you guys to back us! What'd they do—hit the lottery?"

"Well," Danny said, "it's out of my hands now. I just wanted to call you myself and let you know from me what's going on. I'm still your contact for now, but I expect that to change soon and one of the new squad members to contact you. The way they're going about this, it may take a while to get equipped and set up to go up there again. They're still talking about who is going to get selected for the team. Glenn and I told them what kind of conditions they were dealing with and now they may go through a physical testing process. Just making the decisions for this proposal to get authorization is going to take a while. I don't think they're going to get going on this again until March."

"Jeez, Danny! First of all I'm not going up that mountain with any squad of 12 heavily armed and REI-equipped guys on a lark. This has been hard work so far and if this guy is to be caught it will continue to be. The guy isn't dead, you've been up there. Where you were was the easy part—it gets steep after that. There were five of us up there being careful and we were making too much noise! Twelve guys just wouldn't have a chance. I wanted to suggest that I be given authorization to go on up by myself, but knew that wouldn't be possible. Even if he's sleeping, he'd hear a squad like that so far away they'd never even know when he left the mountain. Besides that Danny, we've got him located now. In April he begins to hit places up on the other end of the range, which means that he moves his residence too. We'd have to do all of this all over again. If they fool around for 60 days, they'll more than likely have to start from scratch. He's due to come back down the mountain in about two weeks. *Now* is when we should be working on it. Within two weeks or so he's going to have to come down from the mountain and hit another house."

"They won't give me the okay to go back up there," he said, the exasperation sounding in his voice. "What else can we do?"

"Danny, if we had sensors we could place them on the trail and we would know when he was coming down and maybe grab him down around the houses."

"Yeah," Danny said, "but we don't have sensors."

"How about the Forest Service?" I asked. "We're on either State Department of Natural Resources or National Forest lands. They've got sensors. I know they use them for surveillance of the marijuana patches they find in the woods. They've got a good deal of tech equipment that we might be able to use."

"How do we go about that?" Danny asked.

"Let's make contact with the Forest Service law enforcement officers at Darrington and get them involved in a cooperative effort to make the arrest," I suggested. "This guy is living in the National Forest and using it as a refuge to hide from law enforcement while he endangers the local population."

"Gotcha!" I could hear Danny grinning into the phone. Suddenly he had a burst of adrenaline. "Glenn and I'll go have a cup of coffee with Dick Lamor tomorrow," Danny said, referring to the National Forest Law Enforcement Officer at the Darrington office of the U.S. Forest Service. "I'll call ya and let you know what he says."

A couple days went by before Danny called. "Dick agrees with your assessment of the situation and says that definitely it's a matter under his jurisdiction. We did some checking, drove up to the end of the road with Dick and it's for sure that the trail leads up across the DNR land and onto the National Forest lands. He wants to know what type of sensors you think would work best."

I thought a minute, then said, "Danny I've never had much luck with the infrared, unless they have the newer ones. Let's use the seismic if he has them available. We need to place the sensors along the trail in the area of that first big old fir log that lays downward on the big fern hillside, from there back down the trail on that little ridge. So we may need a transmitter-relay unit too. I would recommend using three units able to transmit on some frequency that that you and Glenn can monitor or have monitored twenty-four hours a day."

"I'll talk with Dick, then get back to you," Danny said.

Shortly afterward Danny called and asked if I was willing to commit another day to the project. I said I would and we met with Dick Lamor and his electronic technician at Darrington. I took them to the end of the logging road where we had been parking the vehicles and we hiked up the hill past the clear cut to the area of the old downed fir log. It took nearly all day to place the sensors, positioned to they would transmit clearly and surely on the correct frequency. I measured the walking time between each sensor to give us an accurate prediction of our guy alerting the sensor so we'd know it wasn't an animal such as a deer walking the same trail. The sensors would transmit their location in sequence as each was alerted, thereby advising the direction of travel up the trail or down to trail to town. We were set.

On March 2, the phone blared in the middle of the night. I caught it on the first ring and glanced at the clock's glow at the same time—3:17 a.m.

"We got him!" crowed an elated Danny. "I wanted you to know because it will be on the news at daybreak. The sensors worked perfectly and alerted us that he was coming down the mountain in the evening. We were all out of position. Glenn was off duty. I was up on another mountain pulling some tourist out of a snow bank and didn't get the message till nearly ten. I finally got the dog unit and another unit up there with me and we sat up on the old railroad grade. We waited a long time and I figured we had missed him, so we started walking down the railroad grade. One of the guys thought he saw something, but wasn't sure, it was raining so hard then. We slowly worked our way along the grade and suddenly there he was—right in the brush in the ditch along the grade!

"He took off running and we were yelling to stop. I was trying to remember how to yell 'Stop—police!' in Bulgarian, because I had practiced it over and over. It didn't make any difference. He was bookin' across the jogging trail and into the brush. We could see he was carrying something long in his hand but couldn't tell what it was. The K-9 unit turned the dog loose and we gave chase, up into the woods. The dog had him stopped, but he was stabbing at the dog with the spear he had. I got to him first and grabbed him and that darn dog grabbed me! I thought I could hang on, but the dog took me down and the guy took off again. He had rain gear on and it was wet and slippery, of course, and the ground was slick in those leaves and junk. The other two guys caught up to the guy and pounced on him and got him down. He had a gun in his hand and they weren't able to get it loose. I finally got free of the dog and I caught up with them. I was able to get the gun out of his hand and threw it into the woods. He then tried to get another gun that he had. He was strong! He fought us and it took all three of us to get his arms behind his back. We had a heck of a time getting the cuffs on him. He had two guns, several long knives, a small meat cleaver and that darn spear he was stabbing at the dog with. But we got him! It'll be in the news, but I wanted you to be first to know!"

Danny was right. The 6 a.m. Seattle TV news was carrying the story of the Snohomish County Mountain Man capture. They didn't have much of the story yet, of course, but what they had was causing a sensation. Donciev was in the hospital, having suffered severe damage to his lower legs and feet that had been inflicted by the police dog during the capture and arrest. (The media didn't mention anything about Sgt. Danny Wickstrom being bitten.) There were hints and speculation as to where the Mountain Man had been living, if anyone had been helping him to subsist and other questions that we had asked each other. The Snohomish County Sheriff's information officer wasn't saying much until after the subject was arraigned. Donciev was charged with numerous residential burglaries and would go to court whenever he was released from the hospital. Several days went by with recurring news articles and additional information about Donciev. He had an attorney, and the TV cameras showed his smiling face with pretty nurses attending to every need.

Danny called to tell me more about the capture. He was off duty for several days to recuperate from the dog bites he had suffered. He had requested time and a couple men to go back up the mountain and try to find the hideout. Danny expected to be back on duty the following week and that we could plan to go then, if I was available. He needed me to try to follow the trail, as Donciev wasn't telling the police anything. The following week, Danny called to report that the word from the sheriff's office was they had their man in custody and had sufficient evidence for a conviction. They didn't feel it was prudent to expend additional officer time trying to find the hideout. We had assured them it was on National Forest lands and therefore it was a Forest Service problem. They said if the Forest Service wanted to pursue the issue, so be it. The disgust at this decision was obvious in Danny's voice and he wanted to know if I was going to go looking for the hideout. I called Dick Lamor and asked if the Forest Service office wanted to support another venture up the mountain to see if we could find the hideout. He replied that he personally wasn't able to do that and the Forest Service wasn't really interested, but if I wanted to do so I had his permission. He asked that if we did go and were able to locate the cabin or hideout or whatever it was, to look around and make an assessment whether or not it would be reasonable or necessary for Forest Service personnel to go in and clean up the place. The Forest Service interest was to protect the public should anyone else happen onto the site. I called Danny and advised that I would get a team together the following Saturday and head up the mountain.

I knew that finding the place would be a good news story, though it might not add anything to the prosecution of Donciev. I called Susan Gilmore, a *Seattle Times* reporter who earlier had taken the time to do a good, lengthy story about search and rescue trackers. Susan and I had become friends and I trusted that if she were permitted to accompany the team on this trip up the hill and there was a story, she'd write it in a positive manner, and if there wasn't a story, there wouldn't be negative fallout. She was delighted to have the opportunity to go. I suggested she could bring along one additional person, a photographer, but that person had to be in good physical shape and willing to carry their own load, and provisions for two or three days and nights on the mountain. We would meet at Darrington at 6 a.m. the following Saturday morning ready to head up the mountain. Kathy and Cindy were both scheduled to work on Saturday, but Matt Condon, another experienced Snohomish County SAR tracker was eager to take their place.

Saturday dawned with sunshine and blue skies. We met at a loggers' restaurant in Darrington—Phil and Matt, Susan Gilmore and photographer Betty Udesen. After getting acquainted over breakfast, we headed up the mountain. We didn't need to be quiet or cautious now. Phil and I helped Matt, Susan and Betty to find and understand the sign that we had found on our last two trips up the trail. Betty took pictures and Susan took notes, Phil, Matt and I enjoyed the freedom to explore and examine without possibly encountering the Mountain Man. Sunshine brightened the woods and air and we made good time working our way up the trail. This time, even burdened with four-day packs, we were enjoying the hike. By noon we were standing on the very spot that a few weeks before on the new years' eve, Phil and I had shared lunch with Kathy and SWAT members Glenn and Tony. The mountain was just as steep, but the sunlit blue sky peeking through the fir canopy above encouraged our progress.

Donciev's sign was as difficult to follow as before, but now we could work more efficiently together and concentrate on the one main trail. We worked uphill from the previous picnic site and were soon working through a small, thick stand of young trees five to eight feet tall with the footprint trail threading between and continuing uphill. Suddenly I noticed, just off to the right, a tin can profusion that seemed to be cascading down from a flattened hump above us. We worked our way up the trail onto the hump, where the sign died. Looking around, we discovered that we were in fact standing on the flat, slightly sloping roof of a small dugout dwelling. A hole about 15 x 18 inches in the corner of the roof provided entrance to the 4-foot-high, 5 x 7-foot room concealed below. The roof was cedar poles covered with heavy plastic, dirt and forest debris in which weeds and small trees had grown and died, with other brush having been cut from time to time and piled on.

I eased myself into the hideout to examine it. It was a tight squeeze and it could hold only one person. The walls of the dwelling were 6- or 8-inch cedar logs interlocked at the corners. The dirt floor was mostly covered with double-thick foam pads and sleeping bags. There were three small bundles of full sets of clothing tightly packed together and tied as though ready for emergency departure. Long nails driven into the cedar logs provided hangers for dozens of items—tools, flashlights, binoculars, hammered-metal spear points, and other odds and ends,. Numerous jars and cans held pieces of gun mechanisms, bits of transistor radios and  other electronic parts and pieces, nubs of pencils, pens, nuts and bolts, and various rounds of ammunition for different weapons. Directly beneath the entrance hole, three opposing metal stakes had been driven into the dirt floor and ashes indicated that this served as the fireplace to heat food. The trash and garbage that I had seen cascading down into the pocket of young trees flowed right from the entrance, showing that Donciev simply threw all trash right out of the entrance.

A 16 x 18-inch hole deeper into the dirt floor beside the fireplace permitted him to sit on the dirt floor and put his feet into the hole and sit upright.

We carefully inspected everything inside the dwelling, then began a systematic examination of the exterior area. The footprint trail from the cave to the small creek for daily water was well defined and marked along both sides between the trees and bushes with shreds of old toilet paper marking his indiscriminate use of the area. We found a stash of jars, washed clean and with lids under a log. Pots and pans nested together were cached under another log, two pair of rubber boots cached in another area under a log, and bit and pieces of other items in scattered caches here or there within a hundred feet of the dwelling. The only rhyme or reason for the many caches seemed to be to so distribute items that if one were found, others would not be. The only well-defined trail resulting from frequent use was the trail to the creek. Outside of a close hundred feet of the dwelling there was no evidence, no sign of the Mountain Man. There was no evidence of chopping, sawing or cutting of wood for fires or other uses. No rocks or other items that could be used for tools, no whittling, no clothes, meat or fish-drying racks, no sitting-in-the-sun places. Donciev spent nearly all his time at this location in the hole in the ground like a gopher. He didn't come out and walk around or enjoy his spacious back yard. The only sign was faint footprint sign found around the dwelling that led us to one of the scattered caches. One very faint sign line led me directly to an old rotten stump. I knew he had to be coming to this pile of rotten wood surrounding this stump for some reason. I began to dig in the pile and uncovered a three-gallon plastic tub, double-sealed to prevent moisture entering. I opened the tub and found a .22-calibre Hornet automatic pistol of foreign make with a hundred rounds of ammunition. The tub held additional rounds of 12-gauge shotgun shells and .9 mm ammunition. This tub I removed to take down the mountain and give to the sheriff's office.

While we were examining everything, Susan had taken copious notes, and Betty had taken many photos. When we felt we were done, we recovered the entrance hole as we had found it and started back down the mountain. On the way, we discovered that on our New Year's Eve search, when we had stopped to have the picnic lunch and whispered to each other so as not to alert the Mountain Man, we were in fact only a hundred yards directly below the dwelling.

Eventually Donciev was brought to court and in a plea agreement pleaded guilty to a half dozen burglaries and was sentenced to serve five years in the Snohomish County jail. His attorney filed a civil damage suit against Snohomish County sheriff's office, the arresting officers, and Phil and me. Phil and I were charged in the complaint with having provided the information by which the sheriff's officers had wrongfully inflicted pain and suffering and the loss of two toes. Ultimately the County settled the suit, much to the embarrassment and frustration of the sheriff's office, for $450,000.

In 2001 Mincio Donciev was released from Snohomish County and released into custody of the Immigration Service for voluntary departure from the United States to Europe.

>—•>—0—<•—<

Chapter Twelve

Military Tracking
Gathering Intelligence for Military Advantage

When we in this country picture military scouts, it's common to think of the tough, crusty U.S. Cavalry scout portrayed in Western movies or the stealthy, stoic, wise-beyond-understanding Native American. This dramatized version of an army scout could usually spit farther, shoot straighter and cuss louder, outfight and outwrestle any mere human. He also could glance at a single, seemingly invisible hoof print from 100 feet away and tell you how many Indians of which tribe had passed, exactly how long ago, what color their horses were and what they'd had for breakfast. A modern military scout is just as colorful, interesting, mysterious, knowledgeable, skilled and unbelievable, but for entirely different attributes.

Historically, tracking has always been an accepted part of military operations. Alexander the Great, Genghis Khan, Napoleon and other greatly respected military leaders of modern times have documented their use of "advance scouts" to bring back useful information to locate and determine the numbers, equipment, morale, intent and condition of enemy forces. Intelligence gathering preparation for battle was and is today a necessary process during any threat of military conflict. Regardless of the advance of technology in our world today, it often remains the duty of military scouts afoot as it has for hundreds of years, to find and accurately interpret the physical evidence of enemy forces.

I remember well the U.S. Navy SEAL teams coming to work with Border Patrol units on evening and night shifts along the border fence at Chula Vista, California in the late '60s and early '70s. For the most part, these were very dedicated people who realized the value of participating with Border Patrolmen prowling the night for illegal entries that came through, under, over and around the border fence. These SEALs received the most viable practical training possible that related to military tactics of contending with surreptitious enemy infiltration. Border Patrol officers used standard daylight binoculars, three-cell flashlights and human ingenuity first to spot then to track and catch the intruders. However this was the height of the Vietnam conflict, and along with development of new military tactics came the development of new, exciting high-tech equipment to fight the mostly jungle war. Military-oriented industries funneled newfangled equipment to the SEAL teams to be tested in the Border Patrol proving ground. Electronic seismic sensors, night-vision equipment lighted by starlight, infrared lights, night sighting devices and heat-seeking sensors appeared. Traditional, but updated, mili-  tary booby traps and other installation security and warning devices all came via these SEALs for their testing with the Border Patrol. Word of this "special" training opportunity soon spread to the other military services and encouraged their participation in the unofficial program.

I thought I was leaving my fledgling tracking career behind when I transferred from the southern U.S. border to the northern border in 1973. However without fanfare, my name and association with tracking and training became known to leaders in the search and rescue (SAR) arena in the Pacific Northwest. Along with this new higher SAR profile for me as a tracker and my subsequent development of a more formal tracking training program came association with military Special Forces personnel.

The dozen years from 1973, when I was stationed at Bellingham, Washington, until 1985 afforded opportunities to gather a great variety of tracking mission experiences. One such opportunity was to meet and incorporate my tracking training with Frank Heyl's *"Universal Training Systems" (UTS)* and the formal introduction to training with U.S. Army Special Operations Forces at Ft. Bragg, North Carolina. I participated with Federal and State law enforcement agencies and the military in such adventures as the capture of Christopher Boyce (written about in the book *The Falcon and the Snowman*), the incident at Wounded Knee, South Dakota the Green River serial murder investigation, and many more. October of1990 I retired from the Border Patrol to devote full time to tracking training and consultation services. May of 1991 brought incorporation of Universal Tracking Services (UTS) with a group of skilled assistant instructors to provide sufficient instructors for a rapidly growing training program. Twenty years had established my tracking training and mission success reputation. That reputation and professional posture quickly garnered ready acceptance of the new UTS program as the foremost tracking training program for search and rescue, law enforcement and specialized military units.

U.S. military trackers have a long and well deserved history and reputation from civil war and western movement periods. Resurrected during WW I, tracking became an accepted and highly respected field skill during World War II. Highly trained Army and Marine scout/sniper and reconnaissance teams gathered critical information specific to residents and enemy elements. Specifically trained military trackers were detailed to locate the sign of human presence or passage and determine whether it was that of friendly residents or enemy combatants. Military trackers were specifically employed in the South Pacific Islands, Europe and the deserts of Africa to locate and eliminate surreptitious individuals or small enemy hit-and run-teams. Military training manuals detailing and instructing the use of tracking and counter-tracking techniques in all field skill specialties were written. A military tracking school was developed in the Philippine Islands with both expert indigenous and military tracking instructors. The Korean conflict brought a resurgence of the need for military tracking skills to find the trails, pathways used by small, elite enemy units to infiltrate and strike allied forces behind their front lines. When U.S. units were drawn into the Vietnam conflict again they had to deal with small, highly effective enemy teams that infiltrated through American lines and caused great loss of American and allied life and material. Trackers were specifically trained to identify evidence of enemy activities and follow them to their camps, underground caves and tunnels or hiding places used by the Viet-Cong and North Vietnam soldiers.

Political and military support for tracking faded during the peace-time reorganization of the military. The Philippine tracking school and that entire Division of the U.S. Army was eliminated after World War II. The allied military components retained a few aging "subject matter experts" who served for the duration of the Vietnam War, but political climate, military tactics and equipment were changing with the advent of new technologies. The Vietnam War dramatized this time of change. The French military commanders, when they were fighting in what was then French Indochina, were first to recognize a need for scout/trackers, and they created a tracking-training center in Malaysia, a neutral country with a tropical environment similar to Vietnam. This became known within international military circles as the Malaysian Tracking School, staffed with dedicated civilian and military instruc-tors. The training curriculum was based primarily on the same military manuals that were written for the Philippine tracking school. The U.S. military sent selected personnel to the Malaysian Tracking School during the Vietnam War era. However by 1985, the school had fallen out of military favor and was considered expensive, outdated and detached from other military training and tactics.

Between 1985 and 1995, many changes were taking place in the world. World events nurtured by the ever-changing political powers and policies of the modern post-cold war period created changing con-cepts of the U.S. military command. One change was to place great emphasis on SERE (Survival, Evasion, Resistance, Escape) training for

Army Rangers personnel. Army Command staff realized that after the Vietnam conflict, natural attrition eroded the numbers of "subject matter experts" in many military field skills, including tracking. A new commander, Colonel Preston "Pres" Funkhouser, was assigned to the SERE school in North Carolina and tasked with updating training to prepare and equip personnel should an armed conflict occur. He knew that training for the regular field tactics of scout/sniper, short/long reconnaissance, installation and unit security, and several other specific field skills were related to basic knowledge and skill of tracking. Col. Funkhouser determined that tracking and counter-tracking were vital assets in preparing Special Operations personnel for successful survival, escape and evasion.

In 1987 Coronel Funkhouser invited me and the Frank Heyl's UTS training program to present a basic tracking seminar at Camp Mackall, North Carolina. Camp MacKall is the home of the U.S. Army SERE school, located immediately adjacent to Fort Bragg at Fayetteville, NC and is directly related to ongoing operational training activities for specialist units. This Army post was established during the World War I era and used extensively in  World War II for final training and as a transit base for Army Airborne units. Students attending this first "official" "Joel Hardin", U.S. Army Special Forces training included the SERE instructor cadre and numerous other interested personnel from various Commands and units at Fort Bragg. Their mission was to evaluate the new and different tracking training methods and to determine the prospective effectiveness as presented by UTS.

UTS instructors introduced military personnel to tracking using the same methods, principles and practices that have been so successful in training search and rescue and law enforcement personnel. These methods differed significantly from previous military tracking school concepts and principles. The UTS program concentrated student knowledge and skill development on recognition, identification and "seeing" any and all physical evidence of any single human presence or passage. Training methods of the Philippine or Malaysian schools were focused primarily on "full footprint, multiple-person trailing." Commander Funkhouser and evaluators recognized the value of the UTS tracking principles, techniques and concepts. They recognized the proven success by civilian search and rescue and law enforcement groups as well suited to the modern mil-  itary concepts of small, highly trained, highly skilled specialist teams. Positive evaluations from students and instructors resulted in a continu- ing program of tracking training for Army Special Forces units at Fort Bragg and the SERE instructor cadre at Camp Mackall.

Military students have included mission specialties of scout/snipers, reconnaissance and long-range surveillance units, as well as other Special Operations units in all branches of the armed services. Tracking knowledge and skills continue to play a very important and traditional role in the training and mission success of these specialized units, as it did a thousand years ago, and probably always will. For me, this training provides a continual updating and insight into current military concepts, strategies, tactical techniques and mission objectives.

As I've researched the historical written accounts of tracking, and especially of tracking training, I've found that tracking itself essentially has not changed in any of the three primary arenas of military, law enforcement or missing-person searching. The knowledge and elemen- tary skills that we give our students are virtually the same as have been passed down for centuries, and in much the same way. Little has changed except the styles of the footgear worn by people who walk. Barefoot prints have changed the least and are essentially the same as they were a thousand years ago. The great difference is that barefoot prints are now exceptional, especially if they travel very far. Most of the barefoot prints found today are made by feet accustomed to shoes, thus providing very distinctive sign. The earth's surface has remained virtu- ally the same as well. Although we've covered a significant portion of it with various types of man-made coverings that are resistant to footfalls, when people get out to the dirt and grass of "nature," which in many cases is everything around them, they still place one foot in front of the other, causing visible disturbance or "sign" to the ground surface. One hundred years ago tracking training was teaching students to study an individual footprint, then follow it for a short distance and discern the person's build, age, intent and time of passage. Today my training program still follows, step-by-step, very much the same tracking instructional concepts with military students.

Counter-Tracking

To teach military students this much-needed technique, I found it necessary to help them to understand the general misconceptions of concealing sign. Reinforcing tracking principles was key to this understanding. The single factor of being unable to move forward, backward or sideways without leaving sign, is a key cause of concern for military specialists who deal with foot soldiering in today's modern environment. How the heck do you enable two- or seven-man units to get where we need them to go and back again safely without leaving sign of their having done so? Everyone wants the answer to that question, the burglar here at home, the terrorist who plants a bomb at the military dining hall, or a sniper shooting at a passing unit. When the tactical objective is to "take out" a particular military figure in the field or on the street, how can the team exit and escape without leaving a trail to be followed to their "safe zone"? The military uses the term "counter-tracking" and we have adapted the term for use in our program. Counter-tracking is defined as the ability or technique of "countering" the opposing forces' ability to track.

Counter-tracking is a somewhat clumsy term. It's accepted as a basic field skill element and is described as "the ability to move afoot leaving the least amount or the most confusing, disguised or camouflaged sign to frustrate and discourage any tracker trying to find and follow." While untrained persons may believe there exists some method of moving without leaving discoverable evidence, my experience leads me to believe that there is no such method. Based on the premise that "wherever persons walk they leave sign" we must deal with how to *minimize*, not eliminate the sign created while traveling afoot. In doing so the sign maker is hoping to counter a tracker's efforts to detect or follow his sign.

My tracking training methods are based on the belief that everyone can learn to see the physical evidence of the presence or passage of persons, friend or foe. Both military and law enforcement objectives necessitate instructing personnel in the art of counter-tracking. For example, a two-man sniper team moves slowly and carefully into position to take a shot, then needs to exit the area quickly without being noticed. Tracking students quickly learn that seeing anyone's normal footprints is a learned skill because they consist primarily of scuffs, scrapes, compressions and so rarely are identifiable footprints. Usually people who want to conceal their tracks don't even know what trackers are looking for. Unless the potential counter-tracker understands at least elementary tracking skills, he has no way of knowing what sign he's leaving for a tracker to find. Tracking education must come first! Only after learning the basic skills do inspiration, ideas, imagination and experience enable counter-tracking effectiveness.

I was first introduced to escape and evasion tactics during my early days with the Border Patrol. That was actually the nature of the game, a very serious game of hide and seek. Illegal entrants into the U.S. knew what trackers were capable of doing and some of them played their parts well. Every night in darkness they would creep across the border and cautiously make their way north toward a metropolitan area, usually getting a seven or eight-hour head start before the tracker began. At first light trackers would try to find their sign and follow it quickly enough to apprehend them before they disappeared into a community. Those crossing the border illegally came from all walks of life and from many different countries, including our own. Many U.S. citizens who wanted to avoid the border check stations for whatever reasons, including bringing in contraband would cross in the night afoot thinking they had it made.

It wasn't hard to tell the first-timers from the veterans. Those new to the "art" of illegal crossings had many misconceptions about tracking that led to some downright silly attempts to cover their trails. An often-told Border Patrol sign cutting story tells of an individual who arrived at the border fence and attached cow's hooves to the bottoms of his shoes to walk on. In the old Border Patrol office there were pictures showing the hooves nailed to the shoe bottoms, as well as pictures of the "cow" tracks going across the drag road. It seemed like a good idea until you realize how noticeable it is for a cow to step through a fence and walk across the road on two legs. Some individuals tore up grass and small brush and placed it on their trail in a way that they thought looked natural. Others used branches and sticks or a jacket to brush out their tracks, not realizing that they were creating far more sign than they were erasing. Some common attempts to obscure sign were walking on a piece of cloth or a blanket to cross roads or trails, walking on tiptoes, heels or the sides of their shoes, and crab walking on toes and fingertips. Some tried pogo sticks or stilts to leave no "tracks" at all, evidently not considering that the sticks themselves were making deep holes that were easily followed. Others affixed carpet, clothes or other items to the bottoms of shoes to walk on so as to not leave shoe marks, leaving instead the more curious and distinctive carpet or cloth footprints. Some suspects changed shoes, thinking that a tracker wouldn't notice. Really imaginative individuals loaded themselves with dirt, small rocks, leaves, or other natural ground cover to sprinkle or place on top of footprints when crossing roads, trails or open spaces.

To those untrained in tracking, some of these methods might seem quite reasonable. The problem with these and other attempts at hiding or disguising footprint evidence is that trackers notice this evidence as quickly as they do normal footprints. Without knowledge and skills of tracking, you have no basis of knowledge for counter-tracking. Another factor seldom considered by those without tracking knowledge and experience is the high stress level of the subject while trying to evade the tracker. The stress level of the sign-maker being pursued is automatically jacked up ten degrees higher than that of the pursuing tracker. If the sign-maker is actually tracking-knowledgeable, he knows how much effort he must put into hiding or disguising the sign story he is leaving behind.

I have encountered a very, very few individuals who were skilled counter-trackers. These few were unique individuals, whose illicit businesses necessitated transiting the border on a regular basis, sometimes nightly. Many of them had studied, trained and gained vast knowledge of tracking methods, manners and techniques which would aid their ability to evade pursuing Border Patrol agents. Those who had successfully persevered in this environment for any period of time became formidable adversaries. Some of these had gained a reputation of being able to successfully evade the Border Patrol sign cutters and had built a thriving business on that reputation. From these skilled criminals, I gained much of what I know of counter-tracking. On only one occasion was I seriously challenged by a military Special Forces-trained adversary in an actual evasion situation. The "evader" had been trained in the old Malaysian Tracking School methods and practices, but his deceptive methods and techniques were known and obvious to me. I was easily able to overtake and apprehend him.

I'm reluctant to write more specifically or in greater detail about counter-tracking for fear that one day our armed forces or civilian authorities might have to contend with someone who has learned to use what I've written to ill advantage. I would much rather that anyone of such mind have only the old military manual teachings to trouble the trackers of today's military or law enforcement.

There are only two methods that I know of to defeat a tracker: one, don't try—run as fast as you can to the closest safe zone, and two, don't make any tracks for the tracker to find and follow.

A Worthy Opponent

I with other members of the El Cajon sign cutters had the oppor-tunity to track one particularly skilled counter-tracker. Out on his morning patrol, one of our men picked up some sign that looked espe-cially interesting. He reported his discovery over the radio, calling for backup, then went back to scrutinizing his find. The sign that he had discovered was on a little-used two-track dirt road that crossed a small saddle in the mountains. The ground surface in the short seat of the saddle was mixed native grasses of fescue, pepper grass, short cheat grass and foxtail where cattle grazed. The grasses in the little flat area gave way to small bushes and open rocky ground sprinkled with cactus as the ground turned up toward the brush-covered hillsides.

A couple more sign cutters and I arrived and were shown where the subject had stepped on several small rocks as he crossed the road-way. As he left the roadway edge he had carefully sprinkled loose dirt and dust over his tracks. Most who try this tactic do a very amateur-ish job that usually highlights rather than obscures the track. This guy however, was obviously not an amateur. In places he had "combed" the footfall-disturbed grasses and weeds back into a more natural-looking condition and only very close examination revealed the footprint damage.

Several of us worked the area, mostly on our hands and knees. It was slow and tedious work, but the sign told us that this person was worthy of our time and attention. Two sign cutters without the same sense of the challenge made several attempts to cut the sign along nat-ural barriers further north, but without success. This was going to be a real tracking contest. It was also quite clear that a person taking such care to hide, cover and confuse his sign wasn't moving any faster than we were as we slowly found each step.

As we continued on our slow-speed chase, we became increas-ingly impressed with the skills of our subject. Many times we had to compare notes and opinions before we could figure out exactly what he had done or where he had gone. Ab Taylor, our old master tracker with great depth of experience, often came through with the proper interpretation that would keep us on the track. Together we very slowly worked this sign across the small saddle and up the adjoining ridge toward a small clump of bushes that commanded a full view of the area. Here we found our subject. We gathered in the sparse shade to congratulate ourselves and to talk with the man for whom we had gained a healthy professional respect. The respect was mutual—he expressed his appreciation for the skills that had led us to him. We adjourned to a small country gas station where we purchased refreshments and sat in the shade, "interviewing" our subject regarding how he had acquired his considerable skills.

As it turned out, the man was from deep in central Mexico. He was the son of a career Mexican Forest Service official and had spent much of his life in the mountains with his father, tracking poachers and banditos and learning to read sign. His father had told him stories of his own travel to the Estados Unidos, and of the famous Border Patrol trackers and how to avoid them. We returned our highly respected adversary to the closest port of entry and released him with our good wishes to Mexican authorities as was customary at that time. We learned from this encounter as did he, and I have no idea to this day whether or not he was able to eventually complete a successful illegal entry into the U.S.

Reconnaissance

The primary mission of a reconnaissance team is to gather all possible information about persons who have been in an area—friendly, enemy or enemy-sympathetic local residents. Military forces depend on knowing all they can about the opposing forces. The numbers, locations, methods and manner of operations, equipment, training, mental and physical conditions of personnel are only some of the factors upon which military leaders make tactical decisions. Commanders are likened to chess players. In order to be successful, one must have not only knowledge of the rules and procedures upon which play is based, but also as much as possible about the opposing player—his style, thinking, morale, training and experience. A general should have knowledge of the opposing general(s), but without the day-to-day information about troop movements and emplacement, he would only be groping in the dark and hoping to be successful. However, if the commander has reconnaissance units in the field that can give him accurate information as to opposing force strength, movements, numbers, equipment, morale and physical conditions, he has a tremendous edge when it comes to making crucial decisions.

Reconnaissance-trained trackers might sign cut various areas of natural and manmade barriers and from the sign evidence found, learn when the people were there, who they were, where they were going and why, and their mental and physical state at that time. These are the same tracking interpretations that search and rescue responders must use to be effective.

Afghanistan – 2002

The American military response following the terrorist acts against the U.S. on September 11, 2001, created a number of tracking opportunities for allied military components. The decade following the Gulf War in 1991 was another time of military downsizing as is common following armed military engagements. Administrations after the Gulf War shorted military budgets and manpower allocations, effectively limiting military units, their training and equipment and thereby operational readiness. Due to continued training with Army personnel, I was aware of the significant loss of entire units and commands. Special Operations units were stripped of senior experienced personnel, who were the backbone of future effectiveness. The continued deployment and relief of Army Special Operations units with combat-experienced personnel to various countries on "peacekeeping" missions resulted in closure of many specialist schools. Our tracking training program seemed to be lost to personnel attrition, transfers and indifference. Then the post-September 11 activation of military reserve units drew several experienced and important tracking participants and proponents into active duty training roles and deployments. I was advised of these activations and deployments in requests for training materials to train and equip field combat units with tracking awareness and elementary tracking skills.

Special Forces units assigned to temporary allied operational bases near Kabul, Afghanistan, were engaged daily in search-and-destroy missions. In the late summer and fall of 2002, one particular student, military advisor and assistant tracking instructor was stationed at this base near Kabul. This experienced team leader was well known to Command for his tracking knowledge and skills during the Gulf War, Kosovo and Serbia assignments. He was called upon to conduct tracking training for allied forces' strike teams assigned to search-and-destroy and reconnaissance missions. During a two-month period, this senior Special Operations sergeant documented training for 98 students completing this program's five-day basic military tracking course. Several successful missions were reported and documented subsequent to and as a result of this training.

Military Special Operations units were specially trained to interact directly with native villagers to encourage and enlist their individual and corporate support and alliance in identifying, locating and appropriate disposal of Al-Qaeda operatives and weapons. Tracking-trained members of these units distinguished themselves in their ability to seemingly possess a "sixth sense" or "clairvoyant intuition" in locating weapons caches. Such caches were usually secreted within residential dwellings, business or  government buildings on the outskirts of small villages. Often it was reported that successfully locating such secreted weapons and ordnance was attributed to a simple sign cutting of the streets and passageways. Those trained in tracking could observe sign of evasion or concealment tactics that often indicated or led to these locations. Tracking-trained observers were able to observe unexplained, unusual or surreptitious activity in and around the villages by people clearly not local residents and not evident by simple observation of the village. Special Operations personnel in many instances were able to follow "fugitive sign" from villages or other central areas into the surrounding territories, hills, mountains and into caves used to conceal Al-Qaeda fighters and their weaponry.

Tracking will remain a crucial inexpensive tool of military intelligence and offensive/defensive tactics. As long as military components consist of personnel afoot, tracking may decide the outcome of conflicts and engagements. In January and February of 2004, the training program received specific training requests from U.S. Army, Marine and Air Force components. The recent military action in the Iraq has emphasized the need to equip specialist personnel with knowledge and elementary skill to locate and follow sign of specific individuals in every type of environment. Contacts requested training to include the knowledge and instruction to enable accurate interpretation or reading the "sign story" and sufficient field practice to achieve proficiency in efficient, effective counter-tracking methods, techniques and tactics.

>─┼─●>─0─<●─┼─<

CHAPTER THIRTEEN

An Outback Trek
The Longest Trail

I awoke in darkness, my senses all in tune. The smells of a hound and old dust drifted over me, and a morning breeze just beginning to blow was softly rippling the tent top. Outside the tent I could hear the slight scurrying of some small creature, probably scavenging for bugs or food scraps. Though my eyes were closed, I could see the entire scene in full detail: a rudimentary campsite in the rugged dry landscape of Australia's Great Sandy Desert. Instantly everything was "real time" and in clear view in my mind. I knew it was still dark, the sky a high inky velvet punctuated by star specks and a fast-fading slice of moon. When I opened my eyes, there was just enough light to see outlines of objects, but the sun would pop very suddenly over the eastern horizon. One minute night, the next minute day in the Outback.

What the heck was I doing here? I was trying to find an American, Robert Bogucki, who'd taken off into the desert 40 days before with the idea of making a spiritual quest into complete isolation. He had not returned when expected. Western Australia Police from the local detachment in Broome with some good native trackers had launched a search, but they had lost the sign two weeks later and ended the effort, believing Bogucki to be dead. Now I was here with an American search team, after another two weeks of steady wind and bleaching sun had further reduced the sign. My best teacher Ab had always said that I brought my good luck with me, and we had found the sign and followed it. The elements had taken their toll on it, and it was a real challenge to follow through unfamiliar desert vegetation and patches of adobe sand packed hard as concrete. Even harder was trying to figure out what this guy was thinking when he deliberately went into the roughest areas. Was he still alive?

Yesterday, nearly 75 miles north of where I was following sign, the rest of the team was coming in vehicles to rendezvous and set up a base camp. They had found barefoot prints on a sandy roadway that disappeared into the bush, as Australia's rough, scrubby vegetation is called, then reappeared going the opposite way on the road. Up for discussion was whether these tracks belonged to Bogucki, which way he was traveling, and when the tracks were made. The tracks were going both ways on the road and the team was unable to determine which ones were coming and which ones were going. When I was brought to examine the tracks, I answered all those questions and could confirm that this was undoubtedly Bogucki. Not only was he alive, but we were not more than one day behind him!

I knew there weren't many in this eight-person team, and certainly none in the police force in Broome, who believed this guy was alive and still walking despite what I said about the footprints on the road. It was a very harsh landscape, and Bogucki had been alone in it for 38 days. I thought he was alive, but was I right? How many times had I been in that situation before, the only one who could see the footprint sign and believe in what I was seeing? One thing was certain, if the tracks were Bogucki's, he was alive and well when he made the tracks on the road, but where the heck was he now? I might have screwed up this time; the sign line was not continuing to go where I thought it would. Bogucki's or not it had to go somewhere from there, but where?

What clouded my thoughts was the big bloodhound that lifted it's head and flopped its chops before dropping it again on my feet. This dog thought the most comfortable place to sleep was on top of my sleeping bag, with me in it. Gad, the dog was heavy! The dog's handler, Vickie, slept peacefully on the other side of the tent. This had been our team's first night in the bush and It was hard to believe that this wasn't a dream, except for the weight of the dog. Heck, here I was, a stranger in the middle of an Australian desert. Who would have believed this? I still didn't know all I wanted to know about this guy Garrison, who had managed to get me here on two days notice. I wondered what Bogucki was doing right then, and I determined to find him, whether he wanted to be found or not.

⊱━⊙━⊰

Garrison St. Clair wasn't good about hiding his feelings, or rather he didn't make any attempt to hide his feelings. He didn't beat around the bush, didn't try to be diplomatic or politically correct. I'd met him in Nashville only a couple months before. My colleague Jerry Darkis and I were doing a classroom presentation on tracking to a group of search and rescue personnel at a national conference in Nashville when he approached me during a break, introducing himself as the commander of First Special Response Group. He asked if he could buy me a cup of coffee after the lecture. He said he wanted to discuss tracking on an international basis and I had been recommended as the person he should talk with. He was about 50 years old, short (probably about five foot seven) and balding, with glasses and a huge cigar. He was dressed in military field uniform camos, with spit-polished boots, and wore a very confident manner. He claimed to be a retired Army lieutenant colonel and sure acted like one.

After the lecture, when we were having a cup of coffee, he said he represented a relatively new organization formed of professional SAR personnel from the United States to respond to emergencies in foreign countries. Principally they would respond to instances in which U.S. citizens were lost or in a rescue situation in a foreign country when local authorities did not have adequate services to answer the need. He explained that many countries didn't have formal SAR organizations, training or equipment and couldn't respond to incidents as we do here domestically. He told me of a couple of 1st SRG responses that had been successful, but added that they had been mostly lucky. Garrison wanted the team to be successful because of its expertise and not dependent upon luck.

Many experienced SAR people had advised him that for the team to be able to respond to international missing person search missions, it needed to have trackers. He began to ask me about tracking, posing hypothetical situations and asking what would I do, how would I handle this or that, what would I expect to see, what could I determine from it? He readily admitted that he knew nothing about tracking and wanted to know what I could do. Finally he seemed satisfied and, sticking out his hand, asked if I'd be interested in joining the group. I hesitated—the last thing I needed was the responsibility to respond with another SAR group. This would be volunteering, of course. Someone would pay the expenses, but I'd be doing it for the fun. I was already having all of that type of fun that I could manage. I said that I 'd consider it, and Garrison said an application packet would be at my office before I got back. He paid for the coffee.

He was right: the packet from 1st SRG was there when I got back to the office several days later. I opened it and looked through a half inch of application paperwork. I didn't have time to even begin filling it all out or getting the medical information to complete those forms. I put the envelope on top of my "get to it one day" pile and forgot about the 1st SRG.

Then late in the afternoon of Thursday, August 12, 1999, I was beginning to think that I had achieved all that was meaningful for the day when the phone rang. I recognized the voice, but couldn't figure out who was saying in an excited, but controlled and gravelly voice, "Got yer bags packed and your passport up to date?"

Stalling for time to figure out who was on the other end of the phone line, I said, "I'm always packed and ready to go and keep two passports just so one doesn't wear out."

He laughed slightly and said in a rush, "Well, we've got a mission for a missing American and I think tracking will be the ticket. I've got a call in to the local authorities there and as soon as they call me back, I'll call you and fill you in on the details." Then it dawned on me this was GARRISON ST. CLAIR!

"Well, wait a minute! Just where is this lost guy?."

"Western Australia, in the Great Sandy Desert. I'll call you back in a few minutes with the details. Just wanted to make sure you were in telephone contact." Then he was gone. Oh heck, I thought and turned to my pile of "get to it laters" and pulled out the buried 1st SRG application envelope. I thumbed through the paperwork and found a medical form for deployment and thought, well, if I get to go, they'll need this. I quickly entered the medical information. I wouldn't have time to do anything with the rest of it.

An hour later, Garrison called again, telling me the Western Australia police had conducted a multiple day search for a 33-year-old American by the name of Robert Bogucki. Bogucki had set out to walk across the Australian Great Sandy Desert, reportedly the most uninhabitable area of Australia. He had been gone for nearly a month. They had searched, been unable to find him, and believed that he was dead. The search effort had gone far into the desert, but was terminated when the team, which included Aboriginal trackers, had lost his tracks. Everyone there assumed he was dead, and Bogucki's parents, who lived in California, wanted their son's body, if it was possible to find it, returned to the U.S. for burial. The family would pay the expenses for the team deployment. The local authorities would cooperate to the extent possible, but would not expend further resources to recover a body. "So," he asked, "this isn't a hypothetical situation. Do you think you can find month-old sign that Aboriginal trackers weren't able to follow?" I didn't know the answer to that, and said so, quickly adding that I was willing to give it a whirl. Garrison said he'd call later that evening with details of the deployment, he needed to talk further with the U.S. Consulate and State Department people.

I sat back and thought over what he had told me. Pretty much the usual SAR mission, except that it was in Australia. As I reviewed what I'd have to take, I thought I'd better check my passport just to make sure that I knew where it was and that it was valid, I hadn't carried it since I retired in September 1990. When I found it and checked the date, I was shocked—it had expired two weeks before! I called

Garrison and told him that I wasn't as smart as I had thought I was. He asked if I had a fax machine and for its number; he'd have someone from the State Department fax an order directing the Seattle passport office to provide an immediate issuance the next day. I was more than a little surprised when the letter rolled out of my fax machine within 15 minutes. The next day, Friday, I went to Seattle and obtained the renewed passport, along with air tickets to join the rest of the team in San Francisco on Sunday the 15th.

Sunday—August 15

The check-in area of San Francisco International at the United counter was crowded with humanity, but I knew it 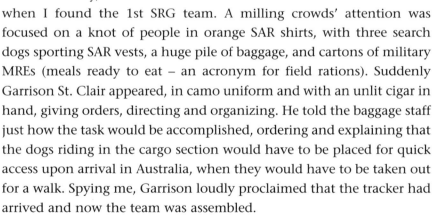 when I found the 1st SRG team. A milling crowds' attention was focused on a knot of people in orange SAR shirts, with three search dogs sporting SAR vests, a huge pile of baggage, and cartons of military MREs (meals ready to eat – an acronym for field rations). Suddenly Garrison St. Clair appeared, in camo uniform and with an unlit cigar in hand, giving orders, directing and organizing. He told the baggage staff just how the task would be accomplished, ordering and explaining that the dogs riding in the cargo section would have to be placed for quick access upon arrival in Australia, when they would have to be taken out for a walk. Spying me, Garrison loudly proclaimed that the tracker had arrived and now the team was assembled.

The team totaled eight people and somehow we all got aboard, though we were scattered around the plane. Early in the 15-hour flight, Garrison came back with team members David Kovar, his second-in-command for field operations, and Amir Findling, an experienced canine handler. Obviously Garrison was well acquainted with and trusted both of these people and had apparently been on missions previously with them, although he seemed to give my opinions and suggestions equal weight. The meeting established that we didn't know any more than when Garrison had first called me, certainly not enough to make any real operational plans. In talking with them, I learned that I had more actual search mission experience than the three of them, and maybe all the other team members to boot. Later in the flight, Garrison asked me to sit with one of the canine handlers to get acquainted. Her name was Vickie Pulver and I found out that though she was a forensics-experienced bloodhound handler, she'd had relatively little missing-person search experience. Like me, she was completely new to the 1st SRG group and didn't know any of the other team members. This was her first meeting with Garrison St. Clair in person, and though she didn't say it, I could tell she didn't know quite what to think about him. She had talked briefly with the other canine handlers and they were SAR search experienced and apparently more acquainted with Garrison.

During the flight a second and third conference was held at Garrison's command in the rear kitchen area of the plane to discuss ideas, plans and protocol. My conclusion at the end of the last meeting was that we simply didn't have the type of information that I would like to have to begin the search for Bogucki. I wanted to talk to someone who might have such information. I made my concerns known to Garrison and David Kovar, explaining that we really didn't know anything about this missing person. Age, color of eyes and hair and what he was wearing simply isn't the type of information that trackers need to begin looking for sign. I wanted to know what was in this guy's head, what he was doing out there and why. I could look without that information, but with it I would know where to look and what to look for, and I asked if there was anyone that could tell us that? Garrison said the person that would have those answers was Bogucki's girlfriend, Janet North, who was staying in Sydney. He had her telephone number, and I asked that we call her during our two-hour layover in Sydney.

Tuesday—August 17

We lost a day to the international dateline and touched down in Sydney two days after departure. The team finally gathered all baggage, equipment cartons and cases of MREs and approached Australian Customs officials, who looked askance at our carts piled high with crates, cartons and baggage. A long discussion ensued between Garrison and the inspectors, which ended with a supervisor cutting open one of the cartons of MREs and looking through one of the packages of field rations. She approved the rest without examination and passed us through to Immigration, which we cleared immediately. The canine handlers broke free and went to retrieve their charges and take them for the well-deserved walk somewhere outside. News media emerged from somewhere taking photographs of the canine units and interviewing the handlers and Garrison. The speakers were announcing boarding of the domestic flight to Melbourne as Garrison finished the last interview. I quickly got him to a pay phone and had him place the call to J anet North.

Janet had a pleasant, shy and slightly raspy voice. I advised her that I had seven minutes for her to tell me whatever she knew that would help me to find and understand Bogucki's trail if she wanted me to find him. I said to her, "Janet, I understand that you know Robert better than anyone else, including his parents, so you're the person that knows what's in his mind—his thoughts, rationale, intentions, ambitions and spirit that will keep him alive. Those are the things that I need to know, and now we have about five and a half minutes for you to tell me these things." Janet quickly said that the first thing I needed to know was that in contrast to what was being said in the media, and what the police thought, Robert wasn't crazy. He was a very deliberate and thoughtful person who had planned carefully to make this trek across the desert. She had been in California when he was in Australia, and they had gone over maps of the area together by telephone. He had carefully planned this venture and had taken with him everything he thought he needed to make the trek successfully. The purpose of his venture was to be totally alone, without resource other than what he carried with him, and to be alone with God and whatever God provided for his needs.

She added that Robert had for many years believed that all persons should have a personal relationship with God, and he felt he didn't. Robert wanted to put himself into a situation in which God would be his salvation or he would perish. They had talked about this possibility and Robert would not want anyone to interrupt or interfere with his quest. She felt that if he thought someone was going to do so, he might hide himself from searchers, and if he felt like he was going to die out there, he would try to get into an area so his body wouldn't be found.

He'd made a plan, and he would stick to it—that was Robert's nature. He had a compass and a map and he would stick to the planned course to be out to Fitzroy Crossing by August 26. "In case you think I'm as crazy as he is because I let him do it, like all the rest of them do, I'm not." she emphasized. "Robert is doing something that he has to do to live, and I love him enough to accept whatever happens. I believe he's still alive and he will come back. I couldn't have stopped him from doing it if I had wanted to, and it wouldn't have been right for me to have tried. If he dies there, that's where he wanted to be." She paused again, and added, "I don't know why he hasn't come out. I've gone there myself and I'm afraid that the area isn't quite like we thought it was from the maps."

I glanced at my watch. Garrison was holding the door to the bus and waving his cigar at me to hurry. I said, "I think you've covered it all. That's the information that I needed. Janet, it was nice talking with you and I'll do the best that I can." I hung up the receiver and ran to climb aboard the bus. Later, aboard the flight on to Melborne and seated with the entire team, I told them what I had learned from Janet. I now had a feeling that I knew Bogucki myself, and I was beginning to get a feel for what we should do. Garrison agreed I should first meet with the local police to find out what they knew, to gain support and assistance from people familiar with the area, and to get on the last tracks and see what Bogucki was doing at that time. I should be able to read from the sign line about his physical condition, mental state, whether or not he was on the planned route and still in control and from that we would know where to focus the team efforts. Garrison looked around at the team members and said, "Sounds like the plan to me."

We would have about an hour more on this flight to Melbourne, a two-hour layover there and then a long flight to Perth, with a four-hour layover, and finally to Broome in the huge state of Western Australia. I could relax a bit now and did so and began to get acquainted with the other team members.

When we landed in Melbourne and emerged through the concourse doors, bright TV lights came on and suddenly the team was on Australian television news. Obviously people in the media in Sydney had contacted correspondents in Melbourne advising them of the elite rescue team from the States that had come to show Australia how to find someone! The reporters were mostly interested in the search dogs and handlers and interviewing Garrison, with his big cigar stuck in the corner of his mouth. I was dressed like the average tourist and no one paid any attention to me as I slipped past the cameras and microphones and went into the airport center. I wandered around into and out of the usual airport shops and into a newsstand. Holy moly! There on the front page were pictures of the canine teams taken at the Sydney airport and a large picture of Garrison St. Clair with cigar flourishing. Headlines announced "American Search Team Lands to Find Bogucki." I produced an Australian dollar and purchased the paper to find out what it was we were going to do. In a quiet corner I read the article, a rehash of the previous stories of the Bogucki search. The only thing new was a statement by the Western Australian Police Superintendent who was neither complimentary nor welcoming. The first part of my little plan was going to be a bit difficult and the media sure wasn't helping.

After some time David came wandering through, spotted me and came to sit. I showed him the paper. "Yes, we know," he said. "The media has already gotten to Garrison and he's on the phone talking to the police, the American Consul and who knows who else. The Consul will meet us at the airport in Perth and will be expected to make a statement to the media." He looked disgusted and said the whole thing had already gotten out of hand, ending with "I'm glad that Garrison's in charge and not me."

One by one the other team members slowly drifted to our location. They'd gotten permission to have the dogs in the terminal and that drew a small crowd of children and mothers. The media flocked to get pictures of the little kids loving the search dogs, pulling their ears and tails. The dogs liked the attention as much as the kids loved the dogs. Long before the first boarding call for our flight, our whole team had gotten tired of the attention and we were glad to have the excuse to gather up gear and head down the concourse to the gate. I was thankful that I was dressed as a tourist and didn't have a dog to draw attention.

It seemed like a long flight to Perth, but not long enough for restful sleep. Upon arrival, TV spotlights blinded all behind me as I walked quickly to the side of the team and passed unnoticed behind the gathered news media. Once past the tangled knot of reporters, cameramen, cords, lines and equipment I was into a relatively empty area of calm in the terminal. The few people were nearly all gathered close enough to see what the media frenzy was all about. I walked outside and found a nice comfortable bench in the shade of a jacaranda tree that was filled to the brim with colorful lorakeets (small birds related to parakeets) that I had come to so enjoy on my previous trip to Australia.

Later I drifted inside and met the American Consul as he waited for Garrison to get free of another telephone interview. The Consul assured me that the police would be cooperative, though the Broome Police Superintendent was huffing and puffing at the issue of a team coming from the States to do what they were unable to do. We would try to minimize that viewpoint I assured him. Finally the call for boarding came to the relief of all and we were off on the last leg of the trip to land in Broome, Western Australia at midnight some twelve hours after leaving Sydney.

Waiting to receive us at Broome was the local police sergeant, Geoff Fuller, with a couple of his men, and the local TV news director

named Troy Hynam. This news director had no reporters, no cameramen, no media fanfare—just a great smile and good wishes for success.
Ah, these were my kind of people—low key, completely accommo-
dating and helpful. No motel rooms were available in the town.
Broome, we quickly learned, was a small, but widely known and
much-cherished tourist and vacation spot. This was the height of the
tourist season and it would be hard to find much of what we would
be needing, including motel rooms and rental vehicles.

Troy was very respectful of our team and mission. His wife and
two children were out of town for a couple days, so he had made
arrangements for us to be taken to his home and bedded down in our
sleeping bags on his veranda. Sgt. Fuller had already arranged an official meeting at the police station for eight o'clock in the morning, with
the huffy and very critical superintendent, who was quoted in the
newest headlines asking "Who Will Pay for the Search for the American
Search Team?"

Wednesday—August 18

Morning came before anyone was ready for it. I heard the rustle
of palm tree fronds and listened to unfamiliar bird talk announcing
that daylight was coming. There was mist in the air and it felt like cool,
cloudy coastal weather. I got up, dressed as quickly as possible, dancing
from one foot to another trying to be quiet and not step on any sleeping bags or dogs and went in to put the pot on to heat water for coffee.
I had gotten permission from Troy to be first up and "on with the pot."
I learned that here when they said coffee, they meant hot water and
instant coffee. After a quick shower—the first in two days of travel and
to be the last for a long week—I found the rest of the group beginning
to stir.

The dogs got up early to go for their constitutional walk and had
to have a handler to supervise which tended to rouse everyone.
Garrison was up and had already left to walk to the police station.
Coffee cup in hand, I managed to get off of the porch. I looked back

at the disarray of bags, boxes and still-sleeping or groggy team members, a couple of whom I couldn't even remember their names and didn't know well enough to wake them up. This was my quiet time and I moseyed around to the back yard only to find two dog handlers asleep on their feet, waiting while their charges, the big bloodhound that looked to me like a mix of some sort, and what looked like a black Labrador, did their morning thing.

The landscape looked much like southern California, with palm trees and shrubs that looked like they needed both water and nourishment. Loose silvery sand held small tufts of grass that served as a lawn. I was sure that I smelled the salt and beach rubble of the ocean in the mist, but wasn't sure that we were close enough; perhaps I was mistaken. I sipped the instant coffee and wondered why places close to where coffee grew never had real coffee. I could hear the little lorakeets having a gabfest down the way and the weird "laugh" of a kookaburra bird. During my second cup of coffee, Garrison came striding back up the drive, his cigar leaving a trail of smoke puffballs. He motioned for David Kovar, standing with his first mug of coffee, and me to join him in the yard.

"Police Superintendent Roust will be at the meeting," Garrison said, "and he's going to give us some crap, so be prepared." Roust's statements in the newspapers the previous day had made it clear he wasn't welcoming us. The police had conducted a reasonable search and officially terminated it, and without new information, it would stay closed.

With a puff on his cigar, Garrison said, "Fuller will run interference for us to the extent possible, but this guy Roust is the superintendent and isn't wanting us to go out there. He's afraid we might find something and make them look bad. The press would crucify him, and it wouldn't be good for us either. We don't have any specifics to plan from, so we'll just have to play it by ear. Got any coffee?" I had already learned that he liked "good" coffee, and this wasn't it and I told him so as we turned to head for the kitchen.

By the time I was ready for my third cup Sergeant Fuller was there to drive us the few blocks to the police station. I thought surely they would have a coffee pot at the police station, declined the refill and readied my gear to leave. Fuller gave us a quick ten-cent tour of the headquarters building, ending at the conference room. Superintendent Roust was sitting at the head of the table in full regalia and looking very, very formal and all serious business. No coffee was offered, there were no coffee mugs on the table, and I began to get the idea this wasn't a coffee-drinking police force. Of course if all they had to drink was the instant, I didn't blame them much. We gathered around the table with Fuller doing the introductions: Corporals Wally Wolfe and Ray Briggs; Western Australia Channel 6 News Director Troy Hynam and the *Western Australia News* reporter Rob Duncan and photographer Ben Martin, Garrison, David and me.

Fuller began with background of the missing-person incident, based on the police investigation and search effort. Robert Bogucki, accompanied by girlfriend Janet North, had come to Australia to tour around Australia by bicycle. Janet grew tired of the bicycle travel and discontinued the trip returning to the U.S. Bogucki continued alone, telephoning Janet in the States from time to time. Somewhere Bogucki got the idea to ride his bicycle across the Great Sandy Desert. He discussed this venture with Janet during their last telephone conversation on July 4. On July 11, Bogucki mailed a card to his parents in California from the Sandfire Roadhouse on the Great Northern Highway. Fuller explained that Sandfire Roadhouse was just a gas stop and small store along the highway about a 150 kilometers south of Broome.

Fuller said they guessed that Bogucki left the highway, apparently on the 11th or the 12th, and headed into the desert on what is known as the Pegasus track. Indicating a map covering most of one wall, he said we'd be able to locate points of interest when he was finished, to which the superintendent harrumphed, but said nothing. On July 23, a tourist group found Bogucki's bicycle and camping gear hidden in the bush along the Pegasus track and reported the find to police. They responded and in searching found Bogucki's name on a rented room receipt, which led them to immigration records and his entry information with Janet. They then managed to locate Bogucki's parents in California and through them made contact with Janet, who told them of Bogucki's intentions to travel across the desert and come out at Fitzroy Crossing.

The police had conferred with Australian Army survival experts and specialists among their own personnel. The general consensus was that anyone walking into the desert in that area would not be able to carry sufficient food and water to remain for more than ten days or two weeks. Bogucki was last known to be at the Sandfire roadhouse on the 11th, and it appeared to the police that the bicycle and other items abandoned by Bogucki had been in the bush for some time. Reasoning that if in fact he had tried to walk across the desert at that point he would be in dire trouble, if not, in fact, dead.

The police mounted a search for Bogucki on July 24 using several Aboriginal trackers, search volunteers and available police officers. The trackers were able to locate what they were sure were Bogucki's footprints walking east on the Pegasus track. The police search followed the footprints for several days and found where the footprints left the Pegasus track and headed northeast. They followed the tracks for three days before losing them during a strong wind storm. They terminated the search on July 31. Fuller described the Pegasus track as an old unused four-wheel-drive road that was rutted, overgrown with brush, and washed out in places. They had broken axles and springs, ruined a dozen tires, punctured radiators, and nearly destroyed three vehicles during this search effort. Altogether they had gone nearly 180 kilometers from the highway following Bogucki's tracks. Their search support was not adequate for this type of search. Available helicopters had a limited range and the last search day's efforts were beyond that range. The search had extended beyond range of communications equipment. They had consulted again with the survival experts and concluded that there was no way that Bogucki could be alive. It would be impossible for him to survive out there for nearly three weeks. Additionally, the Aboriginal trackers had quit the search effort a couple days before the wind storm. They would not have anything to do with a search for a dead person and everyone thought Bogucki was dead, and additionally they were respecting the area of a different tribal group. The police trackers had been able to follow the footprints for two more days, much to the credit of Ben and Rob, who greatly assisted with following the prints. The search was terminated because everyone thought Bogucki was dead and command thought it would be fool-hardy to jeopardize searchers and equipment by continuing. Logistical and communication support was not available to continue further into the desert. Fuller turned to Superintendent Roust and said, "That's about it, sir."

Roust cleared his throat and informed us that he was the official responsible for citizens and natives of Western Australia and, unfortu-nately, for all of the dumb tourists too. He made it clear that he thought Bogucki was irresponsible and had contributed to his own demise in the desert. Sgt. Fuller and the Western Australia Police had spent hundreds of thousands of dollars and endangered many lives in searching for Bogucki. All of the experts agreed that there was no way Bogucki could have survived for the number of days encompassed by the search efforts. Everyone believed that Bogucki was dead. The search had been terminated for sound and justifiable reasons. Bogucki's par-ents and his equally irresponsible girlfriend had agreed with them and they were satisfied. Roust couldn't authorize the reopening of the search unless there was some compelling new information that could support a belief that somehow Bogucki was surviving. He acknowl-edged that the 1st SRG team had come a long way and because of all of the publicity, he was uncomfortable telling us we couldn't go afield on the search. He turned to Garrison and said that as an ex-military offi-cer, Garrison would surely understand his predicament.

Garrison had not taken issue with anything that had been said so far. Now he lowered his cigar and addressed Superintendent Roust. First he complimented Fuller and all of his men on their search effort, and acknowledged that they had terminated the search for sound reasons. He complimented Roust for the job he had done and the support he had furnished to this police detachment. He explained that for the most part we'd already had all of the information that had been presented by Fuller that morning, though we appreciated hearing it from the sergeant. He briefly explained how he'd been contacted at the request of the Bogucki family, and how he'd put a team together with a high level of search expertise. Garrison looked sideways at me and introduced me again as a tracking expert with 30 years of law enforcement experience. He emphasized that I was equally well known for my ability to extract necessary information to ensure tracking mission success. Garrison explained about my conversation with Janet and about what was in Bogucki's mind, and about his personality and will to live. Garrison believed that I had gotten information from Janet that was not previously available to Fuller and his men which would permit our operation to be successful. He turned to me and said, "Why don't you share with the superintendent what Janet told you?"

I recounted my conversation with her, emphasizing her conviction that Bogucki had planned this trip very well. I repeated her explanation that he had a strong desire to place himself in a position in which he would have to trust in God for his survival. He had planned with what he believed would be sufficient provisions, map and compass, etc. She didn't know why he had abandoned his plan to ride his bike across the desert, but she was sure it was for a well-considered reason. During this venture to cross the desert and establish a personal relationship with God, he would not want to be intercepted, interrupted or otherwise contacted by anyone. He had told her that should he come to the point at which he didn't believe he would survive, he would attempt to hide himself, so as to remain forever in the desert. She believed that if rescue teams got close to him, he might in fact hide or otherwise not respond to their efforts.

Garrison then told Roust that it might well be that Fuller and the other searchers had gotten into the right area, but Bogucki didn't call out to them or allow himself to be seen from the air. Bogucki knew where the water sources were, according to Janet, and he planned to drink and replenish his reserves at those sites. To deny our team the opportunity to at least make an effort to find Bogucki and later to find that he had been within reach of the Australian search efforts would be a major error. Garrison said we wouldn't require supplies or support from the police, only their blessing and authorization for our efforts. He concluded, "This is a Western Australia police missing-person incident, and we do not go without your authorization."

Roust cleared his throat again and rose, asking for a few minutes to consult with the sergeant and his men. When they returned, he announced that he would officially reopen the search based on the new information and we were welcome to begin our operation immediately. He added that we would have to have one of the police officers with us at all times, so Constable Ray Briggs would go with us for the first few days. Garrison, David and I all looked at each other and I know we wanted to jump and shout, but we kept our cool.

When the police left, David and I began to look at the wall map to better acquaint ourselves with the search area. We invited Rob and Ben to join us—with their previous search insight we might better understand what we were seeing. Rob quickly pointed out that there were inaccuracies on the map, but he wasn't sure just what was correct and what wasn't. David and I checked to make sure it was an official topographical map of the region and found it published by the appropriate government office. "What's not accurate?" I asked.

"Well," Rob began, "I'm not from here so I'm not too sure, but some of these roads aren't in the right place." Officer Ray Briggs came in and Rob asked about the map. Ray advised that we should get George Messer to discuss this. Ray left the station and returned with George, a likable fellow who said he'd been traveling all over the Great Sandy Desert since it was first surveyed. When he was a kid in the 1940s he hired on with the survey crew contracted by the oil companies to survey the entire region. He worked with them for several years before going on to other work with the oil companies. Then in later years, when they needed someone who knew the original surveys, they had rehired him as a private contractor. I asked that he show us on the map where any discrepancies might be. He laughed, picked up a red felt-tip pen and started drawing on the map's overlay. "Well, for instance, this road wasn't ever made and there's a road here that doesn't show, and this road here goes over this way and up here. This butte isn't here where they put it—it's actually over this way about 50 kilometers and this creek comes over here and runs into this river..."

I said to David, "I'll go find some paper and we'd better make us a map that has the right roads. No wonder Bogucki is out there wandering around somewhere." In another office I received from the secretary 14 x 21-inch sheets of paper. Back at the map, David and I traced a new map that was a combination of the official map and the one drawn by George. We were just finishing when Garrison returned.

"Okay," he said, "we've got a chopper. David, you and Joel will go with Ray to the place where they had the tracks last. The pilot knows the location. He has a GPS way point, and Ray was with the team at the site on the last day of the search. The thing is that the chopper is a little one, and you guys will have to strip your packs to the bare bones. Let's get back to the house and gather up your gear. The rest of the team will head out in the early morning to rendezvous with you. We'll get water, aviation fuel for the chopper, maps, a couple more vehicles and whatever else we need, but the first thing is to get you two headed out there to see what you can find. We have a rendezvous point picked out at an old airstrip that should be easy to find, and George says we can get there in one day's drive so we should be there by tomorrow evening."

It took a two-hour hassle at Troy's house to brief everyone, to have them decide what they should bring, to get arranged and try to get things sorted, taking this and stowing that. The pilot had told Garrison that the total of whatever we took could only weigh ten pounds. We didn't want to be without the necessities of survival or means of communicating with the team. Finally we were rushed to the airport to join Ray and the helicopter owner/pilot, Devon O'Brian. It was a small four-place Robinson helicopter and I quickly understood the ten-pound gear limit. It would barely carry David, Ray, me and the pilot—it was little! David and I had planned to overnight on site and needed minimal gear for that and maintaining ourselves until the helicopter could refuel and return to provide support to us on the ground.

This whole plan was flimsy, as we would be well beyond the operational range of this aircraft. We had another conference, this time including the pilot, who informed us that we'd stop at a cattle station called Dampier Downs Homestead on the way out and refuel from a fuel dump of gas in barrels. Dampier Downs wasn't actually on the way to the place that we wanted to go to, but the pilot assured us that this slight deviation would give the bird fuel enough to return to the cattle station, if needed, for additional fuel in case Garrison didn't get out to the rendezvous point with the fuel he'd be bringing. This kind of thinking made me feel a bit better—they didn't want to get stranded out there without fuel any more than I did.

Devon glanced at our gear, mumbling to himself and stowing it under seat hangers and cushions. I didn't see any gear for Ray or Devon, but maybe there was somewhere else to stuff things in the tiny cabin. A map was spread on the tarmac and Devon confirmed with Garrison and Ray the location of Dampier Downs, Looma Airstrip and a road marked McLarty Track that Garrison was to travel to the rendezvous point. He marked another area on the map with his pen, saying that it was about where the previous search had ended and that's where we'd be going.

We shoehorned ourselves into the little helicopter and I wondered if it would get off of the ground. Glancing at my watch again, I noticed that the afternoon was slipping away quickly, as it was nearly three o'clock. With the rotors straining, we lifted off and I saw the beach only a few hundred yards away over the brushy humps and hollows—I had smelled the ocean! Scattered columns of smoke rose here and there where there were brush fires and I could see that the fires were left to burn until they ran out of brush for fuel.

Reaching flying elevation I could see westward far out to sea with breaking surf on the white sandy beach. Toward the east there didn't seem to be a horizon—the distance stretched further then the eye could see and it all blurred into a gray-green brush colored haze. Here and there, eucalyptus trees in small clumps stretched into the haze of the sky. I glanced at the instrument panel and saw that we were at 500 feet and 110 knots of airspeed. I could see from the treetops and the smoke plumes that we were bucking a headwind and were headed more east than south. The little chopper's motor was working hard and making too much noise for conversation. We had left the highway far behind and occasionally I could see evidence in the brush of an old roadway that the Aussies called "tracks."

We flew for about an hour when I spotted what seemed to be playtoy ranch outbuildings far ahead. As we slowly closed on them and they took on realistic porportions I could see flocks of black cuckoos flying from small groves of trees in the creek bottoms near the buildings. A few head of cattle were scattered in the brush and trees, and a couple horses stood three-legged in the corner of a pale brown pasture. We circled the ranch house and old windmill and settled to the ground near the outbuildings. Devon went through the shutdown procedures and I looked out to see what seemed like a new version of Gary Cooper approaching. The long-legged strolling gait covering the ground unhurriedly brought him quickly toward us. A worn denim shirt showed old sweat stains and his Levi's were threadbare. Once-black boots were the color of the dust he kicked up with each firm step, and a sweat-stained Stetson topped his lean face with its friendly grin. He was every inch an age defying cowboy, sun browned and rawboned strong. He strode up to the little bird and wrenched the door open, nearly dumping Devon out on the ground.

"Well, howdy!" he drawled, with a much wider grin, "sure glad to see you boys!" He pumped Devon's forearm, then turned to greet us just as enthusiastically as we began to climb out. Devon did his best to introduce us to Peter DeLong, the owner-operator of Dampier Downs. Peter knew Ray Briggs and they exchanged greetings. Peter turned to look David and me up and down and then said, "So this is the rescue team! Well, come to the house for tea."

I hesitated, thinking that the morning had fled and now the afternoon was going and we didn't have time to sit and have tea. Ray noticed my hesitation and whispered to David and me that it was expected that we go to the house for tea—to do otherwise would be an unforgivable insult. Peter and Devon were already walking ahead and we certainly weren't going anywhere from here without the pilot, we shrugged shoulders to each other and headed for the fenced yard gate and the walkway to the large and typically Australian ranch house. This looked very much like many ranches in cattle country in the States: a little past their pime with a lack of adequate help and funding. Old farming machinery with peeling, sun-bleached paint were parked here and there, two or three old trucks with heavy, heavy cattle racks, a couple old pickup ruins, and of course several tractors of different styles. The buildings looked serviceable but were all in need of repair, paint and window panes.

A flock of black cuckoos circled and squawked before settling into the upper branches of the trees along the creek bottom as we went inside the gate and were greeted by three blue heeler dogs. The  yard was mostly baked dirt but there were some brilliantly colored flowers in small beds. We followed Peter past a large concrete-floored building that was open and screened on both sides from the two-foot base wall nearly to the eaves by long sections of horizonically hinged shutters. Inside we could see several iron skeleton bed frames with sagging springs, each had a large light-blue mosquito net hung from an overhead beam. Ray explained that this was the drovers' and extra hired help's bunk house when Peter had crews to round up cattle. The same style wooden window shutters of the main house were propped wide open. When we all stood in the middle of the large room of the sparsely furnished house, Peter waved toward slightly open doors, saying, "This is what it is—two bedrooms off to the side, my study in that corner, and we call it home." He told us to make ourselves comfortable and went into the kitchen to put the kettle on. We followed and found chairs around a long wooden ranch table.

Peter came to sit with us, asking all about David and me and our mission. The tea was hot and relaxing. Suddenly I remembered that David and I hadn't eaten anything since whatever it was on the flight from Perth last night. Peter, Ray and Devon discussed the previous search effort affording David and I a more complete picture of what was done and what was not. Searchers had worked long hard days working with the Aboriginal trackers to follow Bogucki's footprints on the Pegasus track. The first few days and a hundred kilometers or so went fairly quickly with good progress, then things began to bog down. The footprints weren't easy to find and follow, the road was washed out or overgrown, and vehicles began to break down. Most of the volunteers had to quit the search and return home and to work. Then the footprints turned north cross country from the Pegasus track and things really got rough. The trackers left the search and it was up to the police and the two newspaper guys. Their third day without the trackers was the last. In the third afternoon of hard wind the tracks just seemed to disappear. Police officer Ted Thompson was considered to be a very good tracker, but he couldn't pick up the sign and they decided to quit. Now the U.S. team was going to go back down there and try to find the sign line and continue to follow it even though it was nearly three weeks later.

The second cup of tea was even better and I began to have thoughts of giving up coffee for tea while I was here. Peter asked where Garrison's convoy with the fuel, water and other team members was going to rendezvous with us to set up the base camp. Devon said we had arranged to meet at Looma Airstrip. Peter nodded, but I noticed a look of doubt skitter across his face. When the conversation lapsed, I asked him if he had a question about meeting at Looma Airstrip.

"No, not really. I was just wondering how they were going to get there. I'm sure that road is washed out and no one has been over it for years."

Ray said he'd been told that the road past the airstrip was used quite often and, though rough in places, was passable. A discussion between them ensued over these points. Much of it had to do with some confusion about the actual location of this airstrip. I suggested we look at the map to assure everyone including me, where we were meeing the convoy. Peter said he had original charts and maps of the entire State of Western Australia and much better ones than the police had. He hurried to the corner study and a large old wooden barrel full of rolled maps. He quickly pulled and unfurled one, then another, sorting through a half-dozen before finding what he wanted and brought it to the table. Spreading the map and anchoring it with the tea mugs, his finger traced the road from Broome to Dampier Downs. Then he pointed to a smaller splinter road that intersected with the Dampier Downs road and headed southeast and seemingly dead- ended. "This here is Looma Airstrip. I know where it is because I made it for the government 30 years ago. I made the road to it and it wasn't ever used, so I know it's not passable now."

"Well," Devon said, "that's where Garrison is going early in the morning and he'll be there by late afternoon tomorrow."

Peter stood up and said slowly, "No, he won't. He might think he will, but he won't, so if you're thinking that you're going to meet him there, he ain't going to be there. If you're going all the way down to the Pegasus track, you'd better figure on coming back here for fuel or you'll be sitting out there somewhere waiting for me to come find you."

Ray injected that he was sure that the road went right past the airstrip. It was grown up and unless you knew where it was you wouldn't be able to recognize it from the ground, but from the air it should be visible.

"Okay!" I said. "Before we go any further, let's make sure that we know where we're going to rendezvous and when. I for one don't want to be stuck out there following Bogucki just to get out of the desert!" They all agreed, and Peter led Ray to the satellite phone in the corner. Forty-five minutes later and after contact with Garrison and Garrison then making contact with George Messer, we learned that there was in fact a second Looma Airstrip. Peter was unaware of the second airstrip but according to George it was indeed close to the passable road that George knew about. Finally to avoid any further confussion George agreed to guide Garrison and the convoy to the site the next morning. Garrison did his best to advise Peter and Devon to about where the second airstrip was with assurance from George that Devon could find it from the air. I drew a long breath of relief.

That taken care of, Peter suggested that we have dinner with him and remain the night there and get an early start in the morning. He quickly pointed out that by the time we fueled up and flew south it would be nearly dark and we would have to sleep on the ground instead of in the bunk house. He said that he had some beef cooking on the stove to make stew and it would be ready in an hour if we'd like to have a beer and relax. It didn't take much convincing to make the decision. Ray used the phone to advise his office and Garrison that we were staying the night at Dampier Downs. Helping hands made quick work of cleaning and cutting vegetables and dumping all into the stew. Another beer was passed around while we waited for dinner. I learned that Peter had only recently returned from Perth and a final goodbye to his wife, who had suffered for two years with cancer. That was largely why the ranch was rundown, but Peter was back now and determined to get things going once again.

We had a good dinner and talked into early night. By moonlight we headed for the bunk house and crawled under the swaying mosquito netting. I learned that both Ray and Devon were very, very much concerned about brown snakes crawling into their beds during the night. They admitted that neither would have spent the night outside of the helicopter cabin if we'd gone on south. Neither one would sleep on the ground anywhere in the desert, but they would let David and me do so if we wanted to! We agreed to be up at daylight and lifting off at six in the morning in order to meet the convoy at 4 p.m. Sleep had been elusive the past couple nights, and both David and I slept soundly, snakes or no snakes.

Thursday—August 19

This morning dawned early with a light misty haze rising as the sun's first rays snapped the birds awake and brought long scraggly tree shadows into the bunk house. After a cold-water wash-up and a hot cup of tea, we topped off the little chopper's fuel tanks and climbed aboard. Devon got the rotors turning and before the sun was shining housetop high, we were waving goodbye to Peter, who wished us well in finding Bogucki and invited us to come back to have tea and tell him all about it. We headed directly south, with Devon watching the compass and the GPS to get us back to the way mark position of the last day of the previous search and the end of the line of tracks.

The flight south took nearly an hour and half and allowed me to get a good view of the landscape over a pretty good share of this desert. It sure didn't look like I thought it would. At first I couldn't recognize the sand dunes they were talking about. But as we flew along I suddenly realized what I was looking at—the sand dunes were not hills of loose sand like I expected to see, but endless ripples of the sand surface like you see in the surf line along the beach and caused by the sea sometime in history long past. However these sand ripples were covered for the most part by brush, grass and scattered trees. I had been expecting to see a sand desert like in the southwest U.S.—miles and miles of harsh, rocky soil so thin nothing but a little brush and cactus will grow, and few mammals are found. Here in the Outback there were wild camels, descended from domestic ones brought here as experimental pack animals, herds of wild burros, kangaroos, wallabies and feral cattle. Animal trails crisscrossed the landscape, and I saw remnants of a few old roads, going straight east and west and intersecting straight north and south.

It took a bit of looking around and considerable discussion between Ray and the pilot before they found the last vehicle tracks from their last search day nearly three weeks before. From that point they had followed Bogucki's tracks for another five to 10 kilometers north before the sign was blown out by the wind. I had been told that

Constable Thompson and newspaper reporter Rob Duncan had been able to stay on the sign until late in the afternoon. Then dark clouds rolled in and obscured the sun. A strong wind began to blow up clouds of sand that burned their eyes and noses. It tore at their clothing and they struggled just to get back to the vehicles, the wind taking any evidence of the tracks that they could see. The whole search team turned around and left the desert and left Bogucki to whatever fate he had called upon himself.

The police Range Rover tracks from the previous search were very faint in the open areas where the wind had done its best work, but from the air above I could see them running in and out of the brush in a continual line south off toward the horizon. I couldn't see any footprints along or around the vehicle tracks. I motioned for Devon to sit us down so I could walk. Devon picked a clear area on the ridgetop and setteled onto the sand and course grass.

Once we were on the ground the tire tracks were almost invisible. Devon and Ray stood by the chopper, while David and I began searching for the tracks. We began to circle to the south and I had my first opportunity to climb up one of the 50-foot sand dunes. This one was covered with brush and clumps of tall, coarse-bladed grass. Small clumps of a tall brush hid the Range Rover tracks until I spied some bark skinned off by the undercarriage and realized that the vehicle had driven right over the brush itself. Then I could see traces of the tire marks well blown out by the wind on this ridge top. The vehicle tracks showed the struggle the search party had been having. The Range Rovers went pretty well over brush and trees, up hill and down on the packed sand, but when they hit the ripples, piles, or loose-sand pockets, they sank to the floorboards. Both footprints and tire tracks on the hard sand were like prints on concrete with a little covering of sand and barely visible at best. Only where they were protected from the wind did any compression still show, a barely visible and unidentifiable outline. I could easily understand why the other trackers had difficulty in following the sign of one person mixed with native animal sign through the brush, loose sand and sand packed as hard as concrete.

Now knowing what to "see," I followed the tracks with David to where the vehicle had stopped in the valley between the dunes. I stopped and tried to tell David everything that I was looking for and why it would look like it should, then we slowly began to search our way northward from the last of the vehicle tracks. I found several footprints before I called to David to come take a look at them. They were badly blown out and I wanted to be sure of what I had and that he would be able to see them. There should be at least two sets of the sign: Ted Thompson's and Rob Duncan's. I slowly walked along waiting for David to catch up, the set of tracks that I was looking at had a definite heel, once I could see that the sole portion of the shoe print began to be visible. These prints would be those of Officer Thompson. David struggled to make out what I was showing him in the first few tracks then suddenly the light was right and he caught it.

Together we worked northward, slowly making sure of each of the constable's prints while looking for Bogucki's prints and quickly acquainting David with what the windblown prints looked like. I could tell that the subject of the prints we were following was sure of where he was going. Suddenly I could see the older set of prints that this one followed. "I believe we've found Bogucki's tracks!" I said, glancing at my watch. It was about 8:30 a.m. and the sun was beginning to warm things up. No one was sure about what type of footgear Bogucki was wearing and no one could describe it in any manner that I could visualize what it might look like. Someone had said that Bogucki was walking the Pegasus track barefoot. This older set of prints that the heeled boot was following were simply flattened places of the right shape and size to be footprints. They couldn't be anything but flat-soled shoe prints, about 11 inches long and three or four inches wide at the ball of the foot. I pointed out the very faint flat spots to David and told him that I thought they were the ones that we were looking for. I stayed with the faint tracks, occasionally losing them for a few steps and picking them up again through the brush and grass clumps. In the open, both sets were pretty well gone and only the heel impression of what I supposed was the policeman's boot still showing, but here and there alongside were slick compressions reflecting the light that had to be the flat-soled shoes.

David and I climbed up a dune and crossed its hump down into the valley and worked our way across the bottom and up the next. David tagged along trying to see what I was seeing, not wanting to slow me down and occasionally asking to be shown what I was seeing. When I requested he hung orange surveyor's tape to flag or mark our trail. As we reached the top of the next dune, I looked back and realized that we were out of Ray and Devon's sight. I asked David to radio the chopper and have them come forward to where we were or soon we'd be out of radio range. We'd probably covered nearly a mile.

The ground surface in the valley bottoms between the dunes was light gray, hard-packed sand with streaks of light pink in some places. The winds blew loose sand on the sides of the dunes and at the top dumped whatever was still being carried leaving ripples and soft drifts and piles. The tracks of both men and animals in the loose sand were simply deep pits, like you see above the high-tide line along the beach, pits that quickly eroded due to earth's vibration and the wind that eventually filled them in, becoming shallow depressions.

David was a good student and quickly learned to "see" the meaningful reflections of light, and recognize them as something I should look at. We soon were working as an effective team. We were moving pretty well, when suddenly there were tracks all over the place. I raised my hand and told David to just stand still till I had a chance to look it over and figure out what this meant. There were three sets of tracks—Bogucki's for sure, and Ted Thompson's and probably Rob's. We were in the the valley between two dunes. I followed the sign one way then the other, and suddenly it made sense. This is where they first lost the sign, went back and forth searching for it, found it, lost it again, then found it and went on. But here Thompson was marking the sign, so if they lost it again they would know where it was last. He was using the same old marking method that we had used in the Border Patrol so many years before—a quick toe marking a half circle behind the heel of the print. Here Thompson's tracks went slower, with more looking around, but finally they crossed the valley and began to climb the dune. I saw a mark here or there, but I couldn't see what had been marked.

We worked our way to the top of the dune following some faint flat spots and an occasional heel impression as Devon and the chopper came hopping up behind us and landed in the next valley north. I thought I had the sign, but just wasn't positive. I could see where Thompson had searched the dune top and down the hillside without success—this was where he had finally lost the sign and had given up the search. I worked my way into the valley, directing David to work off to one side, hoping to cover more area and to find the prints. Then I found something—a very faint flat spot that somehow reflected the light or for some reason looked different than the surrounding surface—then another and another in about the right distance sequence. I wasn't sure that I had the right thing, but it was the best that I could see and I worked along, marking what I could see. In the bottom of the valley, we were among knee-high and waist-high brush and grasses. Clumps grew separately but close enough together so the tops hid the ground surface. Animals congregated here, and parting the grass and bush tops, I could see numerous trails and sign of large lizards, birds and the tail drags and thrusts of young kangaroos called joeys. I was to learn later that the stickery, knee-high bushes were the dreaded spinifex that we had been warned would disable the search dogs.

Then I found it! I called excitedly to David to join me. Beside a small bush, in line with the flagging on the hillside behind us and the flagging I had left in the bottom to mark the first "possibles", was the best track we'd seen yet. This one was definitely a flat-soled shoe: some type of tennis shoe or deck shoe, I guessed. It had no line marking the outline or border around the pattern, and that made it actually look like a shower-shoe track, with adjoining lines of pencil-sized octagon shapes running from toe to heel. No impressive heel strikes or ball of the foot-to-toe push-offs— the foot was contacting the surface almost flat. This indicated a man with a rather tall, somewhat slim physique and strong legs. He walked easily and for distance, endurance not speed, and he was able to step between the grass and brush clumps, his feet finding the ground surface without damaging the plants. I quickly fished a track ID card out of my pack and began drawing the prints. David took this time to call the bird to come forward again, and to have Devon contact Garrison via the on-board satellite phone and tell them we had the sign and were traveling northward. David asked, "How do you know this is his track?"

"Well, if they were on his sign when they lost it, then we're on it now because this track comes right from where they last were marking the sign, and you sure haven't seen any other tracks out here have you?" He grinned and we worked drawing, measuring and capturing the details of the footprint.

The bird came whirling over the hump and settled into the low brush a short distance from us, and Devon and Ray came over to see the sign for themselves. I was able to show them the faint indications of the rows of octagons. Maybe they saw them and maybe they didn't, but Ray said that was the description of the prints that they had originally worked on the Pegasus track, now so many kilometers south. Ray went back to the bird to make the calls to his headquarters and the convoy.

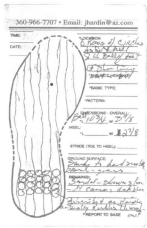

Garrison and the convoy were approximately 100 miles or so northwest of us and well along on the dirt track headed to the rendezvous point. It was a good day for tracking, with a high haze and a gentle breeze blowing and a definite footprint to begin working with. David and I picked up our packs and got back at it. We fumbled a few times, but most of the time, now that we knew definitely what to look for, we went right down the middle of the field like we knew what we were doing. Here the ground cover of small brush and grasses had protected the footprints more from the wind and we could find them quite easily and we moved forward rapidly. When the sign became difficult to find, David would wait at the last known track as I went ahead and cut for another to move him forward. Devon and Ray hip-hopped the chopper along with us, maintaining radio contact via the phone with the convoy.

Working together, David learned more and more about what to look for and we pushed the sign quite rapidly. I was surprised to learn that camel tracks could be easily mistaken for this flat sole we were following. Camels have two toes, or two elongated halves of a padded foot, with no hoof. When we saw only one side of a camel print, it looked very much the same as the month-old flat-sole shower shoe, or whatever it was that Bogucki was wearing. I remember some of the background talk in the police station regarding the possibility that Bogucki was using a camel to carry gear or whatever. Now I understood why someone might make that connection. But he wasn't—the camels walking the same direction either before or after Bogucki weren't paying any attention to him or his footprints.

After we'd gone over one dune top and into the valley before the next one, we had a system going. It helped a lot that Bogucki was going on a straight bearing. I don't think he was using a compass to walk with, but he certainly knew where he was going. We learned to cut the areas where the sand was somewhat soft, but not loose, and the footprint imprints were easier to find. David was flagging to establish the travel route along the top of one dune then the next, then the next. We weren't running on the sign, but we were covering the ground rapidly and I was feeling good! Somewhere ahead it would be down on hands and knees, I was sure, but the key was to run when you could, walk when you have to, and when you can't, you crawl. The sign was still a month old, but we were gaining now!

We watched for the tracks or trails of the brown snakes that Devon and Ray were so concerned about, but didn't see any. We did notice very large bird tracks, supposing that they were those of emus, plus slightly smaller ones the size of turkeys, and here and there tracks

of large lizards with tails dragging. We also
saw small hoof prints of what had to be burros, and of course the joeys. It took me a bit
to figure out some of the joey marks on the
ground. I knew the animals hopped, but I
was unaware until studying the sign, that the
tail contact with the ground surface immedi-
ately under and slightly behind the "elbows" of the hind legs gave as
much if not more thrust than the legs to propel the body up and forward. I was seeing the hopper marks from the hind feet and legs, but
also the deep hard push off from the tail, and then the landing with
the tail coming into contact with the ground before the feet and legs
did. By eleven o'clock, I guessed that we had followed the sign probably ten kilometers (6.2 miles).

The chopper hopped up to and circled around us, alighting on
the sand a few yards away. It shut down and Devon called to David that
Garrison wanted him on the phone. David called to me from the bird,
motioning for me to join him to discuss whatever it was that Garrison
had to say. The convoy had found barefoot footprints on the road that
they were coming in on. Garrison wanted to know if we thought these
could be Bogucki's tracks. I looked at David. How in the heck would we
know? We were nearly 100 miles away from wherever they were! I took
the sat phone receiver and began trying to analyze the tracks as
described by someone who didn't know anything about footprints. In
reply to my questions, Garrison said the footprints were walking west
on the road that the convoy was coming in on. They had overrun them
for several miles before George Messer, who was leading the convoy,
had noticed them on the roadway. Garrison thought the prints were
going off of the roadway into the brush at one point. He was trying to
describe barefoot prints to me and I hadn't seen anything but these
flat-soled shoes.

I asked what details he could see in an attempt to determine the
age of the prints. If he was looking at month-old sign, as we were, he
shouldn't be able to see any detail at all, in fact he shouldn't be able to

see anything but soft depressions in loose sand and nothing on the hard-sand areas. He assured me he was seeing good barefoot prints. In fact, George said he had driven that same road a week before and the tracks weren't there then!

I turned to Ray and asked, "What's the chance that anyone would be in that area walking on that road barefoot?"

"I can't imagine why anyone would be there walking at all, barefoot or not," he answered.

I asked Garrison if anyone with him would know, and what George thought since he was more familiar with the area then anyone else. Minutes ticked by, then Garrison came back on the phone. He said that one of the Aboriginal police officers with them was familiar with the Aboriginal people who lived closest to the area where they were. He didn't think anyone would be there afoot, and offered no chance that any of them would be walking the road barefoot. I told Garrison we'd come take a look at the prints.

David and I marked the last tracks we had with plenty of flagging so we'd not have to look long to find the trail to begin again. David took a way-point on his GPS and, as we piled into the bird, Devon took another way-point once we were airborne. We were in the air 30 minutes or more before we could see the convoy on the roadway far off on the northern horizon. I was busy studying as much of the ground surface as possible, just in case I had to come back and walk the trail. I would have a better idea of what I would find and what the footprint would look like. Almost never did these reports of "possible sign" reported by non-trackers turn out to be worth leaving what sign you were following to go to check it out, but someone had to do it. A hundred times I had done it in the past on missions and sworn that I'd never do it again. But here I was, doing it again!

I watched the countryside go by beneath and wondered what our bearing was and how much we had come off of the north-south line that we had been on at the last sign. I looked for natural barriers that we might sign cut on the way back to shorten the project. Actually everything looked the same for miles and miles. No watercourses, no roads, fence lines—nothing but animal trails here and there, and small patches of open ground amid the brush, grass and scattered scrubby trees. We settled on the ground with dust from the road blowing whatever tracks were there up for the birds to see.

It was nice to see everyone, and the convoy was something to behold. George's big Range Rover in the lead was followed by a 15-passenger Range Rover the likes of which I had never seen before, then another Rover, and finally a five-ton flatbed truck piled high with gear bringing up the rear.

Garrison came to the chopper even before the blades quit turning. He took me to the tracks on the roadway ahead of the vehicles. I walked down the road a bit, looking at the tracks and wanting to get beyond where others had walked and looked. Garrison stood waiting, unlit cigar in hand. These tracks were good, too good to be what we were looking for. The tracks were walking west on the road and then turning around and within a few hours walking back east again. I squatted and looked closely. The sand here was very fine, a light peach color and it held the sign perfectly. These tracks were so good I could see a bit of the cracks, calluses, and cuts in the subject's bare feet. They couldn't be more than 24 hours old because the morning and evening breeze would tend to erode them more than this, even if there was no hard wind during the day or night. These had the effect of the night's dampness, but surely not more than two nights as it wasn't even visible in the fine dust. I looked back, trying to decide just what to say. Just by looking at them, there was no way of telling who had made these prints.

Garrison was now puffing on his cigar and waiting for me to tell him what I thought. I slowly walked further along the double lines of footprints and stopped a couple times to look at them closely, then sat down on the bank along the road and dropped my pack. "Water?" Garrison asked coming up to me, then without waiting for me to answer called to someone to bring a bottle of water. Actually, I just wanted a few minutes to get my thoughts together, add up the 1, 2, 3s. Vickie Pulver and a couple others came running up with water and I said to them, "Just give me a few minutes to put this together," and Garrison motioned gathering them away from the road and from me. First, there was no way of knowing if these were Bogucki's tracks without finding something other than the barefoot tracks to associate them with him. Second, I had only been here for one morning, but I was sure that every morning—just as it had this morning—would dawn with a good breeze, and very probably the sun would set with a similar breeze blowing this loose sand at least slightly. I looked at the tire tracks on the road that weresupposedly George's from the week before. Here and there the barefoot prints had stepped on or had impressed the edge of them, and there was a difference in the color and texture. The tire tracks looked like they were a week old; the barefoot prints looked like they had just been made. They were in the roadbed, that in most places had side banks a foot to two feet high which formed a type of trough for the breeze to blow through, and they would show the wind-blown effects if they'd been here for two days. I got up and put my drawing of the shoe prints that we had been following along side one of the barefoot prints trying to use my imagination to determine if it could be the same person.

Garrison was at my elbow again, impatient. They had been waiting for more than two hours now to get the word on these prints.

"Well, Garrison," I said, "we don't have any way, right now, right here, of knowing who these prints belong to. The only thing to do is to follow them for a ways and see if we can find something that will tell us for sure." I picked up my pack and started walking east.

"Whoa! Where ya going?" he called to me.

"Well, the sign comes from this way and goes back this way last, so we'd just as well be going toward where this person is." "Whoa up", Garrison called, "How do you know it's going that way."

A discussion followed in which it was necessary to find where an eastbound footprint was clearly imprinted upon a westbound track to assure Garrison and the gathered team members that the sign was going east last. I wasn't sure that I convinced anyone, but to me it was obvious and I couldn't see how they couldn't see it for themselves. To satisfy everyone, and most importantly Garrison, it was decided to have one part of the team head back west to cut sign along the road and follow the tracks to where they had turned around, to see if maybe they could find something there that would tell us if this was Bogucki.

I headed east at a fast walk. No need to tarry here—the tracks were relaxed, as though the subject was walking down the beach. David and Vickie followed with radio contact to the convoy where Garrison would wait between the two units, one headed west and the other east. Vickie caught David and me up on the goings-on since we had left them back in Broome the day before, and David filled her in on what we had experienced. I watched the sign and walked as fast as I could, knowing that as long as the footprint stayed on the road like this I could travel four to five miles an hour, and we were burning daylight. Here and there the road had streaks or patches of hard-packed clay, nearly as red as Georgia clay and the same consistency. There was no sand there, no visible footprints, nor the week-old tire tracks. On these strips of hardpan, nothing would dent or scratch the surface, certainly not bare feet. We had quickly gone more than a half mile, when suddenly the tracks were doing a circle dance in the middle of the road on one of these strips of hardpan. Then there it was—shoe prints with little octagons in neat rows of pattern. I whooped! Vickie and David looked shocked.

"It's him!" I shouted. "This is Bogucki! Look, here are the prints!" David whooped and radioed Garrison.

Within minutes, Garrison came roaring up in George's Range Rover. We showed him the prints and my drawing, confirmation. "Let's make up some time!" I said. "Call Devon on the radio and have him fuel up the chopper from the fuel tank on the truck then catch up with us. We'll use the chopper to help run this sign line. Meantime, I'll sit on the hood of this rig and sign cut ahead of the vehicle. Garrison, you drive and watch for my hand signals. When the chopper comes up, we'll have David and Vickie go with Devon and they can sign cut the road ahead two or three miles and radio us if the sign is still headed east. If so, we'll roar up to there and drive the sign while they fly ahead again. We can cover thirty miles in a couple hours this way."

David and I stowed our packs inside, then climbed onto the Range Rover hood behind the "roo guard," and motioned Garrison to go. With him driving 10 to 15 miles an hour, and me motioning for him to slow down here or there, we were moving the sign at a good clip. The chopper soon caught up with us, landed, and took David and Vickie aboard. I had instructed David on what to do and he told Vickie what to look for each time they stopped to check the road for sign. If they couldn't find the sign on one of the hardpan areas, they were to just keep going until they reached the next patch of sand and there the tracks would be. Using this unusual system, with the chopper stopping on the road every three to five miles to check for sign and radioing us to come on if they found it, we covered approximately 20 miles in about two hours. The sign showed that here and there in the soft sand, Bogucki stopped and slipped off his shoes and walked bare-foot, and when the road was mostly hardpan, he would put them back on again. I was able to see where Bogucki stopped to rest, at times lying in the roadway, other times sitting on the shoulder or bank of the road. Occasionally I stopped Garrison and got off to examine the sign closely to make sure what was happening. I carefully examined a large water stain where he had stood and urinated a good volume. Then the tracks ran out.

David radioed Garrison to tell me that they were probably four miles ahead of us and had checked the road and not found the sign going eastbound, though it was still going west. We were now, and had been for some distance, in the middle of a huge burn area in which the entire ground surface was blackened and the brush reduced to black spikes and splinters. This was not an area in which a foot trav-eler would choose to spend the day or night. I waved the onward signal and Garrison roared along the road with me on the hood watching for the prints to turn off or end or something. We came to a sharp bend in the road, the first corner we had come to on this more or less straight road running east and west, and here the road turned about 30 degrees southeast. The chopper was coming back to meet us, so we stopped. I hopped off the hood and could see the footprints walking straight east past the corner and on to an old two-tire track road that continued off into the distance. This was an old road long ago grown over and used only often enough to stunt the sparse tall grass in the tire tracks. The grass reminded me of the sparse wheat grass growing on the dry hills in eastern Washington. In the near distance there were trees and brush, and the tire-track road seemed to disappear into this brush line.

The chopper landed and was shut down; the Range Rover was parked. Everyone could plainly see the footprints walking off of the main road onto the old roadway and they waited expectantly for me to work the sign on the old tire-track trail. David and Vickie tried to work along with me, but this was the hands-and-knees bit, and they were frustrated. We had covered so many miles in such a short time that they had begun to believe that we would overtake Bogucki walking down the middle of the road. I knew it wouldn't be that easy, it never is.

This was very tough. The road had been driven out and back by some vehicle, probably two weeks prior to our being there, leaving behind stirred, crushed and dry vegetation and disturbed gravelly ground surfaces. There was no sign of this vehicle's tracks on the main road from where we had followed the footprints. However the main  road clearly showed George's Range Rover tracks from the week before. The evidence of these tire tracks were most clearly seen in the cured dry damage on the vegetation. In little patches of coarse, dark sand and gravel, I could see some parts of tire tread impressions. The impact of the soft-soled tennis shoes or sandals that Bogucki was wearing left no impression whatsoever on the damaged vegetation and there weren't any sandy patches here to grab the footprints. I made a few walking steps off of the track so my footprints would give me a baseline for comparison. The vegetation alongside the tire tracks was equally coarse, hard and didn't damage easily. The surrounding flat areas were studded with reddish-colored termite constructions that looked like stumps two or three feet tall. This was real tracking and it was tough and slow going.

I found a tiny piece of something here, and another little piece of something there, it had to be Bogucki's sign so I knew that he was still walking the track toward the brush line that we could see ahead. The vegetation alongside the track became more thick and coarse, the spinifex more completely covering the ground surface. The three of us worked along the track, walking the island of vegetation in the center and watching both sides for anything that might be sign. I didn't know what David and Vickie were looking for, but they were both intense and concentrating and from time to time they called my attention to some things that "looked good." We neared the first of a few scattered little trees. Some were spindly eucalyptus; the others looked like some type of scrubby birch.

In a little creek or rain water runoff ditch, sediment had gathered and there was a piece of the heel of the shoe with the octagons. Right On! We were nearly three quarters of a mile from the parked Range Rover and chopper on the main road. We tied flagging to the tallest grass stems and relaxed slightly. We still had Bogucki walking east at this point. At five o'clock, we still had 100 yards to go to where the two-tire track disappeared into the fringe of brush. I wanted to see what he was going to do when he got to the brush. He had continued straight east from the sandy road, so maybe this track went on east for miles. We continued to move the sign, slowly and carefully. The closer to the brush we got, the thicker the vegetation grew. The spinifex covered the ground in most areas like a thick blanket. The native animals made trails through the vegetation where it grew more densely.

The clump of brush that looked like it had swallowed up the tire tracks was growing between the two tire lines and was splayed out and mashed down from the impact of a vehicle passing over it going and returning. I didn't know the name of that brush, but it was oozing a thick, sticky honey-like sap and emitting such a heavy sweet smell that it was sickening. The vehicle had ripped and torn brush in passing through, but it had left a passageway. The old roadway through the brush had created a channel for winter and spring rains and that had created a rutted wash with patches of loose sand and hardpan overgrown with trees and brush. Within another hundred yards the forward progress of the vehicle was stopped by an even heavier growth of brush and it backed up and climbed out of the old roadway and into the spinifex turning around, running over termite mounds and back into the wash headed back west.

We continued following the old roadbed through the thick brush. Here the brush and small trees made an arch completely over the road and in some places leaving only a crawl space beneath. I could see where Bogucki had pushed, pulled and broken branches to go through and we followed the trail. Suddenly, crawling through and over some brush, there was a space of soft sand and Bogucki's prints going both ways, the last ones headed back west. We stopped and looked behind us, but there was a patch of the hardpan where our prints didn't show. Further back, where the vehicle had turned out of the track, we hadn't seen Bogucki tracks, but that was on a long strip of hardpan where the vehicle tracks barely made an impression. Ours didn't show there and neither did Bogucki's.

I had David and Vickie sit down and take a break while I worked the sign further east and found where Bogucki had stopped. The brush opened up and he had taken off his pack and dumped it beside a large brush clump, then he had lain down beside it and slept. He had spent some time there—three, four or more hours, time enough to get some rest. I sat down and thought. We had followed his sign now for at least 30 miles, perhaps more, traveling in both directions. He had stopped to rest a few minutes at a time, but not to really rest anywhere along the road. I wondered just how far he had walked since he last slept before getting to this point. I looked carefully to see if there were any sign of his having eaten anything, but saw no sign of anything.

He had walked into this brush and, finding a good place, had lain down and rested. Then he got up and retraced his steps back westward. But to where? We didn't see his westbound tracks going back out of the brush into the open where the long soft sand strip showed his footprints so plainly, so he had to leave this wash somewhere between here and there. The distance was about 100 feet or so. How far had he gone back west and why did he turn around?

The rest of the crew that had gone west to check the sign had radioed to Garrison that they had found the end where he had turned around. They had been coming back to join with us at the intersection where the road turned. Garrison had waited there for them to find a place to set up camp. It was now 6:30 p.m. This had been one long day, with minimum sleep. This was the farthest that I had ever pushed sign in one day, probably about 90 miles, but we had gained a month in time. I was tired and leaned back and closed my eyes. It had never gotten hot today, probably only 90 degrees or so, just really pleasant. Except for the darn stink of that flowering bush, I could just drop off to sleep. I knew that we were within 12 hours of this guy right now, but where the heck was he? I could see his footprints from where I sat and they looked nearly as good as mine—this guy wasn't that far ahead of us.

David called, checking on me. I could feel the cool beginning to come now and the birds were starting to think it was evening. I couldn't just sit there and began to slowly work the sign back toward where David and Vickie waited, trying to see if there was something that I had missed. I made sure not to mess up the prints. There had to be some part of the story I was missing here somewhere. I told them what I had found and that I didn't know where Bogucki had gone from here. We worked our way slowly and carefully back along the double-track road toward the junction. We could see from the brush line that things were happening back at the main road intersection. The vehicles were all gathered and tents were being set up.

Vickie said she wanted to work her bloodhound Dixie along the track, if we approved. It was getting cooler and perhaps Dixie could pick up the scent in the brush and spinifex, and tell us where Bogucki had left the wash. I agreed it was worth a try. I didn't know anything about Dixie, and I hadn't had any luck with bloodhounds finding anything, but it was worth a try. I didn't think she would hurt any-thing. We returned to where the others were setting up camp at the intersection of the roads. Garrison was in full gale, ordering and directing. He immediately wanted a debriefing, but I put him off, saying that Vickie wanted to run Dixie on the track and I thought it was a good idea, and we needed to get it done before dark. Vickie quickly got Dixie rigged up and we headed out down the track.

Dixie acted to me like she was smelling something. I asked Vickie if it was me, but Vickie just smiled and reminded me that I was the tracking expert and she handled the dog. I had watched many canine teams work search missions, some bloodhounds, some shepherds, and a whole bunch of others. Some looked to me like they knew what they were doing; most didn't. Vickie was obviously "in tune" with the dog, talking to her quietly and confidently. This was the first bloodhound I had been with that actually "worked" the sign. This one didn't just slobber and run, dragging the handler behind. I asked Vickie a couple questions about how the dog was working and she waved me to keep quiet and not bother her. We were nearing the brush and this is where I wanted to see what the dog could do. I was sure that Bogucki had turned north from the double track somewhere in the brushy part of the wash, and Dixie might tell us where.

Dixie kept her nose to the ground, working back and forth, sorting the scents on the roadway. She seemed to know where Bogucki had walked and she consistently came back to that, though she sniffed elsewhere, at my scent and David's, and where Vickie had walked. As Vickie talked quietly to her, Dixie walked the scent to the gap under the branches on the left side of the left tire track. She went under the outstretched branches, outside of the path that one would normally walk if the vehicle had not smashed down the brush. She didn't hesitate and seemed satisfied with the scent trail. The three of us had stepped over and through the middle of the brush, avoiding the branches. Dixie continued to work the scent trail up the wash, past where the vehicle had backed up and climbed out of the wash and turned around. She was now where the visible tracks were going both ways in loose sand. She worked to the place where Bogucki had lain down and beyond, then came back. She seemed confused here, and it was obvious to me that Dixie wasn't reading the footprints that she was walking on. Vickie encouraged her to work back along the north side bank of the wash. She went out of the brush into the spinifex and back again at various intervals, but as far as I was concerned, she couldn't or didn't find the right place. We had been at this for nearly two hours, and darkness was coming. Vickie said that Dixie was getting tired, wasn't finding the right spot, and it was time to call it a day. We headed back to see what kind of a camp had been created.

Three tents were up, and a shelter tarp anchored to the side of the truck provided a room for the radio equipment, operational desk and other necessaries. By  the time we arrived, a small fire was going, and a grill held a five-liter can called a "billy" for boiling water for tea and coffee. Everyone had found seats of some sort and were sitting around the fire getting more acquainted and inquiring of George Messer and Ray Briggs more about the area. Sitting with them was Andrew Jones, owner/operator of the truck that carried tools and equipment for repair of anything we might need on the vehicles, plus all of the MREs, cases of drinking water, the 800 liters of aviation fuel for the chopper and most of the team gear. Rob Duncan and Ben Martin of the *Western Australia News* talked about the previous search effort along the Pegasus track. Garrison stood, cigar in hand, asking questions and facilitating the conversations. Our team consisted of the team medic from Texas, Jan Stalder; communication specialist Mike Priddy from Tennessee; canine handlers Laura Rathe from California and Amir Findling from New York; David Kovar from California and Vickie Pulver from Michigan.

Garrison didn't permit drinking alcoholic beverages during a mission. This was a very good rule, and I would abide by it, but this was Australia—the people here didn't drink water, they drank BEER! I got reintroduced to everyone, though I had met all except Andrew at the police station during the morning briefing the day before. Someone had unloaded my baggage and stowed it in the first tent with my sleeping bag and other paraphernalia. That was taken care of and I could relax, except that Garrison wanted to have a conference, so he, David and I took a walk down the road. This was Garrison's way of having some privacy to discuss things. As we walked, I told him what I knew, with David filling in the gaps. Garrison asked what I intended or wanted to do the next day. I told him I'd like to think about it and I'd have an answer in the morning.

We ambled back to the camp and joined with the others around the fire. The night air was already beginning to settle moisture and coolness along the ground. I sat with the others and watched the night come slowly, the western sky was rose colored and deepening toward the horizon. Night birds were beginning to call. Talk was relaxed and it was easy getting acquainted with the others. A few stars began to show and, one by one, members  got up and retrieved jackets or sweaters while gathering more sticks for the fire. Everyone was tired. It had been a long day for all who came with the convoy too, as they had left Broome at four in the morning.

Friday—August 20

I lay in my sleeping bag going over it all in my mind as I watched the top of the tent take on detail in the coming light. From Garrison's first telephone call to the present, it seemed like a dream, but it was not. I knew that was true by the weight of a big bloodhound across my legs. Why the heck did this big mutt have to sleep on me! Vickie slept peacefully on the other side of the tent, and the dog belonged to her, so why wasn't she over there? The morning breeze was beginning to rustle the tent fabric. I untangled myself from the sleeping bag and the dog, got my pants and shirt on and slipped outside the tent to put on my boots. I shook them upside down to dislodge any little critters that might have spent the night there before pulling them on. I walked off into the black landscape and picked up some of the partially burned brush sticks for the fire and returned to get it going. Boy, this was just like camping out at home. I poured a bottle of water into the billy and set it over the flames. I wanted to have a bit of time to myself to think before I had to tell the others what we were going to be doing for the day. I was amazed looking around to see where the Aussies were sleeping. I'd gone to bed before most of the others and now I could see lumps of sleeping figures on top of the Range Rovers and the back of the truck.

The air was fresh, clean and cool. I had the impression that I could faintly smell the salt air blowing in from the west, but the ocean was over 100 miles away. The sky was still inky, but the east was faintly pink and glowing with golden streaks. On the ground it was light enough to shoot, as they say in the country where I was raised. Looking in the case of MREs I found some little envelopes of instant coffee. I made a cup and walked off west down the road to look again at the tracks coming toward us on the sandy road. I wanted to be sure I was right about the age of the prints. Three vehicles, including Andrew's truck, hadn't wiped them all out and I stopped and got down and examined the near-perfect prints closely. I considered the night's moisture, the morning and evening breeze. I had now experienced it myself, so I knew what it would have been the two days before. I was right, the tracks weren't more than 24 hours old even now. They didn't have more than the one night's moisture on them yesterday when they were found. Bogucki wasn't that far ahead of us. I sipped the coffee and watched the breeze blow grains of sand from the prints and slowly erode the finer detail lines.

When I could hear the camp beginning to stir, I walked slowly back to the fire for another cup of what was almost like coffee. This time I walked down the road the other way toward the southeast, past the still-sleeping team members in the tents following the line of Bogucki footprints coming up the road to meet me. In a quarter mile I came to another old two tire-track road like the one he had turned off on, again running to the east and toward the same brush line in the distance. I turned and walked this road, sign cutting as I went. I reached the brush and scattered trees. The trees were small, scrubby things that reminded me of birch or aspen, with stark white trunks and limbs and small round oval leaves. The birds were busy calling to each other and I could hear a wild donkey braying somewhere off to the east.

I stood and waited for the sun to come over the horizon and through the tree tops to me. As I waited, I was trying to figure out what Bogucki was thinking and what his intentions were. Why did he walk west, probably about 15 miles, then turn around and walk all the way back to the corner? He lay down and slept about four to six hours, then got up and walked back on that little overgrown road and off north somewhere. But where the heck was he going and where was he now? He had walked at least 30 miles or more the day before, so how far did he walk yesterday and how far would he walk today? The sun was now up in the tree tops, and it was time for me to come up with some idea of what to do, so I could get the operation focused for the day. I saw David walking down the road looking for me and I started back to meet him on the main road.

"Well," I said, when we met, "let's talk about what we know. Bogucki is alive and walking. We don't know how far he can walk in a day, but we know he can cover at least 30 miles without stopping for more than just a break. His sign on the road shows strong, steady steps, no sign of real physical difficulties. He pissed in the middle of the road, and it was a puddle bigger than any of mine for the day. He's stopping a bit too often, but then he walks on steadily. His rest breaks are fairly short—about 15 minutes I'd guess. He lay down in the road a few times, maybe to completely rest his legs. I believe it was evening the day before yesterday when he passed this corner going west and perhaps early morning when he got back here. The footprints in this soft, fine sand have a texture that is similar to spraying a fixative on chalk dust. That would explain why the morning and evening breeze didn't distort or erode all of the tiny lines of the octagon pattern. If you look at our footprints from yesterday afternoon on the road right alongside his, ours show more erosion by the breeze then his do.

"He walked west for about 15 miles, then turned around and retraced his steps, walking directly east off on this old track. He knew where he was in relation to where he wanted to be. Somewhere, somehow he saw a landmark or something that he recognized and he knew he was too far west. We don't know where he first hit this road and began to travel northwest—it may be a mile down that way or 15 miles. I'm not sure where we are in relation to a direct north-south line from where we last had the sign down there.

"Remember when we were back there on the road where we first met the convoy, you could see away out north because we were closer to the rim of this plateau? I thought I could see Dampier Downs from there before we landed. This plateau is 900 to 1,000 feet high, The guys that went back west on the tracks said he walked all the way to where an old fence line crosses the road. I think he got to where he could see one of the buttes or something else that he recognized on the map, knew he was too far west and came back here to get back on his original travel line.

"Janet said that she was going to leave on the 25th for her trip to British Columbia. I looked at George's map last night, from here and where we had the sign down south, he would still be heading for Fitzroy Crossing. We're about a 120 to 150 miles from there now—if he's wanting to get out to call her before she leaves on the 25th, he has several days to make it, but he'll have to keep traveling. He left this trail after lying down to rest and headed north—I haven't got the sign, but I'm sure of that. He travels the easy route when it's going the way he wants to go: the animal trails, roads, this old track. I reminded David of the tracker principle that you don't skip ahead but go to the LKP and follow the sign, to not do so was a cardinal sin and basic mistake of tracking, but surely we could catch up a day.

"I think the thing to do is to begin looking down below the edge of this escarpment, cutting ahead for the sign. There's a big creek—it looks like a dry river on the map—that runs diagonally across the lands below, from about where Bogucki turned around all the way to Fitzroy River. Once he hits that creek, all he has to do is follow it to the river, and then up the river to Fitzroy Crossing. He's one full day ahead of us, and at 20 to 30 miles a day, we're not going to catch up by following the sign unless we get real lucky again or unless he stops and holes up somewhere. We're going to have to catch up a day somehow. I say we take the chopper and work the areas north down off of the escarpment toward Geegully Creek." David nodded in agreement, and said, "Let's go tell Garrison."

I had forgotten how difficult it is to make a chopper pilot understand what is needed to help a tracker see sign from the air. Devon was trying, but he was too careful—the wind was blowing a bit and he wanted to fly too darn fast. The creek was big and wide, and for the most part deep, loose sand. Tracks of every type of animal showed in the bottom. In some places there wasn't any sign; in others the terrain funneled all animal travel into the creek in a wide swath of sign. Cattle, burros, camels, huge lizards, emus, kangaroos and I don't know what else all came to the "billabongs," or water  holes. Some were fairly large, others just little puddles, but all drew a crowd. If Bogucki had made it to Geegully Creek, he'd have water every mile or so along the way. The animals came and went up and down the rugged canyons that cut deep into the escarpment. There were hundreds of good trails to sign cut. Flying low and slow, I could separate the burro tracks from cattle tracks from human tracks, on the trails and in the creek bottom, but flying low and slow with the wind blowing scared Devon. If he wasn't confident flying that way, I wasn't confident riding. We decided to have Devon land the chopper here and there and David headed one way while I went the other, checking trails for a quarter to a half mile both directions, but this wasn't an effective way to sign cut. I had explained to David and Garrison that this would at best be a hit-and-miss system, and we'd have to be real lucky to find his prints on one of the trails leading from the escarpment to the creek. One of the problems was that there wasn't any "good" route from the camp area, or where we last had Bogucki's sign to get down the escarpment.

The distance from the bushes where he had lain to sleep and the edge of the escarpment was only about five miles, but it was broken ground with rocky outcrops, canyons and arroyos, some of which ran great distances, serpentining down to the face of the escarpment. Here, at the bottom edge of the escarpment, you could see the rock base that was supporting the flat table top of the desert 1,000 feet above where we had been operating and which extended all the way to the sea, or so it seemed. The landscape below the escarpment was also as flat as a table top, with numerous rocky buttes protruding from the surface. Generally the tops of these were as high as the desert level above the escarpment. It was like a two-level room. Rocky cliffs dominated the break between the two levels—bedrock smoothed by eons of water flow and constant wind erosion had tumbled into debris at the base of the escarpment. Most of the area looked much like various areas of the high desert country I was used to seeing in the mountain states back home. The trees were different:the brush that grew in abundance was much like the sage and buck brush dotting the landscape in Colorado, Utah and Idaho. Just like at home, in the canyons were water holes, some with water and some dried up to a mossy mud puddle. It would be a good place to camp out, so we worked the area until Devon called a halt about three o'clock, saying that the wind was too strong to be flying that close to the ground and the mouth of the canyons. We headed back to camp.

Up on top of the escarpment at the base camp, the wind was really blowing! The tents were flapping like flags, and the team was busy trying to hold everything down and protect it from the red dust. Devon had a real wrestling match with the little chopper, trying to get it to sit down firmly on the ground with the skids down and the rotors up. There was another chopper at the site tied down. This was a bigger, better and more expensive jet-propelled Bell Ranger. Finally we got settled solidly on the ground and secured, and Devon could take a full breath. Other team members came out to meet us and filled us in on the happenings of the day. The Bell Ranger was chartered by the news media who were at the camp doing interviews of Garrison, Ray and others. Rob and Ben had sent their story out last night to the world that we had found fresh Bogucki tracks and that there was a good chance he was alive and still walking. Apparently this was big news in Australia. Gosh, I had forgotten that Rob and Ben were newspaper people—heck they seemed just like part of the team. I had forgotten that they were writing on laptop computers and sending news updates via their satellite phone several times each day.

The media newcomers had a much different attitude and they resented the camaraderie that Ben and Rob enjoyed with us and the rest of the crew. These people were pressed to get a "story" on tape back to Broome in time for the evening news. Lucky for me, they focused on Garrison and the use of the dogs. They had filmed Devon landing the little Robinson in the wind, and they talked Garrison into having the handlers take the dogs out for a bit of a search so they could film them. I later learned that Garrison had made a strong-arm deal with the media: they would get a story, but we would have use of their chopper to help with the search. They would be under the authority of whichever police officer was on scene, and this grated on all of them. The canine units were putting on a show, with the newsmen shooting tape and Garrison tagging along to provide the story line. When the media show returned and immediately shook hands with everyone, assuring they'd return the next morning. They took off to get their film to Broome by the 5 p.m. deadline.

David and I sat in the shade of the flapping tarp of the gear leanto and looked through a box of MREs. We'd eaten nothing all day but a couple of snacks and we were hungry. The meal packages all contained a main dish that could be chemically heated to boiling by inserting the meal pouch into the container envelope and adding a small amount of water. Most meals are hot and ready to eat within 10 minutes. The MREs also contained some type of fruit, dessert such as pound cake, cookies or brownies. All packages contained coffee or tea bags, condiments, gum, matches, and toilet paper.

The wind dropped to a whisper and the air began to cool in the evening. The fire was rekindled to heat the billy and the Aussies had food to cook. George proudly showed me the contents, design and outlay of his specially refitted Range Rover. The rear door opened at the side of the vehicle and exposed a stainless steel built-in, two-door refrigerator/freezer about 30 inches high. The reefer was wired into the vehicle's ignition and battery system that kept it cold with minimal engine on-time. He opened the refer double doors to show me frozen beef steaks on one side and cold beer on the other. He looked around and confided that in consideration of Garrison's "No drinking in the field" policy, the Aussies wouldn't be drinking beer either, or at least would do it discreetly.

The western sky began to take on the hues of orange and red and the sun was a huge golden ball in the middle of it as it sank toward the horizon. David and I took our "command-talk" walk down the road with Garrison. He told us of the events of the day around the camp, the emotions and attitudes of the team members, their willingness to help. We hadn't seen Bogucki's sign, but the circumstances weren't the best and the area to search was huge. This task wasn't impossible, any more than being where we were on two-day-old sign, but we'd need luck and more looking. Garrison wanted to work the canine units the next day between the old track, where the last prints were, and the edge of the escarpment. We agreed. Mike Priddy and Jan Stalder would go as flankers for the handlers; Amir Findling could work alone but in contact with the other two. David, because he had gained more experience in looking for sign than any of the others, would go with me again to continue working the area north of the escarpment and expand the distance out to a perimeter of 20 to 30 miles. I remained as convinced as ever that Bogucki had gone north or near north from where we last had his sign. His ability to climb down into and up out of the canyons, and to know where to get down the face of the escarpment, I believed, would dictate his route of travel.

Saturday—August 21

I awoke again in fading darkness. I had gotten more sleep, having worked out a better understanding with Dixie as to where each of us were going to sleep. She definitely preferred sleeping on top of me. Vickie suggested Dixie was trying to protect her from me, but I knew ole Dix just wanted to sleep on a warm soft doughboy. I rolled Dixie off to the side and pulled myself from the sleeping bag, got my clothes on and stepped out of the tent.

I was eager to be up and going this morning because I knew better than the others what a really large bite we were taking. We had gone over all of the known factors again on the walk-and-talk last night, and I advised Garrison and David that the only choice for a tracker is to begin at the last known point where his footprints left the old two-track road in the brush and work it the slow way. We might eventually have to do it that way, but we all figured it was worth taking another day, hoping to be lucky by making an extensive search of a four- or five-mile stretch along the base of the escarpment where I figured he had to come down. Secondly, we would concentrate on trying to sign cut Geegully Creek, because he had to either cross it or walk right up the middle of it, and that's where we had the best chance of finding the sign. With a pilot who knew how to put the chopper in the right position at a couple hundred feet or less, I would be able to see any human tracks that hit the creek bottom. With Devon, it was going to be a real challenge, and I knew that by noon the wind would be ripping so we'd try that first and work the escarpment base later when we would have to land and work it afoot as we had done the day before. By 3 p.m. we would have to get out of there altogether.

The early morning breeze was brisk and clean, kicking little dust dervishes across the road and causing the sleeping Aussies to pull their swags tighter around their heads and shoulders. They had sheepishly admitted that they were sleeping up high, on top of the vehicles to make sure the brown snakes couldn't get to them. I'd been surprised yesterday morning to see them struggling into winter coats and stomping their feet to warm them. Heck, it was probably about 50 degrees, just nice and fresh. They were impressed that some of us Americans didn't even put on a jacket. We were wearing t-shirts and olive drab camo shirts, and an hour after sunup I thought it was more than warm. With the fire beginning to crackle and the pot on to boil, I rummaged through the MRE box to find the coffee packets and whatever else others had left. Cookies would probably be good later, and peanut butter crackers. I picked out an MRE marked chili and macaroni—it might not be the usual breakfast meal, but it suited me. The others were beginning to stir as I filled my cup and headed off down the road.

The prints were still there, even after three days of wind blowing on them. The dimples were there, but no longer distinct. I sat down on the bank of the road to sip my instant coffee. I couldn't help enjoying being me, sitting on the berm of the dirt road in Australia watching the sunrise. I didn't know where Bogucki was, but right then I hoped that he was looking at the sunrise and enjoying it as much as I was. He had brought me there by taking a walk that no one believed he could finish. No one except his girlfriend Janet. She alone had thought he was still alive.

Camp came to life slowly. One by one the members arose, and everyone headed straight to the fire and the hot water. I watched for Devon to rise. I was eager to get going and knew full well that he wouldn't even think of turning a rotor until the sun was well up and the temperature above 50 degrees. No need to get into a hurry, but I hated the standing around. I slowly walked back to the fire and took another cup of hot water and walked off into the tall grasses to look at the termite towers that looked like old stumps among the grass.

We had decided that this large, flat area alongside the road, where the grasses were mostly the same variety, size and stage of growth, was in fact the derelict Looma Airstrip indicated on the maps. It had grown back in and you'd have to walk on it to realize that it had at one time been bladed out of the brush. I continued walking until I came to an old roadway running east and west at the south end of the old airstrip and began walking east and cutting for sign. My coffee was gone, but the animal sign was interesting and heck, Bogucki could have walked this way. I was more than a mile from the camp when I realized that I'd better get back and grab something to eat. Devon would be getting the little chopper ready to go.

Garrison wanted David to stay and talk with the media, but I wanted him with me because he'd begun to catch on to the sign cutting and would be useful to me. Another pair of eyes might be of great help and we could cover the ground faster when Devon put us on the ground.

Devon finally rolled out of the sleeping bag and came to life with a cup of coffee and a fruit cake to eat. He had topped off the fuel tanks the evening before and began the preflight procedures. David and I gathered our gear and together we lifted off at about 7 a.m. We had talked with Devon about our plan to work Geegully Creek first, low and slow, and then after the wind picked up we would sign cut afoot along the base of the escarpment. Devon was OK with this plan and headed out over the escarpment edge and settling down toward the creek bottom some eight to 10 miles ahead. I explained to Devon that I wanted to begin on the west end and fly into the sun at about 100 feet altitude if possible, just on the north side of the creek. We began and he did pretty well trying to get the bird into any position that I wanted. We worked slowly back and forth across and down the creek bottom. Cattle were already claiming their particular spot of shade under the scrub trees in the bottoms near the billabongs. I never saw any of the burros, but their tracks indicated several herds coming to water during the night. Camel tracks dominated with their large flat prints reflecting the sunlight, but we didn't see any of them either. Here or there we would catch one of the huge lizards out sunning themselves in the open. Huge mounds of sand in the middle of the creek bottom caught my attention and Devon explained that these were dug by the lizards, perhaps burying their eggs. Cockatoos, flights of lorakeets and other birds that I didn't know disliked our disturbance of their air space.

We found sign of all kinds of animals, but nothing of Bogucki. We came to a convergence of two major creeks into Geegully Creek. There was an old road that came in from the northwest, perhaps from Dampier Downs, which came to an iron corral. This was where the rancher gathered his free-range cattle, herding them with choppers and dune buggies. We spent nearly two hours cutting for sign in this area, as it would be a funnel and focal point for anyone coming down the escarpment or following along Geegully Creek. I told David we should check this place each day, as it was such a good sign cutting area. This would be the eastern boundary of our cut and it was time to go back west and begin working the trails.

We were going to concentrate on working in this area about 20 miles long between the bottom of the escarpment and Geegully Creek. The bottom edge of the escarpment was broken ground with small gullies, washes, ridges and a good deal of fallen shale and old rotten rock from the escarpment itself. Animal trails abounded; there was water in many pockets in some of the canyons, but the terrain above wouldn't really funnel anyone coming down the escarpment into a particular area—they could walk out anywhere. We began the search, using one major wash as the west boundary and worked our way north and east. By 3 p.m. we had covered less than half of the strip. Devon was beginning to get a bit frustrated at how many times we wanted to sit the bird down and look. Every couple hundred yards there would be more trails or washes to sign cut. David and I began to walk a lot more as the wind coming down the canyons and draws began to gain strength. Both of us were thinking that soon Devon would say the wind was too strong to fly this low and slow in this area.

The day wore on and we were getting tired. Devon tapped his watch after one foray on the ground and said, "We're getting short of fuel, and the wind is picking up. It's 4:30—what would you two say to a dip in the pond?"

We looked at each other and asked, "What pond?" He added, "I think it's time for me to take a bath. How would you two like a dip in the pool?" I was still puzzled. We'd seen water in many little potholes and puddles in the creeks, but I sure had missed the pool!

"If you know where there's a pool to take a bath in, count me in!" said David. I agreed, trying to think how I could have missed water as big as a pool or pond.

We lifted off and chug-chugged toward the escarpment, climbing and heading for one of the canyons in the near distance. Devon in fact didn't know of a pond, but said to David, "There's got to be a pool somewhere up this canyon that we can sit down and walk to." Devon twisted and turned the little bird in the canyon and found two ponds of seemingly clean, cool water about 20 x 20 or 15 x 30 feet in size. He selected the one with the best landing site nearby and slowly worked

the little bird down onto the sloping hillside below. We hopped out and worked our way to the pool. It was water, though not quite as clear

as it looked from the air, and not cool, but it was wet. We stripped and stepped in. Devon had his towel, soap and razor from his shave kit in the chopper; David and I brought our sweat and dirt. The pond wasn't deep, but it was deep enough to soak, and it had several large rocks of the right size for sit stools for a leisurely wash. We air-dried in a few minutes and dressed, already feeling guilty that we would not tell the others about our refreshing bath. Devon made it clear that he didn't want to ferry all of the others from camp to this pond.

At camp, we found a different Bell Ranger chopper with cameramen and reporters from the other media services. Fortunately, we seemed to be of little interest and, as it was a bit after 5 p.m., they had to get back to Broome with the evening news film. The Ranger had brought in a replacement for Ray, who needed to go out for other official business. The replacement was Constable Lindsey Grateorex, whom we greeted in passing as we just wanted to be left alone, both of us feeling a bit guilty at just having had a bath. We needed to think about what we had not found this day. The Ranger lifted off and then things got quiet. How nice to have no great commotion going on, except for the wind whipping up the dust and flapping the tents. The in-camp team had re-rigged the tarp shelter to better protect the radio desk setup and other items from the wind whipped dust. We gathered in the shelter, mostly out of the wind, and talked about not finding Bogucki's sign. Evening came on with long shadows and slowly everyone gathered quietly around the fire. By the time Dixie was ready to lie down, so was I. I crawled into my bag, shaking off the afternoon wind's deposit of dust, and lay in the tent listening to the quieting of the wind. I heard the three ladies giggling together as they walked off down the road, realizing that the bits of conversation I overheard indicated they were going to take a spit bath, each with a bottle of water.

Sunday—August 22

I awakened to a slight scraping sound that clearly in my mind was something long and snakelike slowly moving against the edge of the tent wall. I opened my eyes and could see that it was still night. The scraping sounds stopped. The snake had to be outside the tent, so that wasn't a problem. I slowly brought my wrist to where I could see my watch and saw it was nearly 5 a.m. Shucks—time to be thinking of getting up anyway. I realized ole Dix was lying alongside my back with her head across the bottom of the sleeping bag. She was pushing me toward the tent wall. I slowly tried to move and heard the scraping sound again and realized instantly that it was Dix's tail inside and not a snake at all. She lifted her head to look at me. I'm sure if a floppy-jawed bloodhound can grin, she was doing so. I pushed her away and got up.

This would be another day of flying out east and north, we had to find his sign somewhere. We would have the use of another of the media choppers, as well as the little Robinson. Where to look, who should go and what to tell them to do? The dogs were of little or no use in this type of operation—the area was too great with no real place to narrow it down to give them any chance of finding the scent. Morning was glowing in the east with the highest stars of the western sky still fading. I again wondered where Bogucki was and if he was also up and enjoying the morning as I was. I picked up an armload of sticks, here and there breaking them from the stalks and spikes, noting how clear and clean the broken slashes were even in the early darkness.

The fire was going and the billy was on to boil. I sat waiting for my first cup with the coffee bag in hand and trying to decide if another mac and chili would do for breakfast when David came to join me. We had taken the "command" walk with Garrison the evening before and listened as he vented and fumed about what the media was doing and not doing and saying, and eventually got around to the fact that we were marking time but not moving ahead. Heck, we well knew that but didn't know what to do differently. Garrison had spent a good deal of time the past couple days when not in company of the news media conferring with George speculating on Bogucki's travels and the terri- tory from base camp to the Fitzroy Crossing. Garrison was convinced that we were not looking far enough east, that Bogucki was headed east on the bit of a road and would continue to go east and north instead of the more northerly route that we were spending so much time checking. He wanted today to be focused on going east from the base camp along the southern edge of the escarpment that slowly dimin- ished in height and perspective in the next 50 miles. He had directed that David and Vickie could sign cut the area north of the escarpment if they wanted, but I was to go in the media's Bell Ranger when it arrived and work as much as 40 miles east then northward to either find the sign or prove his concept wrong. There was no discussion: this was a marching order for the day.

David and I made our instant coffee and wandered west down the road. I absent-mindedly noted the Bogucki footprints were still there, but the designs were fading; the wind was erasing the edges of the prints and all sign of them on the hardpan surfaces. Neither of us talked much, both of a mind that the effort should be concentrated either on the "last known place" (LKP) in search jargon, or sign cut- ting relative to that point, instead of way out east. I well knew we had committed the cardinal sin, but somehow wasn't able to re-do and make it right. Garrison was the boss, so that's what would be done, and heck, we had spent two days already doing what we thought was right and hadn't found anything, so who knows, maybe he was right.

In camp, the rest of the group was beginning to appear and acquire the needed hot tea or coffee to open the eyes and minds. Water from the bottles was splashed and sloshed into faces and over straying stands of hair with one holding the bottle for another. This had been a somewhat dainty activity the first couple of mornings, but now the formality was lost in practicality and anyone grabbed a bottle for anyone else without regard to sex or national origin and they all drip-dried into their first cup of coffee.

We would have to wait until the media chopper came in before departing for our sign cutting assignments and took the time to clean up gear, straighten up the tents and make notes of the previous few days' activities. Garrison was pacing a new trench into the old roadway and sending smoke signals with his cigar that said he was very frustrated with the waiting and depending on media choppers to get the work done. The little Robinson chopper was fueled and ready to go; Devon cleaned and polished windows and checked systems, rotors and control connections. Garrison called another meeting with David, Vickie and me and reaffirmed that we were to find the sign somewhere going east from the LKP.

About 7:30 we heard the whine of the jet Ranger coming low and fast over the rim of the escarpment and bearing directly to the camp. When the blades slowed to a near stop, four people got out, two reporters, a cameraman and the pilot. A big discussion began between Garrison and the Ranger crew as to who was going to go with the chopper and who wasn't. The pilot had not been told that he was to work with our team; he had been hired by the TV station and they told him that the reporter was in charge. The reporter was a nice young lady who looked about 15 years old. Someone at the station had told her that she was in charge and by golly she was going to be in charge. We waited outside the circle for Garrison to resolve the issue. Finally Lindsey

Grateorex stepped forward and said directly to the pilot that in fact he—the Western Australia Police—was in charge of the search and of the air space surrounding the search effort, and the chopper was to stay grounded unless it had a search team member aboard to direct the flight activities. The pilot was to do his best to do whatever the team member wished, so far as it didn't endanger the aircraft. When the pilot and his companions wished to fly, they could either ask Garrison for a team member to direct their flying activities, or they could depart immediately and return to Broome. He would give them five minutes to make up their minds and if the pilot wished to keep his license to fly in Australia, he'd better choose one of those two options.

The constable turned on his heel and gestured to Garrison to follow and they returned to the campfire circle. We waited while a group discussion ensued, with both the Ranger pilot and the young lady raising their voices. It became clear that the pilot was going to fly and the lady reporter was going to go with the cameraman and one member of our team. That turned out to be me.

This whole business had taken an hour or more, Garrison had invited them all over for a cup of coffee to calm things down a bit and it was 9:30 before the signal was given to board the aircraft. Something told me this was not going to be a fun day. The little Robinson lifted off with David and Vickie before we did and they headed north to drop over the escarpment before heading east. We lifted off in the Ranger and headed directly east. The reporter had a sour look on her face and had insisted in riding the front seat, where I could have had a better chance of seeing the ground. She had made it very clear to Garrison that her service had leased the helicopter and pilot, they belonged to her and it was her responsibility to be the first on the scene should Bogucki be spotted. She was to get the first interview and her cameraman had to be there to film the interview. The other reporter was from another media organization and was just a tag-along. The cameraman was an older man who had not gotten involved in the discussion at all.

We flew over the brush and trees at treetop level with the pilot following Garrison's instructions and the cockatoos took to the air.

About 20 miles out— further than we had gone on previous days—the pilot began to look for trails and roads for me to check. We found a few, but certainly not enough to ensure that we would find footprints of anyone walking east or northeast. To double check, I walked the trails and old two track roadways some distance in each direction. The pilot understood what we were trying to do and in a short time was trying to get the bird in the right position for me to see the ground surface. The reporter eventually got the message that what she said didn't have a real bearing on what we did, or where we went, or who flew in the front seat, until we found Bogucki. On one stop the pilot walked with me on a well-used animal trail that was running diagonally toward the northeast for nearly a mile, learning about tracking and what I was looking for.

The wind was strengthening a bit early and by 1 p.m., the trees and brush were waving in a sea of movement that from the air was not just distracting but kicking up little dusty camouflages to hide whatever was down below. It was more difficult for the pilot to find spots to put the bird on the ground, but we continued looking as best as we could. About 2 p.m. there was a radio message from the Robinson that Devon was taking David and Vickie back to base camp as the wind was just too much to try to work close to the ground. We had found an old north-south road about 30 miles east of the camp that from the air, seemed as if it would still be passable by vehicle. We were trying to walk it and check it often enough to be sure that Bogucki had not walked it or crossed it.

Finally the pilot said the wind was just too strong and gusty to be flitting in and out that close to the trees and the ground. We decided to fly along the road to see just where it went for future reference and the possibility of working it the next day. We knew that it must intersect with the rim of the escarpment at some point. Garrison radioed from base camp to inquire how we were doing. The pilot told him where we were and that we had given up trying to get on the ground and would be coming in shortly. The old roadway did come to the edge of the escarpment and wound around until it found a way steeply down from the rim and onto the flatland below. In the flat below it crossed Geegully Creek, then split, with one track heading west to where we had found the cattle-gathering area, and the other track heading almost northwest. It would be a good barrier to sign cut for Bogucki's' sign. If he had stayed on the original travel route, the sign would have to cross this road somewhere. The trouble was that even from the air there were places that the old road wasn't visible through the brush and washed-out areas. What were the chances that Bogucki would just happen to wander across the road in a place where his footprints would remain? Or that he would see the old roadway and follow it for a stretch where the footprints would be visible, like they were on the other road? We headed back for base camp. This was going to be an early day.

When we arrived, the big Range Rover was gone. Garrison was more than agitated that Devon had come in with David and Vickie due to the wind being too strong to work sign cutting. He had unloaded the 12-passenger Range Rover and taking the constable, Andrew and George Messer, tore off east down the two-track road where we last had Bogucki's sign. Garrison was determined to drive the Rover east to the area that he thought Bogucki's footprints would be found. David tried to tell him that the road was impassable in places due to washouts and heavy brush, but to no avail. Garrison would use the Rover like a tank and plow through it all. Andrew was along with his tool box to fix whatever got broke on the vehicle. George was along because he had some idea of the area, and Lindsey because he didn't refuse to go.

After break David and I organized everyone remaining at the camp except the two pilots, but including Rob and the three new media people, into a type of line search operation that would exercise the dogs and give everyone an opportunity to participate in a realistic effort that might produce some positive results. We would sweep eastward in line across the spinifex mesa just north and parallel to the two-track road that Bogucki had walked. There was a real possibility that one or more of these searchers would either find some unmistakable sign, such as a footprint, dropped litter or something that belonged to Bogucki, or one of the canines would suddenly locate the scent and be able to follow it even a short way. We would have a fresh start and probably be able to follow the sign if we could find just one footprint headed north from where he had left the road. Of course if Garrison found it further out east during his thrust we would be doing this for nothing, but at least we were doing something and the canine units and those at camp needed to be doing something practical.

We walked out to the starting line and I gave a short lesson on what they should look for, what the sign should look like and how they should work together to find whatever was there while best using the canine units. We began with great enthusiasm and high spirits. Everyone felt better doing something. I worked back and forth along the line from team to team as they discovered this and that and called for my examination before moving on. Each team had flagging tape to mark any suspected sign for further examination. The canine units worked back and forth, one on each end of the line and one in the center. I paused to enjoy the sight of these people working together without regard to affiliation—media people interspersed with the 1st SRG members, canine handlers helping trackers, trackers helping canine handlers. Amazingly the news people forgot their primary mission and were totally involved in an actual search effort. Time overtook the effort before we reached the eastern edge of where I thought the greatest possibility was. A radio call from Devon recalled David to the base camp to talk by radio with Garrison, which reminded us that it was well past 4 p.m. and the media types still had to get to Broome to make the 5 p.m. telecast. One look at their faces was enough to know that we had made believers out of them. The news broadcast tonight would be a positive statement about the 1st SRG effort. We recalled everyone and returned to base.

Garrison wanted Devon to fly east along the road until he came to the Rover and land to pick up Andrew. They'd had two flat tires on the vehicle, put on the two spares, and now had another flat tire. Andrew would bring one of the flat tires back and repair it to get the vehicle mobile again. David got a bright idea to send the spare tire from Ben's Rover with Devon. The news people loaded into the Bell Ranger and took off for Broome, promising to return in the morning and asking to be on the ground with whatever search effort was conducted the next day. A short time later the little chopper returned and landed easily with Andrew and the first flat tire. Andrew went to work immediately on it, saying that another tire on Garrison's Rover was also going flat. It only took Andrew about 20 minutes to repair the tire, but as he was finishing, Garrison radioed that he had two more flat tires. Andrew whistled and rolled his eyes, muttering that Garrison thought the Big Rover was a tank with tracks instead of a rubber-tired vehicle. He jacked up George's Rover, placing it on blocks to remove a tire and be able to take two good tires to Garrison, less than 10 miles from camp. Andrew was hoping the vehicle wasn't going to have a ruptured radiator, fuel tank or crank case.

He loaded the two good tires into the chopper and Devon cranked it up and lifted off toward the eastern horizon. Probably 40 minutes later, the Robinson returned with Andrew. This time he was really disgusted. Garrison's Rover with two rear tires flat was down on the rear axle and he was unable to get the jack under it to raise it up to replace the flat tires. He retrieved his 10-ton floor jack from the truck and lugged it to the chopper. The jack itself weighed 65 pounds. Devon was unable to land where the Rover was now stopped, so on the last trip out Andrew had dropped the tires onto the ground from a height of about 10 feet. The jack was too heavy for Andrew to move around inside the cabin of the chopper so he determined that it would be best if he carried the jack out to the site on his lap. While Devon hovered the bird, he would push the door open and hold it with one hand, then put his leg out and foot down on the skid and slide the jack out across his leg and over the skid to drop it on the ground without damaging the chopper.

We settled back to await the next radio call as the evening shadows began to lengthen. An hour went by before we heard the Robinson in the distance and realized that it wasn't coming in to land. We finally saw the little bird some distance to the east and apparently hovering above Garrison's vehicle. We concluded that Devon was simply coming along with the vehicle as it was slowly returning on the same route and probably having to push the now-downed brush and trees back the other way to get through. Close to another hour after Devon returned and shut down the chopper, Garrison's Rover emerged from the brush line in the distance and came charging back along the two-track road like a roaring demon. With brush hanging from the Rover's every crevice and protrusion, the crew disembarked. They said nothing, their faces telling the story of a wild ride they wouldn't want to repeat. Andrew said nothing, but piled four flat tires at the truck and quietly went to work. No one asked if they had found anything. Darkness was coming on quickly now and there was no indication from Garrison that he was wanting to take the command walk down the road. We turned our attention to which MRE to heat up. A good hot meal and another night on the hard ground—boy, we could hardly wait. Later sitting by the fire Andrew quietly told us that the plan had worked well to get the jack on the ground. Then, hanging onto the skid by his hands, he dropped onto the ground himself. To return, he had climbed onto the roof of the Rover and Devon had gotten the skid close enough for Andrew to grab hold and climb aboard. He was marveling at his own ability to facilitate and improvise to keep the project moving forward. The adventure with Garrison had made each of them far more appreciative of what it was that we were attempting to do in finding one set of footprints in this vast land.

Monday—August 23

In early morning light, David and I walked out toward the sunrise along the two-track road that Bogucki had walked. We turned silently together off to the north, following another old track through the spinifex and looking toward the rich deep lavender of the mesa below the escarpment. It was a quarter mile to the first of the broken arroyos that would lead to the escarpment face and fall down onto the mesa below. This was a good starting place and we decided to sign cut the edge of this break eastward while we finished our coffee. I was sure that Bogucki had worked his way carefully down the bank of one of these washes somewhere within the next mile and then, little by little down the escarpment toward Geegully Creek. We should have found the sign yesterday with the line-search effort, but we didn't. We hadn't gone very far when we heard Garrison's air horn blasting the morning shadows into light. I didn't know if he was just trying to wake the camp, or if he was calling us. We turned and walked unhurriedly back to camp, but heck the coffee was all gone by the time we got there.

Garrison wanted to talk operations again. He had just learned that the Bell Ranger was coming in today with another media crew from Perth. Sgt. Fuller at Broome had already told the crew that they'd have to cooperate with the search by sharing the airtime with search members if they wanted to get film. This didn't make them happy, but they wanted their share of the story. We decided that once they were at camp, we would send David and Vickie with Devon to work Geegully Creek, and I would go with the Ranger crew as we had done before. Garrison still had it in his head that Bogucki had continued going east because he had left the road headed east and had been walking east on the road for 15 miles.

This wasn't a bad idea and our efforts sure hadn't proved Garrison wrong the day before. I was just as sure that Bogucki was only coming back to his original travel route and that he had gone north from here. I went over it again in my mind while waiting for the chopper to arrive. My idea was that he'd been coming north from where we had the sign way down south and he'd come to this main road and could see the vehicle tracks. He'd stood in the road and looked one way then another, then sat down on the shoulder of the road to consult his map. Then he had gotten up and walked nearly 20 miles northwest on the road. He had stopped at some point, turned around and retraced his steps right back to this road corner near where our camp was. There, without stopping or even hesitating, he walked right off of the road corner and onto the two-track old road headed east. But he only went on this old track until he was well into the brush, where there was shade, then he lay down on a grassy spot under a bush and slept. This meant to me that he had walked the road northwest until he saw something that permitted orienting himself with his map and assuring him that his original direction was correct. He had simply turned around and with determination, walked all of the way back to the beginning of the mistake to erase it. Now he was back where he wanted to be. I thought he was headed northeast to strike Geegully Creek and follow it to Fitzroy River.

Garrison was the boss, and the boss felt very strongly about his hunch, as was clear from the disastrous events of yesterday. Those happenings didn't erase the idea from Garrison's mind. The Bell Ranger was a great machine for a ride and today a different newspaper reporter and a TV news photographer with a big camera would be riding along. They were now settling down to a soft seating while blowing up old grass, weeds and dust before touchdown.

Garrison wanted us to work eastward as far as possible and reasonable, and then north. Today he was just strongly suggestive, not adamant, and I was free to sign cut whatever I thought was worth looking at. I briefed the pilot, who readily understood that I wanted to be able to "see" footprints on the trails, pathways, patches of sand or dirt and roads if we found some. We studied the map and waited for the newspaper reporter to finish an interview with Garrison. The morning breeze was already picking up and taking on the personality of the previous day's wind. I knew this was going to be another short day of sign cutting from the air if this kept up, even though we were going to be a couple hours ahead of yesterday's start . Even this Ranger wouldn't do well in the canyons with a strong wind creating odd drafts up and down—it was difficult enough out on the flat mesa. I always accepted the pilot's judgment. My rule about flying with someone else is if the pilot is nervous, I'm nervous, and if he wants to get on the ground, I want to get on the ground too.

I had told the pilot to go straight east, slow enough that I could note on the map any north-south trails, paths, little roads or anything else that looked like a good cut. We were now four days behind the sign we'd found so fresh on the road, so if we went about 20 miles east and up to 40 miles north, it should put us one or two days behind his travel—if he had continued to walk 20 miles a day. From the line east, I wanted to find the road that went to the cattle corral that we had located the day before and check for sign in the bottom near Geegully Creek. I had in mind that if we found nothing there, we would work back west toward where David and Vickie would be working the trails coming down the escarpment and across to the creek.

It was beautiful country, but there sure was a lot of it! We covered the 20 miles with a few small circles to check sign on trails and occasionally a section of old roadway. Before leaving base camp I had asked George about any roads out the way we were going to work and he didn't know of any usable roads out in that section of the map, but he said roads had been cut out there some 50 or 60 years before. We flew over miles of small scrub trees, brush and occasionally open patches of ground anywhere from 10 to several hundred acres. Cattle roamed most of the area, I could see their sign and that of small herds of burros, camels and who knows what else. I had the pilot sit down in a place or two while I checked sign. I saw everything but human tracks. One good thing though—we covered enough area that if the tracks kept going, they wouldn't all be windblown or tromped out by animals. It was hard for some of the team to comprehend the magnitude of what we were trying to accomplish—finding the prints of one person in an area 20 by 40 square miles is no small task, even if the ground is bare.

We reached an area with several impressive rock formations sprouting from the grazing lands and the reporter informed the pilot that this was where she wanted to land and do an interview with me. I said no, but she said Garrison had promised, so we did. As we neared the end of the interview, the pilot got a radio request to come directly to the landing strip at Dampier Downs. He looked at me and shrugged, saying that he too had a boss and it wasn't his chopper. We loaded up and headed for Pete's ranch, about 100 miles from where we were.

The problem with using someone else's aircraft is that you're not the boss—the guy who's paying the bill for the air time is the boss. We landed at the end of the fixed wing airstrip east of the ranch house and out of sight of where we had landed with the Devon's bird. Two guys dressed in street clothes waited at the end of the runway with a pile of gear. Their boss had sent two videographers in a twin-engine Cessna to replace the two who had come with the chopper he'd leased for the job. The Cessna pilot had made contact with our pilot while still in the air and had dropped the two guys off at the end of the dirt strip. Then he had taken off presumably going back to Perth. The two guys had been waiting nearly an hour when we arrived. The Cessna pilot thought the chopper would be without passengers and could easily take these two passengers and their equipment to the camp. We were only a quarter-mile from the ranch house at Dampier Downs, but there wasn't anyone home there and they couldn't carry all of the video equipment that they had brought anyway. Nothing to do but go back to the camp and drop off two people and return to pick up these two; we couldn't leave them sitting on the end of this dirt strip in the desert. This would end sign cutting operations for this day.

We lifted off and headed south toward the edge of the escarpment that looked like a dark wall between the desert plain and the dusty blue sky. The Ranger climbed quickly heading south. Mowa Butte was in the flight line, a large rock protrusion jutting from the level ground, flat on top and nearly the same height as the top of the escarpment. It was easy to see that at one time this whole region had been the same height, then water had washed and eroded all of the softer material away to a depth of 900 feet. The video crew wanted footage and directed the pilot to circle the butte slowly so they could take what seemed to be endless shots. First in close, then backing away and down close to the treetops below looking at the tumbled rock falls in their array of pinks and rose lavender colors. Some might think the desert drab but this is a colorful country, a virtual color wheel of hues, some soft and others vivid and deep.

I was wearing the cabin earphones that monitored the radio and permitted our in-cabin communication without having to shout and read lips. I heard a radio call to the pilot mentioning my name. The pilot said into the mike, "They've got something up on top south of us and want Joel to take a look at it, so guess we'd better head that way." The camera crew didn't want to give up, but the pilot was tired of this and we headed off toward the escarpment again. I had been try-ing to sign cut the cattle trails below and was unable to see anything of interest.

We spun along, gaining altitude until we were just level with the top of the escarpment. From my rear seat, forward visibility was diffi-cult but as we came up to the steep wall of the escarpment, I could feel the pilot watching something and maneuvering the bird toward it. As he turned slightly west, I saw another Bell Ranger sitting on the ground, surrounded by a dozen people, at least two of them with shoul-der cameras. Others were directing and arm waving, and Devon's Robinson chopper was hovering just outside this arena of confusion. I had no idea what was happening. If they had found Bogucki, it must have been his body, because whatever the object of their attention, it was stationary. I'd learned it was better not to make up things, but rather just to wait and see what was taking place.

When we circled around again, I could see the Robinson on the ground near the Bell Ranger and Garrison out directing everyone. The pilot settled the chopper's skids onto a rocky surface and the pilot held up his hand for us to wait until the engine was shut down before deplaning. When the whine quieted to where we could hear, he advised that the police wanted everyone except me to wait where the other Ranger was sitting until further notice. I was glad to get my feet on solid ground and I was tired of photographers and reporters.

Garrison came hustling to meet me with the story. While return-ing to the camp from a trip to Broome, the other Ranger pilot had spotted something bright blue under a small bush. He was pointing to a small brushy area on the jutting point of the vee between two small, rocky, dry creek bottoms. They had sat down and gone to check out the blue item, discovering it to be some of Bogucki's personal effects wrapped in the blue tarp he had been carrying. They had opened the items and of course filmed the pilot and reporter examining the items before calling into base camp and advising them of the find. They continued to search the  immediate area and, using the Ranger, sent the videographer up to film the location and the reporter doing the "news" story from the air before the police could get there. The police had ordered them to remain at the chopper and not contaminate the area with scent and footprints before our team could get there, but no one was there to stop them from doing whatever they wanted to do. Garrison and the police had to wait until Devon could get the Robinson ready to take them to the scene. Their arrival had been just prior to our getting to the scene and our pilot, hearing all of this on the air, had waited until things were settled down before getting on the ground himself.

Devon was taking off again to bring Vickie and the bloodhound to the scene. Garrison was really hot under the collar and the police-man Lindsey was biting nails to keep from throwing rocks and cussing the media types. He had backed the Ranger pilot up against his bird and talked to him like a father to a son bringing home the family chariot with the front end smashed in. The media types got off with a good scolding because anything you said to them might turn up on TV or in the paper. Taking my pack, I headed along the sign trail already created by the little group to and from the bushes where Bogucki's debris was slightly flapping in the breeze. Undoubtedly there was plenty of sign, but they had managed to contaminate it all by running around checking bushes and staging various "discoveries." I went to the tarp and looked at the pile of items. A well-worn red Bible was prominent—that could mean something. There were also a notebook, a few other miscellaneous papers, a couple items of dirty clothing and a water jug— probably five to seven pounds total weight. I looked around, trying to see what he would have been seeing from this little point. This was the edge of the breaks leading down the face of the escarpment. From the air it didn't seem very far to the steep face, but from the ground it looked like a hiker's challenge instead of a walk to a Sunday picnic. I had flown over these breaks now for two days, but hadn't really tried to sign cut due to the humps, ridges, deep canyons and gullies. I thought of all of the times I have said to students, "Never just go somewhere, cut everywhere you go!" Well, too late for that.

The ground surface underfoot was different from anything I'd seen so far. Here the soil had more clay in it. The rain had wet it thoroughly and the sun had baked it like adobe. Vegetation was sparse on the top of the ridges which were just outcroppings of the hardened clay that looked like rock, except the rocks had color and the clay was just a drab gray and dun brown. I had seen clay like this in many places in the U.S.—that wasn't what was different. This clay had a loose covering of beautiful brown "marbles" from the size of peas to nearly as large as golf balls. I had never seen anything like these before. I picked up several to examine them closely. They looked like glass and were in fact glass, probably created by melting globs of silica into a thousand different sizes of melon balls. They were varying shades of dark brown and nearly all were perfectly round. I couldn't see anything else volcanic around here, and these weren't washed from the clay, these were just sitting on top of the ground. I gathered three or four more in my hands and looked around to see if I could get an idea of what Bogucki would have been seeing and thinking. I sign cut the gully on either side of the point looking for where he had gone. I had his sign coming off of the point and along one side of the arroyo downhill along a faint game trail, but then he had stopped and returned to the point. He had been uncertain, starting and going back, then he dropped off his extra gear under the bush. He hadn't restarted in the same direction, so the sign must go off the brink somewhere else.

I would have to get outside the area contaminated by the film crew to find anything I could be certain of. The marbles didn't dent into the ground surface when stepped on, but instead seemed to scatter and leave small areas clear. They were so hard that stepping on them didn't break, crush or mark them in any way. This was not an easy place even to find a print, let alone get a make or identify it. I slowly sign cut my way out to the point of the vee and began a side hill cut on the fork that led back toward the camp. The ground surface here should have left me something to see—a scuff, slide mark, squashed or mashed vegetation, or anything I would recognize as Bogucki sign. I worked slowly, trying not to miss anything. I figured that this was the area of least probability because it wouldn't be going the direction that he wanted to follow. While studying the debris site, I observed that we were almost straight north of the place where we last had his sign on the two-track road. Leaving that area he most probably headed almost due north to here where he had stopped, recognizing that he was at the southern edge of the escarpment.

Devon returned to drop off Vickie and Dixie, and the competing video crews fought for position to get good shots of the search dog in action. I continued my cut to a point I thought sufficiently far enough south of an east-west line through the Bogucki debris. There I began a west-to-east cut that would parallel that east-west line about 50 to 75 yards south. I'd be making a triangular cut around the debris site, which would permit me to find the Bogucki sign coming to the debris site from the dense spinifex and brush, and possibly give me a better idea of where to look on the downhill north side. This was also something to do while the media crews fell all over themselves creating a story for the evening news at the debris site. I worked slowly and soon was joined by Vickie and Dixie. Vickie said Dixie had worked the scent from the debris area in a large circle around the top of the point, where it had been blown by the hovering helicopter. Beyond that, Dixie couldn't get it started again. Vickie added that the scent that Dixie was working might well have only come from the site of the Bogucki belongings. She might have been able to do something with it if the copter hadn't spent so much time filming from 50 feet in the air directly over the site. Vickie joined me making the sign cut with Dixie trailing.

Suddenly we found the sign! It was faint, but definite partial footprints and walking easily and directly out to the point, though from where we were, we couldn't see that the route ended up at the high point between the arroyos. Bogucki wouldn't have been able to see that either until he actually stepped out of the brush and out onto the point itself. We walked up the sign line toward the debris site but stayed out of sight of the media. I explained to Vickie what I had been able to learn from following the sign away from the blue tarp and being able to point out the various locations to her as I talked from where we were standing.

"Bogucki went down the point and across the arroyo along a little game trail to where it began to drop down steeply to another level below. There he stopped, studied the landscape below and returned to the high ground. There he sat and culled the stuff he was carrying and started out again. I believe he would have gone slightly east but still to the north, probably to right where those choppers are decked now. Let's back out of here slowly so as to not be seen and go over there and make a cut behind them to see if we can pick up the sign."

We backtracked through the scattered bushes and circumvented the media around Lindsey and Garrison and ended up at the line of choppers. I told her to take Dixie around in front of the choppers. "If the media come back over here they'll follow the dog, and I'd rather they don't know what I'm doing."

The spinifex was thick and filled two little water runoff washes ten feet or so apart in the depression behind the choppers. I eased over to take a closer look hoping that the activity at the site had so drawn the attention that they hadn't messed up this area. I found a clean footprint impression crushed into the spinifex in the bottom of the first ditch, then another partial on the bank leading across the depression and away from the choppers. I worked the sign slowly finding here or there some bent or flattened spinifex, a scuff or scrape, rolled ceramic marbles—a lot of maybes, but together they were something. I crossed the second ditch and there was another definite footprint crushing the spinifex. This was flat with a large round toe. No heel showed in the spinifex, but this had to be Bogucki. I worked it as the crowd of media people started packing up to return. They loaded and lifted off, each intent on getting to Broome to file their stories first. Vickie looked questioningly at me. I told her to take Dixie back in with the rest and I would walk in. She asked if I had it and I pointed to the ground and signaled the affirmative. "I'll be in later," I said. "Do me a favor and take Garrison and the rest and give me a break for a bit." She nodded.

I went down into the small arroyo and walked in the dry stream bed a few yards to where it opened like a door to the broken terrain below. Finding a small stone bench to sit on, I watched the lagging afternoon begin to turn into evening and draw long dark shadows down into the canyons. In a while, I heard the Robinson cranking its lift off to return to the base camp. The sun was close to the horizon now and I was losing the light in the arroyo. At last some peace and quiet to be able to think! I quickly picked up the sign again. I could see where Bogucki had stepped up the bank on the other side and I followed. This was definitively him and he was on his northward course. He would be dropping into the breaks where the terrain would channel and permit his descent to the valley flatland below. I stood on the edge, looking down over the humps, ridges and canyons below. A couple ways to go down looked promising, but I'd have to wait till morning to find out where he had gone. I flagged the sign for the morning and turned to hike five miles back to camp that was glowing in the last rays of the sun.

A moody fog of dejection had settled over the camp by the time I walked in a hour and more later. In silence and gloom, everyone felt somewhat glad that the Bogucki debris had been found, but not at all happy about the manner in which it was found. Everyone could imagine what the media was going to do with the story on TV, despite the facts that Rob and Ben had communicated to their newspaper via the satellite phone. I shucked my field gear. To Garrison and David, I said that we should take a walk. At last, it was me saying it to Garrison that we needed to conference. We moved off down the road silently. When we were well out of earshot, I said, "Garrison, I think this is the time to ask George Messer it he would mind breaking out the beer."

He raised an eyebrow, puffing on the cigar and waiting for some explanation from me. "Well," I continued, "the mood of the team sure isn't very upbeat, we've worked long and hard, we're near the end, and with what has happened today, everyone knows what's going to be on TV tonight. It just seems like it's the time. I actually have a pretty good feeling about what we've done. They found the blue tarp because of what we were doing, and now we have the sign headed downhill toward the breaks."

Garrison's mouth slowly drooped open as his mind went from breaking out the beer against his rules to what I had just said. His cigar dangled at half mast. He looked a bit like a bulldog that had just been slapped alongside the head. "Whaddaya mean?"

I explained, and grinned thinking about how to say it made me even more sure and confident. "We spent three days, counting today, looking for sign ahead somewhere and haven't found it. I don't think we've missed the sign anywhere we've looked, and looked in what seemed to be the right places. Maybe we haven't looked in the right place, but maybe he hasn't gotten as far as we thought either. With all the hubbub out there, I found the sign going on from the blue tarp. He went right through where the choppers were parked and on over to the edge and it looks like he's going to head down the escarpment where we've checked below and haven't found his sign. That's as far as I have it at this time, but we have a great start for the morning, and I'm beginning to bet that he's down in one of those canyons and hasn't come out, for whatever reason."

Garrison's mouth closed around the cigar and he puffed a couple times, and asked "You mean that you've got the sign going on past where we were and maybe he's between there and the bottom where you've been cutting sign?"

"That's right. I don't know what the chances are that he's there, but that's a lot better than where we've been for the past couple days. The sign is about a half-day older than the sign where he lay down in the brush. He's still walking and he's going into rough broken country, maybe he fell and broke a leg, turned an ankle, who knows what, but I don't think we missed him coming out down below. That means he's somewhere in the next two, three or five miles, between wherever he chose to try to get down the escarpment and where the choppers were parked. So I think it's a good time to give everyone a beer, boost their spirits, and give a cheer. We won't celebrate, but we'll at least get their spirits back up. We have something to cheer about. We'll either have him or have his sign out on the valley floor below by tomorrow afternoon. I think that rates a beer and a cheer."

David was grinning from ear to ear and we high-fived and turned to Garrison, who was now grinning also. "It'll break my own rules, but I think you're right."

Back at the campfire, Garrison yelled out a command to everyone to gather at the fire pit. We pulled up stools while everyone else seated themselves gloomily, obviously not in the mood to hear a pep talk. Garrison went through the day's events slowly and finished up with the summation of the media circus at the debris site. Then he paused and added, "But, we have good news to work from. Joel has found Bogucki's sign going northeast from where he stashed the stuff under the bush. Joel and David feel good about the fact that we haven't found the sign down below. What that means in simple terms is that there's a real good chance that he's between the Bible and the bottom. Joel says the sign is workable and that it shouldn't take all day to work it down into the canyons and out at the bottom. If Bogucki's not there, we'll know where to look ahead by early afternoon. We've worked hard all week and tomorrow is going to be a hard push, because according to schedule it's the last day of our mission—we need to find him! So, Joel thinks it's time for a beer tonight and an early rise in the morning. George, would you mind passing around the beer?" Even a couple members who'd said they didn't drink beer took one with great enthusiasm. My oh my—was it cold and refreshing! It tasted especially good amid the exclamations of joy and excitement at our news.

When the shouts of appreciation had subsided, I laid out my plan. "Let's get up early. I want to be up and ready to go an hour before daylight so we can hike out to the site and be on the sign as soon as it gets light. My suggestion is for Mike to go with me to work the sign line. Laura, Amir and Vickie can work the tops of the breaks, the draws, gullies, canyons and ridges in between with the dogs. Jan can either wait here or be a flanker for one of the canine units. I think we need to have David on a high point that I have picked out, with radio contact between me and with each of the canine units to coordinate things in the field. Otherwise we don't know where anyone else is, and we need to maintain contact with base camp here if possible. Garrison, Lindsey and George can man the radio here and talk with the media when they get here. Ben and Rob are free to help out wherever they want to. I want to be out and gone from here, hopefully out of sight before any of the media even get close in the morning. Garrison and Lindsey can make up some story to tell them and keep them here until we have a chance to find something. So what do ya think?"

George stood as they looked from one to the other and said, "Well, mates, that calls for another beer!" as he opened the reefer and pulled out the box. Boy did that cold beer taste good! I chose Mike Priddy to go with me because he was a communications specialist and he could keep in touch with the other teams while I worked. I had purposely suggested David for field operations coordinator because he was Garrison's second in command, and thus Garrison would be more prone to supporting my plan, and I had a lot confidence in David's experience to assist the operation by specific instruction and direction in the field.

Everyone was back in good spirits again and ready for the challenge of the next day. We all turned in early. It had been a long, frustrating day and everyone wanted to be rested for the push the next morning.

Tuesday—August 24

Morning found Dixie flopping her chops, wheezing and stirring on my feet. My watch showed half past four and, after a few minutes listening to the night, I crawled out of the sack and into my clothes quietly. I took my usual walk off the road and into the open to gather sticks for the fire. I soon had the fire going and the billy on to boil and looked for the packets of that great, wonderful hot-water coffee. I vowed to myself to raise the next real cup of coffee in my hand in a toast to such common everyday taken for granted and under appreciated gifts. The others were up earlier than usual, getting their gear ready to head out. I stuck a few of the MRE goodies in my pack, thinking that several of us might be together at lunchtime. I had not eaten anything yet in the field and my pack was beginning to fill with goodies. Soon everyone was ready to leave and under Garrison's watchful eye we headed out in file toward the dark of the escarpment with quiet high spirits and determination to have success before the media came on scene. Daylight was coming quickly and I led out at a good pace. I wanted to be where I had flagged the last track by the first good light to give us a good start and a chance to be down in one of the canyons before the media began coming in. The dogs were eager to be out and working and ran ahead and circled around and back to the file. I was heading through the spinifex and brush straight to the last track, it had taken me a bit more than an hour to walk in last evening and that should put us back on track with the sun just over the tree tops.

Once in the immediate area, Amir peeled off first with his dog Radar to begin working the westernmost canyons, then Vickie and later Laura chose overlapping sections to work together to cover the full area. This would be a day of down into and back up out of a good many draws and canyons for all three units. I pointed out the dark outline of the hill, backlit by the coming sun, that I thought would provide the needed radio communications and permit an occasional visual contact with the canine units and for Mike and me as we worked the sign line. Mike and I arrived at the ribbon flag that I had tied to indicate the last sign. The sun was now above the far eastern horizon and while shadows hid all of the bottoms, there was good light where we would begin working. I started by backtracking a short distance to show and tell Mike what we would be looking for, a 15-minute tracking class. As we came to the last track, I began looking for the next. I spotted a scratch in the dirt where one of the little marbles had been pressed onto the adobe and had slid backward slightly, indicating action of the ball of a foot.

I worked the sign over the crest of the rim and down the slope toward where I could see several little watercourse gatherings that formed the head of a creek at the top of an arroyo leading into a canyon. Intermittently finding slight indications of passage, I was sure I was on Bogucki's sign, but it wasn't easy or rapid progress. Finally, near the head of the creek erosion, I found what was definitely the edge of a shoe impression—we were still on it! He was going to follow down this creek to cross the extension of the canyon that appeared to run further east and continue northeast on his original bearing. At intervals, I could hear David talking on the radio with one of the canine units as they continued to work toward our position across the tops of the draws.

I glanced at my watch. It was nearly 7 a.m., and I had wanted to be into one of the draws or the canyons by now, well before the media could come hovering over us. I was sure they'd be arriving early and we'd be near their flight line to and from Broome. I wanted our efforts to be under cover in some canyon bottom so we could work without being observed. David would help with that effort by coding his communications with Garrison, so they wouldn't know where we were. Lindsey would use his police authority to order all media participants to remain at the command post. Garrison would offer a briefing, if and when there was anything to report. We certainly didn't want a repeat of yesterday's experience. I found one mark then another and tried to keep Mike involved and seeing the sign. We were now definitely headed down into the wash as it deepened and ran generally in the direction that Bogucki wanted to go.

David called and wanted me to talk with Vickie on the radio. She was in the bottom of an arroyo with some large trees and heavy brush northwest of our position. I was unable to make radio contact with Vickie but could see David atop the peak. David pointed to where he had last seen Vickie going into a canyon. David advised us that he could see from his high vantage that the draw we were working into would run into the larger arroyo that she was in. He went on to say that Laura had found what she thought was a track well ahead of us in that main arroyo. Vickie had joined her to try to verify that it was in fact a line of footprints going through thick underbrush. Together following the sign they had found a nearly clear footprint in the sandy sediment in the creek bottom. It didn't have the identifying little hexigon markings so they weren't sure and wanted me to come and check it out. I told Mike to flag the last print that we had as I looked for a direct route to where Vickie and Laura were. It appeared that the best route was just the way Bogucki had gone, right on down the draw that we were in to where it ran into the main gully and then west down that main arroyo. We headed out and began noticing here and there the edge, toe or heel of Bogucki's shoe. We were right on the sign. We could see that he came to the junction and turned into the main arroyo following the watercourse, picking his way through the thickening brush in the broader creek bottom. We abandoned following the sign, and hurried along, nearly running where the conditions permitted and abruptly came up to Laura and Vickie waiting at the track in the sand. Yep, it was our guy. Great job! I told them, but let's not slow down.

Then I heard the sound that I had dreaded but had known was coming—an approaching chopper. As I listened, I realized that he must be looking for us. He was working a pattern north of the debris site from the day before. Laura and Vickie were with Mike and me, so the only one left out in sight besides David was Amir working his dog Radar. I didn't know where they were, I couldn't see David but I could hear the chopper getting closer to where we were. It wouldn't do any good to hide; we couldn't work if we were hiding in the brush.

Suddenly the chopper was hovering right over us. The noise was almost deafening in the narrow and deepening arroyo.

"David," I shouted into the radio, "see if you can get this guy to go somewhere else—to camp or somewhere! We can't hear ourselves talk with him hovering over us." In a few moments the chopper moved off downstream, still hovering over the canyon. The pilot was no fool—he knew we wouldn't be coming down this watercourse unless we had the sign. We gathered forces and began moving on the sign downstream as the chopper noise faded off into the distance.

We were quickly getting into a sheer rock-wall canyon whose perpendicular walls grew above our heads and out of sight as we proceeded downhill. All we had to do was make sure the tracks were still going downstream wherever we could find them in the sediment deposits in the bottom—no one was going to try to climb out of this trough. Longer sections of the bottom were rock, smoothed by eons of scrubbing sand, which ended in pools with sandy bottoms and washed gravel. Bogucki had been going right down this bottom, with nowhere else to go until another wash intersected the canyon from the north. At this point the chopper noise came back, and he was hovering right over us again.

"David," I said into the radio, "this guy knows what we're doing and he's going to keep going down the canyon and back to check on us, each time going farther to try to pick Bogucki up ahead of us. See if you can get Garrison or Lindsey to make this guy sit down at search base."

I was trying to watch the sign closely as somehow I didn't think we had missed sign this good on the valley floor below. Somewhere Bogucki had got hung up in this or another of the intersecting canyons. The chopper suddenly pulled up from where it was hovering over us and turned out of our sight and hearing. I noticed that Bogucki had been sitting in several opportune places, on natural seating benches created by the water cascading down the hill. He was thinking, unhurried, almost reluctantly going forward in some places.

We were trying to make quick time. Mike and I were leading and the canine units were bringing up the rear. Then the canyon began to flatten and widen out from the sheer rock-wall area. Now there were small "islands" of scrubby trees. The sign went from island to island; he was checking, looking and continuing onward. Then we came to an area in which the water had washed and eroded inward and up under the creek bank tree roots. Here Bogucki had spent some time. His prints covered the sandy sediment creek bottom and sign showed that he had crawled into the space up under the tree roots. There he had stayed for some time, hidden from the outside in a cave-like space. I looked inside this space. The sign showed that after a long period of time, perhaps as much as a day or more, elapsed, he had crawled out and continued his journey downstream.

The canine units had caught up and together we headed downstream, now following the obvious Robinson Crusoe's "Friday" footprints on the beach as they walked the widening strip of sediment toward what appeared to be the mouth of the canyon. We came out of the creek bottom on a broad, flat rusty-red-colored rock shelf. I walked toward what I could see were the tops of trees protruding at a slight distance ahead of the shelf. Suddenly, we were standing on a long semicircle edge of the shelf above a 100-foot waterfall drop. We backed up a step or two and gazed at the sight. The trees were tall and the tops were barely above the shelf on which we were standing. We stood there, somewhat spellbound. Looking down, I could see footprints in the sand and small gravel at the bottom of the drop, as well as the remnants of what appeared to be a small fire at the base of a tree. The creek bottom where the trees were growing and continuing on down was choked with long bunch grasses and brush and more trees. There clearly were water pockets in the bottom to feed this growth.

"Look!" Laura exclaimed, pointing as we all turned. There, to the side of us, spelled out with more rocks on the shelf, were the letters H E L P. We had overlooked the HELP sign when we walked past it, drawn by the tree tops waving us toward the edge of the shelf. That broke the reverie.

"OK," I said, "let's figure out which way he went to get down in there." I believe we were all thinking that, alive or dead, he was within earshot of where we were standing. We began to look for sign at both corners of the shelf and were working our way down into the bottom when there was a radio call relayed by David from base camp. Laura yelled, "He's been found!" Found? I looked at Mike and he looked at me. Found? Heck, we were all here together—how could someone have found him? Laura was listening to her radio. "The chopper picked him up down the canyon ahead of us!" she shouted.

We climbed back to the shelf and gathered together. We could now see David on the top of the knoll talking into his radio. "The helicopter is taking him to Broome," he said to us. I turned to look at my team. Their faces were crushed with disappointment.

"Well guys, they only found him because we led them to him. Let's not forget that getting him was the objective."

Then Laura, being her usual perky self, seized the moment and excitedly extracted her camera from the pack to take pictures. The search was successful—he'd been found alive! Vickie suddenly caught Laura's mood and they began hugging each of us. This was her first search success with the subject found alive. After pictures were taken, we headed back cross-country toward a rendezvous point with David coming from his high point.

The mood was solemn when we all got together. We all had mixed emotions—elation that he'd been found alive and that we were on the sign perhaps only an hour behind, but sharp disappointment that we hadn't been able to get to him before the press chopper picked him up. David announced that there were no choppers to pick us up because they'd all gone immediately to Broome to get some of the story and the glory. His congratulations brought only "Yeah, same to you" as we began the nearly five-mile hike cross country back to base.

We had hiked a mile or so when the little Robinson chopper appeared headed north over our heads. We stopped to wave and wonder where Devon was going. Surely he wasn't going to abandon us now—he was part of our crew and not the media. David's radio came to life, with Garrison advising that Devon was on his way to pick up Ben, the Western Australia News reporter who had been a part of our crew from the beginning. Ben had been on the chopper that picked Bogucki up and they had kicked him out to make room for Bogucki and left Ben to fend for himself. (We found out later that the pilot of the chopper had called the base camp to advise of Ben's location after learning that the Broome Police were going to be at the airport to take everyone into custody and probably seize his helicopter. The pilot didn't want to have the responsibility for dumping someone without any survival gear in the desert where they had picked up Bogucki.) Garrison said that when Devon returned he would come out and pick up the canine units first, then the rest of us. So we kept trudging up hill and down toward the base camp.

When we hiked into the camp at about noon, mighty preparations were under way to get everything packed up and to head for Broome. Garrison said that Sergeant Wolfe of the Broome Police had already made arrangements for rooms at the best motel and a huge "barbie" was planned for the next day at police department expense. We started to feel better. The happy prospect of going to town for a hot shower, cold beer and nice bed was just too much to keep depressed spirits down. Everyone was grabbing gear and stowing it in vehicles or on the truck. It was going to be a long, hot and dirty drive and everyone wanted to get to the end of it by getting started. Ben and Rob announced that they were heading out ahead of and traveling faster than the convoy could make it so they could get their stories filed, and they had two seats available in their Range Rover. David and I volunteered to go; we might just make the scheduled evening flight to Perth. Garrison had already requested that Sgt. Wolfe contact the airlines to reschedule our flights and Australian Immigration to extend our visas. We were 180 miles out from pavement, George said, but Ben thought Rob was a race driver and we might just make our 11:30 p.m. flight.

We loaded our gear and hugged everyone, including George, Lindsey and even Devon, and were gone in a cloud of dust. It was a wild ride, at least half of it in four-wheel drive through ruts and washouts and long stretches of dusty hard surface sand. We flew around corners, slid sideways to avoid dips and rocks and hit the pavement at 7:30 p.m. We were in Broome at 8:00 and Rob was good enough to take us to a market to buy a couple cases of beer to cool for the others when they came in. Then we found the motel, where we gladly hit the showers between cold beers. An hour later David and I were cleaned up enough for public view and we hung on the balcony and watched the sun sink into the ocean where foamy surf softly caressed white beaches. We drank beer and talked while washing and drying clothes with the in-room appliances before repacking for the homeward trip.

The evening news was full of the news helicopter that had rescued Bogucki from sure death while the American searchers struggled in the desert. We didn't need to watch or hear the news—heck we had been there and knew what the real news was! We arranged for Rob to come to the motel and pick us up at 10:30 for the 11:30 flight. The little airport waiting area was full of people, a number of whom were talking about the rescue of the crazy American but no one noticed either of us as we bought Rob a beer at the bar. Check-in had taken only five minutes, and we were free of baggage all the way home. We sat and talked about the mission and Rob assured us that by the time we arrived in Perth, Ben's story would be front page of the Western Australia News, and this story, complete with Rob's pictures, would tell the truth about Bogucki's rescue.

Suddenly a police vehicle came sliding to a stop at the entrance to the patio and out climbed Garrison, Sgt. Wolfe and Lindsey. They came with huge grins and big hugs to say good-bye. As were doing so, another car drove up and several persons got out. They introduced themselves as the news director and reporters of the Perth TV station that had leased the helicopter which picked up Bogucki. They tried to explain or excuse their actions in snatching Bogucki ahead of us in the canyon and taking him to another location for the filming of the interview without notifying anyone. They apologized and rationalized, but we were not impressed. Sgt. Wolfe advised them to see the

Police Superintendent in the morning at the station. They would have to explain to him their reasoning for rescuing Bogucki but not taking him to base camp where he could have appropriate field medical care. They had also disobeyed direct police orders and abandoned another person (Ben Martin) in the desert and only when it was obvious that they would be found out, notifying anyone that the person was stranded there.

Garrison hotly refused to give them an interview. David and I, though almost overlooked in the shouting of the heated argument and discussion, also refused interviews and the police ordered them to leave the area or face arrest for disturbance of the peace. Things settled down and the police bought us another beer as we waited for our flight to Perth. They assured us that we would miss a very festive barbie the following evening on the beach hosted by the local police detachment, but wished us well. Then we were boarding and off to home.

This time there wasn't anyone to meet us with blinding lights and cameras rolling as we returned in succession to Perth, Melbourne and Sydney. In Melbourne we had time between flights to pick up a copy of the Western Australia News and on the front page was Ben's story about the search. We sat and read the story together, shook hands and felt damn good about what we had accomplished.

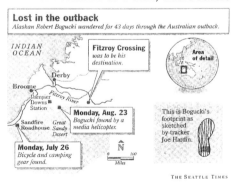

Lost in the outback
Alaskan Robert Bogucki wandered for 43 days through the Australian outback.

INDIAN OCEAN

Fitzroy Crossing *was to be his destination.*

Area of detail

Derby
Broome
Fitzroy River
Dampier Downs Station

Sandfire Roadhouse — Great Sandy Desert

Monday, Aug. 23 *Bogucki found by a media helicopter.*

This is Bogucki's footprint as sketched by tracker Joe Hardin.

Monday, July 26 *Bicycle and camping gear found.*

N

0   100
Miles

THE SEATTLE TIMES

Several months after the search, I had the pleasure of a visit at my home in Everson, WA by Robert Bogucki and Janet North, who had gotten married after returning to the United States. Bogucki came with a grin and a heartfelt thank you, bearing the maps and notes from his 43-day journey. We spent most of the day talking about "our" adventure, and how we both felt about what we had done. We studied the maps and I recounted the route and the sign story that I had read from his footprints—his thoughts, emotions, and physical condition. We compared notes—he talked about his days of meditation and prayer, his hunger and thirst, being tired of walking, the mental struggle to maintain control. He talked of long days sitting and enjoying the surroundings of unspoiled nature, and his being alone within it; nights of long walks in the moonlight with stars overhead. He had achieved the now undeniable spiritual relationship with God that he had so desired. He told us of the mental aspects that he had dealt with in relation to dying, of his suffering, but of his inner joy at being alive surrounded only by what God had created. We spoke of those things that we shared and did not speak of those things that belonged to Bogucki alone. We now share an intimate friendship, linked by a most unusual event, and we continue to communicate through letters and e-mail contact.

This opportunity was a great adventure, challenge and achievement for me personally. I was permitted by the circumstances of this venture to explore my memory, use my imagination, and use the full range of knowledge, experience and skills developed during my tracking career. Many aspects of tracking that are so difficult to explain and demonstrate to others, including experienced trackers, but in which I have total confidence, served me very well in this instance. Talking with Janet North, and believing the subject could be alive, provided me with motivation to approach this mission without even considering the eventual outcome. I had confidence that once on scene, I could find and follow the month-old sign and be able to read the sign story and compare with the furnished information as to the subject's habits, demeanor and personality. I believed that I would be able, in the press of the situation to incorporate willing but untrained team members into efficient tracking team members. I gambled with the concept that Bogucki had continued to walk 15 to 20 miles a day from the last known place. However I always kept in mind that I was gambling, "taking a recoverable risk," and I had confidence that, if necessary, I could go back to the last known sign and follow it to wherever he had gone. The lessons learned in this adventure will serve me well during future tracking opportunities.

⊱━━◦━━⊰

Garrison St. Clair stepped down as Commander of the organization in November of 2002 having established the group as a viable, professional and successful international SAR resource. He asked that David Kovar succeed in the position of commander and that I accept the position of second in command. Subsequently Garrison died of a heart attack January 27th of 2003 while in Baja California, Mexico.

First Special Response Group under David's leadership continues to respond to SAR mission requests with successes in Latin and South America, Europe and the far East. The organization is expanding the nature of request response to include emergency services and the SAR needs analysis for developing countries. Requests for training and program development by experienced professional level SAR personnel provides additional opportunities for 1SRG personnel to deploy to foreign countries. The enthusiastic and experienced 1SRG tracking unit now numbers a dozen members in training to learn of the responsibilities and expectations needed to ensure success for this unusual and extreme mission response.

About the Authors

For 25 years Joel Hardin put his mantracking skills to work as an agent of the U.S. Border Patrol. He learned those skills in the dusty ground and mountains of the southern border as he and his fellow agents tracked down people illegally crossing into the United States. He is considered by most in the world of tracking to be one of the premier mantrackers in the U.S. He is and has been continuously active and responding to tracking missions for more then thirty years. Joel retired from the Border Patrol in 1990 to devote full time to tracking training, consultation services and actual mission response. During this career he has trained thousands of others to become proficient in this ancient art. Search and Rescue groups, military Special Operations and law enforcement agencies around the world have called on Hardin for expert tracking consultations and training their personnel. Over the years Joel Hardin has had many fascinating adventures, including everything from criminal investigations and tracking down escaped fugitives to returning lost children to worried parents. For years his students have encouraged him to write these stories down along with some of his valuable training insights. This book contains many of those interesting case files and adventure stories from a lifetime of tracking. Joel Hardin now resides in Everson, Washington with his wife Janet. He continues to train trackers, provide consultation services and respond to tracking missions all over the world through his company *Joel Hardin Professional Tracking Services.*

Matt Condon is a freelance writer, pastor and counselor living in Missoula, Montana. He began tracking training as a Search and Rescue volunteer in 1990, under Hardin's tutelage, and has become a journeyman tracker. Their friendship and Matt's knowledge of both tracking and writing made him a key asset to encourage and to complete this project.

ORDER FORM

Additional copies of "**TRACKER**"

May be ordered by email, telephone or regular mail with check or credit card at $18.95 each, plus $4.00 shipping and handling.

For 8 or more copies please call 1-800-200-1274-pin-8191 or 8192 for price and shipping information

You may detach and mail this form with
personal check or money order to
JHardin, Inc Publishing, 7133 Mecklem Rd., Everson, WA 98247

You may call 1-800-200-1274-pin-8191 or 8192 to order by telephone and provide your credit card number

You may email to Book@jhardin-inc.com and follow email instructions to order and pay via email with check or credit card

Please send me _____ copies of TRACKER,
@ $18.95 plus $4.00 shipping & handling for each copy.

❑ Check enclosed
❑ Charge my credit card
❑ VISA   ❑ Mastercard

Credit Card Number _____
Name on Credit Card _____
Expiration date _____
Credit Card "V" Number _____
*(last 3 or 4 digits of the credit card number on reverse
side of card above the signature)*

Name _____
Address _____
City _____
State _____ Zip _____
Email _____

Mail to above address ❑   Different address ❑
Please provide:

_____

_____